Human Dignity, Judicial Reasoning, and the Law

This volume explores how national and international human rights courts interpret and apply human dignity. The book tracks the increasing deployment of the concept of human dignity within courts in recent decades. It identifies how human-dignity-based arguments have expanded to cover larger sets of cases: from the right to life or the right to integrity or anti-discrimination, the concept has surfaced in disputes about political and social rights and rule of law requirements, such as equality or legal certainty. The core message of the book is that judges understand, interpret, and apply human dignity differently. An inflation in the judicial recourse to human dignity can saturate the legal environment, depriving the concepts as well as human-rights-based narratives of salience, and threaten the predictability of court decisions. The book will appeal to philosophers of law, constitutional theorists and lawyers, legal comparativists, and international law specialists. While being dedicated specifically to human dignity jurisprudence, the book touches on many aspects of judiciary and as such will also be of interest to researchers studying legal reasoning, interpretation and the application of the law and courts, as well as social philosophers, political scientists and sociologists of law, politics and religion.

Brett G. Scharffs is The Rex E. Lee Chair and Professor of Law and Director of the International Center for Law and Religion Studies at Brigham Young University J. Reuben Clark School of Law.

Andrea Pin is Full Professor of Comparative Public Law at University of Padua.

Dmytro Vovk is Visiting Associate Professor at Benjamin N. Cardozo School of Law and Director of the Center for the Rule of Law and Religion Studies at Yaroslav Mudryi National Law University.

Routledge Research in Legal Philosophy

The Origin of Copyright
Expression as Knowing in Being and Copyright Onto-Epistemology
Wenwei GUAN

Constitutional Imaginaries
A Theory of European Societal Constitutionalism
Jiří Přibáň

Human Dignity and the Law
A Personalist Theory
Michał Rupniewski

Legal Ethics for Lawyers
A New Model
Barbara Mescher

Moral Pluralism and the Complexity of Punishment
The Penal Philosophy of H.L.A. Hart
Nicolas Nayfeld

Sport, Law and Philosophy
The Jurisprudence of Sport
Miroslav Imbrisevic

Cosmopolitanism, State Sovereignty and International Law and Politics
A Theory
Jorge E. Núñez

Human Dignity, Judicial Reasoning, and the Law
Comparative Perspectives on a Key Constitutional Concept
Edited by Brett G. Scharffs, Andrea Pin, and Dmytro Vovk

For more information about this series, please visit: www.routledge.com/Routledge-Research-in-Legal-Philosophy/book-series/RRLP

Human Dignity, Judicial Reasoning, and the Law

Comparative Perspectives on a Key Constitutional Concept

Edited by Brett G. Scharffs, Andrea Pin, and Dmytro Vovk

Routledge
Taylor & Francis Group
LONDON AND NEW YORK

First published 2024
by Routledge
4 Park Square, Milton Park, Abingdon, Oxon OX14 4RN

and by Routledge
605 Third Avenue, New York, NY 10158

Routledge is an imprint of the Taylor & Francis Group, an informa business

British Library Cataloguing-in-Publication Data
A catalogue record for this book is available from the British Library

ISBN: 978-1-032-31057-2 (hbk)
ISBN: 978-1-032-31062-6 (pbk)
ISBN: 978-1-003-30785-3 (ebk)

DOI: 10.4324/9781003307853

Typeset in ITC Galliard Pro
by Apex CoVantage, LLC

Contents

Contributors

Mikhail Antonov, Professor at Law Faculty at HSE University

Zachary R. Calo, Professor of Law at Hamad bin Khalifa University—Qatar

Justin Collings, Professor of Law at Brigham Young University J. Reuben Clark School of Law

Hans-Joachim Cremer, Chair for Public Law and Legal Philosophy at University of Mannheim

Michelle Flynn, Irish barrister and Associate at the Department of Law and Anthropology, Max Planck Institute for Social Anthropology, Halle, Germany

Paul Gowder, Professor of Law at Northwestern Pritzker School of Law

Eugenia Relaño Pastor, Dr. Habil., Professor of Law at Complutense University of Madrid

Andrea Pin, Full Professor of Comparative Public Law at University of Padua

Giorgio Repetto, Professor of University of Perugia

Neville Rochow, Associate Professor (Adjunct) at the University of Adelaide Law School

Brett G. Scharffs, The Rex E. Lee Chair and Professor of Law and Director of the International Center for Law and Religion Studies at Brigham Young University J. Reuben Clark School of Law

Haim Shapira, Professor of Law at Bar-Ilan University

Piotr Szymaniec, Dr. Habil. in Law, Professor at Angelus Silesius State University in Wałbrzych

Eugene K. B. Tan, Associate Professor of Law at Singapore Management University—Yong Pung How School of Law

Christine M. Venter, Teaching Professor at Notre Dame Law School and Affiliated Faculty in Gender Studies at the University of Notre Dame

Dmytro Vovk, Visiting Associate Professor at Benjamin N. Cardozo School of Law; Director of the Center for the Rule of Law and Religion Studies at Yaroslav Mudryi National Law University

Acknowledgments

We are grateful to Pembroke College for hosting the conference, and to the International Center for Law and Religion Studies at Brigham Young University for facilitating the gathering, which was held concurrently with the Center's Young Scholar's Workshop on Religion and the Rule of Law, held across the street in Oxford at Christ Church. There were remarkable synergies between the two gatherings, and we are very grateful to Routledge for the opportunity to work with them on this volume.

We are also grateful to the authors who contributed to this book, to Brigham Young University law student, Alec G. Monson, for his help with the introduction, and to Amy Andrus, Jane Wise, Keylla Ortega, and Elyse Slabaugh for editing support.

1 Introduction

Human Dignity in Adjudication

Brett G. Scharffs, Andrea Pin, and Dmytro Vovk

Overview

In the study of human dignity, one of the most important questions for lawyers and judges is whether human dignity is itself a right or, rather, the foundation of rights. The answer, of course, varies from legal system to system, and sometimes the answer is, unsurprisingly, both.

This book is an effort to contribute to and update scholarly work that has already been done on this topic. This project brings together a remarkable group of emerging as well as established scholars, focusing systematically on the uses of human dignity in the work of courts in a variety of countries. What emerges is not only an enlightening set of comparative law perspectives on an important question, but more importantly, a deepening of our collective understanding of just how generative, foundational, and useful human dignity is as a legal concept.

There were two primary antecedents to this volume. The first was the effort to draft and adopt what became the *Punta del Este Declaration on Human Dignity for Everyone Everywhere*, which was finalized and promulgated in December, 2018, as part of an effort to commemorate the 70th anniversary of the unanimous adoption by the United Nations General Assembly of the Universal Declaration of Human Rights (UDHR).[1] The drafters of the UDHR were representatives of a variety of legal and cultural backgrounds from all over the world who were working at a time when the horrors of World War II were fresh upon the world's memory. They found in the universal value of human dignity a shared commitment to the worth of each human being. Human dignity was the lodestar that guided their three years of discussions and drafting, and it became the organizing heart of the Universal Declaration on Human Rights.[2] Seventy years later, The Punta del Este Declaration focused on the many practical uses of human dignity in the field of human rights.[3] Perhaps it is no coincidence that the post-World War II Constitution of Germany and the Basic Law of Israel emphasize human dignity as a core, foundational value.

The process of drafting and promulgating the Punta del Este Declaration laid the groundwork for a conference, held the following year at Pembroke

DOI: 10.4324/9781003307853-1

College, Oxford University, where a group of scholars gathered to discuss human dignity and the work of courts. The presentations at that conference were of such a high quality that it led to what became this book. The Punta del Este Declaration has also inspired a variety of other initiatives to explore and examine various perspectives on human dignity, including Christian perspectives, religious perspectives more broadly, African perspectives on human dignity, Asian perspectives on human dignity, and Islamic perspectives on human dignity. We hope a series of related books will be published memorializing the work on these projects.

Contents

The book is divided into four parts. Part I focuses on the social meaning, legal salience, and role in the adjudication of human dignity. Paul Gowder of Northwestern University School of Law contributes a chapter titled, "The Rule of Law Sets Its Face Against Humiliation."

As Gowder explains, to humiliate a person is to force them to surrender their dignity by performatively affirming their subordinate status. The rule of law protects persons against the dignitary injury inflicted by the bully, understood as a wrongdoer characterized by a taste for the humiliation of others. This chapter draws out the relationship between this category of dignitary harm and the rule of law through an examination of American White supremacy both in historical context and the author's own experience with racist police bullying.

Understood in this way, the concept of dignity unifies the allegedly disjointed facets of the rule of law. Formal conceptions of the rule of law according to which its core achievement is the avoidance of lawless violence and substantive conceptions that focus on the ideal of equal law turn out, in Gowder's view, to share the goal of allowing subjects of law to live with dignity.

As Gowder elaborates, this conception of dignity also has the potential to be of use in constitutional and human rights advocacy and adjudication, because it permits a connection between observed behavior and the normative status of law: if we observe undignified behavior in response to some legal regime, that gives strong reason to conclude that those who are driven to behave undignifiedly have been reduced to an unacceptably subordinate status. This reason is both epistemic—undignified behavior is evidence that the person so behaving is subject to arbitrary power forcing them to do so—and at least in a weak sense constitutive, in that part of the character of the rule of law is its capacity to permit dignified behavior.

The next chapter, by Neville Rochow of Adelaide University Law School and Hans-Joachim Cremer of the University of Manheim, is a dialogue between the Anglophone common law world and the German civil code world, and features a comparative legal analysis between Australia, Great Britain, the United States, and German jurisprudence. In Germany, dignity is a constitutional mandate. The idea of dignity in Germany comes from Kant—his philosophy laid the legal foundation for human rights. It is the idea that all human beings have the social claim to being valued and respected, which prohibits making the person an object of the state or subjecting citizens to treatment individuals do not deserve.

Rochow and Cremer also note that dignity is the source of human rights law. In the Universal Declaration of Human Rights "equal and inalienable rights" and "the inherent dignity of all members of the human family" are linked. The European Court of Human Rights (EctHR) confirmed that when they said the "very essence of the Convention is respect for human dignity and human freedom" (*Pretty v. United Kingdom*, para. 65).

As they peruse a variety of rulings, Rochow and Cremer suggest the German jurisprudence on dignity should inform appellate courts in Australia, the United Kingdom, and the United States. In *Clubb v. Edwards*, the High Court of Australia ruled that prohibitions on communications around abortion centers respected the dignity of the people there to protect them from uninvited political messages. In *Bull and Bull v. Hall and anor another*, the Supreme Court of Great Britain the United Kingdom faced Christian hotel owners who denied a room to gay partners wanting to stay there. The Court considered the competing right to not be discriminated against by both parties but eventually ruled in favor of the gay couple. But in *Lee v. Ashers Baking Company Ltd.*, the Court refused to force bakers to support gay marriage on their cake. The baker's dignity required the Court to not violate his conscience. In *Masterpiece Cakeshop*, the United States Supreme Court ruled that religious individuals have the right to have their case heard by an impartial judge.

Rochow and Cremer conclude that under the First Amendment, the United States has no concept of human dignity associated with it. They argue that the US should look to Germany and implement human dignity more progressively. The judiciaries of Australia, the United Kingdom, and the United States are consigned to wait for the legislature to effectuate the change to valuing human dignity. German courts, on the other hand, have evolved their jurisprudence to create solutions to these problems.

Justin Collings of Brigham Young University Law School contributes a chapter titled, "Dignity Proper and Dignity Plus: On the Uses of Dignity in German Constitutional Jurisprudence." Collings explains that Germany's Federal Constitutional Court is pivotal in promoting dignity in German society. The Court has placed dignity as the "supreme value in the value system of fundamental rights." Dignity in German jurisprudence is unamendable, the Court says. But an absolute value requires a rigidly narrow scope. The problem is the more Germany has elevated dignity, the less of a role it has played. Dignity proper is absolute and narrow. Dignity plus is relative, limitable, and more applicable in German law.

As Collings describes it, "dignity proper" came from Germany's post-WWII efforts to "never again" have a government without regard for human dignity. Each individual possesses dignity, both living and dead. Dignity does not begin with birth nor end with death, although the need to protect the dead diminishes with time. This meant abortion was illegal. Dignity permits self-development and self-determination. German courts also rely on dignity as a right by itself and a principle justifying other rights without explanation.

In contrast, in Collings' analysis, "dignity plus" is used in three ways: supplemental dignity, hybrid dignity, and jurisgenerative dignity. Supplemental dignity works in conjunction with other constitutional guarantees. Hybrid dignity is when the Court combines the dignity guarantee with the constitutional promise of the development of one's personality. Jurisgenerative dignity is when the Court derives new and unenumerated rights from general claims of liberty. Collings concludes that two criticisms of German jurisprudence remain: 1) the Court is inconsistent. It never explains why dignity requires protection when it does, and why not when it does not. 2) Collings worries that dignity is a mechanism that allows the German Court to discover and invent new rights with no basis.

The final chapter in Part I is by Zachary R. Calo of the Hamad bin Khalifa University in Qatar, on "Dignity, Sexuality, and Moral Order in Legal and Judicial Debates." In Calo's view, human dignity is undefined term that has not been agreed upon and that potentially harms the legal process and progress. An unqualified use of dignity can lead to contradictory results, as happened with the concept of "Dignitary harm." Religious groups have reinforced their view of heterosexual marriage by claiming a dignitary harm to marriage if it is extended to homosexual couples. On the other hand, the Constitutional Court of South Africa found criminalizing homosexual activities to harm gays' dignity. Laws that treat citizens unequally on the basis of sexual orientation damage dignity.

Dignity also coincides with the values of freedom and autonomy. A person has dignity only if they can self-actualize and make decisions for themselves. The United States Supreme Court in *Lawrence v. Texas* held a law banning homosexual relations violated homosexuals' "dignity as free persons."

For Calo, dignity frees from that which limits human potentiality and autonomy. France has dealt with religious headscarves worn by Islamic women. Non-Islamic people normally see it as a violation of the woman's dignity because it dehumanizes them by forcing them to be subservient to men. In contrast, a Sunni Muslim argued that it was her exercise of religious freedom and that the idea that human dignity was based on "chauvinistic logic" that assumes that women who wear the full veil lack agency and autonomy. Calo analogizes that approach to claiming slavery as the ultimate expression of true freedom. The dignity argument on both sides left the legal crisis unresolved.

As Calo sees it, "liberationist dignity" seeks to remove individuals from oppressive religion. Religious dignity is inferior to society's dignity because religion is wrong when it comes to LGBTQ+ and marriage definitions. Preventing homosexuals from self-actualization violates human dignity. The confused nature of dignity leads to dignity wars. Calo concludes that every human being has intrinsic worth, this worth should be recognized by others, and the state exists for the individual and not the individual for the state. The competition between dignities shows the need for a new shared meaning of dignity.

* * * * *

Part II focuses on International and Comparative Perspectives on Human Dignity. It begins with a contribution from Andrea Pin from the University of Padua, titled, "Supranational Dignity: The Court of Justice of the European Union's Conceptualization of a Legal Value." Pin argues that the Court of Justice of the European Union (CJEU) advances human dignity in Europe with an incremental approach. Two legal concepts made its progress possible—first, the doctrine of "direct effect" in its *Van Gend En Loos* judgment and the "European Communities' legal supremacy." Direct effect means the European Communities' (EC) regulations create rights that are directly enforceable by domestic courts without the need for states to execute them. Legal supremacy granted EC and EU law over domestic law and gave domestic judges the power and responsibility to rule EC and EU law.

Although the 2000 European Charter of Fundamental Rights cites human dignity seven times, according to Pin, it is the CJEU that caused the concept of human dignity to take flight. The CJEU has trimmed down the sovereignty of Member States. Since the EU's Charter limits it to economic activities, the CJEU can expand human rights through an economic lens. This leads to problems with conflicting interests, but the CJEU has favored expanding human rights via claims of dignity. For example, the EU protects workers' freedom of movement within its borders, including the right to family reunification. The CEJU ruled in *Coman* that states must recognize same-sex partnerships because failure to do so would discourage gay couples from relocating within the EU, threatening the EU's freedom of movement with the family.

Overall, human dignity in the CEJU's case law protects the individual from public powers and triggers public policies. The CJEU's approach has several consequences. The CJEU views dignity in a constitutional fashion—dignity falls within social justice and equality and calls for a concrete, case-by-case approach instead of rigid rules; it views dignity as a right and principle creating further rights for individuals; it usually rejects formalist understandings of dignity to avoid weakening claims; it allows the concept of human dignity to drive legal innovation and broaden human rights protections.

The following chapter by Eugenia Relaño Pastor from Complutense University of Madrid is titled, "A Multi-Approach to Human Dignity in the European Court of Human Rights." For Pastor, the concept of dignity is vague and undefined. Nevertheless, it is a potent legal tool that courts have relied on despite the lack of consensus as to what it means and how it is applied in contradictory ways. The paper explores the plurality of meanings after WWII and features a typology of conceptions of human dignity as a tool for the ECtHR through the "dignity cases."

In Pastor's typology, dignity has several definitions: 1) dignity operating as the foundation for human rights (German Constitution); 2) dignity understood in reverse order with human rights, meaning dignity does not justify human rights, rather it informs the content of human rights; 3) dignity as synonymous with individuality and self-realization; 4) dignity attached to context, in which case, dignity is contextual and pragmatic but not relativist, and the generalization of particular dignities does not lose its fine distinctions between contexts; 5) dignity as tied to people's self-esteem and worth, which implies their vulnerability, with their vulnerability displaying their dignity; 6) human dignity as a limitation to human rights, in which case individual and collective identities are interconnected—the increase of individual dignity leads to an increase in human rights. This will result in a limited jurisprudence regarding human dignity and will limit dignity rights to the individual and collective.

Although the European Convention on Human Rights and Fundamental Freedoms (ECHR) was completely silent about human dignity, the Strasbourg Court's jurisprudence has developed and interpreted the rights to include human dignity. The first reference to human dignity appeared in the *East African Asian case*, where racial discrimination was an infringement of petitioners' rights. The Court interprets "degrading" behavior in Article 3 of the ECHR to include behavior that violates human dignity. The Court also uses dignity as a bridging notion in Articles 14 (discrimination) and 11 (freedom of assembly and association). The Strasbourg Court's multiple interpretations and their breadth have created a malleable analysis used to protect human rights.

Christine M. Venter, from Notre Dame Law School in the United States, contributes a chapter titled, "Acknowledging Persons and Communities of Infinite Worth: The Concept of Dignity in the Jurisprudence of the South African Constitutional Court." Venter asserts that the South African Constitutional Court is developing a robust dignity jurisprudence, defining dignity as both a right and legitimizing principle. The Constitution declares dignity to be a right of both individuals and entire communities, and the lack of dignity for the individual harms the community. The Court protects dignity in two ways. First, the Court enforces dignity in finding violations of Article 9 of their Constitution, which is the right to equal protection and freedom from discrimination. According to this line of reasoning, discrimination is the crime and dignity is the reason. Second, the Court will declare the right of dignity has been violated as stated in Article 10 of the Constitution, which guarantees each person will have his or her dignity "respected and protected."

The Court has held that dignity rights are required to vindicate: 1) the right to equality and non-discrimination; 2) the enforcement of socio-economic rights; 3) the right to have one's dignity recognized by not being subjected to cruel, arbitrary, or inhumane treatment by the state; and 4) the right to express oneself both as an individual and in community through one's autonomy. For example, in *Dawood v. Minister of Home Affairs*, the Court held that a statute denying married persons the right to live together while their immigrant residence permits were pending was a violation of the dignity right per se. While the decisions defending dignity as a stand-alone right are few, the jurisprudence is growing.

Piotr Szymaniec, from Angelus Silesius University of Applied Sciences in Wałbrzych, contributes a chapter titled, "Human Dignity as Constitutional Value: The Viewpoint of Polish Courts." Szymaniec notes that Article 30 of the Polish Constitution of April 2, 1997, states that human dignity is a source of the freedoms and rights of individuals and citizens, including in the Constitution. Therefore, the Polish Constitution follows the path marked by the German Basic Law of 1949, which in Article 1, Section 1 declares human dignity to be an inviolable value. Szymaniec notes that it is legitimate to question whether Polish constitutional jurisprudence has developed its own approach to the notion of dignity or merely repeated concepts elaborated elsewhere. In his view, it is doubtful that an analysis of the Constitutional Court's judgments reveals a uniform and coherent concept of dignity, utilized by the Court. On the one hand, the Court's views are strongly influenced by the German concept of dignity as a natural law element underpinning the entire positive-law system. Moreover, Gunter Dürig's "object-formula" being itself a transformation of the Kantian understanding of dignity, is also emphasized in Polish jurisprudence. On the other hand, however, statements influenced by personalism and a liberal approach, emphasizing the sphere of individual autonomy as well as the sociological concept of dignity, can also be found in the judgments of the Polish Constitutional Court.

* * * * *

Part III focuses on human dignity, religion, and courts. Michelle Flynn from the Max Planck Institute for Social Anthropology contributes a chapter titled, "Deliberations on Dignity: Irish Case Law Concerning Medical Intervention and Freedom of Religion, Belief and Conscience." The Irish Constitution relies heavily on natural law. From an Irish perspective, human dignity comes from natural law and provides Irish courts the opportunity to expand on the doctrine. Human dignity means the "inviolable intrinsic value, equal to other persons, that the person has and includes the recognition by other persons of such value with respect of that person." While treating human dignity as its own right is appealing it poses problems. When stretched too thin, human dignity's expansion may hurt other human rights.

The Irish High Court has ruled that dignity requires that an adult have the right to choose their medical treatment. In one case, a woman was in a vegetative state for 23 years, so her family chose to remove her from life support. The Irish Supreme Court justified its approval of permitting the death on human dignity grounds. But the problem is more complicated when parents make healthcare decisions for their children. The state has an interest in life but the parents have their religious freedom too. In *Fitzpatrick and Ryan v. F.K. and the Attorney General*, a Jehovah's Witness hemorrhaged after giving birth and losing blood. She refused to consent to receive the blood transfusion. The High Court ruled that "(t)he right to life is the pre-eminent personal right. . . . The respect is absolute." However, the Court justified the hospital's decision to provide the blood and save the woman's life due to objective evidence that she did not have capacity to make a decision about the blood transfusion.

In *North Western Health Board v. H.W. and C.W.*, the High Court ruled that the state has a duty to protect children's rights only in exceptional circumstances where parents had failed in their duty toward their children for moral or physical reasons. Differing opinions between doctors and parents did not warrant the state making healthcare decisions for the child instead of the parent. The screening medical test suggested strongly by doctors did not rise to the level of state intervention. But in *Baby A.B.: Children's University Hospital Temple Street v. C.D. and E.F.*, which involved the baby of a Jehovah's Witness who would die without a blood transfusion, the High Court ruled that the state's interest in life could "prevail even in the face of express and fundamental constitutional rights." (para. 35). In another case, the parent's refusal to administer pain relief drugs to the child was again found within the parent's discretion. According to Flynn's analysis, the expansion of human dignity to protect life is problematic when it contradicts religious freedom. Determining where and to what extent rights exist requires case-by-case analysis to avoid an overly broad expansion forced by judges that would harm other human rights.

Haim Shapira from Bar-Ilan University contributes a chapter titled, "Religious Perspectives of Human Dignity in the Context of Israeli Case Law." As Shapira shows, the notion of human dignity has been of paramount importance in the development of Israeli constitutionalism, as much of what was dubbed the "Constitutional Revolution" stemmed from the passing of the *Israeli Basic Law: Human Dignity and Liberty.*

Shapira showcases the importance and contentiousness of the concept of human dignity within the Israeli Supreme Court's case law. Dignity both bolstered the Supreme Court's activity of reviewing the Parliament's legislation and to develop a panoply of rights. In fact, if the Parliament was reticent in implementing several fundamental rights, the Supreme Court massaged the concept of human dignity to derive a wealth of freedoms. Dignity has been more than a right—it has formed the basis for the jurisprudential creation of more rights.

The list of rights and how to balance them has shifted through the years, Shapira argues, along two different, and often competing, strands of thinking. On the one hand, Aharon Barak and his intellectual progeny fostered an idea of dignity centered around the self-determination and the autonomy of the individual. This Kantian reading of human dignity, however, has long coexisted with a jurisprudence that has read the notion of dignity within the framework of Jewish sources. In Israel, dignity thus became the crisscross of the Janus-faced Israeli and democratic constitutional pedigree.

Mikhail Antonov from the HSE University, contributes a chapter titled, "Human (Personal) Dignity as an Argumentation Tool of the Russian Constitutional Court." Article 21 of the Russian Constitution enshrines human dignity as one of the Constitution's fundamental values. However, the concept of dignity is not firmly established in Russian jurisprudence. In practice, Russian courts tend to stick to the traditionalist definition of dignity prevailing in the communitarian discourse. This discourse, in its turn, is largely shaped by the doctrine of the Russian Orthodox Church. Due to its malleability, this concept is subject to broad interpretations and can be utilized for different purposes, including delimitation of other constitutional rights from certain ideological positions.

Antonov's chapter analyzes the conceptual conflict in the interpretation of dignity: its liberal context in the Constitution and its conservative use in political discourses and in court practice, both being informed by the Russian Orthodox Church's doctrine. Particularly, in the jurisprudence of the Russian Federation's Constitutional Court, this concept was sometimes utilized to restrict constitutional freedoms such as expression, conscience, and speech, and to deny the equal protection principle. The chapter argues that, in this context, argumentative references to "personal dignity" can sometimes justify discretionary delimitation of constitutional rights by courts, so that "dignity"—in the way it is understood by the majority—can become a dangerous rhetorical tool utilized to limit individual freedoms.

* * * * *

Part IV focuses on Human Dignity and Social Rights Protection. It begins with a chapter by Giorgio Repetto from the University of Perugia, entitled, "Between Autonomy and Solidarity: The Use of Human Dignity in Social Rights Issues. A European Perspective." Repetto examines whether and to what extent human dignity is a viable legal basis for promoting social rights and welfare policies. His main concern is that human dignity is at odds with the world—human dignity has high moral ambitions but is aimed at places of the world in political turmoil. The ineffective message sends a reversal of the intended message.

Repetto examines four countries and their judiciaries' enforcement of human rights: Germany, France, Italy, and Great Britain. In his view, Germany's judiciary is the strongest—the Federal Constitutional Court declared a duty on the legislature to provide social services via legislation. But the duty is not enforceable because the objective burden of proof is a high standard. The strong vision of human dignity and social rights has led to undetermined results. Repetto finds human dignity incommensurable with social rights: Germany likely gained social rights from legislative interventions.

In France, legislation in the social field did not per se establish a link to human dignity. The French *Conseil Constitutionnel* claims human dignity in several cases but widespread consensus agrees that human dignity is not yet a basic value. The Italian Constitution mentions human dignity several times, but the Italian Constitutional Court rarely invokes human dignity. Instead, the Court defers to the legislature and limits its intervention in the social field. In Great Britain, human dignity is forced by the ECHR and fundamental freedoms. There is a stance against the empowerment of human dignity through judicial decisions. Again, the judiciary defers to the legislature.

The relationship between human dignity and social rights is not straightforward. In Repetto's view, human dignity is not per se a valid yardstick for social progress but it can still be invoked to protect basic human rights.

Human dignity mediates between freedom and equality. Individual liberty and common good are found in constitutional texts and are built upon by legislation. Judges and legislatures work in tandem—legislatures rely on judges to deal with varied situations and judges rely on legislatures to offer responses on conflicting interests. Human dignity is the "shadow," the underlying value balancing individual autonomy and the pursuit of the common good.

Eugene K. B. Tan from the School of Law at Singapore Management University contributes a chapter titled, "Dignity as a Shield. The Putative Dignitarian Discourse on Protecting Migrant Domestic Workers in Singapore." Tan notes that courts in Singapore in recent years have come out strongly in abuse of female migrant domestic worker (MDW) cases and have imposed deterrent sanctions against employers convicted of abusing their MDWs. For example, in *ADF v. Public Prosecutor* (2010), the Court of Appeal, Singapore's highest court, reviewed the sentencing principles relevant to a person convicted of voluntarily causing harm to an MDW. While the Court in the *ADF* case did not engage in a discourse on rights, it is evident that the principles of human dignity and respect exerted a strong influence in the Court's determination of the outcome of the case and in meting out the appropriate punishment. The considerations of "fairness, respect, and dignity" were given judicial cognizance. As the apex court noted, the regulatory regime has its inherent limitations and reach since the cloistered domestic setting does not always facilitate the enforcement actions that can prevent the mistreatment of the MDWs. This chapter examines the developing judicial discourse on dignity and respect in the context of protecting MDWs in Singapore. It considers whether the dignitarian discourse is adequate in protecting the vulnerable segment of society and whether it can catalyze greater consideration and respect for the well-being, if not the rights, of MDWs.

* * * * *

As the chapters that fill this volume attest, human dignity is a complex, contested, and contestable concept. It is our hope that these chapters enrich and enlighten our collective appreciation of human dignity as a rich and generative value, and an important tool in a variety of adjudicative contexts. As with all tools, of course, human dignity is capable of being used skillfully and well, less well, and even in ways that are inappropriate, disingenuous, or dangerous. This is not to downplay the importance of the concept, but to alert us to the variety of uses of its conceptions.

The notion of human dignity invites conversations about its meaning, roots, and judicial usage. In a world in which relationships are becoming increasingly strained and conversations are turning less friendly and frequent, we hope this volume keeps conversations alive.

Notes

1 The Declaration and the explanatory materials are available at www.dignityforeveryone.org/introduction/.
2 See more on UDHR Founding figures at the 2023 symposium "Essays in Honor of the 75th Anniversary of the Universal Declaration of Human Rights." *Review of Faith & International Affairs* 21 4).
3 Brett G. Scharffs and Ewelina U. Ochab (2022) published a companion volume to this book focusing specifically on the Punta del Este Declaration.

Reference

Scharffs, Brett G., and Ewelina U. Ochab. 2022. *Dignity and International Human Rights Law: An Introduction to the Punta Del Este Declaration on Human Dignity for Everyone Everywhere*. New York: Routledge.

Part I

The Social Meaning, Legal Salience, and Role in Adjudication of Human Dignity

2 The Rule of Law Sets Its Face Against Humiliation

Paul Gowder

Introduction

Scholars of dignity frequently offer their readers a typology of its uses, sometimes to build a unified account, sometimes merely to clarify the conceptual muddle by distinguishing between its senses (e.g. Anderson 2014; Bayefsky 2013; Schroeder 2010). These all seem to cover the same broad territory, more or less, but with an author's unique spin depending on the purpose for which the typology is built.

In that vein, we can sketch out at least three distinct facets of dignity:

1. Dignity as property of persons ("human dignity") in virtue of which they gain moral or political entitlements, as in Kantian or Catholic conceptions of dignity (e.g. Moyn 2014).
2. Dignity in the sense of "dignified treatment," as a way to treat people that is in accord with their status (e.g. Dan-Cohen 2002; Khaitan 2012; Waldron 2012).
3. Dignity in the sense of individual behavior, the "dignified person." For the most part, this idea has been attached to an individual ethical principle, i.e., that one ought not to grovel, flatter, or be a people-pleaser, that one's life goes less well in some perfectionist sense if one does so.[1] As I will be focusing on this third category of dignity, let us give it a separate name for ease of reference: "uprightness."

A person's capacity to live with uprightness can be a source of moral obligations for others. Some areas of our existing moral dialogue seem to rely on such an idea. For example, when advocates of the legalization of assisted suicide speak of "death with dignity," they seem to be at least sometimes claiming that, at a certain level of advanced illness, one is forced by circumstances to function in a non-upright fashion due to, for example, lack of control of one's excretory functions, and that a person who is so forced is wronged by those who keep him or her from choosing death to avoid the indignity (e.g. Street and Kissane 2001).

DOI: 10.4324/9781003307853-3

A wrongdoer can also directly attack another's capacity to live with uprightness. For the most classic example, consider the figure of the *bully*, who routinely beats up her victim until the victim is reduced to a state in which he is driven to grovel to her to avoid a beating. Apart from the moral wrongdoing of the beating in the first place, it seems to me that we can also accuse the bully of an additional form of wrongdoing in virtue of the fact that she has stripped her victim of his dignity as uprightness. She has, in other words, *humiliated* him.

Because of the relativity of status—because it is possible to increase one's own status (whether merely self-perceived or also other-perceived) by degrading another, we can find analytic traction on practices of humiliation in the law by examining their function in contextually significant status negotiations. This chapter draws out some of these features of status, humiliation, dignity, and law through the lens of American race relations and arbitrary police power. In particular, it attempts to shed light on those legal/racial status negotiations through my own experiences of being subjected to a police officer's attempt at humiliation. In doing so, I draw on the techniques of critical race theory in legal scholarship, which has long relied on personal narrative to unsettle hierarchically bound conceptions of the social function of law (Bell 1995, 899; Espinoza and Harris 1997, 1630; Delgado 1989). The reader's indulgence is requested, as this technique requires some development before the intellectual payoff can be reached.

The Orleans Parish Prison

I spent the afternoon of July 24, 2003 in jail. At the time, I was 24 years old, a graduate of Harvard Law School, a member of the bars of Massachusetts and Oregon, and I had just left a job as a legal aid lawyer to move to New Orleans and find something less burnout-inducing to do with my time. I drove a barely functional Dodge with a broken taillight and out-of-state plates, as well as a number of left-wing bumper stickers. I am also Black, although I can pass as White in some contexts.[2]

The broken taillight was the police officer's initial excuse to pull me over.[3] However, rather than writing me a citation for the taillight and sending me on my way, the officer immediately asked me if I had any "drugs or weapons." When I said "no," he ordered me out of the car and began to root around inside.

As I uttered the standard ritual phrases of constitutional self-protection ("I do not consent to this search"), I also tried to signal my status as a lawyer capable of defending myself by showing him one of my bar cards. The moment I did so, he put me in handcuffs and locked me in the back of the police car. He then returned to his search of my car. Several minutes later, he returned to wave a cigarette butt under my nose, asking, "What do you think about this, Mr. Lawyer?" At that point, he told me that I was under arrest for possession of marijuana.[4]

I was taken to the Orleans Parish Prison, which also serves as the New Orleans city jail, and which became internationally notorious two years later during Hurricane Katrina when the Sheriff's Department abandoned hundreds of prisoners who were locked up with chest-high floodwaters, sewage, and no food or water (Human Rights Watch 2005). Mother Jones has characterized it as one of America's worst prisons and aptly describes its epidemic of sexual assaults, stabbings, drug dealing by guards, and similar abuses as "barbaric" (Ridgeway and Casella 2013). My inner experience throughout was a high-speed oscillation between terror that I would be beaten or disappeared by the police who evidently had some kind of grudge and no regard for the legal propriety of their actions, and fury that my legal experience, my bar card, and my Harvard degree didn't protect me from it.

In retrospect, having acted out that terror-fury with shouting and banging on the bars, I'm surprised I didn't leave with broken bones or worse. And given the documented character of the prison and the police, I doubt I could have avoided violence had I stayed locked up for long.[5] I may be alive today thanks to the good fortune that I had been doing some work for a fixture in the local music industry, a (White) woman who happened to be a member of a prominent Louisiana political family. When the deputies eventually permitted me to use the telephone, I called her. She called a judge. The judge signed an order for my release—no arraignment, no bail hearing, no reading of charges, just an order, sight unseen, and I was released from jail four hours after I entered.

Having been arbitrarily sprung by an irregular judicial act, I had not received any of the standard processes, such as an appearance date or an opportunity to enter a plea; consequently, I had no idea of the status of the charges against me. About a week after my release, I called the prosecutor's office to try to ascertain some of this information and was relieved to learn that that charge had been dropped—according to the person on the other end of the telephone, because they tested whatever "joint" the officer had turned in and discovered that there wasn't any marijuana in it.

Reflecting on that experience so many years in the future and from the safe intellectual distance of a tenured position in a well-regarded law school in the north, the primary impression it now makes on me is of the utter lawlessness of the whole interaction. Throughout the entire process, nothing was done legally, everything was just a raw exercise of power. The officer chose to arrest an innocent man, and plant something purporting to be "evidence" in order to justify the action, based on nothing more than evident race and/or political bias and the fact that he had the power to do so; I escaped punishment only by deploying similarly arbitrary power to which I happened to have access, and even the traffic ticket for the broken taillight (which the officer ultimately wrote and slipped into my shirt pocket as I was being booked into the prison) was, I unhappily suspect, eventually resolved other than by ordinary legal processes (more on this later).

But there's also a clear status dimension to the interaction. The officer was, probably, originally provoked by my refusal to hide my politics—by my (admittedly obnoxious) left-wing bumper stickers, and the contrast of that boldness to the race and class signals that my person and my broken-down vehicle sent. But the real provocation, the thing that landed me in Orleans Parish Prison, clearly came when I dared to claim the status, authority, and competence of a lawyer to resist his illegal behavior. It was flashing the bar card that put me in cuffs, and that earned me a snide "Mr. Lawyer" as I was taken to lockup. I was acting out of my place, either falsely claiming to be a lawyer, or, perhaps even worse from the officer's perspective, actually having the temerity to be a lawyer, and to think that made me an important person, all the while bearing the physical markers of lower status on my body and my vehicle. I created status dissonance in the officer, and he sorted it out by reinforcing the hierarchy as he perceived it.

On that reading of the interaction, I could have protected myself by taking on my designated role as a subordinate (or maybe by paying a bribe—it's possible that the stop was originally intended to be a shake-down). I was supposed to grovel a little bit, to supplicate, and certainly not quite literally attempt to play the lawyer card. Like all bullies, he wanted me to surrender my dignity, to behave obsequiously, to say "uncle." Seeing me unwilling to do so, he was happy to use force to enforce his hierarchical position.

And that reading also accommodates the denouement. The story the prosecutor's office gave to me doesn't ring true—it seems unlikely that they found the resources to send every ostensible joint turned in by a police officer to some lab to test its THC content, and certainly not within a week of arrest. More likely, my ad hoc release signaled that I could back up my claims to status—that I had access to the Louisiana power structure, and—shifting from the individual officer's standpoint to the standpoint of the city's criminal justice apparatus as a whole—I was no longer to be treated as a subordinate who could be arbitrarily imprisoned, but as a meaningful threat. Hence, the prosecutor—maybe knowing that the arrest was unwarranted, maybe simply not caring—chose to drop the charges rather than risk whatever political trouble I might be able to make.

I contend that reflecting on this account can help us shed light on dignity as a juridical concept—with its opposite, represented by the police officer's abuse of his authority as a negotiation of status—and commonalities between that interaction and a range of abuses along a spectrum from commonplace schoolyard bullying to Jim Crow.

Dignity: One Conceptual Typology of Many

I propose to begin by making a distinction between second-person dignitary wrongs and first-person dignitary wrongs. A second-person dignitary wrong is an insult, in which Ego assaults Alter's dignity by doing something that one does not do to persons whom one respects (i.e., a violation of dignity in the second sense of the typology in the introduction). For example, if Ego surreptitiously takes naked pictures of Alter and posts them on the internet, Ego has assaulted Alter's dignity because posting naked pictures of someone isn't in accord with their status.

By contrast, first-person dignitary wrongs (humiliations) are acts that Ego takes against Alter which coerce Alter into surrendering his or her own uprightness. Humiliations are wrong because they impose on Alter the practical obligation to violate his or her own dignity, by acting like an undignified, low-status, person.

Humiliation seems to me to be the defining behavior of the bully. The schoolyard bully, to take its quintessential example, doesn't merely want one's lunch money; the schoolyard bully wants one to say "uncle"—put differently, the schoolyard bully has a taste for relative status achieved through the humiliation of others, and a disposition to procure that status through the abuse of power, typically violently. For further expository convenience, I shall use the term "bullying" to stand in for "aggressive first-person dignitary wrong"; a bully is one who is disposed to humiliate others.

One indicator of domination, according to Pettit (2012, 84–87), is the extent to which people can look one another in the eyes. As Pettit explains, domination is a product of inadequately controlled power—one dominates another when one can interfere with their choices without fear of suffering sanctions. Relationships structured by persistent bullying (or its continual latent threat, which amounts to a structural kind of bullying, as further discussed later) violate Pettit's "eyeball test."

My New Orleans experience illustrates the relationship between domination and the eyeball test. In my interaction with the officer, I mistakenly thought that my being a lawyer conferred upon me the capacity to sanction the officer for arbitrary use of power; hence, I didn't engage in the subordinate behavior that was expected of me. I looked him in the eye, metaphorically speaking, without having any right, from his perspective, and the perspective of the larger social context in New Orleans, to do so. Hence, my behavior was status-dissonant, and he punished me to restore our relative places in the hierarchy. Only when both I and the prosecutor learned that I did have access to a meaningful alternate power structure (political connections) was my lack of deference allowed to pass without further punishment.

Put differently, the underlying status relations (reinforced by arbitrary power) created a kind of latent bullying—I was obliged to recognize the police officer's capacity to harm me with impunity, and hence obliged to mollify him with obsequious behavior. My failure to do so led him to deliver on the implicit threat, and, in doing so, make our relative status legible through the bullying exercise of power. Fortunately, I actually had invisible status which conferred on me the long-term power to resist the force directed at me; that status in turn protected me from the long-term consequences of the refusal to supplicate.

Filing Out the First-Person Dignitary Wrong

To sum up the foregoing: a bully gives his victim a strong incentive to surrender her uprightness and behave in an obsequious fashion toward the bully, via the wrongful use or threat of power.[6] The sufferer of a first-person dignitary wrong is obliged by force to act out her subordination, and thereby make the wrongdoer's implicit or explicit claim to superior status legible in her behavior.

Group-based latent humiliations—such as the racial character of New Orleans policing as described earlier—are, I contend, a key mechanism through which social caste is reinforced. By terrorizing all but the most privileged of some subordinate caste into submissive behavior in public, higher castes create a visible expression of their claimed superiority, one which provides continuous evidence of their advantaged status. Consider the Jim Crow era in the American South as a key example: the constant background risk of violence should Black Americans not behave obsequiously to Whites whom they happened to encounter would have reinforced the perceptions of social hierarchy in both races.

Similarly, because of the inadequate enforcement of laws against gender-based violence and patriarchal gender norms which have trained men to respond to frustration or perceived status threat with violence, women in patriarchal societies have reasons to behave obsequiously toward men. This is evidenced, for example, by the fact that women are often afraid to bluntly reject unwanted sexual advances from men (Bohns and DeVincent 2019).[7] All women living in societies with that persistent danger of gender-motivated violence thus have reason to complain of a class-based first-person dignitary wrong.

Such class-based first-person dignitary wrongs are likely to have a self-reinforcing character. The inequality of the classes is reinforced by the behavioral regularities that these power disparities create: superordinated classes become habituated to, and come to expect, small (or large) daily acts of subordination, and experience themselves as affronted when they're not provided; subordinated classes come to adopt self-abnegating beliefs consistent with the continual obligation to behave in a subordinate fashion. Again, we can see part of this in contemporary gender dynamics. For example, some women have observed that many men unconsciously expect them to give way when walking down the street; women's failure to do so leads to actual collisions.[8] These beliefs, in turn, are likely to promote in superordinated classes the growth of their disposition to respond with violence (or other sanctions) when their demands for deference are not met; the anticipation of such sanctions is likely to promote in subordinated classes additional fear and obsequiousness.

However, it is important to note that not all bullying will be reinforced by immediate violence. Sometimes, the violence can be structural, and the humiliation can be a consequence of institutions, including legal institutions, that direct a subordinated class to engage in behavior consistent with that low status.

The quintessential case of such institutional bullying is segregation, in which members of low-status social castes are forced to physically carry themselves into places that are humiliating because they are socially designated as inferior and reserved for undesirables. Moreover, because the segregated are people whose identities are seen as inferior, their presence in those spaces reinforces the inferior status of the places, even as their subjection to warehousing in those spaces reinforces their inferiority, establishing a vicious cycle of stigma and humiliation. This is the dynamic vividly highlighted in the famous doll study, in which Black children during the time of Jim Crow school segregation were led to see their own physical characteristics as representing inferiority, an understanding reinforced, if the Supreme Court in *Brown v. Board of Education of Topeka* is to be believed, by their compulsory occupation of segregated physical spaces.[9]

We should believe the Supreme Court, for first-person dignitary harms have natural connections with a belief in one's own inferiority. One of the most consistent insights of modern psychology is that human cognitions often follow actions, rather than the other way around. This is an abstract-level description of, for example, cognitive dissonance reduction (McGrath 2017); the relationship between behavioral changes, such as smiling, and mood (Alam et al. 2008); and perhaps even the broader phenomenon of adaptive preferences (Elster 1983). The essence of first-person dignitary wrongs is that the subordinated are rewarded for actions consistent with their inferiority and punished for actions consistent with their equal standing. How could one not come to believe that one is inferior over a sustained course of such treatment? Not surprisingly, there is evidence that the humiliated come to believe in their inferior status in real-world examples of deep institutional bullying, such as the enforced servility of bonded labor.[10]

First-Person Dignitary Wrongs and the Rule of Law

There is a highly suggestive passage in Frederick Douglass's account of his famous fight with the "slave-breaker" Covey (Douglass 1857, 242).

> Whence came the daring spirit necessary to grapple with a man who, eight-and-forty hours before, could, with his slightest word have made me tremble like a leaf in a storm, I do not know; at any rate, I was resolved to fight, and, what was better still, I was actually hard at it. The fighting madness had come upon me, and I found my strong fingers firmly attached to the throat of my cowardly tormentor; as heedless of consequences, at the moment, as though we stood as equals before the law. The very color of the man was forgotten.

Observe, first, how Douglass describes Covey in the standard terms of the bully—he's really a coward, like all bullies secretly are, who uses unjust access to violence to extract subordination ("trembl[ing] like a leaf") from his victims. But more importantly, observe Douglass's choice to highlight that it was the lack of equality before the law that had previously prevented him from being able to resist Covey's bullying, and that his newfound ability to resist created a simulacrum of legal equality. For the moment, between Douglass and Covey, there was the rule of law. And that rule of law came from his refusal to submit to Covey's attempts to inflict first-person dignitary wrongs on him, his incredible daring to fight back.

I contend that Douglass was quite right to equate his seizure of uprightness against Covey to a temporary, local, rule of law.

Before we get to that argument, however, we must pause for a moment for some methodological work. What is the point of talking about a concept like dignity? One need not deny that there is such a thing as dignity to be skeptical of the practical utility of spilling ink trying to figure out what it means. In particular, one may be tempted by a strategy of reductionism, in view of the following:

1. The copious literature putting forth numerous different conceptions of what dignity might be and what it might be good for—it may even be an essentially contested concept (Rodriguez 2015);
2. The potential for confusion between dignity as a political obligation and dignity as a way of living (O'Mahony 2012); and
3. The capacity of many if not all of those conceptions of dignity to be explained in terms of the (arguably) lower-level value of equality.[11]

If we are to resist the temptation to just reduce dignity to equality, we must find some use for the troubled concept. There are at least three possibilities.

First, we may have brute instrumental reasons for deploying a concept of dignity in real-world politics. Perhaps the idea of dignity appeals to our fellow citizens, maybe even in part because of its conceptual messiness, in a way that more abstract values like "equality" cannot. Or—a less instrumental version of the same idea—perhaps the fact that dignity captures both an individual virtue of ordinary moral life as well as an abstract political ideal makes it more epistemically accessible to our fellow citizens because their day-to-day lives are shaped by the practical goal of comporting with the virtue side of it.

Second, we may make use of a concept like dignity as an object of something like a Rawlsian overlapping consensus. We might believe, for example, that the multiplicity of conceptions of dignity bear a family resemblance to one another, such that adherents of divergent conceptions of the good can respectfully interact with one another based on the common core of the ideal. For example, liberal and Catholic citizens may find a shared value in dignity that can permit the mutual pursuit of justice. Even if their conceptions of dignity are wildly distinct and even opposed in some applications, there may still be areas of shared application—such as the moral condemnation of torture, perhaps—that may permit some beneficial common ground.

Third the ordinary ("folk") usage of the concept of dignity might offer us distinctive insights into a dimension of the underlying value of equality that mere reference to the underlying value obscures. Its capacity to guide our understanding of equality may justify our taking on the conceptual burden of making use of it.

Here, I draw on the last rationale stated earlier to justify making use of the notion of "dignity" rather than reducing it to equality simpliciter. I claim that we can make use of the ideas about dignity which I've tried to draw out in the previous sections to show why Douglass was right, and why there is an intimate connection between dignity and the rule of law.

This account draws on the account of the rule of law that I have offered elsewhere, in which the ideal of the rule of law is fleshed out in three principles, regularity, publicity, and generality (Gowder 2016). With respect to first-person dignitary wrongs:

The principle of *regularity* requires that those officials who exercise the state's coercive power do so only pursuant to the actual constraint of reasonably specific rules specifying the conditions under which the state's monopoly on coercive force can be used. This is the rule of law principle whose failure was most salient in my experience in New Orleans—a police officer evidently had the power to lock someone up in one of the worst prisons in the country for no reason other than his personal whim and faced no realistic prospect of sanctions after the fact.[12] Regularity is the fundamental principle that keeps state bullies in check. Regularity is also a core principle that forbids violently enforced social hierarchies like that of the Jim Crow South, in which lynch law was deployed by the coordinated behavior of state officials and violent gangs of White civilians to secure the continual subordinate behavior of Black Americans (Gowder 2018, 247–351, 2021, 90–102).

The principle of *publicity* requires that ordinary people in a rule-of-law state be able to operate the rules that govern the use of the state's coercive power. In a state satisfying the requirements of publicity, the people will be able to deploy the rules to challenge the use of the state's coercive power against them, will be able to monitor compliance with those rules, and will be able to act collectively to enforce them.

My New Orleans experience also featured multiple examples of the failure of publicity. First, as noted earlier, I didn't dare try to use the existing internal affairs and civil rights litigation processes to deploy sanctions against the officer who falsely arrested me. Second, I discovered that even something as simple as a trial for a traffic violation (the broken taillight) was impossible to get in the failed legal system under which the city operated. My attempts to get such a trial were thwarted: I spent months on end showing up for repeated trial dates, all of which entailed sitting in a courtroom for hours and then being told that the date was to be rescheduled for more months into the future. Eventually, after several iterations of this runaround, I gave up and left the jurisdiction.[13] At no point in the entire sorry process did I ever lay eyes on a judicial officer of any kind. This also strikes me as having a dignitary aspect. I wanted a trial on the traffic ticket not really to challenge that charge (after all, I was actually "guilty" of having a broken taillight), but to get an opportunity to meet the police officer under oath, in a forum of equals under the law, where I would have the opportunity to question him about the arrest and reveal his criminality without having to risk the prospect of immediate retaliatory violence. In other words, I wanted the protection of the legal system to stand up to my bully, to be able to fight back, not with fists, but with gavels. Because I could not get any kind of trial, I was denied an opportunity to exercise the dignity of standing fearlessly face-to-face with the officer.

The principle of *generality* requires that the content of the rules be consistent with the social equality of those who are to obey them. Core violations of the principle of generality are those where the law requires those subject to it to performatively affirm their own subordinated status, as with laws requiring Black Americans to sit on the back of the bus or attend segregated schools. The idea of first-person dignitary wrongs can serve to elaborate the account of why these laws are particularly objectionable—because there is a moral wrongfulness to requiring someone to *perform* their own subordination (and hence both affirm it to others as well as potentially promote a belief in it themselves), independent of the wrongfulness of imposing that subordination from the outside by brute force.

Understood in this way, the concept of dignity as uprightness can be seen to unify the allegedly disjoint facets of the rule of law. Formal conceptions of the rule of law according to which its core achievement is the avoidance of lawless violence and substantive conceptions that focus on the ideal of equal law turn out to share the goal of allowing subjects of law to live uprightly.

With this in mind, we can easily see what Douglass meant when he said that he and the slave-breaker "stood as equals before the law" when he fought back. A key difference between a regime operated under the rule of law and its opposite is that, in a rule of law regime, people are entitled to fearlessly defend themselves against aggression. By contrast, "trembl[ing] like a leaf in a storm" before the demands of hierarchically superordinated classes is the core experience of a lawless regime. For a moment, the psychic baggage of the lawless condition under which he lived dropped from Douglass, and he was able to act like a legal equal and experience the characteristic cognitions—the courage, the sense of entitlement to dignity—of a legal equal.

The Jim Crow South is another paradigm case of the failure of the rule of law in the United States. The Jim Crow South was organized around racialized violent displays of status. Consider first the widespread understanding of the South as an "honor culture" obsessed with personal status (cf. Hunt 2007). Second, consider the motivation of practices such as violent lynching as methods of ensuring the overall social subordination of one race to another.[14] Third, observe how practices such as lynching, as well as the actual formal criminal justice system, were deployed to punish specific individual deviations from norms of expressed subordination—that is, insufficient obsequiousness on the parts of Blacks to Whites, often further associated with status and dominance-based conceptions of masculinity.[15] Even the social construction of the rationale for felon disenfranchisement under Jim Crow drew on conceptions of indignity associated with Black citizens (Holloway 2009, 956–59).

In a world in which the law and social norms were utterly devoted to preserving what Du Bois famously called the psychological wage of whiteness, it should be unsurprising that Jim Crow combined violations of regularity and publicity to terrorize Black Americans into submissive behavior with legally enforced segregation qua violations of generality intended to force Blacks into physically organizing themselves into subordinate places. This continued violent enforcement of status is a key part of why we do not just understand Jim Crow as an ordinary oppressive regime but as the continuation of slavery by other means: in effect, the regime attempted to re-impose the relationship between Douglass and Covey that existed before Douglass had the courage to fight back; to create a regime of such pervasive legal and hence physical vulnerability that Black citizens were forced to "tremble like a leaf" in the presence of their overlords.

More generally, the existence of pervasive humiliation may serve as a tool to identify rule of law violations, either for the promotion of human rights, or even, potentially, as evidence in actual litigation, because it permits a connection between observed behavior and the normative status of law. This is a lesson that we can draw from the Court's wise example in *Brown v. Board of Education*. The justices recognized that the fact that Black children had been trained to see their physical characteristics as inferior was important evidence of the actual lack of equality in the schools. Similarly, if human rights advocates, judges, and juries actually observe undignified behavior in response to some legal regime, that gives them reason to conclude that those who are driven to behave undignifiedly have been reduced to an unacceptably subordinate status. Thus, for example, the pervasive indignities that women must inflict on themselves for fear of men—letting unwanted suitors down as gingerly as possible, darting out of the way on the street—is, I contend, evidence of a failure of the rule of law with respect to gender. And real-world lawyers and judges ought to devise ways to draw on these facts, for example, in litigation against jurisdictions that neglect the enforcement of laws against rape and other forms of gender-based violence.

The Talk

Fast-forward to fifteen years after my encounter with the New Orleans Police Department. I am accompanying several members of the University of Iowa's Black Law Students Association at the organization's annual "Street Law" presentation to a local high school. The "Street Law" concept is designed to endow teenagers with tools to mitigate the cruel double-bind that persons of color in the United States face when forced into a police encounter: be too accommodating (for example, by engaging in behavior that can be interpreted as consenting to a search), and a Court will soon find that you "voluntarily" surrendered what few constitutional rights you have; be too confrontational and you might end up dead.[16] In trying to impart survival skills to those children in Street Law, I aim to frame the indignities they must suffer to try to keep themselves alive and out of prison as tactical maneuvers. I instruct them to ever so politely resist with their words while surrendering with their bodies—to utter those same magic words that I tried in New Orleans, "I do not consent to this search," even as they complaisantly hand over their backpacks to submit to that very same search—and I tell them that this is merely a move they must play to win in the long run. My catchphrase is "The streets are the police's turf, the courtroom is yours—what you're trying to do is get through the interaction without giving up your rights so your lawyer can beat them later on."

For most of the students, this approach works well enough. But, invariably, some students—almost always Black boys—just tune out. At a recent iteration of Street Law, I pulled aside a student who was ostentatiously listening to loud music on his headphones through the entire session and tried to convince him to engage, but all he would say to me was "They'll do what they want anyway."

I can't blame him for resisting the lesson. It's a hard one to take—to be told that you have to quietly submit to illegal interrogations and illegal searches, and that the only hope in a police encounter is the dim prospect of a subsequent vindication in a judicial system that has never been known to trust the word of Black teenagers over police—and by giving it, however necessary, I too am inflicting a dignitary harm on these students. No matter how hard I work to make it tactical, I'm still telling them to submit when challenged by the heavily armed police officer in a racist system. The public defender who tells the client who insists that she's innocent nonetheless to take the plea deal and act contrite at sentencing must experience similar conflicts. And we must condemn the systems of arbitrary power that constrain the incentives of the student and the defendant so that they have no real choice but to submit to these indignities.

But I have it easy, for I'm not a parent. One of the harshest burdens of Black parents is the felt necessity to give "the Talk" to their children–to discuss what they should do if menaced by police, or by Whites with murderous intentions (Thomas and Blackmon 2014; Whitaker and Snell 2016). Prominent in such discussions is a recommendation to engage in hyper-polite, hyper-compliant, behavior–don't question, don't argue, don't raise your voice. One Black boy described the Talk as follows:

> He walked me through all of the situations in life where I need to make myself smaller to be safe. He told me, "You cannot give police a reason to go any further with you. If they pull you over, be compliant, don't raise your voice, don't ask questions. Just do what they ask of you." I was frustrated because it was unfair. I was 16 years old, just out of boarding school, and I'd just come home to Chicago. He's still coaching me on how you can't be your biggest, boldest self.
>
> (Thompson Plourde and Thompson 2017)

There's nothing new about the Talk. Famous lynching victim Emmett Till's mother gave a version of it to him before permitting him to visit family in the South in 1955 (Onwuachi-Willig 2017, 1138). It couldn't protect Till then, and it can't protect far too many Black children today. Yet Black parents still feel the overwhelming need to give it, to do what little they can to convince their children to surrender their dignity in the hopes that it will spare their lives.

The need to deliver the Talk doubtless inflicts many concrete harms on Black children and parents.[17] But the most salient description of the harm thus inflicted is as a first-person dignitary wrong inflicted by the police and the American criminal justice system as a whole on Black Americans. It is humiliating to have to tell one's children that, simply because of the color of their skin, they are obliged to, in turn, humiliate themselves in the face of violence—to act obsequiously, to fear insisting on their legal rights. In this chapter, I have argued that this wrong is characteristic of lawless social relations, and that we can make the concept of dignity do something useful by applying it to this situation. And I offer the continuing prevalence of the Talk as evidence that the rule of law is deficient in the United States.

Notes

1 This is what Formosa and Mackenzie (2014) describe as "achievement-dignity."

2 My multiracial background (my father is a Black man from Chicago; my mother is a White woman from England) permits me to pass in contexts without a lot of Black people, i.e. where the local Whites are unaware of the diversity of Black physiognomy—and hence partake indirectly and occasionally in some of the benefits of Whiteness. New Orleans is not one of those places in which passing is possible for me.

3 See *Whren v. United States*, which permits "pretextual" stops in which the police stop people for minor traffic violations when their real motive is to investigate or "discover" much more serious crimes.

4 Just for the record, I did not possess any marijuana.

5 On the police, see, e.g., Times-Picayune Editorial Board (2017), recounting the history of egregious police criminality; Peter Scharf and Stephen Phillippi (2015), recounting racialized gangs within NOPD, murders.

6 It is important that the use or threat of power be wrongful. There may be situations where it is entirely legitimate to use power to force someone to surrender their own dignity. For example, the murderer might have a strong incentive to beg the judge for mercy—but I don't want to say that he suffers a *wrong* thereby.

7 For journalistic accounts, see Serina Sandhu (2015).

8 Again in the popular press, see Jessica Roy (2015).

9 Bergner (2009) describes the study and subsequent debates surrounding it.

10 See Satz (2010, 184–85). Moreover, those who do the subordinating have an incentive to promote this internalization of subordinate status in order to reduce the likelihood of resistance or self-assertion, so as to continue extracting rents from the unequal relationship (Schaffner 1995).

11 Of course, it is always possible to argue that equality ought to be defended in terms of dignity. But at least equality has some extra-normative content from which we might begin (such as the idea of sameness); moreover, in liberal democratic

political theory, the folk concept of dignity may be more objectionably perfectionistic, insofar as it seems to bring in ideas about how a life well-lived may look, rather than the concept of equality; this objectionable perfectionism may give us some independent reason to treat equality as prior to dignity.

12 Given the reputation of the New Orleans police, I certainly didn't dare try to invoke sanctions myself, either by litigation or by filing some kind of complaint, for fear of either of the mysterious resurrection of the charge against me or more direct violent retaliation. See, e.g., Times-Picayune Staff (1996), reporting on a New Orleans police officer's conviction for hiring a hit man to kill a citizen who filed an internal affairs complaint against him; U.S. Department of Justice (2012), reporting on sentencing of New Orleans police officers who, in the aftermath of Hurricane Katrina, "opened fire with assault rifles and a shotgun, shooting at an unarmed family walking on the east side of the bridge," then chased down two witnesses and shot them too, and then orchestrated a cover-up involving a conspiracy to falsely claim that the victims had first fired at them; A. C. Thompson (2010), reporting on an indictment alleging that NOPD officers shot another person in the aftermath of Katrina, beat the people who tried to obtain medical assistance for the person they shot, and then torched the corpse to cover it up—although I hasten to note that in this case some of the resulting convictions were overturned on appeal. Illustrating the impunity enjoyed by officers guilty of anything short of murdering someone and torching a car with the body in it, I note that, according to the internet, the police officer who falsely arrested me is, as of this writing, the commander of an entire division, and appears in listings of the department's most senior officials.

13 For all I know, I may have thereafter been under an arrest warrant for failure to appear. Some months later, I hired a "traffic ticket lawyer" from an internet search to resolve the taillight ticket, and received a notice of dismissal in the mail; to this day, I have no idea what the "traffic ticket lawyer" did to dispose of the citation—I can only pray that he filed some kind of motion, as opposed to bribing someone in the clerk's office or bringing some other kind of illegal end to the mess. Given what we have already seen about the New Orleans legal system, however, I hold out very little hope.

14 Garland (2005, 817), describing the system of lynch law: "To allow the matter to go to the authorities and be dealt with by the legal system was to depersonalize the relationship of white to black and to treat the matter of black misconduct as a question of law. By avenging the crime themselves, the lynchers implied that the relationship that counted was between blacks and whites, and that this was a relationship not of laws and citizens but of superiors and subordinates, masters and slaves." The lynching of Black accused criminals "re-established the correlative status of the troublesome black man, which was as nothing, with no rights, no protectors, no personal dignity, and no human worth."

15 For example, Matt Ingram was convicted for "reckless eyeballing" of a White woman (Berry 2008). Emmett Till was brutally murdered for allegedly whistling at a White woman (Onwuachi-Willig 2017).

16 Recently, two American courts have recognized the problem of police violence against Black Americans and have gone so far as to suggest that it is entirely rational, and no particular indication of a guilty conscience, for Black Americans to flee from the police in view of the record of what happens to Black people in police encounters. See *United States v. Daniel Derek Brown* and *Commonwealth v. Warren*.

17 For example, it seems extremely likely to me that it exacerbates the racial disparity in American incarceration, due to different incentives that Black and White citizens face in being solicited by the police to submit to so-called "consent searches"—in which police intimidate civilians into agreeing into otherwise illegal searches.

Those who are subject to being arbitrarily killed by the police have less capacity to say "no." Hence, they are more likely to be convicted for any offenses uncovered by such "consent" searches, notwithstanding the supposed protections of the Fourth Amendment.

References

Alam, Murad, Karen C. Barrett, Robert M. Hodapp, and Kenneth A. Arndt. 2008. "Botulinum Toxin and the Facial Feedback Hypothesis: Can Looking Better Make You Feel Happier?" *Journal of the American Academy of Dermatology* 58 (6): 1061–72.

Anderson, Elizabeth. 2014. "Human Dignity as a Concept for the Economy." In *The Cambridge Handbook of Human Dignity: Interdisciplinary Perspectives*, edited by Marcus Duwell, Jens Braarvig, Roger Brownsword, and Dietmar Mieth, 492–97. Cambridge: Cambridge University Press.

Bayefsky, Rachel. 2013. "Dignity, Honour, and Human Rights: Kant's Perspective." *Political Theory* 41 (6): 809–37.

Bell, Derrick. 1995. "Who's Afraid of Critical Race Theory?" *University of Illinois Law Review* 1995 (4): 893–910.

Bergner, Gwen. 2009. "Black Children, White Preference: Brown V. Board, the Doll Tests, and the Politics of Self-Esteem." *American Quarterly* 61 (2): 299–332.

Berry, Mary Frances. 2008. " 'Reckless Eyeballing': The Matt Ingram Case and the Denial of African American Sexual Freedom." *The Journal of African American History* 93 (2): 223–34.

Bohns, Vanessa K., and Lauren A. DeVincent. 2019. "Rejecting Unwanted Romantic Advances is More Difficult Than Suitors Realize." *Social Psychological and Personality Science* 10 (8): 1102–10.

Dan-Cohen, Meir. 2002. "Defending Dignity." In *Harmful Thoughts: Essays on Law, Self, and Morality*, 129–46. Princeton: Princeton University Press.

Delgado, Richard. 1989. "Storytelling for Oppositionists and Others: A Plea for Narrative." *Michigan Law Review* 87 (8): 2411–41.

Douglass, Frederick. 1857. *My Bondage and My Freedom*. New York and Auburn: Miller, Orton & Co.

Elster, Jon. 1983. *Sour Grapes: Studies in the Subversion of Rationality*. Cambridge, UK; New York: Cambridge University Press.

Espinoza, Leslie, and Angela P. Harris. 1997. "Afterword: Embracing the Tar-Baby-LatCrit Theory and the Sticky Mess of Race." *California Law Review* 85 (5): 1585–645.

Formosa, Paul, and Catriona Mackenzie. 2014. "Nussbaum, Kant, and the Capabilities Approach to Dignity." *Ethical Theory and Moral Practice* 17 (5): 875–92.

Garland, David. 2005. "Penal Excess and Surplus Meaning: Public Torture Lynchings in Twentieth-Century America." *Law & Society Review* 39 (4): 793–834.

Gowder, Paul. 2016. *The Rule of Law in the Real World*. New York: Cambridge University Press.

Gowder, Paul. 2018. "Resisting the Rule of Men." *Saint Louis University Law Journal* 62 (2): 333–59.

Gowder, Paul. 2021. *The Rule of Law in the United States: An Unfinished Project of Black Liberation*. Oxford: Hart Publishing.

Holloway, Pippa. 2009. " 'A Chicken-Stealer Shall Lose His Vote': Disfranchisement for Larceny in the South, 1874–1890." *The Journal of Southern History* 75 (4): 931–62.

Human Rights Watch. 2005. "New Orleans: Prisoners Abandoned to Floodwaters." *Hrw.org*, September 21, 2005. www.hrw.org/news/2005/09/21/new-orleans-prisoners-abandoned-floodwaters.

Hunt, Cecil J. II. 2007. "No Right to Respect: Dred Scott and the Southern Honor Culture." *New England Law Review* 42: 79–108.
Khaitan, T. 2012. "Dignity as an Expressive Norm: Neither Vacuous nor a Panacea." *Oxford Journal of Legal Studies* 32 (1): 1–19.
McGrath, April. 2017. "Dealing with Dissonance: A Review of Cognitive Dissonance Reduction." *Social and Personality Psychology Compass* 11 (12): e12362.
Moyn, Samuel. 2014. "The Secret History of Constitutional Dignity." *Yale Human Rights and Development Journal* 17 (1): 39–73.
O'Mahony, C. 2012. "There is No Such Thing as a Right to Dignity." *International Journal of Constitutional Law* 10 (2): 551–74.
Onwuachi-Willig, Angela. 2017. "Policing the Boundaries of Whiteness: The Tragedy of Being Out of Place from Emmett till to Trayvon Martin." *Iowa Law Review* 102 (3): 1113–86.
Pettit, Philip. 2012. *On the People's Terms: A Republican Theory and Model of Democracy.* Cambridge, UK; New York: Cambridge University Press.
Ridgeway, James, and Jean Casella. 2013. "America's 10 Worst Prisons: NOLA." *Mother Jones*, May 6, 2013. www.motherjones.com/politics/2013/05/10-worst-prisons-america-orleans-parish-opp/.
Rodriguez, Philippe-Andre. 2015. "Human Dignity as an Essentially Contested Concept." *Cambridge Review of International Affairs* 28 (4): 743–56.
Roy, Jessica. 2015. "What Happens When a Woman Walks Like a Man?" *New York Magazine (The Cut)*, January 8, 2015. www.thecut.com/2015/01/manslamming-manspreading-microaggressions.html.
Sandhu, Serina. 2015. "Women Share Their Experiences of Rejecting Men's Sexual Advances—and How They Reacted." *The Independent*, October 25, 2015. www.independent.co.uk/news/world/women-share-the-consequences-of-rejecting-sexual-advances-on-blog-a6709241.html.
Satz, Debra. 2010. *Why Some Things Should Not Be for Sale: The Moral Limits of Markets.* New York: Oxford University Press.
Schaffner, Julie Anderson. 1995. "Attached Farm Labor, Limited Horizons and Servility." *Journal of Development Economics* 47 (2): 241–70.
Scharf, Peter, and Stephen Phillippi. "The New Orleans Police Department was Troubled Long before Hurricane Katrina." *The Conversation*, August 27, 2015. https://theconversation.com/the-new-orleans-police-department-was-troubled-long-before-hurricane-katrina-46381.
Schroeder, Doris. 2010. "Dignity: One, Two, Three, Four, Five, Still Counting." *Cambridge Quarterly of Healthcare Ethics* 19 (1): 118–25.
Street, Annette F., and David W. Kissane. 2001. "Constructions of Dignity in End-of-Life Care." *Journal of Palliative Care* 17 (2): 93–101.
Thomas, Anita Jones, and Sha'Kema M. Blackmon. 2014. "The Influence of the Trayvon Martin Shooting on Racial Socialization Practices of African American Parents." *Journal of Black Psychology* 41 (1): 75–89.
Thompson, A. C. 2010. "The Killing of Henry Glover: Who Else Knew?" *ProPublica*, June 11, 2010. www.propublica.org/article/the-killing-of-henry-glover-who-else-knew.
Thompson Plourde, Arienne, and Amelia Thompson. 2017. "The Talk: Surviving Police Encounters While Black." *Utne Reader*, June 19, 2017. www.utne.com/community/police-racial-discrimination-zm0z17uzcwil.
Times-Picayune Editorial Board. 2017. "NOPD is Under Federal Consent Decree for Good Reasons." *Nola.com*, April 9, 2017. www.nola.com/opinions/2017/04/nopd_consent_decree.html.
Times-Picayune Staff. 1996. "Len Davis Sentenced to Death for Murder of Kim Groves." *Nola.com*, April 27, 1996. www.nola.com/crime/1996/04/len_davis_sentenced_to_death_f.html.

U.S. Department of Justice. 2012. "Five New Orleans Police Officers Sentenced on Civil Rights and Obstruction of Justice Violations in the Danziger Bridge Shooting Case." *Archives.fbi.gov*, April 4, 2012. https://archives.fbi.gov/archives/neworleans/press-releases/2012/five-new-orleans-police-officers-sentenced-on-civil-rights-and-obstruction-of-justice-violations-in-the-danziger-bridge-shooting-case.

Waldron, Jeremy. 2012. *Dignity, Rank, and Rights.* Edited by Meir Dan-Cohen. New York: Oxford University Press.

Whitaker, Tracy R., and Cudore L. Snell. 2016. "Parenting While Powerless: Consequences of 'the Talk'." *Journal of Human Behavior in the Social Environment* 26 (3–4): 303–9.

Case Law

Brown v. Board of Education of Topeka, 347 U.S. 483 (1954).

Commonwealth v. Warren, 475 Mass. 530, 58 N.E.3d 333 (2016).

United States v. Daniel Derek Brown, No. 17-30191 (9th Circuit, June 5, 2019).

Whren v. United States, 517 U.S. 806 (1996).

3 Dignity—Continuation of a Dialogue

Neville Rochow and Hans-Joachim Cremer

Introduction

In this chapter, we compare uses of the concept of "dignity" as a legal and constitutional guiding principle as applied in common law jurisdictions and Germany. We compare its application in recent Australian, UK, and United States cases with its application in German jurisprudence. As will be seen, Germany has dignity as a constitutional mandate: it is incumbent upon each arm of government to uphold human dignity. Its influence on judicial decision-making is constant, subtle, nuanced, and practical. In the common law jurisdictions that we consider, there is no constitutional equivalent to the German mandate. Nevertheless, when required by statute to uphold dignity in a case, the application is likely also to be subtle, nuanced, and practical, even if not consistent. What also becomes apparent is that when a balance has to be struck between a claim for equality and a claim for liberty, the approach of the courts in Germany is to take more factors into account than in the common law courts. Thus, dignity may swing the balance either way more than might occur in a common law setting. Further, in German courts, the concept of "dignity" does not always find its way expressly into reasons for judgment. Instead, it is woven into the fabric of reasoning; in German courts, it is what may manifest as a claim for the protection of a "personality" right.

Regarding "dignity" and its German context, former President of the Supreme Court of Israel, Aharon Barak, has reminded us of the debt owed to the German legal literature and German Constitutional Court for their enrichment of the modern Western understanding of human dignity (Barak 2015, xxii–xxiii). We agree with Barak. While the German Constitution has an undefined concept of "dignity" as an entrenched constitutional principle,[1] among the concepts embraced is Immanuel Kant's legacy in both the categorical imperative and the concept of human worth, or dignity that is significant in the framing of rights under consideration. We read and interpret the German development as drawing some, more indirect than direct, inspiration from Kantian philosophy.

The German dignitarian philosopher with which most Anglophone lawyers and judges are likely to be familiar is Kant. This is a cultural difference that must be accounted for in common law consideration of German usage of

DOI: 10.4324/9781003307853-4

dignity. Indeed, as discussed in more detail later, while the Kantian concept of dignity may be recognizable as an essential background to the German judicial approach, it is found conceptually rather than by express judicial attribution.[2]

For Kant, dignity is an inherent quality, enjoyed independently of the moral worthiness of an individual (Bayefsky 2013; Kant [1785] 1911, 385). Our autonomy and rational nature provide the foundation for the dignity of every human (Kant [1785] 1911, 385). Every individual human being partakes in the dignity of mankind (Kant [1797] 1914, 462).[3] For Kant, this inalienable quality derives from being human; and more specifically, from the ability, equally shared by humans, to have a grasp of *Vernunft* (reason). Thus, to encounter and respect one another as *vernünftige Wesen* (reasonable beings), treating one another not merely as means (*bloßes Mittel*) but as ends (*Zweck*).[4] From Kant to Böckenförde (2017) and Isensee (Quirk 2018), commentators have examined dignity as an organizing principle. Its role in German jurisprudence is played in ways that are at least worthy of consideration, if not emulation, in the common law world.

In *Human Dignity: The Constitutional Value and the Constitutional Right*, Barak (2015) demonstrates the extent of the debt owed to the Germans in his survey of theological, philosophical, social, and historical perspectives, and by his examinations of the constitutions of the United States, Germany, South Africa, and Israel. In his earlier work, *The Judge in a Democracy*, Barak (2006) laid the foundation for dignity as a part of the judicial armory in seeking to administer justice in a democratic state. In *Human Dignity*, he demonstrates its indispensability. Through both works, he contributed to the awareness of the constitutional comparison and started a conversation among scholars and judges that is critical if the resolution of disputes is to be conducted so that no participating party is dehumanized. While we cannot fully canvass the matters raised by Barak in a chapter like this, we do seek, in our modest way, to contribute to that conversation in which Barak is a principal interlocutor.

What we identify as a Kantian influence, we readily concede, is our subjective interpretation and not one with which all German scholars would agree. But Kant's philosophy of the state has undoubtedly made a tremendous contribution to the argument for, and foundation of, the idea of a legal order based on the rule of law and human rights (Dreier 2013). Some scholars even draw direct connections between Kant and the interpretation of the guarantee of human dignity in Article 1 of the *Grundgesetz*, the German Basic Law, and the Federal Constitution (Stern 2006, 10).[5] The German Federal Constitutional Court (*Bundesverfassungsgericht*), however, neither directly resorts to any specific philosophy nor to any specific philosopher or commentator.

Recently, the Court did summarize its jurisprudence on human dignity and its interpretation of Art. 1 of the *Grundgesetz* in a way which, we would submit, places Kant's influence clearly as at least one that the center:

> The guarantee of human dignity is a fundamental constitutional principle in the system of fundamental rights. . .. Human dignity is connected

> with the human being's social claim to being valued and respected, which prohibits making him a mere object of the state[6] or subjecting him to a treatment which in principle calls his subject quality into question. . . . Human dignity in this sense is not only the individual dignity of the respective person, but also the dignity of man as a species. All possess it, without regard to characteristics, accomplishments and social status. Human dignity is something to which everyone is entitled, it is, as to its foundation, inalienable . . . and is not lost even by "unworthy" behaviour . . . it cannot be denied even to those who are accused of the most serious misconduct. . . . What can be violated, however, is the claim to respect that arises from it.[7]

Continuing the conversation on the role of human dignity is as necessary now as at any other point in the history of dignity as a philosophical and jurisprudential concept. The cultural wars surrounding rights to equality and rights to liberty have been, in Anglophone, common law jurisdictions at least, fought and all but lost by those who had opposed equality rights to the extent that they perceived an incursion upon religious liberty (Kirchick 2019). The battles comprising those wars were too rarely framed in terms of human dignity. Dignity cannot now oversee a resurgence of those cultural wars and favor religious liberty. It does not present an opportunity to reclaim lost ground. Rather, it is the key to the aftermath being dominated by respect rather than misplaced tribalism and triumphalism. That outcome must, in large part, be invigilated by the courts that preside over new disputes. In this chapter, we propose to open a new aspect of the conversation as to how dignity, as understood by German philosophers and civil law lawyers, could better inform the work of common law jurists.

Dignity is credited in international human rights law and constitutional instruments as a seminal source of rights and freedoms. In its preamble, the Universal Declaration of Human Rights (UDHR) inseparably links "equal and inalienable rights" and "the inherent dignity and of all members of the human family." If the matter were one of statutory interpretation in Anglo-Australian law, a linkage would likely be found for inherent human dignity with rights and freedoms that are repeated in the preamble to the International Covenant on Civil and Political Rights (ICCPR). The Council of Europe, it could be argued, in the Convention for the Protection of Human Rights and Fundamental Freedoms (ECHR), adopted the UDHR by reference as the foundation for the rights and freedoms it provided for, and emulates the text of the ICCPR. The European Court of Human Rights has helpfully confirmed that: "The very essence of the Convention is respect for human dignity and human freedom" (*Pretty v. United Kingdom*, para. 65).

Despite its obvious eminent position in the framing of human rights, there remains debate as to what place it should have, if any at all. We acknowledge that there are many other contributors to Anglophone literature on dignity. They include Jeremy Waldron (2012),[8] Jonathan Sacks (2002), Francis

Fukuyama (2018), Michael Rosen (2012), and Donna Hicks (2011). These writers have reminded those active in the area that dignity requires examination and re-examination for it to make a meaningful difference to the ways in which human beings and their place in legal and political systems are to be understood. Our contribution is to remind readers that the instantiation of dignity as an organizing principle in jurisprudence is not yet over.

We argue that, from recent decisions of appellate courts in Australia (*Clubb v. Edwards*; *Preston v. Avery*), the United Kingdom (*Bull and Another v. Hall and Another* and *Lee v. Ashers Baking Company Ltd and Others*), and the United States (*Masterpiece Cakeshop v. Colorado Civil Rights Commission*), there is an evident need to consider, perhaps, how German constitutional jurisprudence on dignity, could, in similar cases, inform both reasoning and outcome of common law decision-making. We accept that critics of dignity in jurisprudence and constitutional discourse make the point that "dignity" is too vague a jurisprudential notion to be of any real value. Standing alone, without any reference point, that may well be true. But it is no less true of concepts such as "the rule of law," "justice," "equity," "liberty" and "equality," all of which require context to have meaning and force. Without that context, they tend toward the clichéd or rhetorical flourish. Dignity is no different. It needs context for it to have meaning. Perhaps, we would suggest, the German courts could assist in finding that context.

Dignity in Australian, British, and US Jurisprudence

High Court of Australia: Clubb v. Edwards; Preston v. Avery

In *Clubb v. Edwards* and *Preston v. Avery*, the High Court of Australia heard two appeals from convictions for breaches of prohibitions regarding communications within abortion clinic "access zones." The Court unanimously dismissed both appeals. In both cases, the appellants challenged laws prohibiting certain communications and activities in relation to abortions in "access zones" around abortion clinics. They claimed, *inter alia*, that the access zones surrounding the immediate area of the clinics impinged upon their rights to communicate on governmental and political matters. This included, they claimed, their right to speak up against abortion.

Clubb had been convicted under s. 185D of the Public Health and Wellbeing Act 2008 (Vic) ("the Victorian Act"), which prohibits a person from communicating about abortions in a manner able to be seen or heard by persons accessing or attempting to access premises at which abortions are provided, if the communication is reasonably likely to cause distress or anxiety. Preston had been convicted under s. 9(2) of the Reproductive Health (Access to Terminations) Act 2013 (Tas) ("the Tasmanian Act"), which prohibits protests about terminations that can be seen or heard by a person accessing premises at which terminations are provided. The two prohibitions applied within a radius of 150 meters from the abortion clinic.

The appellants argued that each of the respective provisions was invalid because each provision impermissibly burdened the implied freedom of communication. The issue of dignity arose directly from the wording of the respective statutory provisions under challenge. Section 185A of the Victorian Act has as its purpose "to protect the safety and wellbeing and *respect* the privacy and *dignity*" (emphasis added) of people accessing services and those employed to provide them. Section 185C emphasized the object of "dignity" by setting out principles that apply to Pt 9A. Among those principles was the re-iteration that the services were an entitlement (Public Health and Wellbeing Amendment (Safe Access Zones) Act 2015 [Vic] s 185C(a)); that each "person's safety and wellbeing" needed to be protected (185C(b)(i)); and that there needed to be respect for "the person's privacy and dignity" (185C(b)(ii)). All members of the Court made reference to dignity in their reasons.

The plurality stressed the significance of dignity, first, by reference to the Second Reading speech and observing that "privacy" and "dignity" are closely linked. It was noted by the justices that the protection of dignity was an aspect of the purpose of the communication prohibition. The Court also cited with approval the extra-judicial writings of Barak, where he said, we might add, in Kantian language:

> Most central of all human rights is the right to dignity. It is the source from which all other human rights are derived. "Dignity unites the other human rights into a whole (Barak 2006, p. 85) . . . [h]uman dignity regards a human being as an end, not as a means to achieve the ends of others."
>
> (see *Clubb v. Edwards*; *Preston v. Avery*)

The prohibition was consistent with both the concept of dignity and placing a limitation upon the exercise of the implied freedom of political communication:

> Generally speaking, to force upon another person a political message is inconsistent with the human dignity of that person. . . . *Within the present constitutional context, the protection of the dignity of the people of the Commonwealth, whose political sovereignty is the basis of the implied freedom, is a purpose readily seen to be compatible with the maintenance of the constitutionally prescribed system of representative and responsible government.* Thus, when in *Lange* (*Lange v. Australian Broadcasting Corporation*, at 571) the Court declared that "each member of the Australian community has an interest in disseminating and receiving information, opinions and arguments concerning government and political matters that affect the people of Australia", there was no suggestion that any member of the Australian community may be *obliged* to receive such information, opinions and argument.
>
> Further, a law that prevents interference with the privacy and dignity of members of the people of the Commonwealth through co-optation

as part of a political message is consistent with the political sovereignty of the people of the Commonwealth and the implied freedom which supports it.[9]

The implied freedom is not a guarantee of an audience; a fortiori, it is not an entitlement to force a message on an audience held captive to that message. As has been noted, it is inconsistent with the dignity of members of the sovereign people to seek to hold them captive in that way.

A law calculated to maintain the dignity of members of the sovereign people by ensuring that they are not held captive by an uninvited political message accords with the political sovereignty which underpins the implied freedom.

(*Clubb v. Edwards*; *Preston v. Avery*, paras. 51, 60, 98–99, emphasis added, several references omitted)

Supreme Court of the United Kingdom: Bull and Another v. Hall and Another

The appellants, the Bulls, owned and ran a private hotel that provided accommodation. Hall and Preddy, the respondents to the appeal, were homosexual civil partners who booked a double room at the hotel by telephone. The appellants, devout Christians, believed that sex other than between married heterosexuals is sinful. A preference for married couples was expressed in their online booking form where it was stipulated that "out of a deep regard for marriage" double rooms were to be let only to "heterosexual married couples." When the telephone booking was taken, Mrs Bull did not confirm whether the reservation was for a man and his wife. However, when Hall and Preddy arrived, the Bulls explained the rule and turned them away.

Hall and Preddy brought a discrimination claim at first instance in the Bristol County Court. They succeeded despite an argument by the Halls that the discrimination law could only be applied to the extent that it was compatible with the right to manifest their beliefs as guaranteed under Article 9 of the ECHR. It was found that the Bulls had directly discriminated against the Hall and Preddy. The Court awarded Hall and Preddy each £1,800 for injury to feelings. On appeal to the Court of Appeal, the direct discrimination finding was upheld. While accepting that the hotel policy was an expression of the Bulls' religious beliefs within Article 9 of the ECHR, that freedom had been justifiably limited by the discrimination law, as permitted by Article 9(2). On appeal to the Supreme Court, the decisions of the courts below were upheld. Among other matters, it was held, unanimously, that the prohibition of discrimination under provisions of the Human Rights Act 1998 was justified under Article 9(2). While "dignity" is mentioned only three times in the Court's reasons, and then only while citing other authorities, the UK Supreme Court's Justice Lady Hale does provide insight as to how a court might use dignity to reach a balance between competing rights and freedoms, especially the freedom to express one's religious belief and the right to be treated equally despite one's sexual orientation.

Lady Hale captures the essence of the conflict of rights early in her reasons by reference to the European Human Rights Commission's (EHRC) approach to the case:

> It is a curiosity of the case . . . that the EHRC has prosecuted this case on behalf of parties with one protected characteristic against parties with another. It is understandable that [the Bulls] should feel this way and a more neutral stance of the Commission might have been to seek to intervene in, rather than to prosecute, these proceedings. But it misunderstands the nature of the case. If Mr Preddy and Mr Hall were hotel keepers who had refused a room to Mr and Mrs Bull, because they were Christians (or even because they were an opposite sex couple), no doubt the Commission would have been just as ready to support Mr and Mrs Bull in their claim. Each of these parties has the same right to be protected against discrimination by the other.
>
> The issues in discrimination law are difficult enough, but there are also competing human rights in play: on the one hand, the right of Mr and Mrs Bull (under article 9 of the European Convention for the Protection of Human Rights and Fundamental Freedoms) to manifest their religion without unjustified limitation by the state; and on the other hand, the right (under article 14) of Mr Preddy and Mr Hall to enjoy their right (under article 8) to respect for their private lives without unjustified discrimination on grounds of their sexual orientation.
>
> (Bull and Another v. Hall and Another, paras. 4–5)

Instead of "dignity," Lady Hale spoke of the respondents' entitlement to "respect and esteem." She also spoke of the public benefit of ensuring equal treatment of same-sex couples in civil partnerships in commercial dealings:

> The rights and obligations entailed in both marriage and civil partnership exist both to recognize and to encourage stable, committed, long-term relationships. It is very much in the public interest that intimate relationships be conducted in this way. Now that, at long last, same sex couples can enter into a mutual commitment which is the equivalent of marriage, the suppliers of goods, facilities and services should treat them in the same way.
>
> (*Bull and Another v. Hall and Another*, para. 36)

Supreme Court of the United Kingdom: Lee v. Ashers Baking Company Ltd and Others

Lee approached a Belfast bakery, Ashers Baking Company, to make a cake decorated to depict Sesame Street characters Bert and Ernie over the slogan

"Support Gay Marriage" for a party. The McArthurs, the owners of the bakery, were Christians who did not agree with the statement. Mrs McArthur originally accepted the order, but upon reflection and after discussion with Mr McArthur, decided that they could not produce a cake with a slogan with which they fundamentally disagreed. They called Lee to communicate their decision, apologize, and provide him with a refund. Lee was able to have the cake made elsewhere in time for the party. Lee had succeeded at first instance and on appeal. However, the case was referred to the Supreme Court for a decision on specific points of law.

On the reference of issues by the Attorney General for Northern Ireland to the Supreme Court, the Court concluded that, in this instance, the McArthurs had not discriminated against Lee based on either his sexual orientation or his political belief. They simply disagreed with the statement. Although the law in Northern Ireland prohibits discrimination, the Court held that this must be read in such a way as to not oblige someone to produce a good with a message with which they fundamentally disagree (*Lee v. Ashers Baking Company Ltd and Others*, paras. 35, 46–47, 62).

Lady Hale, in delivering the reasons of the plurality, captured the issue before the Court:

> The substantive question in this case is whether it is unlawful discrimination, either on grounds of sexual orientation, or on grounds of religious belief or political opinion, for a bakery to refuse to supply a cake iced with the message "support gay marriage" because of the sincere religious belief of its owners that gay marriage is inconsistent with Biblical teaching and therefore unacceptable to God. If the prima facie answer to either question is "yes", then questions arise as to the rights of the bakery and its owners to freedom of religion and freedom of expression, under articles 9 and 10 of the European Convention on Human Rights, and what difference, if any, those rights might make to that prima facie answer.
>
> (*Lee v. Ashers Baking Company Ltd and Others*, para. 1)

For current purposes, it is necessary only to refer to parts of the reasons of the plurality that deal with dignity and the freedoms granted under Articles 9 and 10 of the ECHR (*Lee v. Ashers Baking Company Ltd and Others*, paras. 49–58). In this case, a distinction, not necessary to make in *Bull v. Hall*, between holding and manifesting a belief was made by Lady Hale. Lady Hale pointed out that while Article 9(2) permits limitations on the freedom to manifest one's religion or beliefs, it permits no limitation on the freedom to hold them. She went on to cite with approval a dictum from the European Court of Human Rights decision in *Kokkinakis v. Greece*:

> As enshrined in article 9, freedom of thought, conscience and religion is one of the foundations of a "democratic society" within the meaning

> of the Convention. It is, in its religious dimension, one of the most vital elements that go to make up the identity of believers and their conception of life, but it is also a precious asset for atheists, agnostics, sceptics and the unconcerned. The pluralism indissociable from a democratic society, which has been dearly won over the centuries, depends on it.
>
> (*Kokkinakis vs. Greece*, para. 31)

The reference in the *Kokkinakis* dictum to "the most vital elements that go to make up the identity of believers and their conception of life" is clearly inspired by human dignity and concepts closely allied to it. Lady Hale only referred to "dignity" three times in her reasons. But the application of Article 9(2), to draw the distinction mentioned is a preservation of the bakers' dignity.

The balancing of the religious liberty claim against the equality claim is mediated through Articles 9 and 10 on the particular facts of the case in a way that preserves the sanctity of the *forum internum* of freedom of religion or belief. Although the concept of dignity is not mentioned expressly, Articles 9 and 10 are applied so as to preserve the dignity of the bakers:

> Articles 9 and 10 are, of course, qualified rights which may be limited or restricted in accordance with the law and insofar as this is necessary in a democratic society in pursuit of a legitimate aim. It is, of course, the case that businesses offering services to the public are not entitled to discriminate on certain grounds. The bakery could not refuse to provide a cake—or any other of their products—to Mr Lee because he was a gay man or because he supported gay marriage. But that important fact does not amount to a justification for something completely different—obliging them to supply a cake iced with a message with which they profoundly disagreed. In my view they would be entitled to refuse to do that whatever the message conveyed by the icing on the cake—support for living in sin, support for a particular political party, support for a particular religious denomination. The fact that this particular message had to do with sexual orientation is irrelevant to the . . . claim.
>
> (*Lee v. Ashers Baking Company Ltd and Others*, para. 55)

Supreme Court of the United States: Masterpiece Cakeshop v. Colorado Civil Rights Commission

Masterpiece Cakeshop Ltd v. Colorado Civil Rights Commission is one of a suite of recent First Amendment decisions of the Supreme Court, the other two being *Hosanna-Tabor Evangelical Lutheran Church and School v. Equal Employment Opportunity Commission* and *Burwell v. Hobby Lobby*, in which religious liberty was a central issue.

Phillips, the proprietor of the Masterpiece Cakeshop, was a Christian baker. He refused to make a wedding cake for a same-sex couple because of his opposition to same-sex marriage. The Colorado Civil Rights Commission determined that it was unlawful for businesses that offer goods and services to the public to discriminate on the grounds of sexual orientation. Ultimately, the matter came before the Supreme Court. The Court defined the issues before it in *Masterpiece* as follows:

> The case presents difficult questions as to the proper reconciliation of at least two principles. The first is the authority of a State and its governmental entities to protect the rights and dignity of gay persons who are, or wish to be, married but who face discrimination when they seek goods or services. The second is the right of all persons to exercise fundamental freedoms under the First Amendment, as applied to the States through the Fourteenth Amendment.

The majority opinion delivered by Justice Kennedy held that:

> the delicate question of when the free exercise of his religion must yield to an otherwise valid exercise of state power needed to be determined in an adjudication in which religious hostility on the part of the state itself would not be a factor in the balance the state sought to reach. . . . When the Colorado Civil Rights Commission considered this case, it did not do so with the religious neutrality that the Constitution requires.

Where the reasoning of the Court refers to "dignity," in each instance it is in reference to the entitlement of the gay respondents on the appeal to be treated with dignity, and that dignity is the object of the discrimination laws. Nowhere was the dignity of Phillips considered. While the case was decided by reference to the First Amendment right to religiously neutral treatment by government agencies, the essential issue could also have been expressed in terms of apprehended or actual bias.[10] A finding of bias opens up the question of Phillips' dignity and that the Commission had treated him in a manner that violated that dignity.

Whatever motivated the bias, Phillips was entitled to be treated respectfully, fairly, and without prejudice in respect of his beliefs and any other personal attribute because justice must not only be done but be seen to be done (*R v. Sussex Justices ex parte McCarthy*). Not only had this not occurred, but the treatment was not characterized in dignitarian terms. Even if a properly conducted hearing might have decided that Phillip's undignified treatment of his prospective customers was prohibited, he was entitled to a fairly conducted hearing, both under the First Amendment and otherwise.

The majority seemed to have accepted an argument that baking a cake was, as a creative expression, an "expressive statement" involving Phillips' First Amendment rights. The argument based upon the "expressive statement" does not appear objectively compelling and, without the bias of the Commission, may not have been successful. It was not an argument that would likely have held sway in the *Ashers* case.

While bearing factual similarities to the *Ashers* case, it is distinguishable in that Phillips did not permit the discussions to progress to an actual order, or even discussion of the design and message on the cake. Rather, he refused simply on the basis that he did not bake cakes for same-sex weddings. Instead of focusing on Phillips' conduct, the attention of the Court was on the conduct of the Commission. Having found that Phillips had been treated without neutrality by the Commission was sufficient for the appeal to succeed.

Lady Hale, in a postscript to her reasons in *Ashers*, distinguishes the decision of the majority in *Masterpiece* from *Ashers*:

> The majority recognized that businesses could not generally refuse to supply products and services for gay weddings; but they acknowledged that the baker saw creating a wedding cake as an expressive statement involving his First Amendment rights; and contrasted the treatment that he had received, which they perceived as hostile, from the favourable treatment given to three bakers who had refused to produce cakes with messages demeaning gay persons and gay marriages
>
> The important message from the Masterpiece Bakery case is that there is a clear distinction between refusing to produce a cake conveying a particular message, for any customer who wants such a cake, and refusing to produce a cake for the particular customer who wants it because of that customer's characteristics. One can debate which side of the line particular factual scenarios fall. But in our case [i.e., *Ashers*], there can be no doubt. The bakery would have refused to supply this particular cake to anyone, whatever their personal characteristics. So, there was no discrimination on grounds of sexual orientation. If and to the extent that there was discrimination on grounds of political opinion, no justification has been shown for the compelled speech which would be entailed for imposing civil liability for refusing to fulfil the order.
>
> (*Lee v. Ashers Baking Company Ltd and Others, paras. 59, 62*)

Conclusions on the Common Law Jurisdictions and the Concept of Dignity

From the foregoing, while the notion of dignity may be slowly emerging, it has not yet gained a recognizable jurisprudential meaning. Where it is contemplated in judicial reasoning, it is as a part of statutory interpretation rather than as a freestanding concept. This is especially true of the United States under the First Amendment, which has no concept of human dignity associated with it. If pressed for a prediction, one would have to expect a long and slow jurisprudential development until legislatures and constitutional drafters place dignity at the center of statutory and constitutional considerations. This is because, under strict common law doctrine, the courts are bound to apply statutes according to their intended meaning. Judges are, or should be, loath to invent doctrines when the legislature has stayed its hand unless it is necessary to bridge an obvious gap in the law that needs to be filled. To date, there is no indication that the courts will fill any gap in relation to dignity. But if dignity is legislatively supplied as a consideration, they will apply it with full rigor.

The Relevance of Human Dignity in German Jurisprudence on Cases Comparable to the Common Law Cases Discussed

One of the challenges in any comparative approach is that it is impossible to account for all of the different legal and cultural elements that inform the judicial decision-making process. It is not possible to transplant cases from one legal system into another foreign legal system without making allowance for these factors. Transplanting in this sense would mean taking the facts of a case that has occurred in State A and hypothetically discussing how this case might be resolved by the courts of State B. Take the *Masterpiece Cakeshop* case. There might not be an equivalent for the Colorado Civil Rights Commission in, for example, Bavaria. The legal setting would thus have to be modified. We cannot, however, be certain that facts of this kind would ever arise in the foreign legal system. There is, thus, a certain artificiality in the exercise undertaken here in asking whether "dignity" might have made a difference in the judicial decision-making process. Therefore, the foreign cases discussed can, on this understanding, be used as templates to ask how the German understanding of dignity might have informed the judicial decision-making process.

Germany celebrated the 70th anniversary of its Basic Law, the *Grundgesetz*, in 2019. In 1949, the German *Länder*[11] adopted the *Grundgesetz*[12] as a provisional constitution for West Germany.[13] The first part of the *Grundgesetz* is titled "*Die Grundrechte*." It guarantees constitutional rights and liberties, *Grundrechte*, basic rights. From the outset, Article 1 of the *Grundgesetz* declares human dignity to be "*unantastbar*," literally: "untouchable" or "inviolable." The German Constitution thus displays a commitment to human dignity as its highest-ranking organizing principle,[14] which, over time, has developed into a fundamental right.[15] The German Federal Constitutional Court (*Bundesverfassungsgericht*) judges human dignity to be "a fundamental constitutional principle and the highest constitutional value (109 BVerfGE 279)." Article 1(3) of the *Grundgesetz* declares the basic rights to be binding upon the legislature, the executive, and the judiciary. While there remain theoretical questions,[16] there is no doubt that the German Constitution has respect for the dignity, equality, and liberty of all humans as a foundational principle.

In the cases discussed, "dignity" has played a role to the extent required by the statute to be applied. But it is necessarily ad hoc. It is driven as a consideration by what the legislation requires in the application to the facts of a particular case and only if the statute requires consideration of dignity, and then only to the extent required. Since, in the cases considered, it is, unlike in Germany, not a constitutional requirement to apply the notion of "dignity," there are subtly different approaches to "dignity" in German jurisprudence. In the case of common law application, it is not easy to detect a clear difference in the content of the application. As mentioned, we detect the Anglophone application to be Kantian, but as with the German jurists, there is no express attribution. So, while respect for human dignity will likely be important in any legal system, the predominant difference is that, since, in Germany, it is a constitutional guarantee, its application will be constant, even if not expressly so. German courts adopt a practical approach, which is called for when claims to other constitutional guarantees, particularly liberty and equality, are in conflict. With this in mind, we consider the effect of guarantees of respect for human dignity, provided for in the Constitution of the Federal Republic of Germany. We consider how controversies similar to those in the cases discussed fall to be decided by German courts.

The Exclusion Zone Case: Freedom of (Anti-Abortion) Speech and the Right to Develop One's Personality

In the Exclusion Zone Case, as in *Clubb*, the German Federal Constitutional Court was called upon to consider the enforceability of exclusion zones in a civil action brought by a gynecologist against a protester who had targeted his medical practice. Constitutional complaints were brought in the Federal Constitutional Court by a pro-life activist (1 BvR 1745/06).[17] The appellant activist regarded abortions as reprehensible and immoral because of his religious convictions. He had, in the past, protested against gynecologists who perform abortions by standing in the street close to their practices, displaying posters and handing out flyers expressing his opposition to abortion. The appellant activist approached passers-by, especially those whom he assumed to be potential patients, attempting to dissuade them from having abortions.

The appellant activist's constitutional complaints were against judgments at first and intermediate level, which prevented him from all forms of protest, within a 1-kilometer radius of the plaintiff's medical practice. The appellant activist was found in both instances to have seriously interfered with the plaintiff's general "personality" right. The appellant activist had, the civil courts considered, arbitrarily targeted the practice from among a large number of gynecologists performing abortions and had forced upon the practice publicity that had been neither sought nor provoked. Although he was exercising his freedom of speech, this right justified only proportionate acts. Furthermore, his acts of protest negatively affected the basis of confidence between the gynecologist and his patients, a consideration in the protective legislative scheme in abortion law. The case therefore concerned the question of whether the gynecologist's dignitarian rights in the protection of his personality should prevail over the appellant activist's freedom of expression.

The appellant activist claimed the judgments violated his constitutional rights under Article 5(1), freedom of speech, and Article 4(1), freedom of faith, of the *Grundgesetz*. The Federal Constitutional Court, sitting as a three-judge Chamber, found the complaint on grounds of freedom of faith to be unsubstantiated. The Court nevertheless held the judgments by the civil courts of justice to have violated the activist's freedom of speech and, for this reason, the Court quashed the judgments referring the case back to the court of first instance.

Constitutional review of the civil courts' decisions rests upon the indirect third-party effect ("*mittelbare Drittwirkung*"), or indirect horizontal effect, on relations between private parties *inter se*, which, according to the Federal Constitutional Court's standing jurisprudence, the basic rights guaranteed in the *Grundgesetz* are acknowledged to have.[18] While basic rights in principle bind the state,[19] having no immediate impact on relations between private parties, they are regarded as exerting a "radiating effect" even upon private-law relations by way of influencing the interpretation and application of statutory provisions of private law, especially where statutes contain general clauses ("*Generalklauseln*") or indeterminate legal concepts ("*unbestimmte Rechtsbegriffe*").[20]

The Federal Constitutional Court's case law reaches back to its decision in the case of *Lüth*, which it handed down in 1958. This judgment derives the "radiating effect" of basic rights ("' *Ausstrahlungswirkung' der Grundrechte*") from the "objective value system" ("*objektive Wertordnung*") established by the Constitution's basic rights section, reinforcing the legal authority of those basic rights. Interestingly, the Court defines as the center of this value system the free development of the human being's personality *and its dignity* (see 7 BVerfGE 198, 205, 207). Thus, one of the very roots of the "radiating effect" of basic rights itself, and thus of the indirect third-party effect on relations between private parties *inter se*, is human dignity, as guaranteed by Art. 1 of the *Grundgesetz*.

On the appellant activist's constitutional complaint, the Federal Constitutional Court quashed the civil courts' decisions because, in balancing the conflicting constitutional basic rights within the private-law framework of sections 823(1), 1004 of the *Bürgerliches Gesetzbuch* (the *German Civil Code*), they failed to afford correctly these rights their respective meaning and scope.[21]

According to section 823(1) of the *Bürgerliches Gesetzbuch*, someone who willingly or through negligence unlawfully infringes life, body, health, freedom, property, or another right of another person owes this person compensation for redress of damages. One "other right" the violation of which can make a person liable under this provision is the general personality right (*allgemeines Persönlichkeitsrecht*). It needs to be emphasized that this right is a private right that a private individual can claim in relation to any other private-law subject. Despite its identical name, it must not be mistaken for the *constitutionally* guaranteed *allgemeines Persönlichkeitsrecht* (120 BVerfGE 180, 200–201, 214–15), which is "*ein unbenanntes Freiheitsrecht*," a liberty (binding governmental powers including the judiciary[22]) not explicitly granted by the *Grundgesetz*, but rather derived by the Federal Constitutional Court by way of implication from Article 2(1) in combination with Article 1(1) of the *Grundgesetz* (147 BVerfGE 1, 18). However, the *allgemeines Persönlichkeitsrecht* as a constitutional basic right (partly rooted in Article 1, guaranteeing human dignity!), according to the principle of *mittelbare Drittwirkung*, just explained, influences the interpretation of section 823(1) of the *Bürgerliches Gesetzbuch* and must therefore be heeded by the civil courts (and balanced against conflicting basic rights) when they decide cases such as the controversy between the pro-life activist and the gynecologist. In their case, section 823(1) was combined with an analogous application of section 1004 of the *Bürgerliches Gesetzbuch* to derive a right to forbearance.[23]

The complainant's conduct fell within the scope of Article 5(1) of the *Grundgesetz* when he published statements according to which the gynecologist performed abortions and abortions were performed in his practice. Although Article 5(1) of the *Grundgesetz* guarantees the freedom merely to impart and disseminate "opinions," statements of fact nevertheless fall within the scope of this basic right insofar as they have the potential of contributing to the forming of opinions (90 BVerfGE 241, 247).

The freedom to express one's opinion, however, is limited by laws of general application ("*allgemeine Gesetze*"), to which sections 823(1), 1004 of the *Bürgerliches Gesetzbuch* belong.[24] Although the civil courts had discussed the conflict between the freedom of expression and the *allgemeines Persönlichkeitsrecht*, the Federal Constitutional Court found their considerations flawed because they had not taken into account that individuals cannot rely on the constitutionally guaranteed general personality right to demand being presented to the public only in a way which is agreeable to them. As the Federal Constitutional Court points out:

> The plaintiff's mere wish to be kept free from the annoyance of being confronted with his own free decision to perform abortions and of being criticized for this does not, in the light of Article 5(1) of the *Grundgesetz*, deserve recognition.
>
> (1 BvR 1745/06, para. 23)

In the result, the Federal Constitutional Court decided the case on the basis of a balancing test. The Court did not regard the interference by the complainant into the gynecologist's *Persönlichkeitsrecht* (roots of which, as shown, reach into the guarantee of human dignity) as serious enough to justify the prohibition within an area of a 1-kilometer radius around the practice. Rather, the 1-kilometer ban was an excessive burden on the complainant's constitutionally guaranteed freedom of expression, especially, if, and to the extent to which, one is willing to accept the (albeit controversial[25]) idea that all basic rights have a human-dignity nucleus (*Menschenwürdekern*)[26] or emanate from human dignity.[27] Thus, the philosophical notion of human dignity has found its way into German jurisprudence.[28] However, the connection is less blatant than one might expect in the case of a common law court applying a statute. For instance, in *Lüth*, the Federal Constitutional Court comes very close to, but, nevertheless, shows restraint in directly connecting freedom of speech and human dignity by saying:

> The basic right to freedom of expressing one's opinion is, as the most immediate expression of human personality in society, one of the noblest

> human rights which exist (un des droits les plus précieux de l'homme according to Article 11 of the Declaration of human and citizens' rights of 1789). For a liberal and democratic order of the State it is absolutely constitutive as it alone makes possible the constant intellectual debate, the struggle of opinions, which is its vital element (5 BVerfGE 85, 205). In a certain sense, it is the foundation of freedom as such, "the matrix, the indispensable condition of nearly every other form of freedom."
>
> (Cardozo) (7 BVerfGE 198, 208)

Consequently, if we look closely at the "scales" of the balancing exercise, we can detect elements of human dignity in both "weighing pans."

The "Babycaust" Case

In 1 BvR 49/00, the Federal Constitutional Court heard appeals against the criminal convictions of two pro-life activists.[29] As to the facts of the case, on 8 October, 1997, the two activists distributed four-page pamphlets to passers-by in front of a Nuremberg medical center. The front page contained the following text: "'Killing specialist' for unborn children Dr. F. [is] on the premises of the Northern Medical Centre, Nuremberg" (1 BvR 49/00, para. 2). The middle pages contained information on the development of the human fetus and about abortion techniques. It further contained the requests for support: "Please support our struggle against the unpunished killing of unborn children" and "Therefore: No to abortion." (1 BvR 49/00, para. 7–10). The verso contains the following text:

> Stop the murder of children in their mother's womb on the premises of the Northern medical center. Then: Holocaust—Today: Babycaust (*damals: Holocaust heute—Babycaust*). Whoever remains silent becomes guilty too!
>
> (1 BvR 49/00, para. 2–6)

Dr. F and, on behalf of the medical center, the City of Nuremberg lodged a demand for criminal prosecution for defamation. While the Nuremberg District Court (*Amtsgericht*) acquitted them, the Nuremberg Regional Court (*Landgericht*) found them guilty and imposed fines. The two activists were unsuccessful in their appeals before the Bavarian Court of Appeal (*Bayerisches Oberstes Landesgericht*) against the Regional Court's judgment.

The Regional Court found the accused to be guilty of defaming not only Dr. F but also the medical center in respect of which the Regional Court interpreted the contents of the pamphlet as collectively directed against the center's clinical personnel because it referred to the "murder of children . . . on the premises of the Northern Medical Centre" (1 BvR 49/00, para. 13).

However, the Regional Court did not consider the two activists to be defaming Dr. F when they called him a "'Killing specialist' for unborn children." Rather, this was a true, although a one-sided phrasing of a statement of fact. Where the pamphlet spoke of "the murder of children in their mother's womb on the premises of the Northern Medical Centre," the word "murder" was not used in the sense of accusing Dr. F of actually having committed a crime since it was generally known that the abortions concerned here did not come under criminal law. The expression was rather to be understood as qualifying abortion as the reprehensible, intentional, though not criminal killing of unborn children. It did not amount to a vilification (*Schmähung*) and the balancing of values showed freedom of expression to prevail over Dr. F's personality right (1 BvR 49/00, para. 14).

In contrast, the phrase "then: Holocaust—today: Babycaust" was found to be defamatory. In the overall context of the pamphlet, this could only be interpreted as meaning that Dr. F was killing children for damnable and immoral reasons and that the medical center was at least tolerating this. By their choice of words, they equated the doctor's legal activities with the Holocaust as being synonymous with the most heinous and abominable crimes of mankind for which there can be no justification. Using the word "Holocaust" with the associations it arouses could not be justified as a bold exaggeration, and was unacceptable (1 BvR 49/00, para. 15).

The constitutional complaints against their criminal convictions were only partly successful. Pointing to the details of the pamphlet's text, the Federal Constitutional Court concluded that no reader could doubt that the doctor expressly mentioned on the front page was to be identified as the one responsible for what was happening on the grounds of the medical center, and that the reference to this as "Babycaust" and the comparison with the "Holocaust" referred to the doctor's activities. This connection was emphasized by the fact that the pamphlet was distributed on the grounds of the medical center and thus in the area of Dr. F's premises. The Federal Constitutional Court found no fault in the finding of the criminal courts that there was a severe interference with Dr. F's personality right, and also in the conclusion that the interference with the doctor's personality right amounted to a violation of this right (1 BvR 49/00, para. 33, 35–37). In contrast, it does not agree with the Regional Court insofar as this Court qualified the pamphlet as libelous criticism and a vilification of Dr. F, such as *Schmähkritik* being a grave interference with another person's personality right which is absolutely unjustifiable by constitutionally protected free speech (see 82 BVerfGE 43, 51; 1 BvR 2433/17, para. 18). However, the Regional Court, whose judgment was upheld by the Court of Appeal, actually went beyond merely qualifying the pamphlet as *Schmähkritik*. Rather the criminal courts had based their decisions on a balancing test weighing the accused persons' freedom of speech against the severe violation of the doctor's honor ("*schwere Ehrverletzung*") (1 BvR 49/00, para. 38–39). As in the *Exclusion Zone* case, we see the Federal Constitutional Court analyzing the case as a conflict between basic rights which needs to be solved by a balancing exercise. Both sides demand to be taken seriously. Both sides can point to the dignity aspects of their basic rights—freedom of expression on the one hand and the personality right on the other.

The Rent-a-Villa Case—Non-Discrimination as an Emanation of Human Dignity

The 2006 German *Allgemeines Gleichstellungsgesetz* (General Law on Equal Treatment, "AGG") is a federal statute. Its purpose is to prevent, or abolish, discrimination on grounds of race or ethnic origin, sex, religion, philosophy (or view of life, "*Weltanschauung*"), disability, age, or sexual identity. The common denominator of these grounds of discrimination is that the person concerned cannot alter them at will.[30] Thus, from the perspective of Article 1(1) of the *Grundgesetz*, the impugned criteria for differentiation must have no power to reduce the person's dignity. In other words, they shall not affect the equal dignity of human beings. This shows how the AGG[31] connects to the constitutional protection of human dignity.[32] Consequently, constitutional law requires this law to be applied consistently with Article 1 of the *Grundgesetz*, but also with other constitutional provisions granting rights and freedoms.[33]

The AGG's scope of application includes access to, and the supply of, goods and services which are offered to the public. However, it is difficult to spot cases that are in *pari materia* with the *Masterpiece Cakeshop* and *Ashers* cases. Whether this is indicative of greater tolerance in German society of homosexual couples or not, we could only speculate. However, the concept of dignity inheres in the approach taken by courts in cases of discrimination. Among those cases, one can find the *Rent-a-Villa Case*, as we would like to call it, which was decided by the Cologne Regional Court in 2015 (Decision no. 10 S 137/14, November 13, 2015).

In this case, the plaintiffs, a homosexual couple, were denied services by the defendant. As an accommodation case, it bears some factual similarity to the United Kingdom Supreme Court decision in *Bull v. Hall*. It also bears some similarity to *Masterpiece Cakeshop* as it relates to the provision of specialized wedding services. In the *Rent-a-Villa Case*, the plaintiffs contacted the defendant, the owner of a villa, in which he lived with his elderly mother. Their contact was in response to the defendant's online advertisement for the supply of a venue suitable for wedding celebrations. Rent was limited to short-term use. According to the advertisements, the defendant rented out the villa's living rooms, supplied chairs and tables as required, and provided access to the villa's kitchen, according to catering needs. If a wedding celebration was planned, the owner also offered a "*Sonder-Bonus Hochzeit*" ("special bonus wedding"): renters could additionally book the owner's bedroom for their exclusive use for one night at no extra cost. In the course of their inquiry, the plaintiffs asked the defendant whether their homosexuality would be an obstacle to renting the villa. Before they had been invited to inspect the premises, the defendant sent them an email and an SMS declining to contract with them (see paras. 18, 19, 21, 28 of the Decision).

The Cologne Regional Court applied the AGG and allowed the plaintiffs' claim of damages and costs as well as of immaterial damages (paras. 25–30]). As the defendant advertised his villa for rent through public media, there was, according to the judgment, a case under the AGG. The Court's conclusion was confirmed by the fact that renting the villa was a commercial activity that the defendant would repetitively pursue into the future (paras. 6–8).

The AGG protects the dignity of the person by making discrimination on the grounds of race or ethnic origin sex, religion or *Weltanschauung*, disability, age, or sexual identity impermissible in legal relations where the identity of the persons involved is not relevant. In what is referred to as *Massengeschäfte* (mass transactions), or standardized transactions in which the identity of the persons involved is of subordinate relevance, each transaction must be on comparable terms so as not to discriminate in relation to the identity of the persons involved (Article 19(1) of the AGG). Similar to the common law innkeepers' rule, in the public sphere, German law requires all customers to be treated with equal dignity in being able to enter transactions on equal terms (Singer 2022).

The Court found it sufficient that the owner was pursuing a business model according to which the identity of the persons involved was of subordinate importance. According to the Court, from the standpoint of the *allgemeine und typisierende Betrachtungsweise* ("general and simplifying perspective") offering goods and services to the public on regularly available contractual terms entailed that those terms must be made available to all customers, regardless of their identity. The case was different from one where, typically and reasonably, consideration of certain qualities of the contracting partner is relevant, such as the creditworthiness of a person applying for a loan. The Court did not regard the identity of the renter as relevant to the defendant's business. In normal circumstances, the potential customer, after contacting the defendant regarding the offer to let the villa from the defendant's internet site, would be informed of the terms of the contract and availability of the villa. If still interested, the defendant would invite inspection and discussion of the details of the rental agreement (Decision no. 10 S 137/14, paras. 12–13).

The Court denied the defendant's attempt to evade the application of the AGG by claiming that he only rented the villa to people he liked. Objectively, there were no characteristics of the contractual relationship that could justify its exclusion from the scope of the AGG. Commercially renting out a villa for events such as weddings, family celebrations, or press conferences, meant the identity of the contracting partner was, in the view of the Court, of no relevance. The Court also found it irrelevant that the defendant rented out the house in which he himself lived. Since he did so for commercial purposes, he was bound to comply with the legal requirements for the provision of commercial services, including the prohibition of discrimination.[34] The Cologne Regional Court found the commercial character of the rental arrangement evidenced by the "multitude of cases," since he had rented out the villa at least eight times a year for the last five years (before the judgment), thus at least 40 times. The terms of the contract were "comparable," within the meaning of the section; the same rooms were let according to the same standard terms. No special relation of proximity was found, which would exclude, under Article

19(5) of the AGG, the application of the AGG to the case. This included the "*Sonder-Bonus Hochzeit*" as a special additional free-of-charge offer. It did not, in the Court's view, determine the core contractual relationship (Decision no. 10 S 137/14, paras. 15–21).

The Court ruled out any objective reason ("*sachlicher Grund*"), which might justify differential treatment. The Court was not convinced that there was any difference between allowing a homosexual couple to use his bedroom and allowing a heterosexual couple. As to the defendant's mother's personal position, the Court said:

> The sentiment of morality and decency of the defendant's aged mother are not an objective reason for discriminating against the plaintiffs. On the one hand, the defendant has stated that his mother stays in the garden house during the events and thus does not meet the respective customer of the defendant. A provocation, or anything similar, regarding his mother can therefore not be assumed. Furthermore, this highly individual personal feeling [*dieses höchst subjektive Empfinden*] is . . . completely arbitrary [*in jeder Hinsicht willkürlich*].
>
> (Decision no. 10 S 137/14, paras. 23–24)

It is the paragraph of the decision which shows how Article 19(1) of the AGG works. It defines that the law will not accept or tolerate decisions of a discriminatory nature[35] made by private individuals or other private entities[36] in mass transactions and in other transactions occurring in a standardized way.

Thus, in standard, repetitive transactions, the AGG imposes on the providers of goods and services a duty to serve everyone equally. Under German constitutional law,[37] this restricts the providers' liberty, as protected by constitutionally guaranteed basic rights,[38] as it must give way to the basic right of equality.

Generally, basic rights may be restricted by legislation if the restriction serves a legitimate legislative aim and is proportionate.[39] Article 19 of the AGG has the legislative aim to protect the basic rights of others, the potential "transaction partners," or customers of the providers of goods and services. For this reason, Article 19 of the AGG burdens the freedom of contract of the providers of goods and services; thereby restricting their constitutional liberties protected by Article 2 or Article 12 of the *Grundgesetz*.[40] Where the state, by legislation, intends to protect the basic rights of one group of private persons by restricting the basic rights of another group of private persons, the *Grundgesetz* demands the legislature to strike a fair balance between conflicting basic rights; the rights need to be brought into a relationship of *praktische Konkordanz*, i.e., of practical harmony or harmonious coexistence. Where legislation does not provide a clear-cut rule but rather leaves the courts "room for maneuver," the balancing becomes a task for the judiciary, which, under the doctrine of *mittelbare Drittwirkung* of basic rights, needs to be performed informed by constitutional law.[41]

The implementation of the preservation of dignity under Article 1 of the *Grundgesetz* is, in the end, a practical matter. Providers of goods and services in public commercial activities are legally required to put aside personal bias or sentiments concerning potential customers' attributes such as sexual identity. Providers involved in mass transactions must act neutrally and keep their prejudices "behind the curtain." Outside the context of public transactions, the AGG allows them to act as they wish, even arbitrarily or being motivated by prejudices (148 BVerfGE 267, 283, para. 40).

Obviously, in the case of Article 19 of the AGG, the solution to *praktische Konkordanz* involves restricting the providers' basic rights in favor of their potential customers' basic rights. Since Article 20 of the AGG leaves little room for exceptions, Article 19, even under the doctrine of *indirect* horizontal effect of basic rights, operates well along the lines of the proportionality test as it opposes differential treatment where it is based on characteristics connected to a person's identity and thus to his or her dignity as a human being. However, in other private-law disputes (where human dignity is not at risk), basic rights radiate into private law requiring the courts to truly balance the conflicting basic rights with each party deserving equal respect. In this case, there should be no single valid solution for a specific type of conflict, but rather a "corridor" of possible solutions.[42] Nevertheless, with some exceptions as those provided under Article 20 of the AGG, the courts always need to decide each case, being mindful of basic rights provisions on both sides.

According to German constitutional jurisprudence, constitutionally guaranteed basic rights serve to protect private parties against governmental power, but they also guide the legislature and the courts in solving disputes between private parties, providing each party with provisions that need to be taken into account and balanced against conflicting interests of other private parties.[43] One might consider this legal situation in the light of Immanuel Kant's moral philosophy, in the context of which he defined "Recht"—which might be translated as "the right" or as "law"—to be the epitome (i.e., the sum) of the conditions for uniting what one person wills with what another person wills according to a general law of freedom (Kant [1797] 1914, 203).[44] The consequence is the General Principle of Law ("Allgemeines Prinzip des Rechts"): any action is right ("recht") which, or according to the maxim that everyone's freedom (to choose and act in the sense of willing), can exist together with anyone else's freedom according to a general law (Kant [1797] 1914, 203).[45]

Actual legal systems and the practice of law will never fulfill this ideal perfectly. But including basic rights in a constitution and making them relevant wherever public authority is exercised—including in judicial decisions on conflicts between private parties—can bring us a step closer to this ideal.

Unlike in the aforementioned common law systems, where, in the absence of constitutional mandates, the notion of dignity seems to be slowly emerging in response to statutory requirements, under German law, with its constitutional requirements, it is a constant background of German case law. That said, like in the common law systems, in German jurisprudence, dignity has not yet gained a recognizable jurisprudential meaning that is directly traceable back to Kant or any other philosopher or commentator.

Conclusion

One should not doubt the debt that is owed both to German philosophical writing and the German constitutional framework for the concept of dignity. Neither can there be any real doubt that all jurisprudence would be better for having a careful regard for the dignity of all parties to a dispute.

The German decisions that we have chosen for reasons of similarity with the common law cases exemplify that the analysis of conflicts and disputes based on basic rights standards will, quite regularly, lead to a balancing of conflicting basic rights. The consequence is that the interests of all parties involved, insofar as their interests are protected by basic rights, will equally receive attention and respect (although, of course, decisions produce winners and losers). Many of the basic rights can be interpreted as connected to the fundamental constitutional directive laid down in Article 1(1) of the *Grundgesetz*. Thus, brushing away the (legal and factual) details of cases, one can reveal that, more often than not, in cases concerning human beings (in contrast with legal persons) the balance of competing claims for respect for human dignity is at the core.

Unlike arguments based upon equality or liberty alone, the result of a case decided with dignity as the mediating influence has no foreordained result. Instead, the court is required to weigh all factors that will lead to the dignity of both parties being kept intact, even though one's claim will, in the end, prevail.

Even if the word "dignity" does not find its way into every judgment of every court, its spirit is regarding all parties before a court as human beings worthy of respect. Even in disputes concerning corporations, there are still individuals who stand to lose or gain by the way the legal system treats them. While no legal system is perfect, we hope that this contribution to the ongoing conversation will prompt the question of how best to preserve the dignity of all parties, whatever the outcome of the dispute.

As a way forward in common law jurisdictions' statutory interpretation and constitutional adjudication on rights we suggest the following. First, as cited, the European Court of Human Rights has accepted that "[t]he very essence of the Convention is respect for human dignity and human freedom" (*Pretty v. United Kingdom*, para. 65). This acceptance, we submit, could and should be adopted in all jurisdictions in which the principal human rights instruments are predicated upon dignity, as is the case for the UDHR, the ICCPR, and, of course, the ECHR itself.

Second, we would commend to common law jurisdictions an approach adopted by the Australian High Court in the *Clubb* decision. The Court, adopting what we have noted as being a Kantian mode of expression from Barak, declared in passages cited by us (*Clubb v. Edwards*; *Preston v. Avery*, para. 50–51) that dignity "is the source from which all other human rights are derived. 'Dignity unites the other human rights into a whole (Barak 2006, 85) . . . [h]uman dignity regards a human being as an end, not as a means to achieve the ends of others.'" In considering constitutionally conferred human rights, in that case the freedom of political expression, the Australian High Court said that dignity is central to all human rights. Thus, we argue that the adoption of a working model based upon dignity is desirable as a common law approach when called for in the adjudication of rights. It should not be regarded as foreign to the business of common law courts and their constitutional assessments.

Thus, bringing the German cases (with their more explicit resort to dignity-related balancing of basic rights) to the attention of courts and scholars in common law legal systems will—we hope—inspire these to reflect upon the importance of any legal order's respect for human dignity and to adopt, for the solution of cases arising under the common law, if only as a contrasting thought-experiment, a balancing approach similar to that of the German courts. They might well discover that, after all, they actually have been guided by the idea of equal respect for the liberty and dignity of each and all the parties in the cases they have decided or commented on. The German courts, on the other hand, could become aware of the ability of foreign legal systems to develop, by way of jurisprudential evolution, solutions to controversies with a similar level of protection for human dignity (reaching the same result without, or more rarely, using the word "dignity").

Notes

1 Article 1 of the German Basic Law stipulates that a person's dignity is inviolable. To protect it is the duty of all state authorities (authors' translation).

2 Although the *Bundesverfassungsgericht* directly resorts neither to any specific philosophy not to any specific philosopher, its jurisprudence on human dignity (Art. 1 of the *Grundgesetz*) can be interpreted as finding some inspiration in Immanuel Kant's thinking. Cf. recently *Bundesverfassungsgericht* (156 BVerfGE 182, 208–9 para. 60).

3 See also Kant ([1785] 1911, 436).

4 Kant ([1785] 1911) equates the violation of the rights of man with any instance in which one person uses another person merely as a means and not as an end, thus disregarding that this person, too, is endowed with reason (385, 430).

5 According to the analysis of Lörz (1993). there is a comprehensive parallelism between the guarantee of human dignity in Article 1(1) of the *Grundgesetz* and Kant's understanding of dignity (271–91). Riedel (1986) sees the weight of 2500 years of history of philosophy resting on the concept of dignity (473–74), where Kant is, albeit carefully, relied upon in the context of interpreting Article 1(1) of the Grundgesetz.

6 Cf. Kant ([1785] 1911), where Kant points to "*die vernünftige Natur*" (reasonable nature) as existing as an end in itself, in which man and any other reasonable creature partakes (429). From this he derives the practical imperative: act in such a way as at all times to treat mankind, both in your own person and in the person of anyone else, never merely as a means but always simultaneously as an end.

7 Cf., once again, 156 BVerfGE, para. 60, where the German Federal Constitutional Court reiterates its jurisprudence that the guarantee of human dignity is a

fundamental and constitutive principle of the system of basic rights forbidding the state to reduce a human being to a mere object. Before pointing to the inviolability and inalienability of human dignity, it adds that human dignity is not only the dignity of the individual but also the dignity of human as a species.

8 See, on the long tradition of dignity preceding Anglophone analysis, Nussbaum (2019, chapters 1–4) and Lörz (1993).

9 Cf. *McCloy v. New South Wales*, paras. 42–45, 93.

10 See *R v. Sussex Justices ex parte McCarthy*; *Ebner v. Official Trustee in Bankruptcy*; *R v. Watson; Livesey v. New South Wales Bar Association*; *Johnson v. Johnson*.

11 Baden, Bavaria, Bremen, Hamburg, Hessen, Lower Saxony, Northrhine-Westfalia, Rhineland-Palatinate, Schleswig-Holstein, Württemberg-Baden and Württemberg-Hohenzollern.

12 See the proclamation of the *Grundgesetz* in: *Bundesgesetzblatt* [Official Journal of the Federal Republic of Germany] 1949, 1. For the *Grundgesetz*'s entry into force, Art. 144(1) required ratification by the parliaments of two thirds of the German Länder in which it was to apply initially (verbatim: "in denen es zunächst gelten soll"). See also the Letter from the Three Western Military Governors to the President of the Parliamentary Council of 12 May, 1949, approving the constitution for submission to the German people for ratification in accordance with Art. 144(1).

13 The last paragraph of the *Grundgesetz*'s original preamble called upon the entire German people to complete the unity and freedom of Germany in free self-determination. See also: Aust (2021, Art. 146, para. 3). The country remained divided until Reunification in 1990.

14 The German Federal Constitutional Court, pointing, *inter alia*, to the guarantee of human dignity in Art. 1 of the *Grundgesetz*, reads the Constitution as expressing the will of all who were historically involved in its enactment to break with the past of National Socialism; to the Court the *Grundgesetz* is a counter design to totalitarianism and injustice. See 124 BVerfGE, 300, 328.

15 Only rather recently has the Federal Constitutional Court clearly addressed Art. 1(1) of the *Grundgesetz* as a fundamental right, see: 109 BVerfGE 133, para. 78; 125 BVerfGE 175, paras. 133–34. Some scholars disagree with this categorization (Dreier 2013, paras. 121–27).

16 It is a matter of debate how the relationship between the inviolability of human dignity pronounced in Article 1(1) of the *Grundgesetz* and the other constitutionally guaranteed basic rights ought to be construed. Do all basic rights emanate from Article 1(1)? Does every guarantee therefore contain a human dignity nucleus? Or are they at least inspired by the idea and overall guiding principle of respect for human dignity? For an overview see Dreier (2013, paras. 160–66).

17 As to the facts of the case, see 1 BvR 1745/06, paras. 1–12.

18 Both the basic rights standards that the civil courts need to apply in controversies between private parties, and the resulting scope of constitutional review of such decisions are concisely summarized in: 148 BVerfGE 267, 280–81, paras. 32–34.

19 According to Art. 1(3) of the Grundgesetz, the basic rights guaranteed by the constitution bind the legislature, the executive and the judiciary as directly enforceable law ("*als unmittelbar geltendes Recht*").

20 Cf. the summary of its jurisprudence in 148 BVerfGE 267, 280 para. 32 (on a constitutional complaint against civil court decisions concerning a legal controversy between parties, encountering one another as private persons, over the extent of an owner's and possessor's private-law rights in relation to a third party).

21 As to the standards of balancing constitutional values in such cases, cf. 48 BVerfGE 267, 280–81, where the *Bundesverfassungsgericht*'s constitutional review of civil-court decisions is restrained to establishing whether their interpretation and application of provisions of private law "shows flaws resulting from a fundamentally wrong perception of the meaning of the basic rights concerned and the substantial

relevance of such flaws are of considerable weight for the specific legal case, especially, for the reason that they negatively influence the balancing of the respective legal positions within the framework of the private-law regulation."

22 The basic rights "immediately" bind not only the legislature and the executive but also the courts of law (Article 1(3) of the Grundgesetz).

23 Section 1004 of the *Bürgerliches Gesetzbuch* belongs to the provisions defining the rights of property owners, irrespective of whether movables or immovables are concerned. According to section 1004, the owner of property has a right to removal and prevention of infringement: if in cases where the owner is not under an obligation to tolerate, property rights are infringed upon other than by dispossession or ouster, the owner can demand of the infringer to remove the infringement. If further infringements are imminent, the owner can petition for a preventive injunction.

24 Cf. 120 BVerfGE 180, 201. See also the Regensburg Administrative Court's Decision no. RN 4 E 20.2426, October 14, 2020, regarding § 118 of the *Gesetz über Ordnungswidrigkeiten* (the Administrative Offences Act) as law of general application.

25 See, e.g., Dreier (2013).

26 Cf. 54 BVerfGE 341, 357 concerning the basic right to asylum, whose requirements and scope is regarded as being essentially determined by the inviolability of human dignity; and 80 BVerfGE 367, 373–74 that the core of the personality is protected by the inviolable dignity of the human being. Cf. also: Huber (2018, paras. 121–28; Kokott (2004, para. 89).

27 Cf. 93 BVerfGE 266, 293 saying that "human dignity as the root of all basic rights." See also, e.g., Dürig (1958, paras. 80–81, 85), Häberle (2004, paras. 57–58), where the protection of human dignity is called a "fundamental postulate" and describing the specific guarantees of basic rights as the textualization of sorrowful negative experiences of violations of human dignity.

28 However, for some authors, such as, for example, Stern (2006), the *Menschenwürdegehalt* (human dignity content) of freedom of speech is weaker than that of other basic rights.

29 It also heard a constitutional complaint raised by Dr. F, against whom the two activists had been particularly protesting.

30 This corresponds to Article 3(3) of the *Grundgesetz*: "No one may be discriminated against or given preferential treatment because of his or her sex, ancestry, race, language, home country and origin, faith, religious or political views. No one may be disadvantaged because of his disability." Sexual orientation, however, is not included in Article 3(3).

31 The case discussed in this section concerns discrimination on grounds of sexual orientation in the context of the supply of goods and services. The AGG covers such discrimination, thereby going beyond what European Union directives demand (Ernst, Braunroth, and Wascher 2013, para. 1). At least insofar as the AGG is open for interpretation and application in the light of German constitutional law; see, concerning Article 3(3) of the *Grundgesetz*: 2 BvR 1005/18, paras. 31 et seq.

32 As to the close connection between human dignity and equality as protected by Article 3(1) of the *Grundgesetz*, cf. 84 BVerfGE 90, 121, and 23 BVerfGE 98, 106–7. See also Herdegen (2021, para. 120); Höfling (2021, para. 35); Wollenschläger (2018, para. 43).

33 Cf., *mutatis mutandis*, 120 BVerfGE 180, 211–15.

34 The Court discussed whether there might be a relation of proximity or intimacy between the defendant and his customers involved because the defendant used the villa as his domicile but came to the conclusion that this was not the case as his customers only used the villa as the place of an event rather than lived in the villa.

35 Article 19 of the AGG is constitutive in this respect. Mind that Article 3(1) of the *Grundgesetz* (the general basic right to equality) does not bind private parties directly. According to the Federal Constitutional Court (148 BVerfGE 267, 283 paras. 40–43) Article 3(1) does not contain an objective constitutional principle requiring relations between private parties *inter se* basically to be designed in compliance with equality requirements. Rather, in principle, every private person is free to decide according to his or her personal preferences with whom, when, and on which terms, they would like to conclude a contract and how to make use of their property. There is no general principle emanating from Article 3(1) of the *Grundgesetz* requiring private parties to justify their treating others unequally. However, there can be constellations where Article 3(1) of the *Grundgesetz* does affect relations between private parties.

36 See Articles 2 and 3 of the AGG. The AGG applies to direct and indirect discriminations. Article 3 of the AGG provides definitions of these concepts.

37 To show the full picture it would be necessary to go into details of EU law. For reasons of simplification and concentration, EU law will only be touched upon briefly and sparingly.

38 This may include rights protected by Articles 2, 12, and/or 14 of the *Grundgesetz*.

39 Article 12(1) of the *Grundgesetz* allows "the practice of an occupation" to be regulated by or pursuant to a law. According to Article 14(1), the contents of property rights and their limits shall be determined by laws. The guarantee of liberty under Article 2(1) is essentially limited by the "*verfassungsmäßige Ordnung*," the constitutional order, which is interpreted as encompassing all laws formally and substantively compatible with the *Grundgesetz*.

40 Cf., *mutatis mutandis*, the German Federal Constitutional Court: when regulating the legality of contract clauses, the legislator must "bear in mind that restricting contractual freedom, in whatever way, in order to protect one party simultaneously interferes with the freedom of the other party" (81 BVerfGE 242, 255).

41 Cf. *the German Constitutional Court's decisions*: 7 BVerfGE 198, 203–10; 25 BVerfGE 256, 263; 73 BVerfGE 261, 269; 89 BVerfGE 214, 229 et seq.; 119 BVerfGE 1, 29 et seq.; 120 BVerfGE 180, 199 et seq.; 142 BVerfGE 74, 101; 148 BVerfGE 267, 280.

42 Cf. 120 BVerfGE 180, 210; 148 BVerfGE 267, 281.

43 See: 119 BVerfGE 1, 29–36; 120 BVerfGE 180, 199–200; 142 BVerfGE 74, 101; 148 BVerfGE 267, 280–81.

44 See also: Kant ([1793] 1917, 273, 289–90): "*Right* is the limitation of every individual's liberty on the condition of its concordance with everyone's liberty insofar as this [concordance] is possible according to a general law."

45 Here the quality of an action as right ("recht") is addressed. As the requirements of the action's being "recht" are given in the abstract and in relation to everyone else, we think it is proper to speak of the General Principle *of Law* here.

References

Aust, Helmut Philipp. 2021. "Art. 146." In *Grundgesetz Kommentar* [Commentary to the Basic Law]. 7th ed., edited by Ingo von Münch and Philip Kunig. Munich: C.H. Beck.

Barak, Aharon. 2006. *The Judge in a Democracy*. Princeton: Princeton University Press.

Barak, Aharon. 2015. *Human Dignity: The Constitutional Value and the Constitutional Right*. Cambridge: Cambridge University Press.

Bayefsky, Rachel. 2013. "Dignity, Honour, and Human Rights: Kant's Perspective." *Political Theory* 41 (6): 809–37.

Böckenförde, Ernst-Wolfgang. 2017. *Constitutional and Political Theory: Selected Writings.* Edited by Mirjam Künkler and Tine Stein. Oxford: Oxford University Press.

Dreier, Horst. 2013. "Art. 1 I." In *Grundgesetz Kommentar* [Commentary to the Basic Law]. Vol. 1, 3rd ed., edited by Horst Dreier. Munich: C.H. Beck.

Dürig, Günter. 1958. "Art. 1 II." In *Grundgesetz Kommentar* [Commentary to the Basic Law], edited by Theodor Maunz and Günter Dürig. Munich: C.H. Beck.

Ernst, Hildegund, Anna Braunroth, and Angelika Wascher. 2013. "§ 19." In *Allgemeines Gleichbehandlungsgesetz Kommentar* [Commentary to General Act on Equal Treatment]. 2nd ed. Baden-Baden: Nomos.

Fukuyama, Francis. 2018. *Identity: The Demand for Dignity and the Politics of Resentment.* London: Profile Books.

Häberle, Peter. 2004. "Die Menschenwürde als Grundlage der staatlichen Gemeinschaft [Human Dignity as the Basis of State Community]." In *Handbuch des Staatsrechts* [Handbook of Constitutional Law]. Vol. 2, 3rd ed., edited by Josef Isensee and Paul Kirchhof. Heidelberg: C.F. Müller.

Herdegen, Matthias. 2021. "Art. 1 I." In *Grundgesetz Kommentar* [Commentary to the Basic Law]. 53rd ed., edited by Günter Dürig, Roman Herzog, and Rupert Scholz. Munich: C.H. Beck.

Hicks, Donna. 2011. *Dignity: Its Essential Role in Resolving Conflict.* New Haven: Yale University Press.

Höfling, Wolfram. 2021. "Art. 1." In *Grundgesetz* [Basic Law]. 9th ed., edited by Michael Sachs. Munich: C.H. Beck.

Huber, Peter M. 2018. "Art. 19." In *Grundgesetz* [Basic Law]. Vol. 1, 7th ed., edited by Hermann von Mangoldt, Friedrich Klein, and Christian Starck. Munich: C.H. Beck.

Kant, Immanuel. (1785) 1911. "Grundlegung zur Metaphysik der Sitten [Groundwork of the Metaphysics of Morals]." In *Immanuel Kant: Gesammelte Schriften* [Immanuele Kant: Collected Writings]. Vol. 4. Berlin: Preussische Akademie der Wissenschaften.

Kant, Immanuel. (1793) 1917. "Über den Gemeinspruch: Das mag in der Theorie richtig sein, taugt aber nicht für die Praxis [On the Old Saw: That May Be Right in Theory, But It Won't Work in Practice]." In *Immanuel Kant: Gesammelte Schriften Schriften* [Immanuele Kant: Collected Writings]. Vol. 7. Berlin: Preussische Akademie der Wissenschaften.

Kant, Immanuel. (1797) 1914. "Die Metaphysik der Sitten [Metaphysics of Morals]." In *Immanuel Kant: Gesammelte Schriften Schriften* [Immanuele Kant: Collected Writings]. Vol. 6. Berlin: Preussische Akademie der Wissenschaften.

Kirchick, James. 2019. "The Struggle for Gay Rights is Over." *The Atlantic*, June 28, 2019. www.theatlantic.com/ideas/archive/2019/06/battle-gay-rights-over/592645/.

Kokott, Juliane. 2004. "Grundrechtliche Schranken und Schrankenschranken." In *Handbuch der Grundrechte in Deutschland und Europa* [Textbook of Fundamental Rights in Germany and Europe]. Vol. 1, edited by Detlef Merten and Hans-Jürgen Papier. Heidelberg: C.F. Müller.

Lörz, Ralph Alexander. 1993. *Modernes Grund- und Menschenrechtsverständnis und die Philosophie der Freiheit Kants* [Modern Understanding of Fundamental and Human Rights in Kant's Philosophy of Freedom]. Stuttgart: Richard Boorberg.

Nussbaum, Marth C. 2019. *The Cosmopolitan Tradition—A Noble but Flawed Ideal.* Cambridge, MA: The Belknap Press of Harvard University.

Quirk, Patrick T. 2018. "The Undefined Remains Unprotected: Tensions Between Conscience and the Law in Germany by Way of Joseph Isensee." *Tulane Journal of International and Comparative Law* 27 (1): 55–92.

Riedel, Eibe. 1986. "Gentechnologie und Embryonenschutz als Verfassungs- und Regelungsproblem [Genetic Engineering and Embryo Protection As a Constitutional and Regulatory Problem]." *Europäische Grundrechte Zeitschrift* 13: 469–78.

Rosen, Michael. 2012. *Dignity: Its History and Meaning*. Cambridge: Harvard University Press.

Sacks, Jonathan. 2002. *The Dignity of Difference: How to Avoid the Clash of Civilisations*. London: Bloomsbury.

Singer, Joseph William. 2022. "Religious Liberty & Public Accommodations: What Would Hohfeld Say?" In *The Legacy of Wesley Hohfeld: Edited Major Works, Select Personal Papers, and Original Commentaries*, edited by Shyamkrishna Balganesh, Ted M. Sichelman, and Henry E. Smith, 478–93. Cambridge: Cambridge University Press.

Stern, Klaus. 2006. "Die einzelnen Grundrechte—Der Schutz und die freiheitliche Entfaltung des Individuums [The Individual Fundamental Rights—The Protection and Free Development of the Individual]." In *Das Staatsrecht der Bundesrepublik Deutschland* [Constitutional Law of the Federal Republic of Germany]. Vol. IV/1, edited by Klaus Stern, Michael Sachs, and Johannes Dietlein. Munich: C.H. Beck.

Waldron, Jeremy. 2012. *Dignity, Rank, and Rights*. New York: Oxford University Press.

Wollenschläger, Ferdinand. 2018. "Art. 3." In *Grundgesetz* [Basic Law]. 7th ed., edited by Hermann von Mangoldt, Friedrich Klein, and Christian Starck. Munich: C.H. Beck.

Case Law

German Courts

The Federal Constitutional Court of Germany

2 BvR 1845 and 2100/18, December 1, 2020, reported in BVerfGE 156, 182.
2 BvR 1005/18, January 30, 2020, ECLI:DE:BVerfG:2020:rk20200130.2bvr100518.
1 BvR 2433/17, June 14, 2019, ECLI:DE:BVerfG:2019:rk20190614.1bvr243317.
1 BvR 3080/09, April 11, 2018, reported in BVerfGE 148, 267.
1 BvR 2019/16, October 10, 2017, reported in BVerfGE 147, 1.
1 BvR 1585/13, May 31, 2016, reported in BVerfGE 142, 74.
1 BvR 1745/06, June 8, 2010, ECLI:DE:BVerfG:2010:rk20100608.1bvr174506.
1 BvL 1/09, February 9, 2010, reported in BVerfGE 125, 175.
1 BvR 2150/08, November 4, 2009, reported in BVerfGE 124, 300.
1 BvR 1602/07, February 26, 2008, reported in BVerfGE 120, 180.
1 BvR 1783/05, June 13, 2007, reported in BVerfGE 119, 1.
1 BvR 49/00, May 24, 2006, ECLI:DE:BVerfG:2006:rk20060524.1bvr004900.
1 BvR 2378/98, 1084/99, March 3, 2004, reported in BVerfGE 109, 279.
2 BvR 2029/01, February 5, 2004, reported in BVerfGE 109, 133.
1 BvR 1476, 1980/91 and 102, 221/92, October 10, 1995, reported in BVerfGE 93, 266.
1 BvR 23/94, April 13, 1994, reported in BVerfGE 90, 241.
1 BvR 567, 1044/89, October 19, 1993, reported in BVerfGE 89, 214.
1 BvR 1170/90, April 23, 1991, reported in BVerfGE 84, 90.
1 BvR 40/86, 42/86, April 19, 1990, reported in BVerfGE 82, 43.
1 BvR 26/84, February 7, 1990, reported in BVerfGE 81, 242.
2 BvR 1062/87, September 14, 1989, reported in BVerfGE 80, 367.
2 BvR 487/80, April 23, 1986, reported in BVerfGE 73, 261.
1 BvR 147, 181, 182/80, July 2, 1980, reported in BVerfGE 54, 341.
1 BvR 619/63, February 26, 1969, reported in BVerfGE 25, 256.
2 BvR 557/62, February 14, 1968, reported in BVerfGE 23, 98.
1 BvR 400/51, January 15, 1958, reported in BVerfGE 7, 198.

Regensburg Administrative Court

Decision no. RN 4 E 20.2426, October 14, 2020.

Cologne Regional Court

Judgment no. 10 S 137/14, November 13, 2015.

Common Law Courts

High Court of Australia

Clubb v. Edwards; Preston v Avery (2019) HCA 11.
Ebner v. Official Trustee in Bankruptcy (2000) 205 CLR 337; [2000] HCA 63.
Johnson v. Johnson (2000) 201 CLR 488; [2000] HCA 48.
Lange v. Australian Broadcasting Corporation (1997) 189 CLR 520.
Livesey v. New South Wales Bar Association (1983) 151 CLR 288; [1983] HCA 17.
McCloy v. New South Wales (2015) 257 CLR 178.
Preston v. Avery (2019) HCA 11 at 47–48.
R v. Watson; Ex parte Armstrong (1976) 136 CLR 248.
Re JRL; Ex parte CJL (1986) 161 CLR 342; [1986] HCA 39.
Unions NSW v. New South Wales (2013) 252 CLR 530.

Supreme Court of the United Kingdom

Bull and Another v. Hall and Another (2013) UKSC 73.
Lee v. Ashers Baking Company Ltd and Others (2018) UKSC 49.

High Court of Justice (United Kingdom)

R v. Sussex Justices ex parte McCarthy (1924) 1 KB 256.

Supreme Court of the United States

Burwell v. Hobby Lobby, 573 U.S. 682 (2014).
Hill v. Colorado, 530 U.S. 703 (2000).
Hosanna-Tabor Evangelical Lutheran Church School v. Equal Employment Opportunity Commission, 565 U.S. 171 (2012).
Masterpiece Cakeshop v. Colorado Civil Rights Commission, 584 U.S (2018).

Ontario Superior Court of Justice (Canada)

Ontario (Attorney-General) v. Dieleman (1994) 117 DLR (4th) 449.

European Court of Human Rights

Kokkinakis v. Greece, Application no. 14307/88, May 25, 1993.
Pretty v. The United Kingdom, Application no. 2346/02, April 29, 2002.

4 Dignity Proper and Dignity Plus

On the Uses of Dignity in German Constitutional Jurisprudence

Justin Collings

Introduction

Oliver Wurm, a youthful-looking sports journalist from the Sauerland, has turned Germany's post-war Constitution into a surprise bestseller. Having experienced a road-to-Damascus exhilaration when he read his country's Basic Law (*Grundgesetz*) for the first time, Wurm resolved to bring the Constitution closer to the people. Just months before the Constitution's 70th birthday in May, 2019, Wurm produced a sleek, glossy, modernist magazine version of it. The pamphlet has proved immensely popular. Sales number in the hundreds of thousands. Wurm himself has become something of a television and internet personality—an impassioned apostle for the German Constitution. Wurm makes an improbable constitutional patriot: he is neither jurist, nor statesman, nor scholar. But perhaps for that reason, his evangelizing is all the more effective. He presents himself as a simple man who simply loves his Constitution—especially its very first substantive clause. "You know," he said in a recent interview, "when I read that 'human dignity is inviolable' I get goosebumps" (Cleven 2019).

Wurm isn't alone in that response. The eleven-syllable first sentence of the Basic Law's first article is without rival the most iconic phrase in German law, perhaps in German politics. *Die Würde des Menschen ist unantastbar*: an article, noun, and verb, culminating in the rhythmic sorcery of an untranslatable adjective denoting something inviolable, untouchable, sacrosanct. Navid Kermani, a German writer and critic, described it as "a glorious German sentence, so simple, so difficult, at first blush obvious and yet," upon reflection, unfathomable (Kermani 2014).

There have, of course, been countless efforts to fathom it—to plumb its depths and delineate its contours, to trace its philosophical roots and probe its legal application. And there have been correspondingly numerous efforts to mobilize the phrase in support of every imaginable social, philosophical, moral, religious, and political cause—from the burning issues of the day (abortion, immigration, asylum, assisted dying, genetic engineering, data privacy, religious liberty, etc.) to the banal controversies of the judicial backwaters. In German legal and political discourse, dignity is everywhere. It is

DOI: 10.4324/9781003307853-5

the constitutional order's omnipresent "super-norm"—the ubiquitous primal value that informs and trumps all others—a norm so imperiously indispensable that the Basic Law's "eternity clause" (Article 79(3)) proclaims that it cannot be amended (Baldus 2019).

Germany's Federal Constitutional Court (*Bundesverfassungsgericht*) has played no small role in bringing about this state of affairs. From an early date, the Court has insisted on the primacy and supremacy of the Constitution's first article in describing the role of dignity in the constitutional order, the Court has spared no superlatives. It has called dignity "the supreme value in the value system of fundamental rights" (50 BVerfGE 166, 175 (1979)), the "root of all fundamental rights" (93 BVerfGE 293 (1995)), the highest value in all the legal order.[1]

Such superlatives are more than mere rhetorical adornments. They have jurisprudential consequences—not least because the Constitution itself makes the promise of dignity unamendable.[2] So long as the Basic Law remains in force, dignity must be honored and upheld. But the Court has gone even further. Because dignity reigns, unique and supreme, above all other constitutional values, the Court treats it differently from all other constitutional values. Dignity, the Court has said, is not amenable to balancing.[3] The Court that first adopted the proportionality test that swiftly swept the world does not apply that test to the Basic Law's supreme provision (Stone Sweet and Mathews 2008). Dignity cannot be weighed against other constitutional values, nor limited in any way. It is not only the Constitution's foremost value; it is an *absolute* value. It cannot be infringed no matter the justification. It cannot be balanced no matter what lies on the other side of the scale. It is, as they say, *unantastbar* ("inviolable" or "sacrosanct").

Or so the Court, in its more lyrical moments, has maintained. But the inevitable consequence of an absolute value is a rigidly narrow scope. Otherwise, there is no recourse when rights collide. Accordingly, in the Court's jurisprudence, dignity as an independent, stand-alone fundamental right has played only a limited role. Cases in which dignity as such has proved decisive are surpassingly rare—almost nonexistent. Ironically, the more the Court has exalted dignity in principle, the less it has meant in practice—at least as an independent, freestanding constitutional right. But the Court has also invoked dignity—and much more frequently—in conjunction with other constitutional values. When combined with other values or provisions, however, dignity is not absolute and is subject, like those other values, to balancing and to limits.

There are thus, in the Court's jurisprudence, two kinds of dignity. The first—call it *dignity proper*—is absolute and illimitable, but its scope is slender and cramped. The second—call it *dignity plus*—is relative and limitable, but its scope, like Walt Whitman's bard, is "large, [and] contain[s] multitudes." It is also, like Whitman, contradictory. This chapter explores both dignity proper and dignity plus, in that order.

Dignity Proper

Theodor Heuss, an influential member of the Parliamentary Council that crafted the Basic Law and later the Federal Republic's first president, described the Constitution's dignity clause—famously but elliptically—as a "non-interpreted thesis." Heuss's statement has historically been taken to mean that the Constitution's framers deliberately employed a capacious, ambiguous term. In any case, the clause has since been interpreted almost incessantly. The holy grail in this interpretive quest has always been a concise, persuasive, satisfactory definition of dignity. Such a definition had eluded everyone, including the judges of the Constitutional Court. But that is not for lack of trying. For more than six decades now, the Court has offered partial definitions and later combined those definitions in various ways. Over the same period, it has also put those definitions to practical work.

Dignity Defined

So, what is dignity? The Court has answered this question only in roundabout ways. Like other commentators, the Court has found it easier to trumpet dignity's primacy than to define its content. Despite its being easily and (in Germany) almost universally memorized, Article 1(1) GG remains mysterious. A generally accepted definition continues to elude.

Attempts to define dignity often begin with an intuitive recognition of what it *is not*. And in post-war Germany, dignity was most obviously not Nazism. Dignity was the antithesis of a fallen regime. Thus, the Bavarian Constitution of 1946 began by recognizing the "field of rubble" left in the wake of a "State and societal order without God, without conscience, and without regard for human dignity." Article 1(1) of the Basic Law was similarly animated by a tacit "never again" impulse, although it has never been exhausted by that impulse (Isensee 2011). The Constitutional Court remarked in an early judgment that the Constitution's "basic order is a values-based order. It is the opposite of the Total State, which as exclusive ruler rejects human dignity, liberty, and equality" (2 BVerfGE 1, 12 (1952)). In this formulation, dignity supplanted fraternity in the French revolutionary triad—and it moved to first place.

Some commentators have sought further clarity on dignity's ideological ancestry, tracing it variously back to classical antiquity, to Christianity, or to Kant (many more recent writers downplay its Christian origins) (Isensee 2011, Rn 88). The Constitutional Court, by contrast, has never shown much interest in dignity's intellectual history, though it has, as we shall see, made frequent recourse to Kant's famous formula.

The Court's starting point, instead, has been dignity's position in the constitutional text, from which it has derived its primacy in the constitutional order. From a very early date, the Court has consistently and repeatedly crowned dignity as the "supreme value" in the legal and constitutional order,[4] the "highest value" (45 BVerfGE 187, 228 (1997)), a "foundational constitutive principle" (50 BVerfGE 166, 175 (1979), 87 BVerfGE 209, 228 (1992)), one whose protection constitutes "the supreme objective of all law" (33 BVerfGE 1, 10 (1972)). The Court also maintained, at a very early date, that the dignity guarantee arose from a particular vision of humanity—a specific *Menschenbild*—that began with the proposition that humans "possess an inherent, independent value in the order of creation" (2 BVerfGE 1, 22 (1952)). Although every individual possesses such value, the Court has never conceived of dignity in strongly individualist terms. As early as 1953, the justices wrote that the Basic Law's "idea of the human" (*Menschenbild*) was "not that of an isolated, sovereign individual," but rather that of an individual embedded in society and subject to societal limitations (4 BVerfGE 7, 15 (1954)). In this respect, the early Court's conception of dignity gave greater stress to the Basic Law's communitarian strands than to its liberal thrust. Later, the Court explained that the Basic Law's vision of humanity was defined by an individual's "dignity and the free development of his or her personality in self-determination and personal accountability" (41 BVerfGE 29, 50 (1975))[5]

Who Possesses Dignity?

The Court has further approached dignity in terms of who possesses it and when. The answer to the *who* question is, in two senses, *everyone.* Each individual possesses dignity, and so does humanity at large (87 BVerfGE 209, 228 (1992)). This latter proposition emerged in a 1992 case that asked whether public authorities could ban a gruesome horror film called *The Evil Dead.*[6] A specialized court held that they could, ruling that the film's degrading, gory, brutalizing images offended human dignity. The obvious objection to this was that the film offended the dignity of no particular human; it was just a movie. But the Constitutional Court, to the surprise of many observers, upheld the lower court's judgment. Crucially, the justices wrote that "[h]uman dignity . . . is not only the individual dignity of each respective person, but the dignity of humanity as a species" (87 BVerfGE 209, 228 (1992)). The Court has not elaborated this notion of species-wide dignity, and other judgments suggest that dignity is a category determined by the public morality of German society, rather than by natural norms valid at all times and everyone. But this capacious notion of dignity surely has broad implications. Dignity-based arguments against cloning and other forms of genetic design are rooted in the same idea (Isensee 2011, Rn 139).

In the same *Evil Dead* case, the Court also declared that every human possesses dignity "without regard to his or her characteristics, achievements, or social status." The justices added that dignity can be neither stripped nor forfeited. "Even through 'undignified' behavior," they wrote, "it cannot be lost" (87 BVerfGE 209, 228 (1992)). Many commentators have objected that what cannot be lost needs no protection, but the Court maintains that what the

Constitution protects is not dignity itself, but each individual's right to have one's dignity respected (87 BVerfGE 209, 228 (1992)).

When Dignity is at Stake

The Court has made equally striking statements about *when* dignity applies. Dignity, the justices have held, neither begins at birth nor ends with death. In the latter regard, the Court ruled in a landmark 1971 case that a book by the late novelist Klaus Mann, which allegedly affronted the dignity of the late actor Gustav Gründgens, could be banned (30 BVerfGE 173 (1971)). The Basic Law's rights catalog includes limitations clauses for many of its rights, but not for artistic liberty. Nevertheless, the First Senate held, the rights of artists can be limited by the dignity of their subjects, provided those subjects happen to be human beings. This was so even after those subjects were dead since the state's duty "to protect the individual against attacks on his human dignity does not end with death" (30 BVerfGE 173, 1974 (1971)).

This was a dramatic statement in its own right, but what followed was equally intriguing. The Court did two things flatly at odds with its occasional insistence that dignity is an absolute value. First, it balanced Gründgens' posthumous dignity rights against the artistic rights of Mann's posthumous publisher (30 BVerfGE 173, 195 (1971)). (The Senate split evenly on how that balance should tilt, and the tie, per the Court's rules, ran against a finding of constitutional violation; in this case, that meant that it ran against the publisher.) Second, the Court observed that the dignity of the dead—or the state's obligation to protect it—dwindles with time. "[T]he need for protection," the justices wrote, "and hence the duty to protect, vanishes to the degree that the memory of the dead fades and, in the course of time, his interest in not having his life's image falsified subsides" (30 BVerfGE 173, 196 (1971)). This is a startling notion in several respects. What stands out for our purposes is the Court's open relativization of dignity—at least when it shields the honor of the dead.

Four years later, in 1975, the Court considered the other end of the life cycle. For many decades, Section 218 of the Criminal Code had, on its face, banned and sanctioned virtually all abortions under all circumstances during all phases of pregnancy. By the mid-1960s, however, the provision was a dead letter. Illegal abortions abounded. By the early 1970s, there were clamorous calls for reform. In 1972, a sharply divided Parliament legalized abortion during the first trimester of pregnancy. Scores of MPs who opposed the law then challenged it in a constitutional complaint. They argued that the law violated the state's duty to protect unborn life and to uphold its dignity.

The key question before the Court was whether a fetus enjoys the right to life and possesses human dignity. The Court's First Senate said yes. "[D]eveloping life," a majority of justices wrote, "also takes part in the protection that Article 1(1) GG provides for human dignity. Where human life exists, it enjoys human dignity; whether the bearer of such dignity is aware of it or personally able to preserve it is not decisive" (39 BVerfGE 1, 41 (1975)). The Court went on to balance the dignity and right to life of the unborn against the personality rights (about which more anon) of the pregnant woman. As a general matter, a majority of the justices ruled that the balance tilts in favor of the unborn: abortion "annihilates" unborn life, whereas having to carry a child to term against her will is a lesser, though serious, infringement of a pregnant woman's right to the free development of her personality (39 BVerfGE 1, 41 (1975)). The upshot was that, in principle, abortion must remain illegal for the full duration of pregnancy, and that the state must criminalize unjustified abortions.

The Court revisited the abortion question in 1993 in response to post-Reunification abortion reforms. In that later case, the Second Senate modified the First Senate's earlier stance on criminalization but doubled down on the dignity of the unborn (88 BVerfGE 203 (1993)). All human life, the judges reiterated, enjoys human dignity (88 BVerfGE 203, 251–52 (1993)).

The precise content of that dignity, as noted earlier, has always been hazy. But the Court's most consistent effort to define it has involved Kant's famous subject/object distinction. The Court first invoked that distinction in a 1966 case dealing with the state's power to gather statistics about its citizens—the so-called *Micro-census* case. "It violates human dignity," the justices wrote, "to make a human being into a mere object of the State" (27 BVerfGE 1, 6 (1969)). To this arresting statement, the justices appended a pair of irrelevant citations.[7] Within the Court's jurisprudence, the idea was completely new. But it has had impressive staying power—especially in the context of criminal law, in which the Court has insisted again and again that the state must not treat "the individual perpetrator as a mere object of the fight against crime" (28 BVerfGE 386, 391 (1970)).[8]

In a famous 1977 case on life imprisonment, the Court added to such "mere object" language the mantra that "a human being must always remain an end in himself or herself" (45 BVerfGE 187, 228 (1977)). That precept presupposed an "image of the human as an intellectual-spiritual being" capable of "free self-development and self-determination." The precept applied "without limits in all areas of law" because the essence of honoring human dignity was to acknowledge the individual human as a "self-accountable personality" (45 BVerfGE 187, 228 (1977)). All of this drove the Court's conclusion that, consistent with human dignity, even the most appalling criminals must be given an opportunity to reform and allowed, accordingly, some possibility of parole.

Perhaps the Court's most famous 21st century application of the subject/object distinction, or the *Instrumentalisierungsverbot* (ban on instrumentalization), came in its 2006 judgment negating a controversial anti-terrorism law. The law allowed military officials to order hijacked plans shot down when doing so would protect civilians in buildings or on the ground (115 BVerfGE 118 (2006)). As is often true of the Court's dignity cases, there was an independent ground for decision: in the justices' view, the challenged law offended the passengers' right to life. But the Court also ruled that the law offended human dignity. It treated the passengers on the plane as "mere objects" of the state's "rescue operation" on behalf of others (115 BVerfGE 118, 153–54 (2006)).

The judgment elicited both warm praise and sharp censure. Critics objected most vigorously to the Court's unilateral dignity analysis. If the challenged law treated persons on board as mere objects of a rescue object, didn't the Court's judgment do the same to persons on the ground? Clearly, the case involved clashing claims to state protection. Faced with the situation the law envisioned, the state must either sacrifice the passengers to save others or sacrifice others to save the passengers. One way or another, it must be dignity for dignity, life for life. Some sort of balancing was inevitable. The Court avoided balancing only by ignoring the rights and dignity of most of those involved. The justices' insistence that the Constitution's dignity guarantee simply precluded balancing in this context was not really a means of avoiding the question. It was a way of answering it indirectly on the other side.

The *Aviation Security* judgment was a stirring statement of the ban on instrumentalization, and it allowed the justices to preserve the pretense that dignity is absolute and immune to balancing—an especially portentous pretense given the centrality of balancing, via the proportionality test, to German fundamental rights jurisprudence more broadly. But the posture concealed a tragic choice. Employed thus, dignity is the absolute value of the ostrich.

Dignity's Core

At other times and in different humors, the Court has taken a much harder-nosed view. In late 1970, the justices considered a constitutional challenge to a constitutional amendment—a heretical idea to most Americans, but not uncommon in jurisdictions that impose limits even on constitutional amendments (Albert 2019).[9] In the late 1960s, a German parliament ruled by a "Grand Coalition" of the two largest parties (which, in those far-off times, were large indeed) passed a series of "emergency laws," some of which were enshrined by constitutional amendment. The new laws allowed intrusive government surveillance, often without judicial approval, during emergencies. The laws' challengers claimed that it violated human dignity, and therefore Article 79(3) GG, which bars amendments that infringe human dignity.

A divided Court rejected the complaint, ruling that the challenged amendment didn't trench on dignity's core (30 BVerfGE 1 (1970)). Along the way, the Court noted that dignity violations depend on context and cannot be assessed mechanically or in the abstract. General formulas, such as the instrumentalization ban, can only give guidelines. In any case, they cannot be read rigidly or literally. "Humans," the Court wrote, "are not infrequently mere objects not only of social relations and societal development, but also of law insofar as they must submit to it without regard to their own interests. But that alone cannot result in a finding that human dignity has been violated." Instead, such a finding required underlying treatment that placed the victim's "quality as a subject fundamentally in question." There must be an "arbitrary contempt for human dignity," "derisive treatment," or an "expression of disdain for the value owed one on account of his or her being a person" (30 BVerfGE 1, 25–26 (1970)). In other words, to violate the so-called "eternity clause" of Article 79(3) GG, a constitutional amendment must erode dignity at its core. Such an approach avoided balancing only by insisting that dignity as an absolute bar on constitutional amendment applies solely within narrow limits.

"Eternal" Dignity?

There is a certain irony, almost a paradox, in the elusive quality of defining dignity. Dignity, in the Court's jurisprudence, turns out to be an absolute value whose content is fluid. Sometimes, as in the 1977 *Life Imprisonment* judgment, the Court has been explicit about this. Identifying what the dignity guarantee demands, wrote the justices, "cannot be separated from historical development. . . . Judgment about what conforms to human dignity can only rest on the basis of the present state of understanding and can make no claim to timeless validity" (45 BVerfGE 187, 228 (1977)). The dignity guarantee is itself guaranteed by an eternity clause. It will remain in force as long as the Basic Law endures. But only future generations will know what it means for them. The current generation has enough trouble defining what it means now. Sufficient unto the day is the interpretive conundrum thereof.

Dignity at Work

The Basic Law's rights catalog is organized in such a way that dignity stands out in more ways than one. First, and most obviously, it comes first. Second, the text imposes an explicit duty on "all state authority" to uphold and protect dignity. Third, a subsequent constitutional provision shields it against future constitutional amendment. Fourth, its status as legal norm is ambiguous. The dignity guarantee appears in Article 1(1) of the Basic Law. Article 1(2) declares the German people's devotion to "inviolable and inalienable human rights." And Article 1(3) decrees that the "following fundamental rights bind the legislature, the executive, and the judiciary as immediately valid law."

"The *following* fundamental rights." Does that include dignity, which precedes this clause and is not identified as a right? Is dignity a right? More concretely, can it give rise to an individual constitutional complaint? Many commentators have answered these questions in the negative. Their number includes Hermann von Mangoldt, one of the Basic Law's framers, who maintained that dignity furnished the foundation of all fundamental rights but was not a fundamental right itself (Isensee 2011, Rn 121). The Constitutional Court, by contrast, would have it both ways. The Court has made it clear that dignity is indeed the "root of all fundamental rights,"[10] but it has also insisted that dignity is an independent fundamental right and can support a constitutional complaint.[11] It has not, however, explained why. Unsurprisingly, the Court's willingness to accept dignity as an independent basis for constitutional complaints has prompted thousands of complaints, most of them quixotic, improbable, or bizarre. The deluge began early. In 1953, for instance, the Court held that, however distasteful, it does not violate one's human dignity to have to pay taxes or fees (2 BVerfGE 292, 295 (1953)).

Nearly all complaints invoking dignity alone are rejected by three-justice panels without full Senate review. This is unsurprising for two reasons. First, the success rate for *all* individual complaints is abysmal. Thousands of complaints flood the Court each year; only a few get full Senate review, and fewer still are granted. Dignity is no different. Second, and more to our purpose, complaints invoking only dignity often lack merit because, as Günter Dürig noted more than sixty years ago, a state encroachment on dignity almost surely violates some other, more specific constitutional right (Dürig 1956, 117, 122). When that is so, dignity need not do its work alone.

Dignity proper decides very few cases. An absolute value necessarily has a narrow scope. And a vague value gives little guidance in concrete cases. As a result, dignity does most of its work in connection with other constitutional provisions. Its operation is almost always mediated. Almost always, dignity does what it does as dignity plus.

Dignity Plus

In the Court's jurisprudence, dignity is mediated in three principal ways. I call these *supplemental dignity*, *hybrid dignity*, and *jurisgenerative dignity*. (These are my terms, not the Court's. I am offering a *post hoc* classification of what the Court has done in a very ad hoc way.) In the case of *supplemental dignity*, the dignity guarantee operates "in conjunction with" (*in Verbindung mit*) another constitutional guarantee. In the case of *hybrid dignity*, the Court combines the dignity guarantee with the constitutional promise of the free development of one's personality (Art. 2 GG) to create two rights of a more general character—the general "personality" right (*Persönlichkeitsrecht*) and the general liberty right (*allgemeine Freiheitsrecht*). In the case of *jurisgenerative dignity*, the Court derives new and unenumerated rights from the general rights of liberty and personality. I take these types in turn.

Supplemental Dignity

When the Parliamentary Council was drafting the Basic Law, Hermann von Mangoldt explained that dignity needed to come first in order to establish a proper relationship between dignity and all other constitutional rights (Isensee 2011, Rn 121). For von Mangoldt, as noted earlier, dignity formed the basis of all other rights but was not a right itself. Josef Isensee has written in this regard that dignity gives constitutional interpreters a "teleological compass" by which to steer (Isensee 2011, Rn 121). Similarly, although the Constitutional Court also treats dignity as an independent right, it usually adduces dignity in connection with something else.

The link between dignity and other rights is a theme the Court has sounded repeatedly. It has been said that the Basic Law's "confession [*Bekenntnis*—a term with religious valence] of human dignity" must "govern" the interpretation of every other constitutional provision. Dignity, the Court has said, is "the root of all fundamental rights" (93 BVerfGE 266, 293 (1995)), and all other rights flow from the Basic Law's dignity-based image of humanity (*Menschenbild*) (30 BVerfGE 173, 196 (1971)). Because dignity intersects other rights, the Court often employs the formula "in conjunction with"[12] when introducing dignity into its analysis. It might, for instance, state that the case before it raises the question of whether the challenged law is "compatible with Article 4(1) GG [religious exercise] in conjunction with Article 1(1) GG [dignity]."

It's not always clear what function such conjunctions serve. If dignity really is the source of all other rights, don't all other rights operate at all times "in conjunction with" dignity? If that is so, why deploy the formula in some cases but not others? Why not employ it in every case? And if it applies in every case, why employ it at all?

Perhaps linking a right to dignity is a way of signaling that right's importance. The Court seems to be providing such signals when it presents a given right—such as the right to a hearing before a Court (55 BVerfGE 1, 5–6 (1980))—as an expression of dignity. But again, if all rights are expressions of dignity, it's hard to see why the Court sometimes singles out certain rights as such expressions and not other rights at other times. And it is even harder to tell whether such signals merely provide ambience or actually inform analysis. In the case of religious liberty, the Court has suggested that its roots in dignity should give it special strength (32 BVerfGE 98, 108 (1972)).

Just how much strength is anybody's guess. But in recent landmark cases, the Court has again invoked dignity in connection with other rights to bolster controversial decisions. In a judgment dated 26 February, 2020, for instance, the Court invoked dignity as a supplement to the general personality right of Article 2 as the basis for asserting a general constitutional right to assisted dying/suicide (153 BVerfGE 182 (2020)).[13]

Sometimes the Court connects a right to dignity for purposes of separation rather than strengthening. This can be seen, for instance, in the Court's controversial asylum jurisprudence. The Court has, to be sure, connected the right of asylum to the value of dignity. But it has also stressed the limits of that connection, ruling, for instance, that persecution must reach a certain level of intensity and singularity before it triggers the right of asylum *as an expression of human dignity*. More pointedly, the Court has held that the bond between dignity and asylum is not so compact that abolishing the right of asylum would violate Article 79's eternity clause, which makes the dignity guarantee unamendable (see 94 BverfGE 49, 103 (1996)).

As we saw earlier, the Court's occasional insistence that dignity cannot be balanced against other rights is often merely rhetorical. When it comes to dignity in conjunction with other rights, even the rhetoric drops out. To conjoin a right to dignity is not to immunize that right against limitation or balancing. Quite the contrary. Rights read "in conjunction with" Article 1(1) remain subject to constitutional limitations and to proportionality balancing. Supplemental dignity doesn't always supplement. Sometimes its function is less to strengthen the conjoined right than to relativize dignity itself.

Hybrid Dignity

The Court most frequently employs the "in conjunction with" formula when enforcing the "general personality right" and the "general liberty right"—hybrid rights that fuse the enshrinement of human dignity in Article 1 of the German Basic Law with Article 2's promise that "everyone has the right to freely develop his personality, so long as he doesn't violate the rights of others or offend against the constitutional order or the moral law." In the famous 1957 *Elfes* case, the Court ruled that these two core guarantees, taken together, form a general right of liberty that shields the whole gamut of human acts and omissions from unreasonable state interference (6 BverfGE 32 (1957)). The right provides a seamless shield of protection. It covers all human behavior and all mortal indolence. In practice, it requires the state to give reasons. It entitles all rights-bearers to a proportionality analysis.

Predictably, the general liberty right has given rise to endless complaints stretching from the imperative to the pedestrian and from the sublime to the ridiculous. The general liberty right has been asserted in every context under the sun. Nearly all such claims fail. The Court has held, for instance, that the right is not infringed when the state requires motorcyclists to wear helmets (59 BverfGE 275 (1982)) or forbids equestrians to ride through public woods (80 BverfGE 137 (1989)). Some observers think such cases should never arise at all. Prominent voices have suggested that the Court has gone too far and should pare back. In an important 1989 dissent, Justice Dieter Grimm objected that fundamental rights should cover only acts and omissions that are, well, *fundamental*, and that the Court's everything-under-the-sun approach had fostered a certain "trivialization" (*Banalisierung*) of the very idea of rights (80 BverfGE 137, 168 (1989)). It was a powerful argument. But Grimm's colleagues declined the invitation to reconsider first principles. Thirty years on, the Court's approach remains unchanged.

Within that approach, the unenumerated general liberty right "complements" the liberty rights specifically named in the Constitution (54 BverfGE 148, 153 (1980)). It prevents the state from placing unjustified constraints on what one chooses to do or to avoid. Article 2(1) itself limits the free development of one's personality in terms of (1) "the rights of others," (2) "the constitutional order," and (3) "the moral law," and the Court incorporates these limits in its application of the general liberty right.[14]

The liberty right, it should be stressed, is not the same thing as the personality right, which the Court derives from the same constitutional provisions (72 BverfGE 155, 170 (1986)). The general personality right is somewhat narrower. It shields the central core of an individual's life—what the Court sometimes calls the "intimate sphere" (*Intimsphäre*)—from any state intrusion whatever. Within that sphere, the personality right is as un-balanceable and illimitable as dignity itself is supposed to be.[15] "Insofar as the general personality right is an immediate product of human dignity," the justices wrote in 1987, its "limitation [on artistic expression] is absolute, without the possibility of a weighing of interests" (75 BverfGE 369, 380 (1987)). This view has made the Court much more willing than, say, the US Supreme Court, to uphold limits on artistic or journalistic expression—whether that expression involves photographs of vacationing royalty (101 BverfGE 361 (1999)), scurrilous attacks on prominent politicians (75 BverfGE 369 (1987)), or even a *roman à clef* about a famous actor (30 BverfGE 173 (1971)) or the author's former lover (119 BverfGE 1 (2007)).

As with dignity proper, the Court has declined to define either of the hybrid rights in any definitive way. The rights are there, the Court has explained, to respond to new dangers to dignity and liberty that the framers of 1949 could never have foreseen. Accordingly, the Court has left the rights' contours open and refused to delineate exclusively the protections they comprise (79 BverfGE 256, 268 (1988)). The justices have thus left themselves considerably leeway—more than in other areas of fundamental rights, where the Court's doctrine can be quite detailed—to answer the exigencies of the times.

Jurisgenerative Dignity

Some of the times' most troublesome exigencies stem from technology. From an early date, the Court has flagged the dignitary dangers posed by mammoth data. And in a landmark 1983 judgment, the justices discovered—some say invented—a new right: the right to "personal data self-determination" (65 BverfGE 1, 41 (1983)). The case dealt with a census planned for early 1984—the "Orwell Year," as critics ominously noted. The census would ask citizens scores of questions on a range of topics, including (horrors!) their vacation plans. Popular mobilization against the law was tremendous, and the Court thrilled the populace by striking portions of the law deemed incompatible with the newly christened "right of personal data self-determination" (65 BverfGE 1 (1983)). The Court noted that the technological age raised real and unprecedented risks for human dignity and personal integrity. In that context, the general personality right entailed a right of personal data self-determination—an unwieldy phrase that fired the opening salvo in an international fight for privacy in an age of endless data. Similarly, and for similar reasons, the Court later announced and enforced a right (take a deep breath) to the "warranty of the confidentiality and integrity of information-technical systems" as a subset of the right to informational self-determination (141 BverfGE 220, 264 (2016)).

The Court presented these cumbersomely named rights as emanations and derivations of the general personality right. But none could deny that the rights were new. They thus serve as particularly illustrative examples of what I call *jurisgenerative* dignity—new and independent rights derived from dignity in its hybrid roles. Such rights form the basis of a complex and expanding jurisprudence.[16]

There are other such rights. One of the most controversial of these has been the citizen's right to democracy—not the right to vote, but the right to vote for a legislature endowed with meaningful powers (123 BverfGE 267, 341 (2009)). This right was first recognized in the Court's 2009 judgment approving, with caveats, the European Union's Treaty of Lisbon. In its *Lisbon* judgment, the Court placed explicit limits on German participation in European integration. The Court's linking of democracy and dignity was much criticized—not least because democracy itself is already shielded from amendment by Article 79(3) GG. In subsequent judgments, the Court acknowledged the criticism but refused to budge (129 BverfGE 124, 169–70 (2011)).

Another consequential right derived from dignity—this time in conjunction with Article 20 GG's guarantee that Germany will remain forever a "social state"—is the right to a "minimum subsistence level compatible with human dignity" (*menschenwürdiges Existenzminimum*).[17] The translation is unavoidably clunky, but the concept is powerful. The Court has invoked it, in recent years, to strike down core social relief programs and send the legislature back to the drawing board (cf., 125 BverfGE 175 (2010).[18]

There are many, many more. From the same hybrid combination of the dignity guarantee and the social-state provision, the Court has derived, for instance, an affirmative duty for the state to foster the social reintegration and rehabilitation of those it imprisons (35 BverfGE 202, 235–36 (1973); 36 BverfGE 174, 188 (1973)). Other rights are of such specificity that it's hard to know whether to classify them as new rights derived from the hybrid rights or simply applications of the hybrid rights to specific cases. In any case, the Court has grounded in the hybrid rights, among other things, a right to the protection of personal honor (93 BverfGE 266 (1995)); the privacy rights of medical patients (32 BverfGE 373, 378–79 (1972)); a right to the knowledge of one's parentage (79 BverfGE 256, 268 (1989)); the right to bequeath one's children a hyphenated surname (104 BverfGE 373, 387 (2002)) or retain a surname of one's own from a previous marriage (109 BVerfGE 256, 265 (2004)); protections regarding how third parties use one's name and image (101 BverfGE 361, 380 (1999)); and, of particular cultural-political salience, the right of sexual self-determination.[19]

In many cases, the Court has held that specific, enumerated rights take precedence over hybrid or progeny rights when they overlap or collide (113 BverfGE 348, 364 (2005); 125 BverfGE 260, 310 (2010)). But not always (115 BverfGE 166, 187 (2006)). In any event, the most striking features of the Court's jurisgenerative approach to dignity are its flexibility, its creativity, and its daring. In effect, the Court has combined two of the Constitution's vaguest rights provisions (one of them only ambiguously a "rights provision" at all) and derived from them a lengthy list of specific and sometimes sweeping rights unknown to the Basic Law's text. It is an astonishing edifice erected on the foundation of a constitutional super-clause that neither the Court nor anyone else has ever satisfactorily defined.

Conclusion

The jurisprudence I have briskly surveyed has elicited sharp criticisms. The bill of particulars has been ably summarized by Manfred Baldus, the author of an excellent book surveying German debates about dignity—judicial and otherwise—since 1949 (Baldus 2016, 47, 56–58).

There are two principal criticisms. The first is that the Court's dignity jurisprudence is inconsistent. The Court insists that dignity cannot be lost but never explains why, then, it requires protection. The Court maintains that dignity cannot be balanced, but in practice, it has balanced dignity again and again (such as in the *Aviation Security* and *Surveillance* cases). The Court says that dignity appertains to everyone, but hasn't explained how, if that is so, the right to vote can be anchored in dignity. The Court says that the state cannot treat individuals as objects, but elsewhere admits that the law does so all the time (Baldus 2019, 57). The second critique is that the Court's dignity jurisprudence is imprecise. The Court has never precisely defined what dignity is, and its efforts to identify its violation in the absence of such a definition seem doomed (Baldus 2019, 58).

It would be hard to exonerate the Court from these charges. But it is also hard to imagine a jurisprudence on a concept as fraught as dignity—with a position as prominent as that of dignity in the German Basic Law—that was entirely consistent and precise. Where the dignity guarantee is concerned, the only route to total consistency and absolute precision would likely be to ignore it. This is not to absolve the Court of its most glaring exuberances. But I do suggest that the inconsistency and the imprecision of the Court's dignity jurisprudence stems from the fact that, within that jurisprudence, the Court is nearly always engaging with dignity indirectly and in a mediated way. It is nearly always engaged, as I have been at pains to show, with dignity plus. And the Court's turn to dignity plus has been driven at every step by the inevitable imprecision of dignity proper.

And yet. It should be clear by now that although dignity plus ensures flexibility and responsiveness to new challenges and unforeseen threats, it also enables a vague and free-floating judicial invention of new rights. Many Germans and outside observers celebrate the rights the Court has thus far "discovered." But none can deny that dignity plus has vastly expanded the powers of the Constitutional Court. Dignity plus has always also meant Karlsruhe plus—a capacious conception of dignity has always meant an expanded role for the Constitutional Court.

As should be clear from this brief discussion, the Court's dignity jurisprudence is at once rich, stimulating, and disquieting. It forms one of the richest mines of modern constitutional law. But it doesn't form a coherent whole. The Court hasn't offered a consistent and uncontested definition of dignity, which would seem to be a precondition for its rational application. And perhaps the desire for a constitutional absolute has placed a burden on dignity that no legal norm can successfully bear. As a result, dignity does both too much and too little. The proliferation of dignity plus is a product of the shriveling of dignity proper. The consequence is that the north star of German constitutional jurisprudence beams an uncertain signal. The iconic status of Article 1(1) GG is indisputable. But its practical fuzziness now equals its oracular fame. Everyone knows what it says. Nobody knows what it means. Periodically, however, somebody tells us what it does. That somebody is a sixteen-headed tribunal whose judges wear scarlet robes, sport white bibs, and sit in judgment in a quiet, comfortable city on the eastern bank of the Rhine.

Notes

1. See: 6 BVerfGE 32, 41 (1957); 27 BVerfGE 1, 6 (1969); 30 BVerfGE 173, 193 (1971); 32 BVerfGE 98, 108 (1971); 45 BVerfGE 187, 227 (1977); 72 BVerfGE 105, 115 (1986); 109 BVerfGE 279, 311 (2004).
2. See Art. 79(3) GG.
3. See, e.g.: 109 BVerfGE 279, 313–14 (2004); 93 BVerfGE 266, 293 (1995); 80 BVerfGE 367, 373–74 (1989); 34 BVerfGE 238, 245 (1973).
4. Cf.: 5 BVerfGE 85, 204 (1956); 6 BVerfGE 32, 41 (1957); 27 BVerfGE 1, 6 (1969); 30 BVerfGE 173, 193 (1971).
5. A note on translation: The German term for "human" is *der Mensch*, and the term for "human dignity" is either *die Würde des Menschen* or *die Menschenwürde*. *Der Mensch* refers to all humans, male and female, but because it is a masculine noun, its possessive pronouns are masculine as well. I have consistently used "his or her" as the possessive pronoun for *Mensch*. "His" might be more technically exact, but it would wrongly suggest that the original is gender exclusive.
6. The German version of the film was called *Der Tanz der Teufel*, or "Dance of the Devils."
7. The citations were to the 1956 *Communist Party* judgment and the 1958 *Lüth* judgment, neither of which breathed a word about the subject/object distinction.
8. See also: 63 BVerfGE 332, 337 (1983); 64 BVerfGE 261, 272, 281–84 (1983); 72 BVerfGE 105, 115–16 (1986); 131 BVerfGE 268, 287 (2012); 133 BVerfGE 168, 200 (2013).
9. For the latest, definitive treatment of varying approaches to constitutional amendment, see Richard (2019).
10. Cf.: 93 BVerfGE 266, 293 (1995).
11. Cf.: 1 BVerfGE 332, 343, 348 (1952); 12 BVerfGE 113, 125 (1961); 15 BVerfGE 283, 286 (1963); 61 BVerfGE 126, 137 (1982); 109 BVerfGE 133, 149 (2003); 117 BVerfGE 71, 89 (2006).
12. For examples, see: 6 BVerfGE 389, 433 (1957); 35 BVerfGE 202, 236 (1973); 45 BVerfGE 187, 228, 239 (1977); 46 BVerfGE 160, 164 (1977); 65 BVerfGE 1, 41 (1983); 79 BVerfGE 256, 268 (1988); 97 BVerfGE 228, 268 (1997); 98 BVerfGE 218, 257 (1998); 101 BVerfGE 361, 384–85 (1999); 104 BVerfGE 373, 387 (2002); 105 BVerfGE 313, 333 (2002); 109 BVerfGE 256, 265–66 (2004); 109 BVerfGE

279, 311, 315, 318 (date); 113 BVerfGE 88, 108–9 (2005); 113 BVerfGE 348, 364 (2005); 115 BVerfGE 166 (2006); 117 BVerfGE 202, 225 (2007); 120 BVerfGE 378, 397 (2008); 121 BVerfGE 69, 89 (2008); 123 BVerfGE 90, 101 (2009); 123 BVerfGE 267, 341 (2009); 125 BVerfGE 175, 221 (2010); 125 BVerfGE 260, 310 (2010); 133 BVerfGE 277, 320 (2013); 141 BVerfGE 220, 264 (2016).

13 See also Collings (2020).

14 The role of the "moral law" clause has steadily declined, however, until by now its significance is asymptotically small.

15 Cf.: 34 BVerfGE 238, 245 (1973).

16 See, e.g.: 115 BVerfGE 166, 188 (2006); 120 BVerfGE 378, 397 (2008); 124 BVerfGE 43, 69–70 (2009); 128 BVerfGE 1, 42 (2010); 133 BVerfGE 277, 317–20 (2013).

17 See: 40 BVerfGE 121, 133 (1975); 45 BVerfGE 187, 228 (1977); 82 BVerfGE 60, 85 (1990); 113 BVerfGE 88, 108–9 (2005); 125 BVerfGE 175, 222 (2010); 132 BVerfGE 134, 159 (2012); 137 BVerfGE 34 (2014).

18 Cf., 125 BVerfGE 175 (2010).

19 See: 49 BVerfGE 286, 298 (1978); 60 BVerfGE 123 (1982); 120 BVerfGE 224, 238–39 (2008).

References

Albert, Richard. 2019. *Constitutional Amendments: Making, Breaking, and Changing Constitutions.* Oxford: Oxford University Press.

Baldus, Manfred. 2016. *Kämpfe um die Menschenwürde: Die Debatten seit 1949* [Battles over Human Dignity: The Debates since 1949]. Berlin: Suhrkamp Verlag.

Baldus, Manfred. 2019. "Erst antitotalitäre Grundnorm, nun rätselhafte Supernorm. Artikel 1 Absatz 1 GG [First an Antitotalitarian Basic Norm, Now a Mysterious Super Norm: Article 1, Paragraph 1 of the Basic Law]." In *70 Jahre Grundgesetz. In welcher Verfassung ist die Bundesrepublik?* [70 Years of the Basic Law: How is the Constitution of the Federal Republic?], edited by Hans Michael Heinig and Frank Schorkopf, 47–65. Göttingen: Vadenhoek & Ruprecht.

Cleven, Thoralf. 2019. "146 Artikel, neu entdeckt [Article 146 Newly Discovered]." *Dresdner Neueste Nachrichten*, May 16, 2019. www.nw.de/nachrichten/thema/22463034_70-Jahre-Grundgesetz-146-Artikel-neu-entdeckt.html.

Collings, Justin. (2020). "The German Constitutional Court and the Right to End Life." In *Talk About: Law and Religion. The International Center for Law and Religion Studies Blog*, May 26, 2020. https://talkabout.iclrs.org/2020/05/26/the-german-constitutional-court-and-the-right-to-end-life/.

Dürig, Günter. 1956. "Der Grundrechtssatz von der Menschenwürde: Entwurf eines praktikablen Wertsystems der Grundrechte aus Art. 1 Abs I in Verbindung mit Art. 19 Abs. II des Grundgesetzes [The Fundamental Rights Principle of Human Dignity: A Proposal for a Practicable Value System of Fundamental Rights based on Article 1(1) in Connection with Article 19(2) of the Basic Law]." *Archiv des öffentlichen Rechts* 81 (2): 117–57.

Isensee, Josef. 2011. "Die Würde des Menschen [Human Dignity]." In *Handbuch der Grundrechte in Deutschland und Europa* [Handbook of Fundamental Rights in Germany and Europe]. *Vol. 4: Grundrechte in Deutschland—Einzelgrundrechte I* [Fundamental Rights in Germany—Individual Fundamental Rights I], edited by Detlef Merten and Hans-Jürgen Papier, 3–137. Heidelberg: C.F. Müller.

Kermani, Navid. 2014. "Es gilt das gesprochene Wort [The Spoken Word Counts]." Speech Presented at the Feierstunde 65 Jahre Grundgesetz [Memorial Celebration of the 65th Anniversary of the Basic Law]. www.bundestag.de/dokumente/textarchiv/2014/280688-280688.

Stone Sweet, Alec, and Jud Mathews. 2008. "Proportionality Balancing and Global Constitutionalism." *Columbia Journal of Transnational Law* 47 (1): 72–164.

Case Law

The Federal Constitutional Court of Germany

1 BverfGE 332 (1952).
2 BverfGE 1 (1952).
2 BverfGE 292 (1953).
4 BverfGE 7 (1954).
5 BverfGE 85 (1956).
6 BverfGE 32 (1957).
6 BverfGE 389 (1957).
12 BverfGE 113 (1961).
15 BverfGE 283 (1963).
27 BverfGE 1 (1969).
28 BverfGE 386 (1970).
30 BverfGE 173 (1971).
32 BverfGE 98 (1972).
32 BverfGE 373 (1972).
33 BverfGE 1 (1972).
34 BverfGE 238 (1973).
35 BverfGE 202 (1973).
36 BverfGE 174 (1973).
39 BverfGE 1 (1975).
40 BverfGE 121 (1975).
41 BverfGE 29 (1975).
45 BverfGE 187 (1977).
46 BverfGE 160 (1977).
49 BverfGE 286 (1978).
50 BverfGE 166 (1979).
54 BverfGE 148 (1980).
55 BverfGE 1 (1980).
59 BverfGE 275 (1982).
60 BverfGE 123 (1982).
61 BverfGE 126 (1982).
63 BverfGE 332 (1983).
64 BverfGE 261 (1983).
65 BverfGE 1 (1983).
72 BverfGE 105 (1986).
72 BverfGE 155 (1986).
75 BverfGE 369 (1987).
79 BverfGE 256 (1988).
80 BverfGE 137 (1989).
80 BverfGE 367 (1989).
82 BverfGE 60 (1990).
87 BverfGE 209 (1992).
88 BverfGE 203 (1993).
93 BverfGE 266 (1995).
94 BverfGE 49 (1996).
97 BverfGE 228 (1997).
98 BverfGE 218 (1998).
101 BverfGE 361 (1999).
104 BverfGE 373 (2002).
105 BverfGE 313 (2002).
109 BverfGE 133 (2003).
109 BverfGE 256 (2004).
109 BverfGE 279 (2004).

113 BverfGE 88 (2005).
113 BverfGE 348 (2005).
113 BverfGE 348 (2005).
115 BverfGE 118 (2006).
115 BverfGE 166 (2006).
117 BverfGE 71 (2006).
117 BverfGE 202 (2007).
119 BverfGE 1 (2007).
120 BverfGE 224 (2008).
120 BverfGE 378 (2008).
121 BverfGE 69 (2008).
123 BverfGE 90 (2009).
123 BverfGE 267 (2009).
124 BverfGE 43 (2009).
125 BverfGE 175 (2010).
125 BverfGE 260 (2010).
128 BverfGE 1 (2010).
129 BverfGE 124 (2011).
131 BverfGE 268 (2012).
132 BverfGE 134 (2012).
133 BverfGE 168 (2013).
133 BverfGE 277 (2013).
137 BverfGE 34 (2014).
141 BverfGE 220 (2016).
153 BverfGE 182 (2020).

5 Dignity, Sexuality, and Moral Order in Legal and Judicial Debate

Zachary R. Calo

Introduction: From Culture Wars to Dignity Wars

The modern history of human dignity begins with the Universal Declaration of Human Rights. While the long genealogy of human dignity runs through Classical, Catholic, and Enlightenment sources, it is the Universal Declaration that names dignity as a central moral category within political and legal discourse. It is with the Universal Declaration that the anthropology of dignity is offered as the foundational warrant for the post-war human rights movement. Yet the way in which dignity is used within human rights discourse has shifted markedly since the 1948 promulgation of the Universal Declaration, which invokes dignity as a general theoretical justification for human rights and a concept around which moral consensus might be forged. Unlike the Universal Declaration, in which dignity provides only a minimalist ground for consensus, dignity is now more commonly used to affirm specific and often highly contested rights claims (McCrudden 2008, 670). Robin Lovin (2019), for instance, observes that "human dignity has become a central idea in contemporary thinking both about *what* rights persons have and *why* they are entitled to those rights" (473). As such, dignity no longer operates as a background assumption for grounding human rights in general, but as a basis for decision-making across a range of controversial legal and constitutional questions. What are often framed as culture wars might more properly be seen as dignity wars, for what is at stake is the contested meaning of human personhood and the requirements of dignity.

Although widely invoked, dignity remains poorly understood and undertheorized. The resulting limitations become apparent when dignity is used as the basis for legal decision-making. Christopher McCrudden (2008) summarizes the problem by observing that human dignity "does not provide a universalistic, principled, basis for judicial decision-making in the human rights context, in the sense that there is no common understanding of what dignity requires" (655). In other words, the proposition that "all human beings are born free and equal in dignity" (Article 1 of the Universal Declaration of Human Rights) provides little guidance as to what legal rights this dignity in turn demands. Not only is there a lack of consensus about the meaning of

DOI: 10.4324/9781003307853-6

human dignity, but the law has proven a poor context for establishing such meaning. When dignity is used in legal argument, it is typically asserted as if its authority and implications are self-evidently justified. Dignity operates as a weapon to bolster disputed political positions and its use reveals more about culture than jurisprudence.

From this perspective, dignity operates as a source of division rather than consensus. Riva Siegel (2012) correctly observes that "claims of dignity have become part of a contest over social ordering that is of transnational dimensions" (377). Rather than offering resources to resolve issues of cultural contestation, dignity more often deepens them. This is particularly apparent in the way that dignity has been used to support irreconcilable legal positions. Along these lines, one court spoke of the "conflict of dignities" revealed in opposing legal positions that both appealed to dignity (*Brockie v. Brillinger (No. 2)*). Under such conditions, can dignity serve a constructive jurisprudential purpose? Have the meanings of dignity become so disparate and incompatible that dignitary claims are unhelpful and even counterproductive? Has dignity simply become a means to provide a patina of moral depth and legitimacy to legal positions? Is it prudent, absent a greater degree of shared cultural understanding, to utilize dignity as a resource to develop constitutional morality?

To explore such questions, this chapter considers two legal debates in which dignity has played a central role: LGBT rights and bans on Muslim head coverings. These case studies reveal the inconsistent and sometimes confused ways in which dignity is used. They also reveal the two broad understandings of dignity operating within legal discourse, what are termed the liberationist and teleological accounts.[1] The law does not create these dignities but rather illuminates their grounding in divergent accounts of human nature.

There are reasons to be troubled by the inconsistent and often imprecise ways in which dignity is casually invoked, but it should not be dismissed as a meaningless jurisprudential concept.[2] There might be little consensus on what dignity means and requires, but dignity is still performing constructive work within legal and constitutional debate. In fact, it is precisely the contested nature of dignity that reveals the ways in which the concept operates as a vocabulary for expressing complex anthropological worldviews. In ways that the interlocutors do not even necessarily intend, competing uses of dignity represent divergent accounts of moral order struggling for primacy within the law. In particular, this chapter proposes that dignity can serve as a tool to identify fundamental cultural divides over the nature and meaning of freedom within late modern culture. Dignity has become the language through which competing normative claims are made about what it means to be authentically free and authentically human. Dignity as now employed refers not to a state of being, that is an account of fixed qualities that characterize human nature, but to a process of becoming fully human. To have dignity is to live with and toward dignity. It requires the capacity to realize and express that dignity in freedom. It is the work of law to affirm this freedom and facilitate its realization. Through the legal discourse on dignity, competing visions of the modern self are revealed, negotiated, and refashioned.

Dignity and Sexual Orientation

No debate has more directly implicated dignitarian concerns than that involving the legal rights of LGBT persons, especially how these rights relate to other claims such as religious freedom. The lines of debate are often expressly framed around dignity. Those who oppose the extension of marriage rights to same-sex couples, for instance, invoke dignity to defend the normativity of heterosexual marriage. Dignity in this context often carries theological overtones.[3] One can see this in the Manhattan Declaration, a 2009 statement of Christian leaders and scholars supporting traditional sexual norms.[4] The Declaration speaks of "the dignity of marriage as a union of husband and wife" and the "equal dignity of every human being as a creature fashioned in the very image of God." Dignity as used in the Manhattan Declaration undergirds an anthropology in which "the creation of man and woman, and their one-flesh union as husband and wife, is the crowning achievement of God's creation." Dignity represents a way of ordering and ultimately limiting freedom in accordance with divine purpose and human nature. It is by limiting sexual freedom that human dignity is respected.[5]

Another such line of argument advanced by Sherif Gergis, Ryan Anderson, and Robert George (2011) offers a natural law defense of heterosexual marriage that does not facially depend on religious assumptions. In their framing, the normativity of heterosexual marriage can be "discerned from our common human reason, whatever our religious background" (247). According to this position, what is proper to the human person in sexual conduct reflects the outworking of dignity. Dignity equates with freely coordinating human actions with the ends of human nature that reason discloses. As George states elsewhere, defining marriage to accommodate homosexual unions licenses a form of sexual conduct "traditionally regarded in the West and many other places as beneath the dignity of human beings as free and rational creatures" (Lopez 2011). To operate outside the boundaries of nature and reason is to impair the dignity proper to human beings.

From this starting point, the authors reject the idea that dignity provides a coherent ground for recognizing homosexual unions. In their book *What is Marriage? Man and Woman: A Defense* Gergis, Anderson, and George (2012) critique the concept of "dignitary harm." Dignitary harm is typically understood as a diminishment in status that arises from unequal legal treatment. However, against the claim that "people are stigmatized when their *marriages* are not recognized while others are," the authors argue that insofar as homosexual marriage is not properly speaking a marriage, there can logically be no dignitary harm in denying legal recognition. Dignity serves a dual purpose in this position: it supports an account of human nature consonant only with heterosexual marriage and it denies the rationality of appealing to dignity in support of the legal recognition of homosexual marriages.[6]

While this account of dignity is used to blunt the expansion of LGBT rights, judicial decisions across a range of jurisdictions have used dignity to advance the contrary position. Courts do so in several ways. Dignity is often invoked to describe a quality of human personhood that is damaged by the failure to recognize marriage equality.[7] This account of dignity is never unpacked, nor is its relation to sexual identity established.[8] Dignity is simply asserted to be a characteristic feature of human nature that demands certain legal conclusions. The focus is not on what dignity is so much as what dignity requires. For instance, the Constitutional Court of South Africa found that a law criminalizing same-sex activities between men to be an "invasion of their dignity." While acknowledging that "[d]ignity is a difficult concept to capture in precise terms," the Court still concluded that "it is clear that the constitutional protection of dignity requires us to acknowledge the value and worth of all individuals as members of our society." Laws that treat persons unequally on the basis of sexual orientation damage the ideal of "moral citizenship" (National Coalition for Gay and Lesbian Equality and Another v Minister of Justice and Others, paras. 28, 107).

The concept of dignitary harm plays a particularly important role in these decisions. At work is the idea that the capacity to have dignity is elevated or diminished based on whether the law extends recognition to same-sex persons. The Supreme Court of Canada, in the 1998 case *Vriend v. Alberta*, speaks of "potential harm to the dignity and perceived worth of gay and lesbian individuals" when there is unequal treatment based on sexual orientation. Along similar lines, the Ontario Court of Appeal held in *Halpern v. Canada* that a definition of marriage that does not encompass same-sex relationships "offends the dignity of persons" (para. 48), while the Ontario Superior Court in *Brockie v. Brillinger (No. 2)* concluded that discrimination on the grounds of sexual orientation "has the effect of demeaning the . . . personal dignity of homosexuals" (para. 48) The Canadian Supreme Court in *Law Society of British Columbia v. Trinity Western University* likewise asserted that LGBT students at a Christian law school could "suffer harm to their dignity" by having to agree to engage only in sexual conduct within a heterosexual marriage. In these and other such cases, dignity undergirds a jurisprudence of sexual equality. Equal dignity requires equal treatment at law without regard to sexual orientation.

Courts also invoke dignity in connection with the values of freedom and autonomy. This usage has particular importance in connection with the capacity of persons to become fully human through the outworking of sexual identity. To be dignified is to have the freedom, facilitated by law, to pursue the self-actualization of one's sexuality. Mexico's Supreme Court of Justice of the Nation, for instance, linked dignity with "the free development of personality" and the "right of every person to choose, in a free and autonomous manner" how to exercise "their free sexual option." Dignity is the right of a person to "live her life" in a manner that gives expression to sexuality (*Acción de inconstitucionalidad 2/2010*).[9] Similarly, the United States Supreme Court proposed in *Lawrence v. Texas*, a 2003 decision that held unconstitutional state laws banning consensual same-sex activity, that the right to enter homosexual relationships is expressive of "dignity as free persons." Citing language from a prior decision, the Supreme Court identified "personal dignity" as the "liberty . . . to define one's own concept of existence, of meaning, of the universe, and of the mystery of human life" (*Planned Parenthood of Se. Pa. v. Casey*). To have dignity, in other words, is to be able to explore and express one's sexuality. It is to become the person one wishes to be. This dignity is not narrowly associated with sexuality and yet sexual identity is presented as a uniquely significant aspect of human experience that demands protection. As the Constitutional Court of South Africa observed, "[t]he way in which we give expression to our sexuality is at the core" of the "sphere of private intimacy and autonomy" in which relationships are lived out (*National Coalition for Gay and Lesbian Equality v. Minister of Justice*, para. 32). This position implies that limits on sexual freedom are, as such, demeaning to human dignity. Moreover, it is the role of the law to promote dignity by facilitating the pursuit of sexual authenticity. The law creates space within which persons might become more fully themselves—that is, more fully dignified—through exercising sexual freedom. As the Court in *Brockie* asserted, laws that discriminate on the basis of sexual orientation limit the ability "to achieve . . . dignity." This language of "achieve" is especially revealing in that it speaks to an understanding of dignity, not as a fixed characteristic of human nature, but as a consequence of self-actualization. Dignity is not bestowed but made. It is a process constantly being worked out.

Dignity and Religious Dress

Dignity has also played an important role in the debate over laws that ban Muslim women from wearing headscarves and face coverings. The European Court of Human Rights has ruled on a number of cases involving such bans. Perhaps its most significant decision in this area was the 2014 Grand Camber decision in the case of *S.A.S. v. France*, which involved a French ban on wearing face coverings in public (the so-called burqa ban). As in the cases that preceded it, the Court upheld the permissibility of the ban (Calo 2010). Yet while *S.A.S.* shared many similarities with these previous decisions, it was notable for the central role of dignity in shaping the underlying legal debate.

The case of *S.A.S. v. France* offers another example of the Janus-faced character of dignity, in which debate is shaped around incompatible dignitarian appeals. On one hand, dignity was widely used by those who defended the law. A parliamentary commission tasked with issuing a report on the wearing of the full veil described the practice as "a form of subservience" that "by its very existence negated . . . the equal dignity of human beings" (*S.A.S. v. France*, para. 17). A similar use of dignity is found in a Resolution adopted unanimously by the French National Assembly in May, 2010, asserting that radical practices such as wearing the full-face veil were undermining dignity and equality between men and women.[10] An "explanatory memorandum" that accompanied the draft law prohibiting concealment of the face in public places likewise proposed that French values of liberty, equality, and fraternity "underpin the principle of respect for the dignity of individuals and for equality between men and women." The memorandum noted that it was permissible to prescribe practices such as concealment of the face when they "offended against the dignity of the person" and "cannot be regarded as inseparable from the exercise of a fundamental freedom" (para 76). Respect for the principle of dignity is connected, according to this line of reasoning, with using the force of law to free women from the veil in order to realize gender equality. As the government argued, women who wore the veil had been "effaced" from the public space. Even if this "effacement" was done freely out of religious conviction, "it was necessarily dehumanizing and could hardly be regarded as consistent with human dignity" (*S.A.S. v. France*, para. 82). Wearing a face covering diminishes one's dignity and personhood, and it is the obligation of the state to deny women the freedom to do so. In describing veiled women as effaced, the government implies that it is necessary for the law to impose dignity upon those deprived of it. The niqabi must be made free, in spite of herself.

These various documents invoke dignity without ever explaining its meaning. By one measure, dignity seems to equate with equality, not only before the law but in the deeper sense of social ontology. That is, dignity represents the normative terms on which persons relate to each other in society. Dignity also expresses an account of individual freedom. To have dignity is to be free, and to be made free if necessary. This dignitary freedom is both negative and positive. It is negative in identifying that from which women must be freed and positive in the sense of making women into free citizens of a certain sort. Within this understanding, the ban did not restrict freedom but rather used state power to liberate women from the grip of oppressive religion (Calo 2018). Dignity frees from what limits human potentiality.

This account of dignity contrasts with the one advanced by the applicant, a Sunni Muslim woman born in Pakistan, who claimed "to have sustained a serious interference with the exercise" of her right to religious freedom (*S.A.S. v. France*, para. 25). As the Court summarized her position, the applicant "found it ironic that an abstract idea of gender equality could run counter to the profoundly personal choice of women who decided to wear veils." Moreover, claiming that the ban promoted "respect for human dignity" was based on a "paternalistic" and "chauvinistic logic" that assumes women who wear the full veil lack agency and autonomy (para. 77). In her framing of the issue, dignity represents the capacity to make free choices concerning the manifestation of religious belief. She was not "effaced" but expressing her own experience of freedom.

The claim advanced by the applicant is notable in that it appeals to freedom, autonomy, and self-determination to defend the wearing of the veil. This is a subversive line of argument that reclaims and reappropriates the language of freedom. In the applicant's framing, the government is wrong to equate wearing the veil with a lack of freedom. The choice to cover oneself is freedom-enhancing rather than freedom-diminishing. The idea that authentic freedom can be achieved through self-limitation echoes the conservative position in the sexuality debate. This account of freedom is not understood in terms of removing strictures but entering truth. Freedom has an end and it is by orienting oneself thusly that authentic selfhood is experienced and achieved. What the government sees as slavery becomes the ultimate expression of true freedom.

The parties in this dispute appeal to dignity in order to advance diverse and ultimately incompatible accounts of freedom rooted, in turn, in incompatible anthropologies. For the French government, dignity is advanced by promoting a freedom premised on equality and liberation from restraint. This dignitary equality is flat. It grants primacy to universal liberal values over particularistic loyalties.[11] The individual is located within a social context that presumes an understanding of the modern self—what it means to be free, what it means to be a woman, and what it means to be religious. For the applicant, by contrast, dignity is the equal right under law to be a Muslim, to be a woman, to be and become a self on terms she defines. It is not, at least for the applicant, a mere subjective freedom in which the individual alone is the arbiter of the good. Quite the opposite. Dignity for her is found in the capacity to limit one's freedom as an act of submission to God.

For all the controversy this case occasioned, the rationale the Court provided for accepting the law's permissibility under Article 9 of the European Convention on Human Rights is rather banal. The majority opinion accepted the ban as being justified based on the principle of "living together" (*S.A.S. v. France*, para. 142). While acknowledging that the law "has to a certain extent restricted the reach of pluralism, since the ban prevents certain women from expressing their personality and their beliefs," the Court nevertheless concluded that the state has the authority to "protect a principle of interaction between individuals" (para. 153). In the end, however, the judgment in *S.A.S.* is less significant as a statement of law than of how dignitarian tensions are playing out through law. Regardless of the legal status of headscarf bans, these underlying tensions remain unresolved. In the end, this debate is less about Islam and Muslim women than would at first appear. The veil reveals and accentuates a crisis already long present within liberal society over the contested meaning of freedom and authenticity. Islam thus becomes what Olivier Roy (2007) terms "the mirror in which society now sees itself" (16).

Dignity and Contested Modern Selves

Viewed against the backdrop of these various cases, dignity is not the hopelessly vague concept some have alleged (Pinker 2008). While there is no common understanding of what human dignity means, nor how it should inform law, these competing dignities express deep moral claims about the human person. Precisely because of its contested nature, dignitarian language clarifies rather than obfuscates what is fundamentally at stake. In the end, these legal debates are not primarily about sexual orientation, gender, or religion. These legal debates occur downstream from a more elemental anthropological debate.

Dignity provides a way to narrate two competing anthropologies. One is liberationist. The liberationist account emphasizes dignity as a project of self-creation, that is the self-freed from the boundaries of moral tradition in order to pursue authenticity within the open space of possibility. The seeds of this liberationist anthropology have long been pregnant in the modern project, but cultural and social dynamics have now pushed it more nakedly to the fore. Liberationist dignity imposes no end of freedom other than the pursuit and realization of authenticity.[12] The task of the liberated self is to be true to itself.

The other anthropology is teleological. This account defines freedom in terms of an orientation toward defined and knowable human goods. To be dignified is to order one's life in accordance with norms that exist outside the subjective aspirations of the self. As such, freedom is not liberation to pursue self-fulfillment. It is an occasion to achieve authentic selfhood by submitting to moral authority, an authority that is often rooted in ongoing forms of collective moral reasoning. Authority in this respect is not a limit on freedom, properly understood, but a means of directing persons toward the end of dignity and human flouring.

This divide over the nature and experience of freedom structures debate about both LGBT rights and religious dress. Dignity gives expression, in and through law, to anthropological assumptions that precede law. It is not surprising that sexuality and religion have been at the forefront of this process, for legal debate in these areas revolves around contested understandings of selfhood and dignity in a uniquely powerful way.

The trend has been for legal decisions to privilege the liberationist account of dignity. This anthropology is particularly dominant in cases involving sexuality. Time and again, courts frame sexual identity not only as a preference but as something inseparable from authentic selfhood. To have dignity is to have the freedom to fully express one's sexuality. For instance, the State Supreme Court of Washington, in its 2017 decision in *State of Washington v. Arlene's Flowers*, rejected the idea that there exists a "distinction between status and conduct." In this case, a party that refused to provide wedding services to a same-sex couple was held to have engaged in discrimination on the basis of sexual orientation. The connection between status and conduct is such that failing to provide the services (conduct) is equated with rejecting the sexuality of the customer (status). Implied in this position is the idea that self-identity is so deeply intertwined with expressions of sexuality that it is improper and indeed impossible to distinguish the two. This perspective taps into the ways in which notions of sexual selfhood inform the late modern experience of self, the experience of freedom, and the pursuit of authenticity. To be an authentic self is to be authentic to one's sexuality. To impede the sexual self is to impede the capacity to be truly and fully human. It is to undermine what it means to live with dignity.

Courts notably frame religion differently. While sexuality is presented as an essential aspect of identity, religion is framed as chosen and incidental. It is a private and largely interiorized aspect of human experience and identity. For instance, in the lower Court decision in *Ashers Baking Company*, the shop owners argued that making a cake in support of gay marriage did not entail a mere commercial exchange but a "betrayal of faith" (*Lee v. Ashers Baking Company*, para. 37). However, the Court rejected this claim on the grounds that "[t]he fact that a baker provides a cake for a particular team or portrays witches on a Halloween cake does not indicate any support for either" (para. 67). One can segregate religious commitments from commercial exchange because it is an autonomous sphere of activity that has no bearing on one's religious commitments. The decision in *Brockie* was even more direct, asserting that "freedom of religion does not extend to the practice of religious beliefs in the public marketplace" because it is "peripheral" to commercial activities (*Brockie v. Brillinger (No. 2)*, paras. 16, 56). Defining religion on these terms is quite different from defining sexual identity as something whose expression is essential to living with dignity. Status and conduct, tethered in matters of sexuality, are severed when it comes to religion.

The problem with religion is that operates as a barrier to authentic selfhood by making claims that limit authentic freedom. It is a carrier of moral tradition, associated with the teleological account of dignity, that imposes norms about what the self should be and become. When confronted with a strong religion conviction that advances a determined account of human flourishing, whether arising in connection with sexuality or religious dress, the force of law often pushes back. The law guards the free self. The decision in *S.A.S.*, for instance, can be interpreted as upholding the authority of law to free women from the weight of illiberal and oppressive religion. In the end, few cultural resources remain to resist the expansion of a liberationist dignity against teleological conceptions, especially those connected with religion. Teleological dignity is too contrary to the modern impulse, expressed and reinforced in law, to expand space for self-mastery and self-fulfillment. What Michael Ignatieff (2003) said of human rights might properly be said of dignity. It has become "the language through which individuals have created a defense of their autonomy against the oppression of religion" (54).

Conclusion: The Future of Dignity

In this fragmented environment, can dignity help achieve greater moral agreement on disputed issues of public significance? Does dignity serve a constructive role in constitutional and legal discourse? This chapter has perhaps offered little reason for optimism. Indeed, the very fact that dignitarian disputes are being negotiated in courts reveals the extent to which debate has broken down and consensus become ever more elusive (Klein 2010). Dignity has become a contested legal language because it lacks common meaning at the level of culture.

While courts are advancing an account of dignity that pushes the needle more in the liberationist direction, this does little to resolve the underlying roots of the tension. Dignity remains a conversation stopper, a blunt instrument that ends debate rather than a cultural salve that extends it. Perhaps, in time, a dominant meaning of dignity will be "forged," to borrow the term coined by Riva Siegel (2012, 379), from out of these cross-border legal debates? Perhaps dignity will no longer be contested, at least in its application to certain contested questions. Yet this possibility should not obscure the fact that current usages of dignity in law accentuate rather than heal division. To the extent dignity forges any consensus it is through force rather than suasion.

Can a different, older use of dignity find currency? Is it possible to recover what Christopher McCrudden (2008) terms a "minimum core of human dignity," which might ground shared norms in the fashion of the Universal Declaration of Human Rights? McCrudden (2008) is fairly sanguine that there is such a minimum core and he defines it by reference to three principles: first, the ontological claim that every human being has intrinsic worth; second, the relational claim that this worth should be recognized by others; third, the political claim that the state exists for the individual and not the individual for the state (679).

This account of dignity has the benefit of modesty and restraint. It offers a theory of the human person in which to ground organizing political commitments, without tethering dignity to specific conclusions of law. Conclusions must still of course be rendered, but a minimalist dignity inaugurates the process rather than ends it. It provokes bottom-up conversations rather than imposing top-down determinations. This minimum core of dignity thus has the advantage of pulling dignity back from the culture wars and creating distance between dignity and specific legal claims. At the same time, it is doubtful such a dignity offers a realistic pathway to overcoming the problematic use of dignity in contemporary law. Dignity is simply too enmeshed in contentious debate to be so easily extracted, and the dignity wars too advanced to allow for easy retreat.

If a more determined account of dignity remains a feature of contemporary legal debate, perhaps it is possible to change how the term is used. Instead of framing dignity as an anthropological proposition about human nature and flourishing, perhaps dignity might instead be used to seek recognition and to invest debate with moral depth. This dignity severs, or at least circumscribes, the immediate link between dignity and rights. It is an appeal to the common experience of being human. It is a demand to be heard. Dignity of this sort operates as an interruptive vocabulary that can undermine entrenched expectations and beliefs and thereby create space for being addressed by others.

This use of dignity might not go far in resolving entrenched legal debates but offers a way for it to unfold on different, and perhaps more humane terms. The purpose of this dignity is not to enshrine a triumphant account of the rights-bearing person but to create conditions in which persons can speak and be heard across difference. This dignity is a conversation starter instead of a conversation stopper. It is a provisional rather than absolute discourse that invites consideration of the diverse ways people understand and actualize their humanity. By resisting the idea of dignity as a final ontological declaration and viewing it rather as an indeterminate appeal for respect, new possibilities emerge for realizing shared meaning across seemingly intractable divisions.

One reason for the confused nature of dignity is that the word has become so omnipresent as to be increasingly void of content. Dignity is used to bolster an ever more comprehensive account of rights, reducing debate to a competition between dignities. The result is an unsatisfying and ultimately muddled legal discourse that does little to illuminate dignity itself. Pulling dignity back from the thicket of legal decision-making need not make dignity any less important to the adjudication of legal and constitutional claims but might resituate its place and role therein. This is liberal dignity of a different sort.

Notes

1 As Meir Dan-Cohen (2011) remarks, “there appear to be a number of concepts of dignity in circulation, too dissimilar even to be thought of as different conceptions of one concept” (9).

2 In an oft-referenced article, Steven Pinker (2008) describes human dignity as a “squishy, subjective notion, hardly up to the heavyweight moral demands assigned to it.”

3 While it is the case that dignity as used in contemporary legal debate about matters of sexual ethics has traditionalist overtones, it would be wrong to frame dignity as an exclusively conservative theological category. As Lisa Sowell Cahill (1989) observes in the context of Catholic social thought, dignity “is used by traditionalists and revisionists to advance quite different understandings of sexuality” (120).

4 The 2009 Manhattan Declaration is available at www.manhattandeclaration.org.

5 A similar position is set forth in the *Catechism of the Catholic Church*. In addressing matters of human sexuality, the Catechism speaks of “self-mastery” as “training in human freedom.” “Man’s dignity,” the Catechism continues, “requires him to act out of conscious and free choice . . . and not by blind impulses in himself.” One “gains . . . dignity” by overcoming “the passions” (§2339). Human sexuality is “naturally ordered” to certain goods and it is an offense to dignity to act contrary (§2535).

6 This understanding of dignity, whether rooted in appeals to religious ethics or natural law, has little place in contemporary legal debate. To the extent that a version of this dignity appears, it is more commonly found in connection with defending religious exemptions. The right to religious liberty is connected to human dignity in a manner that warrants protections for conscience with respect to matters of sexuality. As the United States Conference of Catholic Bishops (N.d.) proposed, in quoting a 1991 encyclical letter of Pope John Paul II, religious liberty is “the right

to live in the truth of one's faith and in conformity with one's transcendent dignity as a person." Dignity as it relates to matters of sexual ethics appears indirectly in the form of dignitary claims to protect the freedom of persons and institutions to refuse endorsing same-sex relations.

7 In *Naz Foundation v. The Government of NCT of Delhi and Others*, the Delhi High Court points out: "Indian constitutional law does not permit the statutory criminal law to be held captive by the popular misconceptions of who the LGBTs are . . . [I]t is the recognition of equality which will foster the dignity of every individual."

8 This point was vigorously made by the dissent in the Trinity Western decision, in which it was noted that "*Charter* 'values', as stated by the majority, are amorphous and, just as importantly, undefined. Lacking the doctrinal structure which courts have carefully crafted over the past 35 years to give substantive meaning to *Charter* rights (including the right to equality) and to guide their application, *Charter* values like 'equality', 'justice', and 'dignity' become mere rhetorical devices by which courts can give priority to particular moral judgments, under the guise of undefined 'values,' over other values and over *Charter* rights themselves" (*Law Society of British Columbia v. Trinity Western University*).

9 See generally, Madrazo and Vela (2011).

10 In its opinion, the European Court of Human Rights also referenced Resolution 1743 (2010) and Recommendation 1927 (2010) of the Parliamentary Assembly of the Council of Europe and Viewpoint of the Commissioner for Human Rights of the Council of Europe. In the Resolution, the Assembly "[called] on all Muslim communities to abandon any traditional interpretations of Islam which deny gender equality and limit women's rights, both within the family and in public life. This interpretation is not compatible with human dignity and democratic standards" (*S.A.S. v. France*, para. 35).

11 This is a point that judges Nussberger and Jäderblom made in their partly dissenting opinion, which stated that, "the applicant is right to claim that the French legislature has restricted pluralism, since the measure prevents certain women from expressing their personality and their beliefs by wearing the full-face veil in public (see paragraph 153 of the judgment). Therefore the blanket ban could be interpreted as a sign of selective pluralism and restricted tolerance" (*S.A.S. v. France*, Dissenting Opinion, para. 14).

12 As Patrick Deneen (2018) observes, liberalism has "successfully disembedded us from relationships that once made claims upon us but also informed our conception of selfhood, our sense of ourselves as citizens sharing a common fate" (17–18).

References

Cahill, Lisa Sowle. 1989. "Catholic Sexual Ethics and the Dignity of the Person: A Double Message." *Theological Studies* 50 (1): 120–50.

Calo, Zachary R. 2010. "Pluralism, Secularism and the European Court of Human Rights." *Journal of Law and Religion* 26 (1): 261–80.

Calo, Zachary R. 2018. "Law and Religion in a Detraditionalized Europe." In *Law, Religion and Tradition*, edited by Jessica Giles, Andrea Pin, and Frank S. Ravitch, 135–51. Berlin: Springer.

Dan-Cohen, Meir. 2011. "A Concept of Dignity." *Israel Law Review* 44 (9): 9–23.

Deneen, Patrick. 2018. *Why Liberalism Failed*. New Haven: Yale University Press.

Gergis, Sherif, Ryan T. Anderson, and Robert P. George. 2012. *What is Marriage? Man and Woman: A Defense*. New York: Encounter Books.

Gergis, Sherif, Robert George, and Ryan Anderson. 2011. "What is Marriage?" *Harvard Journal of Law & Public Policy* 34 (1): 245–87.

Ignatieff, Michael. 2003. *Human Rights as Politics and Idolatry*. Princeton: Princeton University Press.

Klein, Laura K. 2010. "Rights Clash: How Conflicts Between Gay Rights and Religious Freedoms Challenge the Legal System." *Georgetown Law Journal* 98 (3): 505–33.

Lopez, Kathryn Jean. 2011. "Sex and the Empire State: Losing Marriage to Sexual Liberalism: Interview with Robert P. George." *National Review*, June 28, 2011. www.nationalreview.com/article/270662/sex-and-empire-state-interview.

Lovin, Robin. 2019. "Human Dignity and Public Reason." *Political Theology* 20 (5): 437–45.

Madrazo, Alejandro, and Estefanía Vela. 2011. "The Mexican Supreme Court's (Sexual) Revolution?" *Texas Law Review* 89: 1863–93.

McCrudden, Christopher. 2008. "Human Dignity and Judicial Interpretation of Human Rights." *European Journal of International Law* 19 (4): 655–724.

Pinker, Steven. 2008. "The Stupidity of Dignity." *The New Republic*, May 28, 2008. https://newrepublic.com/article/64674/the-stupidity-dignity.

Roy, Olivier. 2007. *Secularism Confronts Islam*. Translated by George Holoch. New York: Columbia University Press.

Siegel, Riva. 2012. "Dignity and Sexuality: Claims on Dignity in Transnational Debates Over Abortion and Same-Sex Marriage." *International Journal of Constitutional Law* 10 (2): 355–79.

United States Conference of Catholic Bishops. N.d. "FAQ: Religious Liberty and Marriage." www.usccb.org/issues-and-action/marriage-and-family/marriage/promotion-and-defense-of-marriage/upload/Handout-Religious-liberty-FAQs-2.pdf.

Case Law

Constitutional Court of South Africa

National Coalition for Gay and Lesbian Equality v. Minister of Justice, 1999 (1) SA 6 (CC).

Court of Appeal for Ontario (Canada)

Halpern v. Canada, [2003] 65 OR 3d 161.

Court of Appeal in Northern Ireland (United Kingdom)

Lee v. Ashers Baking Company, [2016] NICA 39.

Delhi High Court (India)

Naz Foundation v. The Government of NCT of Delhi and Others, WPI no. 7455/2001

European Court of Human Rights

S.A.S. v. France (GC), Application no. 43835/11, July 1, 2014.

Ontario Superior Court of Justice (Canada)

Brockie v. Brillinger (no. 2), 2002 CanLII 63866 (ON SCDC).

Supreme Court of Canada

Law Society of British Columbia v. Trinity Western University, [2018] 2 SCR 293.
Vriend v. Alberta, [1998] 1 SCR 493.

Supreme Court of Justice of the Nation (Mexico)

Acción de inconstitucionalidad 2/2010, Pleno de la Suprema Corte de Justicia de la Nación, Novena Época, 16 gostosto de 2010.

Supreme Court of the United States

Lawrence v. Texas, 539 U.S. 558 (2003).
Planned Parenthood of Se. Pa. v. Casey, 505 U.S. 833 (1992).

Supreme Court of the State of Washington

State of Washington v. Arlene's Flowers, 389 P. 3d 543 (2017).

Part II

Human Dignity

International and Comparative Perspectives

6 Supranational Dignity

The Court of Justice of the European Union's Conceptualization of a Legal Value

Andrea Pin

Introduction

The jurisprudence of the Court of Justice of the European Union (CJEU)[1] is institutionally and theoretically influential, as it is regarded as "the most powerful supranational court in world history" (Kelemen 2016, 117–18). Institutionally, the CJEU issues judgments that have binding effects, are immediately enforceable at the domestic level, and interpret legal texts in an incremental, progressive way. Theoretically, the CJEU has pioneered the legal integration of European countries that used to be deadly rivals. It has balanced the necessity of harmonizing domestic legal systems while preserving national peculiarities. It has addressed contentious topics such as economic competition, customs, tariffs, and markets with the overall goal of ensuring peace, a decent life, and even prosperity in a continent that has suffered mass atrocities and two World Wars. It has played an important role in the construction of a network of institutions to prevent Europe from falling into a third spiral of hatred, violence, and war. Its role has been so central and even prophetic that the great comparativist Mauro Cappelletti saw the revival of "natural law" in Europe in its judgments (Cappelletti 1985, 31).

The CJEU has also influenced global narratives about human dignity. The CJEU first incorporated human dignity in its rulings in ways that preceded and anticipated by decades the increasing roles of dignity in European law. More recently, the CJEU has exploited the strong protection that the European Charter of Fundamental Rights gave to human dignity in the 2000s. Only one case discussed dignity in the CJEU during the1960s, two did so in the 1970s, four in the 1980s, and two in the 1990s (ratio: 0.2%). Later on, when its case-load took off, the number of rulings on dignity became more substantial: in 2010, the CJEU discussed human dignity in roughly 1% of the cases.

This chapter will first situate the CJEU within EU law and explain the nature of the CJEU's judgments. Then it will distill the growing importance of dignity within EU constitutionalism. Finally, it will focus on the case law revolving around the concept of dignity.

DOI: 10.4324/9781003307853-8

The Court of Justice of the European Union

The CJEU has played an important role in the constellation of the European Communities (EC) and the European Union (EU), which replaced the EC in the 1990s. Far from merely interpreting EU law while adjudicating disputes, it has also developed EU law since its very beginning (Itzcovich, 288–89; Stein 1981, 1–2). Legal ideas that EU Treaties and other EU rules enshrined were first conceived by the CJEU while adjudicating cases (Lenaerts 2007, 1030). The centrality of the CJEU has thus heeded the call of "EU lawmakers," who frequently write "legislation that invites the [CJEU] to play a central role in governance." The centrality of the CJEU, in turn, has made "private litigants into acting as the eyes, ears, and long arm of Brussels, encouraging the litigants to bring enforcement actions before national and EU courts" and also to advance the legal integration among the EU Member States (Kelemen, 121).

The pivotal role that the CJEU has historically played would have never been possible without two key legal concepts that the CJEU deployed in its early years. In the 1960s, the CJEU developed the doctrine of "direct effect" with its *Van Gend En Loos* judgment. This judgment established that EC regulations create rights that are directly enforceable by domestic courts without the need for the states to execute them (C-26/62). Thanks to this doctrine, individuals and groups could and still can claim EU rights, liberties, and privileges from their domestic institutions without the need for their country to implement EU regulations.

The concept of "European Communities' legal supremacy" has become also paramount in securing the enforcement of EU law. Here, again, the CJEU played a groundbreaking role. With its 1964 *Costa* decision, the CJEU stated that when a domestic and an EC rule conflict, the latter should prevail (Horspool, Humphreys, and Wills-Greco 2016, 70). This judgment prioritized EC and later EU law over domestic law and gave domestic judges the power and responsibility to administer justice in the name of EC and EU instead of domestic law.

The concept of human dignity has played a role in three types of CJEU's judicial proceedings: (1) when the CJEU was called to strike down EC and EU institutions' acts; (2) when it was confronted with EU's employees' issues; and, most importantly, (3) within the "preliminary ruling procedure" (Itzcovich 2017, 278). Through this procedure, domestic courts that are uncertain about how to interpret an EU rule in a given case can pause their judicial proceedings and refer the interpretative question to the CJEU. The CJEU will then deliver a judgment clarifying the correct interpretation of the EU rule at stake (Horspool, Humphreys, and Wills-Greco 2016, 70). The domestic judge will then resume the dispute and decide the case under the interpretation of EU law given by the CJEU.

The writing style of the CJEU tends to be concise and formulaic. Its judgments seldom offer lengthy prose or deep intellectual speculations. This is largely understandable, as the CJEU does not allow separate opinions and therefore judgments tend to synthesize the various judges' viewpoints while focusing on the areas upon which they agree. In contrast, much of the theoretical exploration that the CJEU offers is found in the opinions of the Advocate General (AG). The AG is a member of the CJEU but is not a judge; he or she intervenes in the proceedings to advise the judges about the legal interpretation(s) that would best fit the EU's legal integration (Baudenbacher 2003, 524). While the AG may summon litigants for informal hearings, his or her more important role is to deliver an opinion on an impartial and independent ground from the parties to the underlying suit—a role that is normally credited with being influential for the judges (Craig and De Burca 2011, 62). The AG normally uses a more personal, detailed, and colorful style (Itzcovich 2017, 286), which helps the reader to understand the complexities of the case at stake and the theoretical issues surrounding a dispute.

While the CJEU's writing style is moderate and rigid, its method of interpreting EU law is not. The CJEU's interpretive pattern does not lie within the three corners of the wording, the spirit of the law, or its own precedents. Since its beginning, it has "set sail from the secure anchorage and protected haven of 'plain words' [of the law] to explore the wider seas of purpose and context" (Fennelly 1997, 657). The CJEU normally blesses one interpretive option as the correct one in light of its ramifications for the EU (Rasmussen 2008, 94), as its main preoccupation is to secure the ordered development of legal integration among the Member States. This forward-looking approach thus makes the CJEU's jurisprudence relatively proactive and non-formalistic (Itzcovich 2017, 289).

The supranational status of the CJEU, its institutional role, the binding force of its judgments, and its patterns of legal interpretation provide important context for its interpretations and applications of the concept of human dignity. Because the CJEU often intervenes in domestic disputes, it must be attentive to the contexts in which its judgments are deployed. The binding force of these judgments requires the CJEU to anticipate their potential effects. The CJEU's basic legal philosophy, however, does not just warn against rulings that may have disrupting consequences; it also requires interpretations of EU law that best advance legal integration. Such a task is particularly delicate in the context of human dignity. Dignity has a universal appeal, which must be balanced with the fact that the EU Member States are not uniform in how they understand or balance legal concepts: a factor that the CJEU seems to have often taken into consideration within its case law on the subject.

Dignity and the EU

Paradoxically, in the 1990s, the multi-decade success of the EC and EU pushed the EU to reframe itself. The EC and the EU cultivated peace, political and economic cooperation, and prosperity within an area of the continent that had been plagued with wars and hostilities for centuries. Borders, tariffs, and diplomatic struggles were replaced with open borders, a common market, and diplomatic cooperation on a large scale. Later on, Eastern Europe joined Western Europe within the EU, making Cold War political-ideological rivalries obsolete. With peace and decent living conditions taken for granted, human rights emerged as a new, appealing ideal and an engine for more legal integration (Pin 2019, 236). A rights-based narrative took hold of the legal discourse and led to a reinterpretation of the meaning and goals of European integration.

It is within this context that the idea of dignity gained momentum. The EU's narrative of human rights magnified the idea of human dignity that was on the rise globally. As the CJEU's AG once stated, the EU came to perceive itself as being based on "the confidence . . . that each Member State shares with all the other Member States, and recognizes that they share with it, a set of common values on which the Union is founded, such as respect for human dignity, freedom, democracy, equality, the rule of law and respect for human rights" (*Pál Aranyosi and Robert Căldăraru v. Generalstaatsanwaltschaft Bremen*, para. 112).

The AG's bold statement resonated with the EU's constitutional developments. The EU ratified the European Charter of Fundamental Rights in 2000 and later incorporated it within the EU Treaty in 2007. Within the Charter, the EU cited human dignity seven times.

The Charter's first reference to human dignity is in its Preamble, which states:

> Conscious of its spiritual and moral heritage, the Union is founded on the indivisible, universal values of human dignity, freedom, equality, and solidarity; it is based on the principles of democracy and the rule of law. It places the individual at the heart of its activities, by establishing the citizenship of the Union and by creating an area of freedom, security, and justice.

The Charter also entrenches dignity within its Articles. Its list of liberties entitles Title I as "Dignity." This Title includes "human dignity" itself, the right to life, the right to "the integrity of the person" (Art. 3), the prohibitions "of torture and inhuman or degrading treatment or punishment" (Art. 4), and of "slavery and forced labour" (Art. 5). Within this list, human dignity stands out as the first and most fundamental right: "Human dignity is inviolable. It must be respected and protected" (Art. 1). The Charter further cites dignity in the context of the rights of the elderly ("The Union recognizes and respects the rights of the elderly to lead a life of dignity and independence and to participate in social and cultural life," Art. 25), and of workers' rights ("Every worker has the right to working conditions which respect his or her health, safety, and dignity," Art. 31).

As historians and legal philosophers have pointed out, dignity may function as a foundational principle of a legal system (Brownsword 2014, 7); as a legal principle inspiring the whole edifice of rights (critically, Sangiovanni

2017, 2); as a protection from public powers (Barak 2013, 362); or as a compass for public policies (Dupré 2015, 10). Within the Charter, dignity functions as all of the above. Firstly, it has a foundational value for the whole edifice of the EU. Secondly, it is a general principle that inspires many basic rights. Thirdly, it is a right in itself—indeed, it is the first right to be protected, coming even before the right to life. Fourthly, protecting dignity requires that vulnerable people are treated with respect and that workers are enabled to live a decent life.

The Charter's manifold references to human dignity reflect also the variety of legal and political cultures that inhabit the EU, as well as the malleability of the concept itself. In fact, within the Charter dignity is the seedbed of the negative freedoms that common law jurisdictions have taught to the world, as well as of the typically continental welfare policies: the workers' right to a dignified life strikingly parallels the 1919 Weimar Constitution's command that the economy preserves human dignity.

When the Charter was drafted, however, the concept of dignity itself was not new to the EC and the EU. EU rules often come after a series of "recitals." Recitals do not lay down rules; but they certainly provide a context, sharing the ideals and purposes that inspired the rules. Because of the interpretive style of the EU, which focuses on the purpose of the law rather than on its meaning, recitals are certainly relevant to the rule's interpretation. Such non-dispositive parts of EC pieces of legislation had been referencing dignity for decades before the Charter came into existence.

Dignity was also well known to the EC and the EU early on because of their Janus-faced nature and their cultural roots. Although the CJEU has constantly emphasized that the EC was born as a new, autonomous legal order, it never cut the EC's or the EU's ties with their Member States (*Flaminio Costa v. E.N.E.L.*). The CJEU knew that the EC and the EU drew force and legitimacy from their domestic constitutional traditions. As countries such as Germany, Italy, and France were very sensitive to the ideal of human dignity, the CJEU also had to keep it in consideration while adjudicating.

It is significant, however, that the EU did ground itself explicitly upon dignity only after economic growth had become a constant within most of the EU territories and a robust welfare net seemed to have fulfilled the promises of social rights. Despite the strong social and economic components of human dignity within the European legal culture, the narrative of European integration that revolved around dignity took off outside the social and economic rights agenda.

The post-2000 emphasis on rights did not have immediate effects on the scope of the EU. The EU's powers encompass a variety of fields, from agriculture to tariffs, from the environment to public procurement, immigration, and refugees. EU's competencies and the way the CJEU has interpreted them have substantially trimmed down the sovereignty of its Member States. However, the EU's powers do not extend beyond those granted by the EU Treaty. The EU still devotes most of its attention to economy-related fields. This gives the

Charter of Fundamental Rights a limited scope: since it inspires and controls the EU's activities, it does not control beyond the EU's reach.

The success of the EU narrative of rights, however, is expanding beyond the economic sphere through the support of parties, domestic judges, and the CJEU that increasingly prioritize the EU perspective when they litigate. They read EU rights—including the Charter's rights—into fields that are only loosely related to them and traditionally belong to the states. Fundamental rights litigation thus enters the CJEU through a relatively narrow economic lens. But this economic distortion of human rights often has broad implications: the winning party at the CJEU benefits from a decision that overrides domestic laws within all EU territories. For example, since the EU protects workers' freedom of movement within its borders, including the right to family reunification, the CJEU has ruled that all the Member States must recognize same-sex partnerships (*Relu Adrian Coman and Others v. Inspectoratul General Pentru Imigrări and Ministerul Afacerilor Internet*). This ruling reasoned that a state's failure to recognize such partnerships would discourage gay couples from relocating within the EU, thereby threatening the EU's freedom of movement with the family.

The EU and the CJEU are not alone in patrolling the supranational space in the Old Continent. The Council of and the European Court of Human Rights (ECHR) have been policing the European states' compliance with the European Convention on Human Rights since the 1950s. Since they focus directly on human rights, they would seem to be the ideal place for dignity- and rights-based claims. But the ECHR suffers from institutional and stylistic flaws that make it less than ideal. Institutionally, the ECHR is less powerful than the EU, although it encompasses 46 states since Russia was expelled from the Council of Europe in 2022. When the ECHR finds a Conventional violation, it is up to the Member State to remove it. The domestic effectiveness of the ECHR's judgments thus relies on the states' willingness to implement them. EU laws and the CJEU's judgments are very different. They do not just bind the Member States on the international plane, but actually can override domestic laws.

Stylistically, the ECHR is more erratic than the CJEU in its case law. Its judgments are sometimes inconsistent with each other, and rarely constitute a coherent body of law from which it is possible to draw theoretical consideration. While it is generally forward-looking rather than attached to its precedents, the CJEU has the reputation of being quite disciplined in its reasoning, and attentive to developing its jurisprudence incrementally to promote a smooth legal integration among its Member States. The CJEU's case law on human dignity reflects this incremental approach.

Dignity at the CJEU

The Meaning of Human Dignity

The CJEU's judgments hardly deal squarely with the meaning of the concept of human dignity or with its ramifications. Even among AG's opinions, theorizations of dignity do not abound. This is quite unsurprising. Explorations in such a contested, debatable concept are prone to generate controversy of a magnitude that Europe can hardly handle. As has been noted, post-World War II European Countries have slowly developed a unified constitutional infrastructure and peaceful relations through the abandonment of substantive conceptions of goodness and truth. The mutual relinquishing of claims of moral or epistemological superiority among political and national factions was a key factor in securing enough stability for Europe (McCrudden 2015, 112; Pasture 2015, 193). The rise of fierce inter-state confrontations in the name of key concepts such as dignity can be perceived as potentially resurrecting the moral, spiritual, or religious rivalries that the slow development of the EU tried to dodge.

The only two AGs' opinions that have embarked on intellectual reflections on dignity, with their deeply diverging approaches, witness how shaky it can be to base the EU's legal reasoning on this concept. It comes with no surprise, then, that the CJEU did not explicitly endorse either of the two AGS's theorizations. Since it did not bless or repudiate either of them as the correct interpretation of human dignity, it left the door open for diverging explorations and theorizations, avoiding any attempt to reconcile the different views on the matter.

In the *Omega* case, the AG explored the idea of human dignity from a genealogical perspective, to identify its characters and normative ramifications. Such an exploration was necessary because the CJEU was confronted with the very delicate issue of squaring human dignity *with* EU liberties.

This case revolved around the importation and use in Germany of toy weapons made in the UK. In Bonn, a local undertaking imported harmless laser guns and target vests, which players used to shoot each other in a laser tag game. Under pressure from the public, local authorities prohibited the activity, alleging that it was against public order. A judicial proceeding ensued. On the one hand stood the freedoms of establishment and of movement of goods, which are key parts of the fundamental liberties of the EU. On the other hand stood the principle of human dignity; German domestic authorities thought that the game trivialized this principle, as it consisted of playing at killing.

Both the EU and the German legal orders magnify the role of dignity. As noted, the EU's Charter of Fundamental Rights has a strong focus on human dignity. For its part, the German Constitution enshrines dignity within its opening article (Art. 1). Although both legal orders identify dignity among their core legal principles, however, the case was particularly delicate for the CJEU. As seen, the EU entrenched dignity within its constitutional framework only *after* securing the free market and consolidating the basic freedoms that revolved around it. Implementing dignity was thus intended to add a layer to the EU's edifice and boost its legitimation, not to alter its nature.

The conflict pitted the EU's first layer of economic freedoms of movement and establishment against the protection of human dignity. The CJEU was thus confronted with a serious challenge. It had to decide whether and how to square its foundational ideals, which gravitated around the ideal of a free market, with the later narrative of dignity. In other words, *Omega* challenged the simplistic belief that dignity would add something to the EU rather than change its nature: a belief that the CJEU was quick to celebrate when it stated that dignity was now "a fundamental right" (*Kingdom of the Netherlands v. European Parliament and Council of the European Union*).

The AG Stix-Hackl's opinion magnified the concept of dignity while downplaying the conflict between EU law and German law. She acknowledged that dignity was "the respect and value to be attributed to each human being on account of his or her humanity." "Mankind itself [was] reflected in the concept of human dignity; it [was] what distinguish [ed] [humans] from other creatures." It was "the underlying basis and starting point for all human rights," and "the point of convergence of individual human rights in the light of which they [were] to be understood and interpreted" (para. 75). This conceptualization of dignity was very familiar throughout Europe, the AG continued, as "human dignity ha[d] its roots deep in the origins of a conception of mankind in European culture that regard[ed] man as an entity capable of spontaneity and self-determination. Because of his ability to forge his own free will, he [wa]s a person (subject) and [could] not be downgraded to a thing or object" (para. 78).

The AG went on to describe how the Old Continent came to appreciate human dignity:

> From a religious perspective, the dignity of man [wa]s based on his creation in the image of God and the universal promise of salvation for all mankind. It was political thinking during the 18th century that recognition that all mankind has its nature and reason in common was the cornerstone from which stemmed the demand that human dignity and human rights should be recognized.
>
> (fn. 50)

Such was the meaning of human dignity for the EU, too. The AG, however, acknowledged that human dignity meant something more for the German legal order. Unlike other contexts, in the German legal order dignity functioned as a "separate fundamental right" or "an independent head of claim" (para. 90). It was more than a principle: it was a right (Petersen 2019, 93).

The AG persuaded the CJEU. The latter did not explicitly endorse the AG's reading of the historical development of dignity. It did not depart, however, from the AG's conclusion. The AG and the CJEU shared the view that the difference between dignity as a right and dignity as a principle allowed the coexistence of different national variations of the same concept. Germany could prohibit the laser-tag game, as it was repugnant to its unique perception and understanding of dignity.

Albeit well crafted, the AG and the CJEU's legal reasoning was somewhat a sleight of hand. As seen before, when *Omega* reached the CJEU, the EU Charter's rich language already enshrined dignity *both* as a right and as a principle.

The AG and the CJEU, however, probably exploited the fact that the Charter was not yet in full force and de-emphasized its powerful phrasings about dignity.

Omega and the AG Stix-Hackl clarified how dignity became so important in contemporary constitutional discourse and how the EU tolerated different conceptualizations of it. However, it was AG Maduro in *Coleman* who tried to explain what dignity truly meant.

Interestingly enough, Maduro took pains to explain precisely what human dignity entailed, although there was no need for him to undertake such a task. The issue at stake could have been decided on much narrower grounds—as the CJEU did. Ms. Coleman was employed at a law firm when she got pregnant and gave birth to a disabled son. The attention that her son required made it particularly difficult for her to balance her private life with her employment duties. In her view, the firm reacted in a hostile way, and she filed a complaint for having been discriminated against because of her son's disability.

The domestic judge referred the case to the CJEU, which had to decide whether the directive that prohibited various types of discrimination, including disability (2000/78/EC of 27 November, 2000), applied to Ms. Coleman's case. The interpretive doubt stemmed from the fact that Ms. Coleman was not technically a disabled person; it was her son who suffered from a disability. The CJEU quickly concluded that the directive protected Ms. Coleman, as the case originated in a form of discrimination that was based on disability.

Maduro took a different and winding path. Although the directive spoke of human dignity very tangentially,[2] he emphasized the harm caused by the firm's hostility to Ms. Coleman. Building explicitly upon the work of Ronald Dworkin and Joseph Raz, he focused on the dignitary harm caused by the discrimination suffered by Ms. Coleman. Human dignity, in Maduro's view, included the respect and protection of "personal autonomy," namely the possibility that all "individuals . . . design and conduct the course of their lives through a succession of choices among different valuable options." Mistreating Ms. Coleman because of her son's disability meant degrading her dignity and violating her autonomy.

Maduro's opinion did not differ from the CJEU's judgment in its outcome. Rather, the difference was in his rationale. Maduro tried to bring the argument into the field of human dignity—which was unnecessary for the CJEU to decide and probably even debatable, given the paucity of references to dignity within the directive. Maduro's line of reasoning, however, shows how dignity had become a powerful concept by the time he penned his opinion. By using it, he tried also to give dignity a certain shape—a shape that it did not have in the relevant EU text.

The shift between *Omega* and *Coleman* was major. Within the former, the AG *had* to give dignity meaning to decide the case; she could not avoid addressing the argument of what dignity entailed. Within *Coleman*, the AG *deliberately chose* to employ dignity. What started as an interpretive burden soon became a powerful, appealing intellectual tool that it was possible, even useful, to manipulate.

The CJEU also had a chance to briefly focus on the meaning of dignity later. It is worth mentioning it especially because it was the CJEU, and not its AG, that tried to capture the significance of the concept of dignity. In *Fédération des maisons de repos privés de Belgique*, the CJEU sought to articulate the meaning of dignity and connect it with the traditional economic and welfare fields from which the EU developed. The CJEU then stated that the "right to human dignity and integrity" fleshed out the principles of "social cohesion and solidarity." Although for the sake of the ruling this statement is *obiter dictum*, it is still doubly relevant. On the one hand, it portrays human dignity as a "right." On the other hand, it connects dignity with the idea of "social cohesion and solidarity," thereby repudiating individualist notions of dignity while embracing the typically Continental attention to the social dimension of markets and democracies. The CJEU tried to reconcile its constitutional layer centered around economic freedoms with the continental tradition of the welfare state and the newer narrative centered around human dignity.

Dignity and Legal Interpretation

Although only rarely, the judicial branch of the EU has also given hints about how legal interpretations focusing on dignity can push EU law into the future. On one early occasion, which took place in the 1990s, when the language of dignity and even of rights was not so pervasive, the CJEU and its AG made a significant contribution. The *Cornwall County Council* case revolved around the application of a directive that fought various types of discrimination within employment-related fields (Council Directive 76/207/EEC of 9 February, 1976). A male employee (P.) notified his employer that he would undergo a multi-step process to become a woman. This process began with him dressing as a woman and then continued with a series of surgical operations. However, during the process, the employer terminated his contract. P. then complained that the employer's actions were a form of sexual discrimination.

The directive indeed fought sex discrimination (Art. 2(1)), but its application to the case at stake seemed uncertain. Because P.'s contract was terminated before the completion of the gender reassignment process, P. was still biologically and legally a male. It was unclear whether the prohibition of sex discrimination covered P. throughout this process, or was more narrowly limited to the discrimination between sexes (para. 10).

AG Tesauro noticed the novelty of the case. The CJEU was confronted with "a transsexual [who wa]s seeking to rely on the directive" (para. 1). Future cases that revolved around the same topic would "inevitabl[y]" come to the CJEU: it was just a matter of time, Tesauro noted. In the AG's view, this required the CJEU to "keep up with social change" (para. 9): "[i]n society as it is today, in which customs and morals are changing rapidly, citizens are guaranteed ever wider and deeper protection of their freedoms and social and legal studies are increasingly taking on present-day—and, for that very reason, real—values, on the principle that it is effective to do so, it would be unjustifiable to reject out of hand the problem of transsexuality . . . or simply to condemn it and consider it contrary to the law" (para. 9). "[O]utdated views" could not "cut [the law] off from society as it actually is." In addition, for Tesauro, the CJEU had to heed the call coming from the many Member States that were recognizing transsexuality through legislative or judicial means (para. 10).

The AG thus concluded that it was "necessary to go beyond the traditional [sex] classification and recognize that, in addition to the man/woman dichotomy, "there was "a range of characteristics, behavior, and roles shared by men and women, so that sex *itself* ought rather to be thought of as a continuum" (para. 17). "[T]he idea that the law should take into consideration, and protect, a woman who has suffered discrimination in comparison with a man, or vice versa, but denies that protection to those who are also *discriminated against*, again by reason of sex, merely because they fall outside the traditional man/woman classification," had to be regarded as "obsolete" (para. 17).

The AG reasoned that the 1976 directive had to be interpreted in light of contemporary circumstances, not according to the meaning that was attached to it when it was drafted. The directive could not anticipate what society would become in the span of only a few years: in the mid-1970s, transsexualism was "only just beginning to be 'discovered' " (para. 23). Now transsexualism was becoming a visible phenomenon, which had to stay within the radar of the directive. Protecting transsexuals would also embody the ideals of "social justice and European integration" (para. 24). All in all, the CJEU could not miss the "opportunity of leaving a mark of undeniable civil substance," and "taking a decision which [wa]s bold but fair and legally correct, inasmuch it [wa]s undeniably based on and consonant with the great value of equality" (para. 4).

The CJEU's judgment was much shorter and narrower than Tesauro's broad observations on the nature of discrimination and how it changed over time. However, it ruled that the directive had to cover "discrimination arising . . . from the gender reassignment" (para. 20). The employer had treated P. "unfavourably by comparison with persons of the sex to which" P. belonged "before undergoing gender reassignment" (para. 21).

Despite its conciseness, the CJEU's judgment found room to explicitly link dignity with sex discrimination. It reasoned that "[t]o tolerate such discrimination would [have been] tantamount, as regards such a person, to a failure to respect the dignity and freedom to which he or she [wa]s entitled" (para. 22). This argument is particularly remarkable insofar as the directive nowhere spoke about dignity. The CJEU's evolving conceptualization of dignity prompted an evolving legal interpretation. The need to protect the dignity of individuals as they are, and/or as they aspire to be, boosted an evolving pattern of legal interpretation.

Dignity and the Beginning of Human Life

Scarce explorations of the concept of human dignity did not prevent the CJEU, however, from employing it in extremely sensitive fields. Biotechnological innovation and its achievements have given the CJEU opportunities to reflect and rule over the protection of human life and its relationship to human dignity. As often happens, the CJEU has been confronted with such an ethically hot and politically sensitive topic only indirectly, through the directive 98/44 on the legal protection of biotechnological inventions. Although the directive technically focuses on the patentability of biotechnological inventions, it indirectly touches upon the status of the embryo. Art. no. 6 excludes embryos for industrial or commercial purposes from patentability, while one of its recitals requires that patenting respects human dignity.

The *Brüstle* case dealt with the difficult question of what had to be considered an embryo. Technological development has made fertilization possible outside the human body and with a variety of cell types. The scope of patentability of such cells thus depended on the definition of an "embryo." The AG tackled the issue by pointing to the "principle of dignity" (para. 46). This principle thus became the AG's compass, and was later followed by the CJEU, albeit more succinctly.

Although they were aware of the variety of national opinions on the subject, both the AG and the CJEU determined that the EU could not delegate the definition of an embryo to each of the EU Member States. This would have meant that "an invention . . . could be granted a patent in some Member States, while the patentability of such an invention would be excluded in others" (*Oliver Brüstle v. Greenpeace eV.*, para. 28, AG opinion, para. 56).

The AG suggested starting with scientific evidence. Science made clear that "development from conception [began] with a few cells. . . . They [held] within them the full capacity for subsequent division" (para. 84). Totipotent cells had to be considered "the first stage of the human body which they will become" (para. 85). Since they could develop into a human being, they enjoyed the protection of the dignity and integrity of the person (AG para. 96; *Oliver Brüstle v. Greenpeace eV.*, para. 35).

According to the AG and later to the CJEU, a cell's capacity to develop into a full human being was therefore the basis and guide for the protection accorded by human dignity. Such protection, in turn, excluded the patentability of the cell (para. 35). This set of considerations brought the CJEU to exclude the patentability of embryos, while later making clear that the prohibition of patenting embryos did not hinder or prejudice the development of the scientific research on embryos (para. 40; see *Patrick Grégor Puppinck and Others v. European Commission*, para. 107).[3]

Human Dignity as a Shield

Human dignity has two faces in the CJEU's case law: a shield that protects the individual against public powers, and a trigger for public policies. Dignity renders inhumane or degrading treatments inadmissible under all circumstances (the *Petruhin* case). The breadth of this prohibition has led the CJEU to elaborate on the idea of an "absolute" human dignity, which does not allow exceptions. This aspect of human dignity has been investigated mostly within the case law that revolves around the process for asylum seekers (*C. K. and Others v. Republika Slovenija*, para. 59; the *Cimade* case, para. 56, AG opinion, para. 55), repatriations (*M.P. v. Secretary of State for the Home Department*, para. 36; the *Landkreis Gifhorn* case, AG opinion, par. 45), extraditions (the *Petruhin* case, para. 56), the execution of the European Arrest Warrant that automatizes extradition among EU countries (the *M.L.* case, paras 90–92), and the range of sanctions that states can implement to deter misbehaviors among applicants for international protection (*Zubair Haqbin v. Federal Agentschap voor de opvang van asielzoekers*). Dignity has thus become an important factor in domestic disputes revolving around non-nationals, especially when it comes to how a certain procedure must be carried out (the *Zakaria* case; the *McCarthy* case, para. 33).

The absoluteness of dignity in this context paradoxically requires a case-by-case assessment of the conditions of human beings. If an individual who is about to be extradited in pursuance of the European Arrest Warrant complains that the extradition could put her life at risk, this claim cannot be taken at face value: domestic institutions must investigate the actual conditions that the extradition would entail for the individual (*Pál Aranyosi and Robert Căldăraru v. Generalstaatsanwaltschaft Bremen*, paras 85, 90).

The CJEU has applied the same approach consistently: examples abound here (among many, see *K. v Staatssecretaris van Veiligheid en Justitie and H.F. v. Belgische Staat*, paras 46, 60, 65).[4] Minors' unique vulnerability may require an exception from the parity of arms in judicial proceedings: their testimony may take place before a trial begins to preserve their memory and their personality (the *Criminal proceedings against X. case*, AG opinion, paras 15–19; the *Pupino* case, para. 5). Finally, the enforcement of the Dublin rules—according to which asylum seekers must be deported to the EU country of first entry to file their application—can be suspended if it translates in a degrading treatment (the *N.S.* case, paras 86–89 and AG, para. 112). Such deportations and the eligibility for refugee status have become a matter of grave concern starting in 2010 when massive numbers of people fleeing famine, persecution, and war crossed the Mediterranean Sea: a topic that has caused controversy among states, to the extent that the AG once warned that a human dignity issue was being dealt with as it was "a game of ping-pong" among the EU Member States (*Abubacarr Jawo v. Bundesrepublik Deutschland*, AG opinion, para. 97).

In *A. and Others v. Staatssecretaris van Veiligheid en Justitie*, the CJEU also had to deal with the extremely sensitive topic of sexual orientation, which it tackled from a very specific angle. Once in the Netherlands, some individuals sought asylum, alleging that in their countries of origin they were exposed to persecution because of their homosexuality. The CJEU had to clarify how domestic institutions could assess the claimants' allegations about their own sexuality without infringing upon their dignity.

AG Sharpston noted that "sexuality [wa]s a highly complex issue that [wa]s integral to [one's] personal identity and the sphere of human life" (*A. and Others v. Staatssecretaris van Veiligheid en Justitie*, AG opinion, para. 38). It was difficult to verify an "averred sexual orientation; and it [wa]s unlikely that there [would] be documentary or other evidence to support an applicant's self-declared statement of . . . sexual orientation" (para. 43). However, the *Charter of Fundamental Rights* permitted the Member States to assess the applicants' credibility (paras 44–45). There were severe limits on what the states could do: any interference "with an individual's right to his sexual orientation" was admissible as long as it was proportional to his "right to privacy and family life" (para. 61). The applicants could not "be required to support requests for refugee status in a manner that undermine[d] their dignity or personal integrity" (para. 52).

After these preliminary remarks, AG Sharpston ruled out some options. Since "[w]ithin the [EU], homosexuality [wa]s no longer considered to be a medical or psychological condition," there was "no recognized medical examination that [could] be applied in order to establish a person's sexual orientation" (para. 60). Also "explicit questions concerning an applicant's sexual activities and proclivities" (para. 63), or requests that applicants produce evidence such as films or photographs, let alone that they perform sexual acts in order to demonstrate their sexual orientation" were impermissible (para. 67).

In deciding *A. and Others v. Staatssecretaris van Veiligheid en Justitie*, the CJEU was even more prone to use the concept of human dignity than the AG. The CJEU started with the Charter's bold affirmation of the necessity of protecting human dignity. This legal value, the CJEU said, made some means of assessing one's sexuality impermissible. For one, requiring the performance of sexual activities would infringe upon human dignity, regardless of the probative value that such a method could have (para. 65). In turn, dignity required that the institutions take "into account of the individual situation and personal circumstances of the applicant" (para. 57). Dignity thus protected the applicants from some inhumane practices but also required a contextual analysis of their cases.

Shortly thereafter, in a similar case, the CJEU was called on to determine the role that psychologists could play in evaluating the asylum seeker's sexual orientation (*F. v. Bevándorlási és Állampolgársági Hivatal*). Again, using psychologists was not "inconsistent with human dignity" (para. 33). But they could not be used to analyze one's personality, to derive the sexuality from it (para. 72): as the AG pointed out, scientific literature did not link the personality with sexuality (para. 36). Psychologists, however, could help the applicants talk about their fears, their past experiences, and assess the credibility of their narrations, the AG noted (para. 33). Throughout the process, the CJEU reasoned that human dignity had to be given the highest regard (para. 35).

The aforementioned cases demonstrate the large role that dignity can play in adjudication. Despite its broad application, however, human dignity is not an all-encompassing concept, and cannot be overstretched. In a case about price policies of low-cost airlines, which charged customers for a variety of what they considered extras, the AG argued that charging clients for their carry-on baggage was a severe legal violation. In the AG's view, forcing passengers to either pay for items of very personal use or store them with their checked baggage ran against the respect of their "personal dignity." The idea that dignity connected with such a petty detail had no purchase in the CJEU's opinion, which reached the same conclusion as the AG about carry-on luggage but avoided talking about "personal dignity" (the *Vueling Airlines SA* case, AG opinion, par. 55).

Human Dignity as a Sword

Within the CJEU, human dignity has also functioned as an effective tool to implement and shape domestic welfare policies and to actively protect people in need. In fact, attentiveness to the economic dimensions of human dignity has found its way into CJEU case law when it justified limiting the legal capacity of vulnerable people who could harm themselves by making counterproductive financial dispositions (*E.Q. v. Administration de l'Enregistrement, des Domaines et de la TVA*, para. 64). Dignity also justified the requirement that EU citizens living in in another EU country enjoy the basic means to live a decent life (*Jobcenter Berlin Neukölln v. Nazifa Alimanovic and Others*, para. 45; AG opinion, para. 72): a statement that the CJEU has reiterated making human dignity the point of reference to measure whether a state has provided for the "minimum means of subsistence" (*C.G. v. The Department for Communities in Northern Ireland*, para. 69). Considerations around dignity have driven the CJUE to rule that third-country nationals who applied for international protection have a right to access the local labor market also while a decision on their transfer to another state is pending (*K.S. and Others v. The International Protection Appeals Tribunal and Others*, paras 69–71). Finally, thanks to the horizontal effect of EU law, the CJEU has also applied dignity to private individuals and institutions. This has happened repeatedly within the context of labor relations, as the CJEU established a connection between the concept of dignity and the workers' rights to maximum working hours, daily and weekly rest, and paid leave (among many, *Academia de Studii Economice din București*, para. 41).

The context-based approach, however, also works the other way around, as the *Dano* case illustrated (*Elisabeta Dano and Florin Dano v. Jobcenter Leipzig*; see also the *Vestisce Arbeit Jobcentre* case, para. 52–53). The CJEU was confronted with the case of a family of EU nationals who moved to Germany where they benefited from social welfare but did not engage in work activities. Since the local institutions denied them the additional benefits that the law made available to nationals, they filed a complaint alleging that such discrimination was impermissible because they enjoyed EU citizenship. On the contrary, the CJEU justified the discrimination on the basis that the basic welfare protection they already enjoyed was sufficient to protect their dignity. Since they did not participate in the national economic life, they could be afforded fewer benefits than other EU citizens. Finally, the CJEU emphasized that leveling up welfare services to people who chose not to participate in the economic life of a state would have put "a burden on the social assistance systems of the Member States" (paras 77–78).

A similar approach is visible in a variety of subjects. The Court has made abundantly clear that human dignity does not rule out differences in treatment. For instance, the Court has stated that the duty that all EU Member States secure international protection for refugees does not entail, according to them, a unified set of benefits across the EU territories: states can legitimately offer different levels of treatment, as long as such individuals are not refused the fulfillment of their "basic needs, such as, inter alia, food, personal hygiene and a place to live, and that undermines his or her physical or mental health or puts him or her in a state of degradation of human dignity" (*XXXX v. Commissaire général aux réfugiés et aux apatrides*, para. 32).

The deployment of dignity in cases of welfare is all but marginal in the development of the EU's legal integration. As seen, EU law incorporated dignity later in the game, when its achievements in the fields of welfare and market threatened to make it obsolete. Grounding its identity on dignity was supposed to resurrect its legitimation and appeal. As seen in *Omega*, the priority of dignity soon clashed with the traditional EU market freedoms. The emergence of a thread of cases that have used the idea of dignity to square the circle of limited resources with the expectations of a decent life is proof that the CJEU is trying to reconcile its earlier social rights narratives with its later human rights priorities.

Conclusion

The increasing success of human dignity as a hermeneutical tool at the CJEU does not dispel doubts around its core or marginal features. Dignity has so many faces and fields of application that it is hard to pin down what it means. Within the preceding sketch of the CJEU's case law, however, it is possible to identify some themes and patterns.

First, the CJEU has a sort of primacy in the dignity-based narrative within the EU. As often happened, the CJEU anticipated EU legal developments by entrenching dignity among its core values and ideas within its reasoning. The CJEU adopted and adapted the concept of dignity even before the concept and ideal took off within EU law.

Second, the CJEU conceptualizes dignity in ways that are consistent with the typical Continental approach to constitutionalism. In the CJEU's jurisprudence, dignity embodies the idea of social justice and equality, economic emancipation, and the protection of vulnerabilities. It calls for concrete, case-by-case approach rather than for rigid rules. Its case law is probably even more preoccupied and busy with securing the legal and social integration among peoples than with shielding individuals from public powers. The Anglo-Saxon culture of rights has, however, a place within the CJEU's case law on dignity, as is reflected in the CJEU's strong opposition to all humiliating and degrading treatments.

Third, the dignity that the CJEU and its AG have in mind is both a principle and a right. It started as a principle when the CJEU credited it as a pillar of European constitutionalism. But dignity is also increasingly conceived of as a right, although parties tend not to make freestanding dignity-based claims in litigation, instead linking it to other, more specific rights.

Fourth, the context-based type of reasoning that the CJEU usually adopts rejects formalist understanding of dignity in ways that can both reinforce and weaken individual claims. As seen, dignity does not entail complete equality of welfare treatments across and within countries. Dignity has therefore a different meaning from equality.

Finally, the concept of human dignity drives legal innovation and change, even as the meanings of dignity continue to evolve and clash with each other. On the one hand, it yields legal patterns of interpretation that broaden the protection of human rights beyond the plain meaning of legal texts. On the other hand, it is prone to reinterpretation in light of the prevailing intellectual trends. Such flexibility, however, may morph into several, sometimes conflicting, conceptualizations. For instance, the idea of "national dignity" that Euroskeptical platforms have been promoting surfaced once in an AG's opinion (the *Mittelbayerischer Verlag KG* case, para. 84). Such an opinion was delivered a little before the CJEU noted that the concept of the rule of law requires that everyone is treated by policy-makers "with dignity" (*Hungary v. European Parliament and Council of the European Union*, para. 230; *Republic of Poland v. European Parliament and Council of the European Union*, para. 325)—a statement that explicitly draws from the Venice Commission and is implicitly inspired by Dworkin's autonomy-centered intellectual framework (Dworkin 2011, 205–6). The CJEU's attentiveness to human dignity is likely to attract more dignity-based arguments and the clashes of values and principles that come with them.

Notes

1 The CJEU's original name was the European Court of Justice; it took on its present name after the birth of the European Union. For the sake of brevity and simplicity, the chapter will always talk of the CJEU, regardless of its official title at the time each judgment was issued.

2 Art. 2, no. 3: "Harassment shall be deemed to be a form of discrimination within the meaning of paragraph 1, when unwanted conduct related to any of the grounds referred to in Article 1 takes place with the purpose or effect of violating the dignity of a person and of creating an intimidating, hostile, degrading, humiliating or offensive environment. In this context, the concept of harassment may be defined in accordance with the national laws and practice of the Member States."

3 Mainly due to scientific and technologic development, the CJEU had to review a later case on the same topic and Directive. This time, the *International Stem Cells* case revolved around the possibility of producing pluripotent human stem cell lines from parthenogenetically-activated oocytes, which were incapable of developing into human beings. The DNA of such oocytes, in fact, is only maternal and thus cannot give birth to an individual. Following *Brüstle*, parthenogenetically activated oocytes could not be comprised among embryos (paras. 63–67, which the CJEU followed quite closely).

4 *N.S. v. Secretary of State for the Home Department* emphasizes the importance of flexibility in processing asylum applications for the sake of respecting human dignity (see especially AG opinion, paras 105, 106, 110–12).

References

Barak, Aharon. 2013. "Human Dignity: The Constitutional Value and the Constitutional Right." In *Understanding Human Dignity*, edited by Christopher McCrudden, 361–80. Oxford: Oxford University Press.

Baudenbacher, Carl. 2003. "Judicial Globalization: New Development or Old Wine in New Bottles?" *Texas International Law Review* 38 (3): 505–26.

Brownsword, Roger. 2014. "Human Dignity from a Legal Perspective." In *The Cambridge Handbook of Human Dignity*, edited by Marcus Düwell, Jens Braarvig, Roger Brownsword, and Dietmar Mieth, 1–22. Cambridge: Cambridge University Press.

Cappelletti, Mauro. 1985. "Repudiating Montesquieu—The Expansion and Legitimacy of Constitutional Justice." *Catholic University Law Review* 35 (1): 1–32.

Craig, Paul, and Grainne De Burca. 2011. *EU Law*. Oxford: Oxford University Press.

Dupré, Catherine. 2015. *The Age of Dignity. Human Rights and Constitutionalism in Europe*. Oxford; Portland, OR: Hart.

Dworkin, Ronald. 2011. *Justice for Hedgehogs*. Cambridge, MA; London: Belknap Press.

Fennelly, Nial. 1997. "Legal Interpretation at the European Court of Justice." *Fordham International Law Review* 20 (3): 656–79.

Horspool, Margot, Matthew Humphreys, and Michael Wills-Greco. 2016. *European Union Law*. 9th ed. Oxford; New York: Oxford University Press.

Itzcovich, Giulio. 2017. "The European Court of Justice, Comparative Legal Reasoning." In *Comparative Constitutional Reasoning*, edited by Andras Jakab, Arthur Dyevre, and Giulio Itzcovich, 277–322. Cambridge: Cambridge University Press.

Kelemen, Daniel R. 2016. "The Court of Justice of the European Union in the Twenty-First Century." *Law & Contemporary Problems*, no. 29: 117–40.

Lenaerts, Koen. 2007. "Interpretation and the Court of Justice: A Basis for Comparative Reflection." *The International Lawyer* 41 (4): 1011–32.

McCrudden, Christopher. 2015. *Litigating Religions*. Oxford: Oxford University Press.

Pasture, Patrick. 2015. *Imagining European Unity since 1000 AD*. New York: Palgrave Macmillan.

Petersen, Niels. 2019. "Germany." In *Duelling for Supremacy*, edited by Fulvio Maria Palombino, 89–105. Cambridge: Cambridge University Press.

Pin, Andrea. 2019. "The Transnational Drivers of Populist Backlash in Europe: The Role of Courts." *German Law Journal* 20 (2): 225–44.

Rasmussen, Morten. 2008. "The Origins of a Legal Revolution—The Early History of the European Court of Justice." *Journal of European Integration* 14 (2): 77–98.

Sangiovanni, Andrea. 2017. *Humanity without Dignity*. Cambridge, MA; London: Harvard University Press.

Stein, Eric. 1981. "Lawyers, Judges, and the Making of a Transnational Constitution." *American Journal of International Law* 75 (1): 1–27.

Case Law

The Court of Justice of the European Union

A. and Others v. Staatssecretaris van Veiligheid en Justitie, case C-148/13, 149/13 and 150/13, December 2, 2014.
A. v. Daniel B. and Others, case C-649/18, October 1, 2020.
Abubacarr Jawo v. Bundesrepublik Deutschland, case C-163/17, March 19, 2019.
Academia de Studii Economice din București v. Organismul Intermediar pentru Programul Operațional Capital Uman—Ministerul Educației Naționale, case C-585/19, March 17, 2021.
Aleksei Petruhhin, case C-182/15, September 6, 2016.
C.G. v. The Department for Communities in Northern Ireland, case C-709/20, July 15, 2021.
C. K. and Others v. Republika Slovenija, case C-578/16, February 16, 2017.
Cimade and Groupe d'information et de soutien des immigrés (GISTI) v. Ministre de l'Intérieur, de l'Outre-mer, des Collectivités territoriales et de l'Immigration, case C-179/11, September 27, 2012.
Criminal Proceedings Against X., case C-507/10, December 21, 2011.
E.Q. v. Administration de l'Enregistrement, des Domaines et de la TVA, case C-846/19, April 15, 2021.
Elisabeta Dano and Florin Dano v. Jobcenter Leipzig, case C-333/13, November 11, 2014.
F. v. Bevándorlási és Állampolgársági Hivatal, case C-473/16, January 25, 2018.
Fédération des maisons de repos privées de Belgique (Femarbel) ASBL v. Commission communautaire commune de Brussels-Capitale, case C-57/12, July 11, 2013.
Flaminio Costa v. E.N.E.L., case C-6, July 15, 1964.
Fulvio Fonzi v. Commission of the EAEC, case C-27/64 and 30/64, July 8, 1965.
Hungary v. European Parliament and Council of the European Union, case C-156/21, February 16, 2022.
International Stem Cell Corporation v. Comptroller General of Patents, Designs and Trade Marks, case C-364/13, December 18, 2014.
Jobcenter Berlin Neukölln v. Nazifa Alimanovic and Others, case C-67/14, September 15, 2015.
K.S. and Others v. The International Protection Appeals Tribunal and Others, case C-322/19 and C-385/19, January 14, 2021.
K. v. Landkreis Gifhorn, case C-519/20, March 10, 2022.
K. v Staatssecretaris van Veiligheid en Justitie and H.F. v. Belgische Staat, case C-331/16 and C-366/16, May 2, 2018.
Kingdom of the Netherlands v. European Parliament and Council of the European Union, case C-377/98, October 9, 2001.
M.L., case C-220/18, July 25, 2018.
M.P. v. Secretary of State for the Home Department, case C-353/16, April 24, 2018.
Margherita Macevicius v. European Parliament, case C-66/75, May 20, 1976.
Maria Pupino, case C-105/03, June 16, 2005.
Mittelbayerischer Verlag KG v. SM, case C-800/19, June 17, 2021.
Mohamad Zakaria, case C-23/12, January 17, 2013.
N.S. v. Secretary of State for the Home Department and M.E. and Others v. Refugee Applications Commissioner and Minister for Justice, Equality and Law Reform, case C-411/10 and C-493/10, December 21, 2011.
N.V. Algemene Transport. En Expeditie Onderneming Van Gend & Loos and Nederlandse administratie der belastingen (Netherlands Inland Revenue Administration), case C-26/62, February 5, 1963.
Oliver Brüstle v. Greenpeace eV., case C-34/10, October 18, 2011.

Omega Spielhallen und Automatenaufstellungs-GmbH v. Oberbürgermeisterin der Bundesstadt Bonn, case C-36/02, October 14, 2004.

P. v. S. and Cornwall County Council, case C-13/94, April 30, 1996.

Pál Aranyosi and Robert Căldăraru v. Generalstaatsanwaltschaft Bremen, case C-404/15 and C-659/15, April 5, 2016.

Patrick Grégor Puppinck and Others v. European Commission, case C-418/18, December 19, 2019.

The Queen, on the Application of Sean Ambrose McCarthy and Others v. Secretary of State for the Home Department, case C-202/13, December 2, 2014.

Relu Adrian Coman and Others v. Inspectoratul General pentru Imigrări and Ministerul Afacerilor Interne, case C-673/16, June 5, 2018.

Republic of Poland v. European Parliament and Council of the European Union, case C-157/21, February 16, 2022.

S. Coleman v. Attridge Law and Steve Law, case C-303/06, July 17, 2008.

Vestische Arbeit Jobcenter Kreis Recklinghausen v. Jovanna García-Nieto and Others, case C-299/14, February 25, 2016.

Vueling Airlines SA v. Instituto Galego de Consumo de la Xunta de Galicia, case C-487/12, September 18, 2014.

XXXX v. Commissaire général aux réfugiés et aux apatrides, case C-483/20, February 22, 2022.

Zubair Haqbin v. Federaal Agentschap voor de opvang van asielzoekers, case C-233/18, November 12, 2019.

7 A Multi-approach to Human Dignity in the European Court of Human Rights

Eugenia Relaño Pastor

Introduction: Dignity as a Controversial Concept

Many legal scholars, practitioners, and judges could easily agree that human dignity is central to law and simultaneously disagree on why the concept is relevant. As Schroeder notes, "pessimistically speaking, one might argue that the power of the concept lies in its vagueness" (Schroeder 2012, 326). The variety of meanings of the term "human dignity," its lack of legal definition, as well as its ambiguousness from a philosophical point of view, have rendered human dignity a more controversial concept than human rights (Macklin 2003; Pinker 2008; Ullrich 2003). Although the concept can be clarified significantly, it is accepted that dignity has diverse meanings (Donnelly 1982; Schroeder 2010; Sensen 2011).

The plurality of meaning and the lack of objective criteria to define the term "human dignity" have not prevented courts from using the term as a legal tool. Indeed, the concept has become essential in judicial making and plays a fundamental role in the adjudication of human rights' claims (McCrudden 2008). However, judicial interpretation of the concept of human dignity has not contributed to sketching a discernible common notion (McCrudden 2008, 712). As discussed further in this chapter, human dignity in courts has evolved as a subsidiary notion that reinforces specific human rights discourse and as a normative-axiological stand meaning, the ultimate legal value or a value of humanness (Riley 2010).

The complexity of debates surrounding human dignity is vast, since dignity has been discussed extensively in legal and political philosophy from different perspectives (Donnelly 2015; Habermas 2010; Shultziner 2003; Waldron 2013). Historically, the notion of human dignity has unfolded in many directions. An aristocratic use of dignity developed in ancient Roman times, particularly in Cicero's *De officiis*. Cicero argued for a universal *dignitas*, which imposes on human beings the duty to act conforming to reason (Sensen 2011, 83). In a similar vein, Pope Leo the Great's sermons contain the earliest known usages of the Latin *dignitas* by a Christian thinker and depict human beings as elevated over the rest of nature and created in the image of God, with the duty to act accordingly. Human dignity also emerged as a prominent topic

DOI: 10.4324/9781003307853-9

during the Renaissance. In his *Discourse on the Dignity of Man* (1486), Pico della Mirandola introduced notions of capacity and morality to the concept of human dignity. He underlined the duty of all humans to realize fully their dignity but did not refer to dignity as a value property, as do contemporary paradigms of human dignity. Similarly, Kant connects dignity to duties toward the self and asserts that the reason one should respect others is not because others possess a value property called "dignity" but because the Categorical Imperative demands such respect: "the duty of respect for my neighbor is contained in the maxim not to degrade any other to a mere means to my ends" (Hill 1992; Sensen 2019, 192).[1]

These traditional conceptions of dignity (Cicero, Leo, Pico, and Kant) do not focus on the dignity of others but on the realization of one's own dignity as a duty to oneself. In contrast, the most extended contemporary usage of human dignity refers to human dignity as an inherent value of human beings and as the justification for human rights.

The first part of the chapter discusses the expansion of human dignity's plurality of meanings after World War II in legal philosophy, in order to outline a typology of six notions of human dignity. Taking into account human dignity's multivocal features, this typology serves as a convenient tool for unearthing the different usages of human dignity in the European Court of Human Rights (ECtHR) jurisprudence. This controversial term has been invoked both by parties in cases heard by the Court, dissenting judges of the Court, third parties, and national authorities in the framework of the margin appreciation doctrine. Since analyzing the vast number of Strasbourg cases concerning human dignity is an arduous task, I have selected key cases in which human dignity has played a significant role in elucidating current trends in so-called "dignity cases."

Toward a Typology for Human Dignity: Six Notions of Dignity

It was only after World War II that the philosophical concept of human dignity, which had already existed in antiquity and acquired its current canonical expression in Kant (Hill 1992), found its normative way into texts of international law and post-war national constitutions. Deriving from the United Nations Charter, the Universal Declaration of Human Rights, and the two core UN international human rights instruments—the International Covenant on Civil and Political Rights and the International Covenant on Economic, Social and Cultural Rights—dignity appears not to have had a specific cultural meaning. Nevertheless, the connection between human dignity and human rights was openly recognized in both covenants when declaring that the rights therein derive from the inherent dignity of the human person.[2] Human dignity seems thus to be characterized as a kind of ground normativity within the system, although there is no international texts specify how dignity could be realized through norms or law (Le Moli 2019; Riley 2010, 122).

Even though the concept of dignity has been accepted as a starting point for many constitutions, many philosophical and legal questions remain open and undecided: How do we understand human dignity in connection to human rights? Should courts apply the concept as a universal meta-principle or is it a contextual-relational concept? How can legal practitioners distinguish when dignity is rhetorical or fundamental to a person's claim?

Dignity as a Foundational Notion

As a foundation for human rights, dignity has been included in many constitutions and has become the source and supreme value on which all rights, duties, and state actions depend (Shulztiner and Carmi 2014). The constitutions of Germany, South Africa, Greece, Portugal, Spain, Belgium, Sweden, Switzerland, and other liberal-democratic states voice a strong affinity between human dignity and human rights, since the former is considered justification of the latter. When the individual is the source of normative claims that are not conditional on any state or government, the person is considered as a whole, rather than as possessing individual, divisible rights. This is what Michael Walzer (1994) calls "the thick meaning of human dignity." This thick meaning encapsulates a whole moral worldview and is crucial when debating important issues such as self-worth, the death penalty, abortion, bioethics, torture, and degrading human treatment. The main criticism of the foundational concept of human dignity is that without reference to religious authority, it is much more difficult to justify that all human beings have inherent dignity than to justify that all human beings have human rights (Waldron 2013). Multiple religious and philosophical theories seek to justify an assumption that every human being has intrinsic worth. However, for some philosophers, such as Richard Rorty (2000), it is unclear why respect for human dignity must presuppose the existence of inherent worth.[3] In any case, a foundational notion of human dignity presupposes a certain idea about human beings and affords an equal dignity to all human beings (Masferrer 2016).

Dignity as a Bridging Notion

Jeremy Waldron and Jack Donnelly developed the idea that the relationship between human rights and dignity should be reversed. Dignity is then no longer the foundation for human rights but rather informs the content of human rights and plays a role as a connector among human rights (Donnelly 2015; Waldron 2013). Waldron states that dignity is a status concept, not a value concept, and as status, dignity comprises a given set or list of rights. The list is not arbitrary. Instead, it should be a list that rationally relates to some underlying idea that informs the status in question; it is a matter of having a common rationale explaining how various rights and duties go together. If human dignity is a status, then it comprises not just a set of human rights but an underlying idea that explains both the importance of each right in relation to our being human and the importance of their being packaged together in this regard. This notion of dignity points not just to the rights that constitute a particular status but the underlying idea that unifies them. Consequently, as Waldron writes, "we can stress that we do not have human rights because we have human dignity, but our having human dignity is our having human rights" (Waldron 2013, 25). Likewise, Donnelly notes that "rather than human rights growing up out the ground of human dignity, human rights have reached down into the ground of human dignity, rooting themselves there and, in the process, have reworked and reshaped that ground" (Donnelly 2015, 14).

Dignity as a Progressive and Self-realization Notion

Identifying dignity with self-worth also implies respecting individuals' well-being throughout their lives. From this perspective, dignity is synonymous with individuality and is an "animating factor" that provides meaning to a continuous and dynamic positive sense of self-worth. It is important to distinguish between two sub-concepts of human dignity to fully understand dignity as a progressive notion. On one hand, "status dignity" (the foundational approach to dignity) grounds respect for dignity on the inner worth of every human being. Status dignity is not a matter of degree; but permanent because "everyone has dignity." In contrast, achievement dignity refers to the respect-worthy status of a person's beings and doings and is a matter of degree. It is generally not a permanent or stable property since it can come and go. For example, in certain situations, we may say an individual "lost his/her dignity" or "was undignified."

From a self-realization perspective, dignity is additionally a facilitator of choice, whether in relation to sexual orientation, personal expression, or personal self-fulfillment. When human dignity is understood in terms of the human need for positive self-worth, we should prioritize the "sense of our worth" as an essential primary good and a criterion of justice in Rawlsian terminology (Rawls 1971), based on attributes of human personality acquired through a lifetime (Shulztiner and Rabinovici 2012). If Habermas underlines that "the infinite dignity of each person consists in his claim that all others should respect the inviolability of this domain of free will" (Habermas 2010, 474), Nussbaum adds that free will requires some minimal capacities for the agency since the "notion of dignity is closely related to the idea of active striving" (Nussbaum 2011, 31). In Martha Nussbaum's capabilities theory, capabilities and dignity are intertwined concepts, and the ten central capabilities on her list are ways of realizing a life with human dignity (Nussbaum 2006, 161).

Dignity as a Descriptor Attached to a Specific Context

"Dignity as a descriptor" is a contextual and cultural concept of human dignity and a pragmatic approach to this concept. Being contextual and pragmatic does not mean being relativist. Waldron (2013) merges the two apparently incommensurable approaches to human rights—universalism and relativism—in a theorization of dignity. He draws attention to the paradoxical fact that the egalitarian concept of human dignity results from a generalization of particularistic dignities that must not lose the connotation of "fine distinctions." The issue is the individual's worth in horizontal relations between different human beings in context, not the status of "human beings" in a vertical relation to God. Therefore, human dignity is inseparably understood as granting all citizens equal rights without any sort of discrimination. Charles Taylor (1992) observed that "with the move from honor to dignity has come a politics of universalism, emphasizing the equal dignity of all citizens, and the contents of this politics has been the equalization of rights and entitlements" (37). But such equality can only be possible by taking into consideration the specificities and diversities of each human being. Indeed, as Taylor explained, the politics of difference are themselves part of the politics of dignity. Instead of demanding equal rights and treatment, individuals demand recognition of their distinctness and unique identity (Cooke 2009).

This social-historical move has generated two tendencies in politics: the politics of equal dignity and the politics of difference. "With the politics of equal dignity, what is established is meant to be universally the same, an identical basket of rights and immunities; with the politics of difference, what we are asked to recognize is the unique identity of this individual or group, their distinctness from everyone else" (Taylor 1992, 38). Indeed, the Inter-American Court of Human Rights has developed the unwritten right to identity through case law in claims related to arbitrary arrest, mass expulsion, or disappearance of persons.[4]

It is important to note here that the development of identity can be hampered due to a lack of material and non-material resources. Following Nussbaum's capabilities theory, many human beings do not lead lives of human dignity due to socio-economic deprivations or various forms of social oppression. Nussbaum equates dignity with flourishing; thus, access to resources and developing of capabilities up to an ample threshold are necessary to lead a dignified human life (Formosa and Mackenzie 2014, 879).

A Subjective Approach to Dignity: The "Vulnerability Card"

The notion of human dignity also protects individuals from humiliation and other threats to people's self-worth. There is a close affinity, as Shultziner and Rabinovici (2012) point out, between dignity and individuals' perception of their self-esteem and worth (109). This approach to dignity implies recognition of individuals' dignity through their vulnerability. Violations of dignity are acts that humiliate and injure or diminish a person's or group's self-esteem. In degrading treatment situations, human dignity may be precisely defined not only by a list of concrete immoral conduct but also through the victims' eyes. Therefore, instances of humiliation can involve diminution—of lowering the person who is being humiliated relative to the person who humiliates. In other cases, the diminution of self-worth may involve passive behavior, apart from or in addition to active behavior, that injures self-worth, excludes socially, or fosters the feeling or perception of such injury or exclusion.

Perceptions vary significantly between individuals and between groups across society, but one key aspect to consider is the way people perceive their vulnerability and interpret the laws that affect them (Henkin 1992, 226). Additionally, it must be noted that the vulnerability of individuals should be seen in light of the abilities that constitute their autonomy and their particular context. Acknowledgment of vulnerability implies not only acknowledging individuals' subjective perceptions of their vulnerability but also acknowledging the dignity of so-called "vulnerable populations": the elderly, children, disabled persons, and others (Haugen 2010, 209).

Human Dignity as a Limitation on Human Rights

As mentioned, dignity relies on the assumption of the intrinsic worth of every human being, and human dignity has been the standard for protecting and safeguarding the rights of people. In this respect, the notion implies positive obligations on the state's part to guarantee the protection of everyone's dignity. However, dignity could also be used as a significant constraint to human rights when states impose limitations on human dignity and human rights on behalf of public interest, morals, or safety.[5] Public morals often reflect a collective identity, the majoritarian one, and a particular understanding of what individual human dignity should entail. Identity theories place individual and collective identity in a mutually constitutive relationship. "Collective identities are in constant interplay with personal identities," Polleta, Francesca, and James M. Jasper (2001) argue (298); therefore, individual human dignity realized through personal identity can be reinforced by the collective identity. However, collective ascriptions could also shape the abstract concept of public morals and constrain agency and critical distance for individuals within that collective by oppressing their autonomy and self-determination (Mende 2016, 140).

Furthermore, two sides of a dispute often employ dignity to support their respective rights claims. Many freedom-of-expression cases have dealt with competing claims and interests, for example, and dignity arguments have become a rationale on both sides. In that context, courts have played an essential and decisive role in Western democracies when applying state arguments to public orders or public morals exceptions. Therefore, tensions between conflicting interests and rights exist between individuals and society or between individuals' and states' interests. The latter can potentially restrict a person's rights by applying an illiberal dignity reading. Illiberal applications of dignity happen when general limitations—some constitutions include dignity as a restriction to specific rights[6]—override basic fundamental rights or impose citizen duties toward the state.[7]

The typology of six dignity notions is neither exhaustive nor intended to be categorical. Assessing the approaches of Strasbourg Court judges to dignity claims is challenging. In addressing them, they may mix some of the described categories in a single judgment or combine approaches for rhetorical purposes, to reinforce the relevance of the dispute to human rights included in the European Convention. Additionally, the following case studies not only show that the concept of dignity varies among Council of Europe (CoE) member states but also reveal that enforcement of the notion in each national jurisdiction—as a norm, right, value, or inspiring principle—is very diverse. By analyzing Strasbourg jurisprudence through the lens of the six understandings of human dignity, I aim to add clarity to the discussion of judicial interpretation of the concept of human dignity, to provide avenues for further understanding of dignity in courts.

Human Dignity in the European Court of Human Rights

Human dignity was explicitly included in all major human rights declarations and treaties except the European Convention on Human Rights and Fundamental Freedoms (ECHR). The preamble of the ECHR speaks of justice, peace, democracy, and the rule of law, but not of dignity.[8] The first time "dignity" in the European Convention system's constantly extended treaties as late as 2002. In Protocol No. 13 on the abolition of the death penalty, the text states that such abolition is essential for the full recognition of the inherent dignity of all human beings. Despite this absence, European human rights law comprises an extensive depository of references to human dignity. For example, the European Social Charter includes dignity language and even a specific right to dignity at work, as do provisions in the Convention on Human Rights and Biomedicine. As a result of the prominence of human dignity in human rights discourse, Art. 1 of the EU Charter of Fundamental Rights proclaimed: "Human dignity is inviolable. It must be respected and protected." Thus, the dignity of the human person is recognized not only as a fundamental right in itself but as the real basis of fundamental rights. In fact, the EU Court of Justice has confirmed that a fundamental right to human dignity is part of EU law (Netherlands v European Parliament and Council, par. 70–77).[9]

The Strasbourg Court's jurisprudence has developed and interpreted the rights enshrined in the European Convention on Human Rights and, even though that the Convention lacks explicit mention of human dignity, the Court engages the notion of human dignity in several contexts: the right to life and the end of life (Art. 2); prohibition of torture and cruel, inhuman, and degrading treatment (Art. 3); right to respect for private and family life (Art. 8); freedom of expression (Art. 10); prohibition of slavery and forced labor (Art. 4); health-related cases and biomedical issues (Arts. 2, 3, 8 and 14); immigration and human trafficking (Arts. 3 and 4); discrimination (Art. 14); prohibition of abuse of rights (Art. 17), and others.

However, the Court has not used the notion of human dignity systematically; on the contrary, the Strasbourg Court's jurisprudence shows that the Court understands human dignity in various ways reflecting the typology described. The remainder of this chapter discusses how the Court has applied different notions of human dignity and how Strasbourg judges often rely exclusively on one concept of human dignity or, at other times, use several approaches to dignity in a single case.

According to Kuteynikov and Boyashov (2017), the number of judgments involving "dignity" and "human dignity" in the 20th century did not exceed a dozen in a year. Since 2001, dignity-related judgments have steadily increased in number. From 2001 to 2005, the Court delivered 126 dignity judgments; from 2006 to 2010, the Court published another 412 dignity judgments; and from 2011 until June, 9, 2015, the Court issued 553 such judgments (89). Most cases in which dignity appears involve Article 3 of the ECHR. In fact, out of 1482 judgments (through May 1, 2018) dealing with Art. 3, 852 mention dignity (Bedford 2019). Human dignity became an essential reference in judicial adjudication in the 21st century. Applicants, government representatives, and judges articulated different legal formulations interpreting human dignity at the ECtHR.

One may ask, why the increasing importance of dignity at the Strasbourg Court in this century? There is no single answer; rather, the increase is likely due to a combination of factors. First is the impact in the CoE region of the prominent role of dignity—as a chapter and an article—in the 2000 European Union Charter of Fundamental Rights. When the EU Charter became part of the treaty establishing a constitution for Europe, it developed into a legally binding document for EU Member States that are also part of the CoE. In the EU Charter, human dignity achieves an axiological and normative meaning and also becomes a "framework right" or "mother-right" for other, more specific rights based on it (Barak 2015, 156). Second, before 1945 only five countries used the term "dignity" in their constitutions, while 162 did so in 2012 (Shulztiner and Carmi 2014, 461), indicating that constitutional jurisprudence concerning dignity has gradually increased in this century. Third, judicial practice and doctrine have converged around its presence in various fields of study, including legal philosophy, political science, human rights, and international law.

A Foundational Notion of Dignity

In the first category, dignity is seen as providing the foundation for human rights in general, as key support for why humans should have rights and the limits of these rights. Dignity is the basis for human rights to exist (Carozza 2008; McCrudden 2008); indeed, the Strasbourg Court has reiterated that it is the essence of the European Convention. The foundational role of dignity could be applied to any right of the Convention, but in the context of Art. 3, human dignity becomes integral to the very essence of the ECHR

(Riley 2010, 124). Interpretations of the European Commission and Court of Human Rights of the Art. 3 ECHR have drawn extensively on the concept of human dignity as a basis for their decisions.

The first reference to human dignity appeared in the Commission's decision in the *East African Asian* case where the racial discrimination, the applicants were subjected to constituted an infringement of their human dignity and, due to the particular circumstances of the case, amounted to degrading treatment. In another case, *Ireland v. The United Kingdom*, Judge Sir Gerald Fitzmaurice provided a separate opinion in which he identified the concept of human dignity as central to the idea of what constituted "degrading" treatment under Art. 3 of the ECHR.[10] And Judge Evrigenis, in his separate opinion, insisted on the development of an extensive notion of torture that includes dignity as a key to identifying what is protected under the prohibition on inhuman treatment.[11]

Since 1973, the interpretation of the content of Article 3 has evolved with jurisprudence. One of the most important cases involving the threshold for what constitutes ill-treatment or inhuman or degrading treatment is *Bouyid v. Belgium*. In this case, the Grand Chamber overturned the Chamber's judgment and declined to follow previously established case law. It concluded that an unjustified and unnecessary slap in the face of a (17-year-old) person arrested by a police officer was sufficient to cross the threshold. The Grand Chamber considered the concept of dignity in detail, taking into consideration several international human rights texts and stating that "although the Convention does not mention that concept—which nevertheless appears in the Preamble to Protocol No. 13 to the Convention, concerning the abolition of the death penalty in all circumstances—the Court has emphasized that respect for human dignity forms part of the very essence of the Convention" (*Bouyid v. Belgium*, par. 89). In finding that the punishment in question was degrading within the meaning of Article 3 of the Convention, the Court noted that:

> although the applicant did not suffer any severe or long-lasting physical effects, his punishment—whereby he was treated as an object in the power of the authorities—constituted an assault on precisely that which it is one of the main purposes of Article 3 to protect, namely a person's dignity and physical integrity.
>
> (*Bouyid v. Belgium*, par. 90)[12]

The Court applied a strict foundational notion of human dignity in which no human being can be treated as an object because of the absolute intrinsic value of a person regardless of "whatever the impact [referring to the physical force] on the person in question" (*Bouyid v. Belgium*, par. 101). One year after *Bouyid*, in *Khlaifia and Others v. Italy*, a case involving the removal of a large group of Tunisian sea-migrants after each had been identified individually, the Grand Chamber clarified when treatment falls within Art. 3 of the Convention and emphasized that adjudicating the severity of ill-treatment requires taking into account a variety of circumstances within which it took place.[13]

The foundational approach to dignity has been challenged in French and US courts by the controversial dwarf-tossing cases. Dwarf tossing has served as a test case to rethink the theory of human dignity (McGee 1993). The rights of dwarves to earn an income and do what they want with their own bodies must be balanced against the interests of society in not allowing people to engage in dehumanizing activities. Applying a negative rights argument, dwarves have an absolute right to do with their bodies whatever they want so long as they do not violate others' rights (Leget, Borry, and de Vries 2009). In contrast, a positive rights argument starts with the assumption that someone other than the dwarf ("mankind") has rights that conflict with that of the dwarf. However, those who argue that the right of "mankind" not to be dehumanized should be balanced against the right of dwarves to bodily autonomy must also consider that "mankind" has no rights as such. "Mankind" is a collective term with no independent existence.

In *Manuel Wackenheim v. France*, the European Commission of Human Rights declared inadmissible the claim of Mr Wackenheim, who suffered from dwarfism and worked in the "dwarf tossing" business. The appellant brought his claim to European human rights institutions alleging violation of his right to freedom, employment, respect for private life, an adequate standard of living, and right to non-discrimination. Before the Commission's decision, the French Council of State had upheld a "dwarf-throwing" ban by the mayor of Morsang-Sur-Orge because the activity undermines the dignity of the human person, which is a component of public order. The case later reached the UN Human Rights Committee, which did not address the balancing of rights and concluded that the ban on dwarf tossing was based on objective and reasonable criteria.

Dignity as a Bridging Notion

Another important role that dignity can play is to connect different human rights at play. In *Identoba v. Georgia*, the Chamber held that there was a violation of Art. 3 in conjunction with Art. 14 (prohibition on discrimination) and, unanimously, that there was also a violation of Art. 11 (freedom of assembly and association) in conjunction with Art. 14. The case concerned a peaceful demonstration in Tbilisi in May, 2012, to mark International Day Against Homophobia, which was violently disrupted by counterdemonstrators outnumbering the marchers. The Court noted that authorities knew or ought to have known the risks surrounding the demonstration; therefore, authorities had been obligated but failed to provide adequate protection for it to be held peacefully. *Identoba* suggested that human dignity is the touchstone for determining whether discriminatory treatment violates Art. 3. The Court recognized that bias-motivated verbal abuse, or hate speech, combined with aggressive behavior that arouses feelings of fear and anguish, is incompatible with human dignity. More specifically, the Court highlighted that "treatment which is grounded upon a predisposed bias on the part of a heterosexual majority against a homosexual minority may, in principle, fall within the scope of Article 3" (*Identoba v. Georgia*, par. 65); therefore, authorities had a duty to provide "heightened protection" for a vulnerable community on the state's part. In *Identoba*, human dignity appears as a connector notion that glues together human rights with situations of vulnerability and discrimination as well as with the state's obligation to protect its citizens.

A similar case on discrimination, in which human dignity demanded positive duties from the state, was *Nachova v. Bulgaria*, a case concerning a fatal shooting by military police soldiers of two Roma persons. The Court's ruling made clear that European states have an obligation to investigate possible racist motives behind acts of violence because:

> racial violence is a particular affront to human dignity and, in view of its perilous consequences, requires from the authorities special vigilance and a vigorous reaction. It is for this reason that the authorities must use all available means to combat racism and racist violence, thereby reinforcing democracy's vision of a society in which diversity is not perceived as a threat but as a source of its enrichment.
>
> (*Nachova v. Bulgaria*, par. 145)

Another representative case that brings together three articles from the Convention, with human dignity in a bridging role, is *Behar and Gutman v. Bulgaria*. The Court dealt with the positive obligations of the state to protect specific groups—Jewish and Roma—from discriminatory public statements made by a politician. The question was whether negative public statements about a social group could affect the "private life" of that group's individual members and the applicants' honor or dignity, owing to their ethnic identity, to the point of triggering the application of Art. 8. The Court reasoned, based on its prior case law (see *Perinçek v. Switzerland*; *Lewit v. Austria*; *Aksu v. Turkey*). that negative stereotyping of the group had to reach a certain level. The "certain level" will depend on the impact on the sense of identity of an ethnic or social group and the circumstances of each specific case.

A final area in which dignity is pivotal to determining connections among human rights enshrined in the ECHR is in violations of physical, psychological, or moral integrity. The Court indicated for the first time that the concept of private life covered the physical and moral integrity of the person in *X and Y v. The Netherlands*. The case concerned a sexual assault of a mentally disabled 16-year-old teenager. Regarding the protection of a person's physical and psychological integrity from another individual, the Court held that authorities' positive obligations include a duty to apply an adequate legal framework affording protection against acts of violence by private individuals. Therefore, Arts. 2 and 3 were considered in combination with Art. 8.

Dignity as a Progressive and Self-realization Notion

Dignity as a principle requires respect for the free development of human personality since the capacity of self-transformation is constitutive of a human person. As a self-realization notion, dignity appears in many complex cases involving the right to life and the end of life, and, in the context of biomedical sciences, issues regarding medically assisted procreation, pregnancy, birth, the right to know one's biological identity, transgender surgery, etc. In such cases, appeals to *dignity as liberty* invoke the values of autonomy and free development of personality, whereas appeals to *dignity as life* relate to claims associated with the regulation of birth, sex, or death—acts that symbolically express the value of human life itself (Siegel 2013, 513).

Concerning the right to life and protection of the unborn life, the Strasbourg Court has declined to rule on when life begins or whether the unborn child is a person or has intrinsic dignity for purposes of Art. 2. In *Vo v. France*, a doctor performed a medical procedure on the applicant intended for another person. As a result, the applicant had to terminate her pregnancy. The applicant complained that her unborn child's lack of criminal-law protection violated Art. 2 of the Convention since there was no clear legal definition of the unborn child or a European consensus on the status of the embryo. As the Court stated, "in French law the Court has yet to determine the issue of the 'beginning' of 'everyone's right to life' within the meaning of this provision and whether the unborn child has such a right" (*Vo v. France*, par 85).

End-of-life cases put the Strasbourg Court in a difficult position. Even assuming states have positive obligations under Art. 8 (private life and family life) to take measures to facilitate suicide with dignity, the question is how to measure when a respondent state fails to comply with that obligation.[14] The Court analyzed the question of assisted suicide for the first time in *Pretty v. The United Kingdom*, involving an applicant dying from a degenerative disease. Because the latest stage of the disease would leave the applicant in an undignified condition, she wished to be able to control how and when she would die. She complained to the Court that the authorities refused to give an advance undertaking not to prosecute her husband if he assisted her in committing suicide, since she could not do so by herself. The Court stated that the consistent emphasis in all cases before the Court had been the obligation of the state to protect life. The Court was not persuaded that:

> the right to life guaranteed in Article 2 can be interpreted as involving a negative aspect. . . . Article 2 of the Convention is phrased in different terms. It is unconcerned with issues to do with the quality of living or what a person chooses to do with his or her life. To the extent that these aspects are recognized as fundamental to the human condition that they require protection from State interference, they may be reflected in the

> rights guaranteed by other Articles of the Convention or other international human rights instruments. Article 2 cannot, without a distortion of language, be interpreted as conferring the diametrically opposite right, namely a right to die; nor can it create a right to self-determination in the sense of conferring on an individual the entitlement to choose death rather than life.
>
> (*Pretty v. The United Kingdom*, par. 39)

In *Pretty*, the Court also gave an overview of the meaning of "private life" as an area that "covers the physical and psychological integrity of a person" that will "sometimes embrace aspects of an individual's physical and social identity" (*Pretty v. The United Kingdom*, par. 193).

Many dignity-based complex cases are examples of intra-rights conflicts in which values are "balanced" against each other. For example, a problem of incommensurability appeared in *Evans v. The United Kingdom* between two dignity claims grounded in a person's self-realization and the right to have a family, each invoked by a party in the conflict (Mrs Evans and Mr J). Mrs Evans complained that domestic law permitted her former partner effectively to withdraw his consent to the storage and her use of embryos created jointly by them, preventing her from ever having a child to whom she would be genetically related. She relied on Arts. 2, 8, and 14 of the Convention. The Grand Chamber held no violation of Art. 2 and Art. 8, or a breach of Art. 14 in conjunction with Art. 8. The Court held that the applicant's right to choose to be a genetic parent did not trump her partner's right to choose not to be a genetic parent.

This approach unveils a dilemma. On the one hand, by allowing the destruction of Mrs Evans' eggs, the woman is effectively deprived of the right to decide to have a genetically related child, which inflicts "such a disproportionate moral and physical burden on a woman that it can hardly be compatible with Article 8 and the very purposes of the Convention protecting human dignity and autonomy" (see joint dissenting opinion of Judges Türmen, Tsatsa-nikolovska, Spielmann and Ziemele in *Haas v. Switzerland*, par 13). On the other hand, the genetic father's dignity could also be impaired since an IVF treatment with his genetic material without his continuing consent infringes on his private life and life plan. As McCrudden explained by quoting Adler, "One approach to conflicts of this kind is to say that resolving such conflicts is not a role for the courts . . . when reaching the stage where values conflict we must employ emotions to resolve the conflicts" (McCrudden 2008, 715).

Another dignity-related case involving an individual's capacity for self-realization, transformation, and development is *Vinter v. The United Kingdom*. The Court considered whether imposing a whole life sentence without the possibility of release or case review was a violation of Art. 3. The Court's opinion echoed the concept that capacity for self-transformation is constitutive to the human person, and therefore, the destiny of the human life should not be predetermined (Bedford 2019, 186). In the concurring opinion, Judge Power-Forde explained that:

> Article 3 encompasses what might be described as 'the right to hope'. . . . The judgment recognizes, implicitly, that hope is an important and constitutive aspect of the human person. . . . Long and deserved though their prison sentences may be, they retain the right to hope that, someday, they may have atoned for the wrongs which they have committed. . . . To deny them the experience of hope would be to deny a fundamental aspect of their humanity and, to do that, would be degrading.
>
> (*Vinter v. the United Kingdom*, Judge Power-Forde's Concurring Opinion)

Such reasoning suggests that dignity as a self-realization or progressive notion is also based on a fundamental principle that dignity includes hoping for dignity.[15]

Dignity as a Descriptor Attached to a Specific Context

In a collection of case law, context is crucial in deciding dignity claims involving detention, prisons, extradition, hospital internment, and asylum seeking. In such cases, living conditions and personal circumstances are essential to identifying a violation of human dignity. In the first case involving Art. 3, *Tyrer v. The United Kingdom*, a 15-year-old boy was sentenced to three strokes of a birch rod (Finer and Wadham 2019, 158–59). The applicant was required to lower his trousers and underpants and lean over a table. His father and doctor were present when the police carried out the sentence. The Court stated that although the physical effects of the punishment were not severe, the situation involved a particular level of humiliation and debasement. The Court relied on the context as well as the subjective perception of humiliation. It observed that:

> publicity may be a relevant factor in assessing whether a punishment is 'degrading' within the meaning of Article 3 (art. 3), but the Court does not consider that absence of publicity will necessarily prevent a given punishment from falling into that category: it may well suffice that the victim is humiliated in his own eyes, even if not in the eyes of others.
>
> (*Tyrer v. The United Kingdom*, par. 32)

Another set of cases where context is crucial to adjudicate a claim under Art. 3 involve the living conditions of immigrants and asylum seekers. A number of cases have reached the Strasbourg Court addressing the degrading conditions in which would-be immigrants and asylum seekers were held (inter alia, *Tarakhel v Switzerland*; *S.D v Greece*; *Tabesh v Greece*). In *M.S.S. v. Belgium and Greece*, the Grand Chamber recognized that exposure to certain conditions can be incompatible with human dignity. Here, the Court emphasized that the applicant's emotional suffering and difficult living conditions, "combined with the prolonged uncertainty in which he has remained and the total lack of any prospects of his situation improving, have attained the level of severity required to fall within the scope of Article 3 of the Convention" (par. 263). In such cases, vulnerability is a key concept in the lives of asylum seekers who face a lack of support, uneasy economic conditions, no access to employment, inability to meet physical needs, and a lack of any realistic options for overcoming their abased situation.

Detention facilities for the mentally ill are another vulnerable context where degrading treatment is more likely to occur. *M.S. v. The United Kingdom* considered whether the transfer of a person with a psychiatric disorder from a police cell to a mental health facility constituted a violation of Art. 3. The conditions of detention played a role in conjunction with the vulnerability, and the structures of detention as a whole demonstrated a lack of concern for the needs of the applicant (Bedford 2013, 77–78). The Court held that:

> the applicant was in a state of great vulnerability throughout the entire time at the police station, as manifested by the abject condition to which he quickly descended inside his cell. He was in dire need of appropriate psychiatric treatment, as each of the medical professionals who examined him indicated. The Court considers that this situation . . . diminished excessively his fundamental human dignity.
>
> (*M.S. v. The United Kingdom*, par. 44)

Therefore, transfers from detention facilities to correctional facilities or medical centers are often situations where the transfer's context and circumstances are inhumane for the detainees. In *Tomov and Others v. Russia*, the Strasbourg Court reiterated this approach and found a violation of Art. 3 where authorities adhered to outdated standards in prisoner transportation, including transporting some detainees in solid metal cubicles in prison vans.

Dignity Implies a Subjective Approach to Dignity

In some of the cases involving Art. 3 scrutiny, subjective criteria and the context in which applicants were placed are intertwined, and both become key factors in establishing a breach of Art. 3. Human dignity is violated when a person is subjected to various kinds of physical or psychological abuse, humiliation, and debasement, irrespective of the perpetrator's intention.[16] Although Art. 3 has been invoked in a large number of cases, two in which vulnerability played a determining role are highlighted here. In *Identoba*, the Court recognized the intense fear and anxiety suffered by one applicant before any physical assault and found that the absence of any injuries to other members of the group was "less relevant" in determining a violation of Article 3 (*Identoba and Others v. Georgia*, par. 70). And in *Oršuš and Others v. Croatia*, the Court noted that humiliation triggered by discriminatory segregation in education, based on Roma children's ethnic background, amounted to treatment contrary to Art. 3. The Strasbourg Court found the placement of applicants in situations that denied respect and value in their own eyes and in society's eyes to constitute a violation of dignity.

The subjective approach to dignity can be identified in a set of cases related to the right to private life (Art. 8) and freedom of expression (Article 10), where the ECtHR based its rulings on psychological harm suffered in conjunction with harm to the applicant's reputation. The Court also took into account the dignity inherent in an artist's manifestation of the freedom of expression. In some cases, the dignity argument appears on both sides of the conflict. One Art. 10 case with a relatively large number of references to dignity is *Vereinigung Bildender Künstler v. Austria*.[17] The applicant association alleged that the Austrian Court's decision forbidding it to continue exhibiting a collage painting by Otto Mühl violated its right to freedom of expression under Art. 10 of the Convention. The Court found that the Austrian Court's injunction was disproportionate to the aim it pursued and, therefore, not necessary in a democratic society within the meaning of Art. 10. Thus, the Court concluded that the injunction violated freedom of expression.

The joint dissenting opinion of Judges Spielmann and Jebens refers to two concepts of human dignity: an "abstract or indeterminate concept of human dignity—a concept which can in itself be dangerous since it may be used as justification for hastily placing unacceptable limitations on fundamental rights" (par. 9), and a concrete concept of the "fundamental personal dignity of others," which was central to the debate in the present case. Judges Spielmann and Jebens noted that including of Mr Meischberger's photograph in the collage painting without his permission caused him to feel profoundly humiliated and degraded. They further asserted:

> a person's human dignity must be respected, regardless of whether the person is a well-known figure or not. . . . The right to one's own image is in our view covered by Article 8 of the Convention, which protects the right to private life. Article 8 protects the right to an identity and the right to personal development, particularly in relation to the notion of personal autonomy.
>
> (*Vereinigung Bildender Künstler v. Austria*, Judges Spielmann and Jebens' Joint Dissenting Opinion, par. 14)

According to Judges Spielmann and Jebens, Mr Meischberger's dignity should be protected on the grounds of "protection of the rights of others."

The Strasbourg Court has also considered a collective and subjective perception of dignity associated with "the protection of rights of others" as the legitimate aim in Art. 10 cases where public morals were at stake (the dignity of Orthodox believers in *Mariya Alekhina and Others v. Russia* and offenses to intimate personal convictions of the population within the sphere of morals, in *Sekmadienis Ltd. v. Lithuania*). Consequently, when artistic freedom conflicts with the abstract concept of human dignity, one can observe a dignity concept linked to personality rights and another notion of dignity subordinate to public morals. Both include a subjective approach to dignity by relying on the person's and society's perception of their self-esteem and worth.

Another cluster of judgments involving dignity from a subjective point of view deals with transgender and transsexual issues. These judgments could also be considered under the self-realization category, as vulnerability and self-realization are often connected. In *Sheffield and Horsham v. The United Kingdom*, the applicants argued without success that the failure of British legislation to recognize their new gender was an affront, to their dignity and caused them enormous distress. However, five years later the ECtHR reversed the *Sheffield* decision. In *I v. The United Kingdom* and *Christine Goodwin v. The United Kingdom*, which were handed down together, the Strasbourg Court linked the concept of human dignity and the right to private life and upheld that:

> the very essence of the Convention is respect for human dignity and human freedom. Under Article 8 of the Convention in particular, where the notion of personal autonomy is an important principle underlying the interpretation of its guarantees, protection is given to the personal sphere of each individual, including the right to establish details of their identity as individual human beings. . . . In the twenty first century the right of transsexuals to personal development and to physical and moral security in the full sense enjoyed by others in society cannot be regarded as a matter of controversy requiring the lapse of time to cast clearer light on the issues involved.
>
> (*Christine Goodwin v. The United Kingdom*, par. 90)

Human Dignity as a Limitation to Individual Personal Dignity

As previously noted, human dignity can also manifest as an aspect of the Convention's general limitations to override manifestations of fundamental rights, particularly as a legitimate aim necessary in a democratic society for the protection of morals. Hence, the notion of dignity can quickly become a screen behind which paternalism or moralism are elevated above individual freedoms.

In *Kharin v. Russia*, the applicant alleged that his unlawful detainment in a sobering-up center was a breach of his right to liberty and security. The government held that the individual's appearance while intoxicated offended human dignity and public morals, which implicated principles of public morality in terms of the protection of public dignity. Although not disputing the state's interest in protecting public morality, the Court found that detention of an individual for the mere reason that his physical appearance, under the influence of alcohol, presents an insult to public morals, is incompatible with the purpose of Art. 5 of the Convention. The Court explained that "this rationale would be only a step away from introducing a system of compulsory confinement for any abnormal appearance which might be perceived by some as offensive or insulting to human dignity and public morality." However, the Court found no violation of Art. 5. The joint dissenting opinion of Judges Rozakis, Spielmann, and Jebens highlighted that equal dignity is the basis for the equality of people and that the Court's role is to find a balance between the rights of an individual and the rights of the others. The dissent asserted that, in Kharin's case, an offensive physical appearance was not a sufficient ground on which to justify detention and that "mere public intolerance or animosity cannot justify the deprivation of a person's liberty" (Kharin v. Russia, Judges Rozakis, Spielmann, and Jebens' Joint Dissenting Opinion, par. 7–8).

The full-face veil ban cases at the Strasbourg Court highlight the conflict between the protection of the rights of others, public morals, and personal autonomy rights. In *S.A.S. v. France*, the Court upheld France's ban on the full-face veil and found that wearing the veil was a valid exercise of religion but one that prevented people in France from "living together." The applicant explicitly claimed that the ban affected her private life because her ability to wear the full-face veil was essential for her social and cultural identity. However, the Court agreed with France that when a woman covers her entire face except for her eyes, she is breaching the right of others to live in the space of socialization, which renders living together more difficult. Although "living together" is not present as a potential limitation on rights in Arts 8 and 9, the Court found that the notion of "living together" falls under the category of "protection of the rights and freedoms of others."

In *S.A.S*, and in subsequent full-face veil cases, human dignity takes on multifaceted meaning. First, human dignity implies the recognition the person's unique identity (Cooke 2009); thus, the applicants argued that the right to develop one's identity falls under the scope of Article 8. Second, the French Government insisted that the ban in *S.A.S.* had the legitimate aim of "respect for human dignity" and the measure was justified under the abstract assumption that women who wore veils were "effaced" (*S.A.S. v. France*, par 77). Contradicting this argument, the Court took the view that respect for human dignity cannot legitimately justify a blanket ban on wearing the full-face veil in public places. And third, a majority of the Court in *S.A.S.* upheld that "a legitimate aim in ensuring 'living together', through 'the observance of the minimum requirements of life in society'," is one facet of the "rights and freedoms of others" within the meaning of Art. 8.2 and Art. 9.2 of the Convention. The latter argument implies a particular way of socializing in the public sphere (free of full-face veils), which inevitably involves a certain type of public morality and leaves aside other social interactions. Therefore, respect for the minimum requirements of life in society, translated into the abstract principle of "living together," becomes a sort of "public dignity" adopted by the legislator. In this manner, a particular and non-neutral "public dignity" works as a limitation on individuals' dignity manifested through expressing of their cultural identities and religious affiliations.

Finally, it is worth mentioning another dimension of dignity that the Strasbourg Court endorses as a limitation of individual rights: the collective dignity of a group and the dignity of ancestors. In *Perinçek v. Switzerland*, a doctor in law and political activist was convicted for rejecting the legal characterization of atrocities committed by the Ottoman Empire against the Armenian people in 1915 as "genocide." The applicant's conviction intended to protect the human dignity of members of the Armenian community, who identify themselves through their cultural history, which includes the 1915 genocide.[18] The Court struck a balance between two Convention rights: the right to freedom of expression (Art. 10) and the right to respect for private life (Art. 8). While addressing the legitimate aim of protecting the rights of others by restricting freedom of expression, the Court distinguished, on one hand, the dignity of the deceased and surviving victims of the events of 1915 and subsequent years and, on the other, the dignity, including the identity, of present-day Armenians as their descendants (*Perinçek v. Switzerland*, par. 155). The Court noted the rights of Armenians to respect their and their ancestors' dignity, including the right to respect their identity constructed around the understanding that their community has suffered genocide. Interestingly, the Court accepted that both ethnic identity and the reputation of ancestors were rights protected under the "private life" of Art. 8 (*Perinçek v. Switzerland*, par. 227).

Conclusions

Dupre remarked that human dignity considers people in their unique and entire humanity, and "it is a most useful tool to protect against cumulative or compound human rights breaches" (Dupre 2019, 118). Indeed, the practice of human rights has captured the concept of human dignity, metonymically superseding its meaning and providing a broad spectrum of notions of human dignity beyond the intrinsic value of human life. This chapter has shown the plural understandings of human dignity at the European Court of Human Rights. Despite dignity's absence from the European Convention of Human Rights, the Strasbourg Court has advanced an evolutive interpretation of the Convention, according to the light of "present-day conditions" (*Tyrer v. The United Kingdom*, par. 183), and has connected the Convention's human rights to contexts by evolving and broadening the grammar of human dignity (Dzehtsiarou 2011, 1731).

The judgments analyzed here demonstrate not only that the concept of dignity varies over time and depending on the circumstances of cases but, as McCrudden highlighted, that human dignity has a polymorphous nature. Due to this nature, dignity has acquired a solid and stable role in the legal reasoning of the European Court of Human Rights. The six notions outlined here reveal that a single conception of human dignity is not discernible from the analysis of the jurisprudence. Despite this lack, the Strasbourg Court's interpretation has proven that dignity plays a fundamental role in judicial crafting. The identification of human dignity's usages and understandings could be a starting point for new "entries" in a *Dignity Dictionary* for judges and a constant reminder of how relevant this concept is, beyond its rhetorical uses, for human beings.

Notes

1 In his published writings, Kant uses the term "dignity" 111 times. The works in which the word is used most often are (ordered by the number of appearances): the *Doctrine of Virtue* (21 times), the *Groundwork of the Metaphysics of Morals* (17 times), *Religion within the Boundaries of Mere Reason* (11 times), and the *Lectures on Pedagogy* (10 times) (Sensen 2011, 92).

2 The Universal Declaration of Human Rights includes five references to human dignity (two in the Preambles and in Art. 1, 22 and 23.3) and refrains from giving a specific definition of human dignity. See Preambles of the International Covenant on Civil and Political Rights and the International Covenant on Economic, Social and Cultural Rights: "Considering that, in accordance with the principles proclaimed in the Charter of the United Nations, recognition of the inherent dignity and of the equal and inalienable rights of all members of the human family is the foundation of freedom, justice and peace in the world; Recognizing that these rights derive from the inherent dignity of the human person."

3 Rorty (2000) believes that all foundationalist attempts at justifying human rights on human dignity are doomed to fail.

4 In 2014, in *Expelled Dominican and Haitian Persons vs. The Dominican Republic*, the Inter-American Court decided that the Dominican Republic violated, among others, the right to judicial personality, a name, a nationality, and an identity. Previously, in 2005, in the case of the *Serrano-Cruz Sisters v. El Salvador* regarding the disappearance of seven- and three-years old sisters, the dissenting Judge, A. A. Cancado Trindade lamented that the Court lost an opportunity to develop the question of the right identity.

5 After September 11, 2001, the rhetoric of dignity was imposing restrictions on civil rights as part of the "war of terrorism" with the argument that the state has a duty to protect the dignity of individuals who could be affected by terrorism. See former President George W. Bush's speech when he addressed the United Nations General Assembly, United Nations Headquarters in New York: "By deliberately murdering the innocent to advance their aims, these extremists defy the fundamental principles of international order They show contempt for all who respect life and value human dignity" (Bush 2008).

6 Lebanon, Laos, Moldova, Ukraine, Azerbaijan, etc. (Shulztiner and Carmi 2014, 484).

7 See examples of illiberal uses of human dignity arguments in Mikhail Antonov's chapter in this volume.

8 What explains this absence? A former president of the European Court, Jean-Paul Costa (2014), suggested that the reason may be found in the intention to create a pragmatic, practice-oriented instrument: being pragmatics rather than dreamers.

9 See more on human dignity in jurisprudence of the CJEU in Andrea Pin's chapter.

10 Judge Sir Gerald Fitzmaurice points out that "in the present context it can be assumed that it is, or should be, intended to denote something seriously humiliating, lowering as to human dignity, or disparaging, like having one's head shaved, being tarred and feathered, smeared with filth, pelted with muck, paraded naked in front of strangers, forced to eat excreta, deface the portrait of one's sovereign or head of State, or dress up in a way calculated to provoke ridicule or contempt" (*Ireland v. United Kingdom*, Judge Fitzmaurice's Separate Opinion, para. 27)

11 Judge Evrigenis points out that "[B]y adding to the notion of torture the notions of inhuman and degrading treatment to other categories of acts causing intolerable suffering to individuals or affecting their dignity rather than to exclude from the traditional notion of torture certain apparently less serious forms of torture and to place them in the category of inhuman treatment which carries less of a 'stigma'" (*Ireland v. United Kingdom*, Judge Evrigenis's Separate Opinion).

12 There is an extensive number of judgments that have highlighted the close link between the concepts of "degrading treatment" and respect for "dignity": for example, *Kudła v. Poland*; *Valašinas v. Lithuania*; *Yankov v. Bulgaria*; and *Svinarenko and Slyadnev v. Russia*.

13 "According to the Court's well-established case-law, ill-treatment must attain a minimum level of severity if it is to fall within the scope of Art. 3. The assessment of that level is relative and depends on all the circumstances of the case, principally the duration of the treatment, its physical or mental effects and, in some cases, the sex, age and state of health of the victim" (*Khlaifia and Others v. Italy*, para. 159)

14 See *Haas v. Switzerland* regarding the refusal to provide medication necessary to the suicide of a person who had a mental illness. Unlike *Pretty v the United Kingdom*, in *Haas*, the applicant alleged that his life was difficult and painful. If he did not obtain the substance in question, the act of suicide itself would be stripped of dignity.

15 The importance of the ground of rehabilitation and reintegration has become a mandatory factor that Member States need to take into account, see *Khoroshenko v. Russia* and *Murray v. the Netherlands*, and in the post Vinter's Chamber on the subject: inter alia, *Öcalan v. Turkey*; *László Magyar v. Hungary*; *Čačko v. Slovakia*.

16 In *Rachwalski v. Poland* the Court stated that "if it sufficient if the victim is humiliated in his or her own eyes."

17 Other cases involving reputation and dignity are *Uj v. Hungary* and *Lindon and others v. France*.

18 The Coordinating Council of the Armenian Organisations in France (CCAF), acting on behalf of the 600,000-strong Armenian community in France, stated that "under international law, genocide was recognized as an attack on human dignity, which the French courts saw as a component of ordre public. Its denial likewise infringed that dignity; it affected not only history but memory, which was an integral aspect of the right to dignity" (*Perinçek v. Switzerland*, para. 184).

References

Barak, Aharon. 2015. *Human Dignity: The Constitutional Value and The Constitutional Right*. Cambridge: Cambridge University Press.

Bedford, Daniel. 2013. "'MS v United Kingdom': Article 3 of the ECHR, Detention and Mental Health." *European Human Rights Law Review* 72 (1): 77–78.

Bedford, Daniel. 2019. "Key Cases on Human Dignity under Article 3 of the ECHR." *European Human Rights Law Review* 2: 185–94.

Bush, George W. 2008. "President Bush Addresses United Nations Assembly." https://georgewbush-whitehouse.archives.gov/news/releases/2008/09/20080923-5.html.

Carozza, Paolo G. 2008. "Human Dignity and Judicial Interpretation of Human Rights: A Reply." *European Journal of International Law* 19 (5): 931–44.

Cooke, Maeve. 2009. "Beyond Dignity and Difference. Revisiting the Politics of Recognition." *European Journal of Political Theory* 8 (1): 76–95.

Costa, Jean-Paul. 2014. "Human Dignity in the Jurisprudence of the European Court of Human Rights". In *Understating Human Dignity*, edited by Christopher McCrudden, 393–402. Oxford: Oxford University Press.

Donnelly, Jack. 1982. "Human Rights and Human Dignity: An Analytic Critique of Non-Western Conceptions of Human Rights." *The American Political Science Review* 76 (2): 303–16.

Donnelly, Jack. 2015. "Normative Versus Taxonomic Humanity: Varieties of Human Dignity in the Western Tradition." *Journal of Human Rights* 14 (1): 1–22.

Dupre, Catherine. 2019. "Making Human Dignity Work." *European Human Rights Law Review* 2: 115–18.

Dzehtsiarou, Kanstantsin. 2011. "European Consensus and the Evolutive Interpretation of the European Convention on Human Rights." *German Law Journal* 12 (10): 1730–45.

Finer, Louise, and John Wadham. 2019. "Dignity, Ill-treatment and Detention." *European Human Rights Law Review* 2: 155–71.

Formosa, Paul, and Catriona Mackenzie. 2014. "Nussbaum, Kant, and the Capabilities Approach to Dignity." *Ethical Theory Moral Practice* 17 (5): 875–92.

Habermas, Jürgen. 2010. "The Concept of Human Dignity and the Realistic Utopia of Human Rights." *Metaphilosophy* 41 (4): 464–80.

Haugen, Hans Morten. 2010. "Inclusive and Relevant Language: The Use of the Concepts of Autonomy, Dignity and Vulnerability in Different Contexts." *Medicine, Health Care, and Philosophy* 13 (3): 203–13.

Henkin, Louis. 1992. "Human Dignity and Constitutional Rights." In *The Constitutions of Rights: Human Dignity and American Values*, edited by M. J. Meyer and W.A. Parent. Ithaca: Cornell University Press.

Hill, Thomas E. 1992. *Dignity and Practical Reason in Kant's Moral Theory*. Ithaca: Cornell University Press.

Kuteynikov, Alexander, and Anatoly Boyashov. 2017. "Dignity Before the European Court of Human Rights". In *Human Dignity: Establishing Worth and Seeking*, edited by Edward Sieh and Judy McGregor, 83–101. London: Palgrave Macmillan.

Le Moli, Ginevra. 2019. "The Principle of Human Dignity in International Law." In *General Principles and the Coherence of International Law*, edited by Mads Andenas, Malgosia Fitzmaurice, Attila Tanzi, and Jan Wouters, 352–68. The Hague: Brill Nijhoff.

Leget, Carlo, Pascal Borry, and Raymond de Vries. 2009. "'Nobody Tosses a Dwarf!' The Relation Between the Empirical and the Normative Reexamined." *Bioethics* 23 (4): 226–35.

Macklin, Ruth. 2003. "Dignity is a Useless Concept: It Means No More Than Respect for Persons or Their Autonomy." *British Medical Journal* 327 (7429): 1419–20.

Masferrer, Aniceto. 2016. "Taking Human Dignity More Humanely". In *Human Dignity of the Vulnerable in the Age of Rights: Interdisciplinary Perspectives*, edited Aniceto Masferrer and Emilio García-Sánchez, 221–56. New York: Springer.

McCrudden, Christopher. 2008. "Human Dignity and Judicial Interpretation of Human Rights." *European Journal of International Law* 19 (4): 655–724.

McGee, Robert W. 1993. "If Dwarf Tossing Is Outlawed, Only Outlaws Will Toss Dwarfs: Is Dwarf Tossing a Victimless Crime." *American Journal of Jurisprudence* 38 (1): 335–58.

Mende, Janne. 2016. "Collective Identity." In *Right to Identity*, edited by Paul Tiedemann, 129–50. Stuttgart: Franz Steiner Verlag.

Nussbaum, Marta. 2006. *Frontiers of Justice*. Cambridge, MA: Harvard University Press.

Nussbaum, Marta. 2011. *Creating Capabilities: The Human Development Approach*. Cambridge, MA: Harvard University Press.

Pinker, Steven. 2008. "The Stupidity of Dignity." *The New Republic*, May 28, 2008. https://newrepublic.com/article/64674/the-stupidity-dignity.

Polleta, Francesca, and James M. Jasper. 2001. "Collective Identity and Social Movements." *Annual Review of Sociology* 27: 283–305.
Rawls, John. 1971. *A Theory of Justice*. Cambridge, MA: Harvard University Press.
Riley, Stephen. 2010. "Human Dignity: Comparative and Conceptual Debates." *International Journal of Law in Context* 6 (2): 117–38.
Rorty, Richard. 2000. "Human Rights, Rationality and Sentimentality." In *The Politics of Human Rights*, edited by The Belgrade Circle, 67–81. London: Verso Books.
Schroeder, Doris. 2010. "Dignity: One, Two, Three, Four, Five, Still Counting." *Cambridge Quarterly of Healthcare Ethics* 19 (1): 119–25.
Schroeder, Doris. 2012. "Human Rights and Human Dignity. An Appeal to Separate the Conjoined Twins." *Ethnical Theory and Moral Practice* 15 (3): 323–35.
Sensen, Oliver. 2011. "Human Dignity in Historical Perspective: The Contemporary and Traditional Paradigms." *European Journal of Political Theory* 10 (1): 71–91.
Sensen, Oliver. 2019. "How to Respect Someone's Dignity." In *Kant's Concept of Dignity*, edited by Yasishi Kato and Gerhard Schönrich, 159–76. Boston: De Gruyter.
Shultziner, Doron. 2003. "Human Dignity-Functions and Meanings." *Global Jurist Topics* 3 (3): 1–21.
Shulztiner, Doron, and Guy E. Carmi. 2014. "Human Dignity in National Constitutions: Functions, Promises and Dangers." *The American Journal of Comparative Law* 62 (2): 461–90.
Shulztiner, Doron, and Itai Rabinovici. 2012. "Human Dignity, Self-Worth and Humiliation: A Comparative Legal-Psychological Approach." *Psychology, Public Policy and Law* 18 (1): 105–43.
Siegel, Reva. 2013. "Dignity and the Duty to Protect Unborn Life." *Proceedings of the British Academy* 192: 513–27.
Taylor, Charles. 1992. "The Politics of Recognition." In *Multiculturalism: Examining the Politics of Recognition*, edited by Amy Gutmann, 25–74. Princeton: Princeton University Press.
Ullrich, Dierk. 2003. "Concurring Visions: Human Dignity in the Canadian Charter of Rights and Freedoms and the Basic Law of the Federal Republic of Germany." *Global Jurist Frontiers* 3 (1): 1535–653.
Waldron, Jeremy. 2013. "Is Dignity the Foundation of Human Rights?" *New York University School of Law, Public Law Research Paper*, 12–73. https://doi.org/10.2139/ssrn.2196074.
Walzer, Michael. 1994. *Thick and Thin: Moral Argument at Home and Abroad*. Bend: University of Notre Dame Press.

Case Law

European Court of Human Rights

Aksu v. Turkey (GC), Application nos. 4149/04 and 41029/04, March 15, 2012.
Behar and Gutman v. Bulgaria, Application no. 29335/13, February 16, 2021.
Bouyid v. Belgium (GC), Application no. 23380/09, September 28, 2015.
Čačko v Slovakia, Application no. 15018/11 and 61199/12, July 22, 2014.
Christine Goodwin v. The United Kingdom (GC), Application no. 28957/95, July 11, 2002.
Dakir v. Belgium, Application no. 4619/12, July 11, 2017.
East African Asians v. The United Kingdom (3 E.H.R.R. 76), December 15, 1973.
Evans v. The United Kingdom (GC), Application no. 6339/05, April 10, 2007, Eur. Ct. H. R.

Haas v. Switzerland, Application no. 31322/07, January 20, 2011.
Identoba and Others v. Georgia, Application no. 73235/12, May 12, 2015.
Ireland v. United Kingdom, Application no. 5310/71, January 18, 1978.
Kharin v. Russia, Application no. 37345/03, February 3, 2011.
Khlaifia and Others v. Italy (GC), Application no. 16483/12, December 15, 2016.
Khoroshenko v. Russia (GC), Application no. 41418/04, June 30, 2015.
Kudła v. Poland (GC), Application no. 30210/96, October 26, 2000.
Lászlό Magyar v. Hungary, Application no. 73593/10, May 20, 2014.
Lewit v. Austria, Application no. 4782/18, October 10, 2019.
Lindon and Others v. France (GC), Applications nos. 21279/02 and 36448/02, October 22, 2007.
Mariya Alekhina and Others v. Russia, Application no. 38004/12, July 17, 2018.
M.S. v. The United Kingdom, Application no. 24527/08, May 3, 2012.
MSS v. Belgium and Greece (GC), Application no. 30696/09, January 21, 2011.
Murray v. Kingdom of the Netherlands (GC), Application no. 10511/10, April 26, 2016.
Nachova and Others v. Bulgaria (GC), Applications nos. 43577/98 and 43579/98, July 6, 2005.
Öcalan v. Turkey, Applications nos. 24069/03, 197/04, 6201/06 and 10464/07, March 18, 2014.
Oršuš and Others v. Croatia (GC), Application no. 15766/03, March 16, 2010.
Oussar c. Belgique, Application no. 37798/13, July 11, 2017.
Perinçek v. Switzerland (GC), Application no. 27510/08, October 15, 2015.
Pretty v. The United Kingdom, Application no. 2346/02, April 29, 2002.
Rachwalski v. Poland, Application no. 47709/99, July 28, 2009.
S.A.S. v. France (GC), Application no. 43835/11, July 1, 2014.
S.D. v. Greece, Application no. 53541/07, June 11, 2009.
Sekmadienis Ltd. v Lithuania, Application no. 69317/14, January 30, 2018.
Sheffield and Horsham v. The United Kingdom (GC), Application nos. 31-32/1997/815-816/1018-1019, July 30, 1998.
Svinarenko and Slyadnev v. Russsia (GC), Application no. 32541/08, July 17, 2014.
Tabesh v. Greece, Application no. 8256/07, November 26, 2009.
Tarakhel v. Switzerland (GC), Application no. 29217/12, November 4, 2014.
Tomov and Others v. Russia, Applications nos. 18255/10, 63058/10, 10270/101, 73227/11, 56201/13 and 41234/16, April 9, 2019, Eur.
Tyrer v. The United Kingdom, Application no. 5856/72, April 25, 1978.
Uj v. Hungary, Application no. 23954/10, July 19, 2011.
Valašinas v. Lithuania, Application no. 44558/98, July 24, 2001.
Vereinigung Bildener Kunstler v. Austria, Application no. 68354/01, January 25, 2007.
Vinter v. the United Kingdom (GC), Applications nos. 66069/09, 130/10 and 3896/10, July 9, 2013.
Vo v. France (GC), Application no. 53924/00, July 8, 2004.
Wackenheim contre la France, Commission (Second Chamber) Decision, Application no. 29961/96.
X and Y v. Kingdom of the Netherlands, Application no. 8978/80, March 26, 1985.
Yankov v. Bulgaria, Application no. 39084/97, December 11, 2003.

European Union Court of Justice

Case C-377/98 *Kingdom of the Netherlands v. European Parliament and Council of the European Union*, Judgment of October 9, 2001.

Inter-American Court of Human Rights

Expelled Dominican and Haitian Persons v. The Dominican Republic, August 28, 2014 (Preliminary Objections, Merits, Reparations and Costs).
Serrano Cruz Sisters v. El Salvador, March 1, 2005 (Merits, Reparations and Costs).

UN Human Rights Committee

Wackenheim v. France, Communication no. 854/1999, U.N. Doc. CCPR/C/75/D/854/1999 (2002).

8 Acknowledging Persons and Communities of Infinite Worth

The Concept of Dignity in the Jurisprudence of the South African Constitutional Court

Christine M. Venter

Introduction

South Africa, along with the Federal Republic of Germany, has been at the forefront of creating an explicit "dignity canon." Given the history of oppression and the denial of dignity that was manifested in the apartheid system (Abel 1995), it is not surprising that dignity features prominently in the South African Constitution and has become a foundational norm for many of the most significant decisions delivered by the South African Constitutional Court. While international human rights law is also predicated on the concept of dignity, as evidenced by the Universal Declaration of Human Rights and other foundational documents, the core content and requirements of dignity had, until recently, remained somewhat ambiguous in that arena. However, where international human rights law has lagged, the South African Constitutional Court has been ahead of the curve in developing a dignity jurisprudence. While scholars in other parts of the world have been divided about the content of the right to dignity and are still debating how it informs other rights, the South African Constitution and its Court have firmly established dignity as a content-laden actionable right.

While the Court has developed traditional dignity-related rights primarily centered around humane treatment, non-discrimination, and equal protection rights, as well as socio-economic rights, it has gone even further than these traditional categories. The Court has construed the Constitution and its own role as requiring the restoration and preservation of the dignity of the "previously disadvantaged" (Article 9(2) of the Constitution), as well as restoring the common good. Mindful of the deprivations of rights and liberties, and the humiliating indignities imposed on the majority of the population by the apartheid system, the Court has construed dignity as a means of healing and reforming society. It has not only recognized wrongs done to individuals and relational dignity (McCrudden 2008), but it has also acknowledged the harm done to the community and the resulting violation

DOI: 10.4324/9781003307853-10

of the community's dignity when the dignity of an individual is violated. It has thus created a social and community-based dimension to dignity—one of the more unique jurisprudential contributions that has been made by the Court.

The Court has accomplished this primarily by acknowledging, as it did in *Carmichele v. Minister of Safety and Security* (2001) that "our constitution is not merely a formal document regulating public power. It also embodies, like the German Constitution, an objective normative value system." Part of the normative South African value system is the importance of community. People are social beings, and the Constitution speaks to the value of *ubuntu*—the recognition of a bond that connects all members of society based on their common humanity and dignity. Another important value recognized in the Preamble of the South African Constitution, is the need for societal transformation, with the goal of creating a transformed society based on "democratic values, social justice and fundamental human rights."

This is not to suggest that the Court's path to implementing dignity has always been smooth and consistent. The earlier Court decisions illustrate the justices' struggle to find the appropriate language to define and enforce dignity in a consistent way as an independent right in and of itself, despite the Constitution's explicit mandate to that effect articulated in Article 10. In some areas, the Court has preferred to decide cases using dignity as an informing precept and has analyzed the law in terms of violations of Article 9—the right to equal protection and freedom from discrimination, rather than as violations of Article 10. The Court has demonstrated greater facility with its language and analysis in opinions wherein it relied on equal protection and even socio-economic rights rather than pure dignity violations. This may be because Article 39 of the Constitution explicitly authorizes the Court to look to international human rights and the laws of other countries in interpreting its own laws; the Court has thus been free to borrow from the jurisprudence of German and Canadian courts, or supranational courts. However, even in cases where the Court's language or reasoning do not fully do justice to the notion of dignity, its commitment to that concept remains unshakable. The Court has demonstrated this commitment not only by means of several important opinions but also through its choice of artwork at Constitutional Hill—the seat of the Court. Many of the paintings and sculptures chosen by the justices speak to human dignity in a profound and compelling way, reinforcing the importance of the concept for all who enter.[1]

The dignity canon of the Court is now sufficiently extensive to provide a model for other legal systems seeking to implement a juridical concept of dignity; particularly those jurisdictions attempting to restore human dignity to their societies in the wake of gross violations of human rights, or those seeking to foster dignified lives for their citizens by guaranteeing socio-economic rights.

Dignity in the South African Constitution and the Jurisprudence of the Constitutional Court

The Constitutional Court was created in 1994 and heard its first case in 1995. It is the ultimate arbiter in all constitutional issues and was charged with interpreting the newly drafted Bill of Rights by means of the guiding principles articulated in the Constitution, among which dignity features prominently, both as a guiding principle and a specific right.

Dignity in the Constitution

Dignity is the cornerstone of the South African Constitution. Not only is it referenced as a core founding concept in Article 1(a), but it is also specifically enshrined in the Bill of Rights in Article 7(1) where the "democratic value of human dignity is affirmed." Moreover, Article 10 guarantees the right of each person to have his or her dignity "respected and protected." Additionally, the Table at the end of the Bill of Rights provides that the right to dignity is non-derogable. This signifies that dignity is not only a principle that should inform the Court's understanding of the Constitution but is a specific right in and of itself. Given this, it is not surprising that many of the Court's landmark decisions have been devoted to developing the concept.

The African National Congress ("ANC"), South Africa's governing political party, has long placed dignity at the forefront of the struggle for freedom. The party was committed to the creation of a Constitutional Court to guarantee the rights that people had been denied under the apartheid system. In 1956, the ANC and its allies drew up the Freedom Charter, a document in which the party essentially committed itself to the creation of a constitution founded on dignity. Although many of the rights contained in the Freedom Charter revolved around socio-economic rights, the Charter also recognized equality and non-discrimination rights, as well as communitarian rights (South African Congress Alliance 1955).[2] The importance of the Court in giving effect to these rights should not be underestimated. At the opening of the Constitutional Court in 1994, Nelson Mandela proclaimed:

> [t]he last time I appeared in court was to hear whether or not I was going to be sentenced to death. Fortunately for myself and my colleagues we were not. Today I rise not as an accused, but on behalf of the people of South Africa, to inaugurate a court South Africa has never had, a court on which hinges the future of our democracy.
>
> (Mandela 1995)

In 1996, the new post-apartheid Constitution went into effect. Designed to be the antithesis of the pernicious race-based apartheid laws, Article 1 provides that "[t]he Republic of South Africa is . . . founded on the following values: (a) Human dignity, the achievement of equality and the advancement of human rights and freedoms." In one aspect, the South African approach was consistent with countries like Germany, in that dignity was incorporated as a value informing the Constitution. However, the Constitution then went on to demarcate dignity as more than just an interpretative value, as Article 10 provides that "Every person shall have the right to respect for and protection of his or her dignity." The Constitutional Court has not shied away from its obligation to interpret the concept of dignity in deciding numerous cases. It has held that dignity rights are indispensable in respect of: one, the right to equality and non-discrimination; two, the enforcement of socio-economic rights; three, the right to have one's dignity recognized by not being subjected to cruel, arbitrary, or inhumane treatment by the state; and four, the right to express oneself both as an individual and in the community through the recognition of one's autonomy and individual preferences and through one's cultural choices lived in community. This section will examine each of these rights and posit how various cases decided by the Constitutional Court bespeak a commitment to the development of these rights and provide a model for international human rights jurisprudence to emulate.

Dignity in the Jurisprudence of the Constitutional Court

From the outset, the Constitutional Court established that it was cognizant of the fact, at least in theory, that dignity is a right in and of itself, not merely an informing principle. In *Dawood v. Minister of Home Affairs* (2000), the Court noted, "dignity is not only a value fundamental to our Constitution, it is a justiciable and enforceable right that must be respected and protected." The Court acknowledged the multiple roles of dignity in the Constitution, noting how "human dignity . . . informs constitutional adjudication and interpretation at a range of levels. It is a value that informs the interpretation of many, possibly all, other rights . . . such as the right to equality, the right not to be punished in a cruel, inhuman or degrading way, and the right to life." Moreover, the *Dawood* case was one of the earliest cases to find the primary violation in that case was the right to dignity and not any other right. In determining that the statute that denied married persons and families the right to live together while their immigrant residence permits were pending was a violation of the right to dignity *per se*, Justice O'Regan asserted "[i]n this case, however, it cannot be said that there is a more specific right that protects individuals who wish to enter into and sustain permanent intimate relationships than the right to dignity in section 10." The Court found that:

> The decision to enter into a marriage relationship and to sustain such a relationship is a matter of defining significance for many if not most people and to prohibit the establishment of such a relationship impairs the ability of the individual to achieve personal fulfilment in an aspect of life that is of central significance. In my view, such legislation would clearly constitute an infringement of the right to dignity.

The Court thus recognized one's right to autonomous choices and to live in a community, whether it be with one's family or the broader community.

However, prior cases shied away from finding violations solely based on Article 10 and instead based their decisions on Article 9 of the Constitution—the right to freedom from discrimination—while also referencing the right to dignity.

Equal Protection and Non-Discrimination Rights

One of the earlier cases that came before the newly formed Court was *Hugo v. President of the Republic of South Africa* (1997), a case where the applicant alleged that the first statute enacted into law by newly elected President, Nelson Mandela, was unconstitutional because it discriminated based on gender. Cognizant of its mandate to give effect to the concept of dignity, the Court noted, "[a]t the heart of the prohibition of unfair discrimination lies a recognition that the purpose of our new constitutional and democratic order is the establishment of a society in which all human beings will be accorded equal dignity and respect regardless of their membership of particular groups. The achievement of such a society in the context of our deeply inegalitarian past will not be easy, but that that is the goal of the Constitution should not be forgotten or overlooked." Despite that proclamation, the Court neglected to fully engage in an analysis of the right to dignity.

As it was early in the Court's existence, the justices may have lacked confidence in their ability to fully articulate the parameters of a dignity violation and instead focused on dignity as a value informing the Constitution, resting their analysis on the discriminatory aspect of the case under Article 8.[3] The statute at issue in *Hugo* purported to grant a presidential pardon to all mothers of children under the age of twelve, who had been incarcerated for nonviolent crimes. President Mandela, who himself had been incarcerated during his own children's formative years, recognized the hardship imposed on children whose primary caregivers (usually mothers, per the testimony of expert witnesses in the case)[4] were incarcerated. The plaintiff, Hugo, the father of a son under the age of twelve, challenged the constitutionality of the statute on the basis that it violated Article 8 of the Constitution, which prohibited unfair discrimination on gender and other grounds. Justice Goldstone recognized that the concept of dignity generally mandates equality and non-discrimination. While the Court acknowledged that the statute might appear discriminatory, given that it offered the possibility of pardon and release to female prisoners but not to males, the Court nevertheless found it constitutional because the President's pardon power was very broad and that it was a social fact that women were generally caregivers of young children, so favoring them did not constitute "unfair" discrimination. The Court also noted that Hugo, as a male, was not a member of a previously disadvantaged group. The dignity of the male prisoners, who were not being released, was not discussed in detail; perhaps in part because the Court lacked the terminology or juridical basis to discuss dignity in this way.

Similarly, in *Prinsloo v. Van der Linde* (1997) the Court once again discussed dignity only in the guise of equal protection and not as a separate justiciable right. The Court did, however, recognize that the acknowledgment of dignity was integral to the transformation of society. It contrasted the new constitutional era with the apartheid era and implicitly recognized a Kantian concept of dignity when it explained:

> [w]e are emerging from a period in our history during which the humanity of the majority of our inhabitants of this country was denied. They were treated as not having inherent worth; as objects whose identities could be arbitrarily defined by those in power rather than as persons of infinite worth. In short, they were denied recognition of their inherent dignity.

The Court ultimately found the statute at issue to be constitutional, despite the fact that it created a legal presumption of negligence on the part of landowners on whose land fires had broken out. The Court reasoned that, although the statute treated landowners differently from other members of the public in creating the presumption of legal liability, it did not discriminate against them unfairly. The Court opined, "[i]n our view unfair discrimination, . . . in the context of section 8 as a whole, principally means treating persons differently in a way which impairs their fundamental dignity as human beings, who are inherently equal in dignity."

The complex ways in which dignity and other constitutional rights intersect in many of the South African dignity cases is best expressed through the example of *Minister of Home Affairs v. Fourie et al.* (2006), a case in which two women challenged the constitutionality of the common law definition of marriage, which described it as a union of one man with one woman. In rejecting that definition of marriage, the Court noted, "[discrimination] denied to homosexuals and lesbians that which was foundational to our Constitution and the concepts of equality and dignity, which at that point were closely intertwined, namely that all persons have the same inherent worth and dignity as human beings, whatever their other differences may be." In using this language, the Court seemed to acknowledge that any violations of these two rights may constitute separate and distinct violations. This case built on the jurisprudence of a prior case, *National Coalition for Gay and Lesbian Equality v. Minister of Justice* (1999), where Justice Ackerman stressed the extent to which the common law criminal offense of sodomy was an infringement of the right to dignity, as well as equality, and the right to privacy. There, the Court noted the broad and pervasive negative repercussions that adhere to the affected individuals and the community as a whole when dignity is denied. The Court added:

> There can be no doubt that the existence of a law which punishes a form of sexual expression for gay men degrades and devalues gay men in our

> broader society. As such it is a palpable invasion of their dignity and a breach of section 10 of the Constitution. . . . The harm caused by the provision can, and often does, affect his ability to achieve self-identification and self-fulfillment.

Thus, the Court has shown itself willing to find a breach of the right to dignity as a separate constitutional violation. It also acknowledged the relationship between dignity, autonomy, and self-fulfillment—the ability to make autonomous choices reflecting who one is, is crucial to dignity. The Court also acknowledged a relational aspect of dignity; one finds meaning and dignity in the relationships one forms with others and inherent dignity entitles one to acknowledgment of those relationships and respectful treatment by the community. Thus, the Court has evinced an incorporation of McCrudden's (2008) notion of "relational dignity"—a dignity of recognition.

The Court's difficulties in determining the precise relationship between dignity and other constitutional rights were made evident by the *Jordan* case (2002). There the Court struggled to reconcile whether criminalizing prostitution was consistent with the constitutionally guaranteed rights to equality, privacy, as set forth in Article 14, autonomy, as referenced in Article 11, and economic activity, contained in Article 22 of the Constitution. The case involved the constitutionality of a criminal anti-prostitution statute, which penalized the prostitute for providing sexual services but not the customer who purchased them. Several sex workers had challenged its constitutionality, contending that it discriminated based on gender (as most prostitutes are women) and thus violated the sex workers' right to equality before the law. The applicants also asserted that it violated their rights to economic activity and privacy. The majority of the Court ignored the dignity aspect of the claim and upheld the statute as non-discriminatory because it applied equally to both male and female prostitutes. The majority's opinion pointed out that, "[t]he stigma that attaches to prostitutes attaches to them not by virtue of their gender, but by virtue of the conduct they engage in." Two dissenting justices found, however, that the statute discriminated based on gender, as the majority of prostitutes were women. The dissent further noted that criminalizing their conduct without penalizing the conduct of their male customers, created a "stigma [which] is prejudicial to women, and runs along the fault lines of archetypal presuppositions about male and female behaviour, thereby fostering gender inequality." The dissent went on to assert the Kantian view that despite violating the equality clause, the statute did not however violate the applicants' right to dignity, as engaging in prostitution did not dignify the human body.

Along with non-discrimination and equal protection rights, the Court has placed great emphasis on upholding socio-economic rights as inherent to dignity in cases like *Nokotyana v. Ekurhuleni Metropolitan Municipality* (2010). South Africa was one of the earliest domestic jurisdictions in the world to develop the concept of the "progressive realization" of socio-economic rights.

This juridical development accords with international human rights law in this area in the sense that it has always urged that socio-economic rights are integral to human dignity. However, the South African Court has taken that concept even further by placing socio-economic rights on a par with civil and political rights; an approach that has not always been ascribed to in international human rights law.

Socio-Economic Rights

Those who suffered under the apartheid system and its racially based distribution of goods and benefits have always been keenly aware of the link between socio-economic rights and dignity. In his Trafalgar Square speech, Nelson Mandela (2005) argued that "[o]vercoming poverty is not a gesture of charity. It is an act of justice. It is the protection of a fundamental human right, the right to dignity and a decent life." The relationship between socio-economic rights and dignity had been a consistent campaign of the ANC since the Freedom Charter days, when that document reflected the desire of the people to strive for both dignity and better conditions of life. Mandela (1993) had similarly recognized that dignity, equality, and socio-economic rights go hand-in-hand, when he posited in a speech at Soochow University, "[w]e do not want freedom without bread, nor do we want bread without freedom. We must provide for all the fundamental rights and freedoms associated with a democratic society."

The Court showed that it was cognizant of the symbiotic link between socio-economic and civil and political rights in the 2001 *Grootboom* case, where it acknowledged, "[t]here can be no doubt that human dignity, freedom, and equality, the foundational values of our society, are denied those who have no food, clothing or shelter. Affording socio-economic rights to all people therefore enables them to enjoy the other rights enshrined in [the Constitution]." The Court also went on to stress the indivisible interrelationship between equal protection rights and socio-economic rights when it stated, "[t]he realization of these rights is also key to the advancement of race and gender equality and the evolution of a society in which men and women are equally able to achieve their full potential." The Court further recognized the Kantian approach of acknowledging the inherent value of human beings, when it explained that "[t]he right to adequate housing is entrenched because we value human beings and want to ensure that they are afforded their basic human needs. A society must seek to ensure that the basic necessities of life are provided to all if it is to be a society based on human dignity, freedom and equality."

Similarly, in *Daniels v. Scribante* (2017) the Court further solidified the connection between dignity and a home, when it upheld the right to security of tenure. The Court found that "[a]n indispensable pivot to that right [the right to secure housing] is the right to human dignity. There can be no true security of tenure under conditions devoid of human dignity." It went on to point out that "[t]he importance of dignity as a founding value of the new Constitution cannot be overemphasised." This principle was echoed by Judge Zondo in his dissenting judgment in *Malan v. City of Cape Town* (2014) where he noted that "having a home is very important to the dignity of any person."

Although Article 27 of the Constitution provides that "[e]veryone has the right to have access to health care services, including reproductive health care; . . . sufficient food and water; and . . . social security" the Court has declined, however, to delve too deeply into precisely what is required for human dignity in terms of provision of a "minimum core" of economic rights, such as access to a specific amount of water under the Limburg Principles (UN Economic and Social Council 1987). In the *Mazibuko case* (2010), the applicants requested that the Court specify exactly how many liters of water per day were necessary to live a life with dignity, suggesting that the Court should set a minimum requirement of 50 liters per person per day, which roughly corresponds to the World Health Organization Guidelines on Sanitation and Health (2018). The Court refused to do so, noting "[t]his is a matter, in the first place, for the legislature and executive, the institutions of government best placed to investigate social conditions in the light of available budgets. . . . Indeed, it is desirable as a matter of democratic accountability that they should do so." The Court adopted a reasonableness approach, assessing whether the government was acting reasonably in the way in which it allocated water to poor residents of the townships.

However, in 2020, the South African High Court (Gauteng Division) in *Minister of Education v. Equal Education*, demanded as a matter of dignity that the government feed hungry children during the Covid pandemic. The case involved the responsibility of the state to continue providing school lunches to children who were not in school because of the pandemic. The High Court held that:

> [i]f there was not a duty on the Department to provide nutrition when the parents cannot provide the children with basic nutrition, the children face starvation. A more undignified scenario than starvation of a child is unimaginable. The morality of a society is gauged by how it treats its children. Interpreting the Bill of Rights promoting human dignity, equality and freedom can never allow for the hunger of a child.

The Right to be Free from Cruel, Inhumane, or Degrading Treatment by the State

The Constitutional Court has also been vigilant about guarding the dignity of individuals from any encroachment by the state in the form of cruel or inhumane treatment. In *S. v. Makwanyane* (1995), a case challenging the constitutionality of the death penalty, the Court noted, "this court has already acknowledged the importance of the constitutional value of dignity in interpreting rights such as . . . the right not to be punished in a cruel, inhuman or degrading way, and the right to life. Human dignity is also a constitutional value that is of central significance in the limitations analysis." The Court invoked a Kantian approach in invalidating the death penalty when it reasoned that:

> capital punishment strips the convicted person of all dignity and treats him or her as an object to be eliminated by the state. [It] destroys life, which is protected without reservation under section 9 of our Constitution, it annihilates human dignity which is protected under section 10, elements of arbitrariness are present in its enforcement and it is irremediable.

The Court reiterated that the rights to life and dignity were "the most important of all human rights." Pursuant to that approach, the Court found that treating people as a means by making an example of them to deter others from criminal conduct was inconsistent with human dignity, as it objectified them.

The Court went even further in upholding the right of individual human dignity vis-a-vis the state, when it permitted a terminally ill prisoner to be released so that he could die at home. In the *Stanfield v. Minister of Correctional Services* (2003), the Court found that the refusal of the Bureau of Prisons to release Stanfield "amounts to an infringement of section 10: From this it is clear that the . . . respondent has failed to accord the applicant the dignity inherently forthcoming to him."

Individuals, Communities, and Ubuntu—The Transformative Social Dimension of Dignity

It is evident from its pronouncements that the Constitutional Court has embraced Kantian notions of dignity; however, it has taken these concepts even further in imbuing the constitutional right to dignity with African notions of communitarianism. These notions are predicated on the idea that individuals are inextricably connected to their communities; therefore, actions inflicted upon an individual reverberate through society and affect other members of the community by diminishing the communal sense of societal dignity. As Michael Onyebuchi Eze (2008) has argued, in African society, "the relationship between the individual and community is dialogical, for the identity of the individual and the community is dependent on this constitutive formation" (386).

The Court laid the foundations for this innovative approach to dignity through its recognition of the social nature of human beings expressed through their relations with others. The Court first articulated this principle in the *Makwanyane* case through its endorsement of the African precept "*umuntu ngumuntu ngabantu*," which translates as "a person is a person because of other people." Since that case, the Court has developed this line of reasoning in multiple ways. First, it has articulated the principle that the violation of the rights of the individual also has a detrimental impact on the community. This understanding derives not only from cultural mores but also from the concept of *ubuntu*, a term that was used extensively in the 1993 South African Interim Constitution. Moreover, as Chemhuru (2018) argues, the Court has further adopted an approach that "gives accommodation to the communal values, as well as to values of individuality, to social commitments as well as to duties of self-attention" (38).

The community's interest in dignity is perhaps best encapsulated by the language and purpose of the 1995 Promotion of National Unity and Reconciliation Act. That statute was enacted to establish the Truth and Reconciliation Commission ("TRC") that would permit victims and their families to testify about the gross violations of human rights that they had suffered during the apartheid regime. Perpetrators, who had repented of their crimes could come forward, testify, and seek amnesty if they could show that they had disclosed everything about the crime and were truly sorry. The TRC was predicated on the idea that the community as a whole suffered when an individual's dignity was violated and restoring the dignity of an individual helped heal society. When these types of violations occur, it is not only the victim's rights that need redress, but the community must also acknowledge what has occurred and be made whole by being reconciled with the victim or her family. Article 3 of the TRC's objectives thus included "establishing and making known the fate or whereabouts of victims and . . . restoring the human and civil dignity of such victims by granting them an opportunity to relate their own accounts of the violations of which they are the victims, and by recommending reparation measures in respect of them." The Commission explicitly viewed this as necessary because "the pursuit of national unity, the well-being of all South African citizens and peace require reconciliation between the people of South Africa and the reconstruction of society." (Preamble of the Promotion of National Unity and Reconciliation Act). The Commission believed that healing the injury to both the individual and society could not occur until a full accounting of the violations had been provided. This idea, that insults to dignity do not happen only to the individual but diminish the dignity of the community as a whole, opens a new area of exploration in dignity jurisprudence.

The Constitutional Court has also recognized the importance of group solidarity and how an insult to the dignity of one can injure the community. In *Hoffman v. South African Airways* (2001), a case involving the right of an HIV-positive individual to be employed as a flight attendant, the Court reiterated that the interests of the community lie in the recognition of the inherent dignity of every human being. That understanding had first been articulated in *National Coalition for Gay and Lesbian Equality* (1999) where Justice Ackerman, in invalidating South Africa's anti-sodomy laws, identified the communal harm that resulted from the denial of dignity. He noted that this impacts society as a whole, not just gay men, stating, "[t]he harm also radiates out into society generally and gives rise to a wide variety of other discriminations." In finding violations of the right to equality, the right to dignity, and the right to privacy, Ackerman cited with approval, a decision of the Canadian Supreme Court which had held that "so soon as we say any . . . group is less deserving and unworthy of equal protection and benefit of the law all minorities and all of . . . society are demeaned."

Justice Sachs, in concurrence, also reflected on the injury done to the gay community and not just individual gay men. He pointed out that the sodomy laws, by denying "full moral citizenship in society because you are what you are, impinge on the dignity and self-worth of the group." Sachs went on to invoke South Africa's apartheid past in justifying the need to protect the dignity of the claimants. "At the heart of equality jurisprudence is the rescuing of people from a caste-like status and putting an end to their being treated as lesser human beings because they belong to a particular group." Sachs' articulation is consistent with a truly African approach to communitarianism and human rights based on the common good. Recognizing the dignity of the individual and restoring him or her to full membership in the community does not only make the victim whole but restores the integrity of the community. This approach reveals the Court's commitment to not only redressing the wrongs done to the particular applicants or the group that the applicant represents, but also to transforming society as a whole through upholding dignity.

The understanding that the protection of dignity is both a community obligation and a community benefit was echoed by the Court in the 2006 gay marriage case, *Minister of Home Affairs v. Fourie et al.*, where the Court held, "[a]ccordingly, what is at stake is not simply a question of removing an injustice experienced by a particular section of the community. At issue is a need to affirm the very character of our society as one based on tolerance and mutual respect." In finding the common law, which defined marriage as being between a man and a woman, unconstitutional, the Court noted that the denial of equal protection to the individual applicants detrimentally impacted society as a whole.

Another area in which the South African Constitutional Court has furthered our understanding of the juridical notion of dignity, is in articulating the importance to the individual of living in a community and identifying with a particular community. This shows that the Court embraces an African communitarianism approach, rather than Mill's concept of the autonomous individual in society. Mill ([1848] 1965) asserted that a just regard for the good of all was best attained by creating an environment whereby the "individuality of that person ought to reign uncontrolled either by any other individual or the public collectively" (943). In contrast, in *National Coalition for Gay and Lesbian Equality v. Minister of Justice* (1999), Justice Sachs explained that autonomy means more than "the right to occupy an envelope of space in which a socially detached individual can act freely from interference by the state." He added that individuals are not "isolated, lonely, and abstract" entities but rather, they are people who "live in their bodies, their communities, their cultures, their places and their times."

The concept of expressing one's affiliation with a community was also at issue in *MEC for Education: KwaZulu-Natal v. Pillay* (2008), a case involving a high school student's right to wear a nose stud to school as an expression of her South Indian Tamil Hindu culture. Although wearing a nose ring was not required by the applicant's religious affiliation, the Court nevertheless upheld her right to wear it. Writing for the Court, Chief Justice Langa reminded the parties that human dignity encompasses not only the "unique set of ends" of each individual but also one's common cultural aspirations. He went on to point out that "[d]ignity and identity are inseparably linked as one's sense of self-worth is defined by one's identity. Cultural identity is one of the most important parts of a person's identity precisely because it flows from belonging to a community and not from personal choice or achievement."

This understanding of the role of culture and community as an integral part of human dignity is a truly African contribution to the Western understanding of the concept, which tends to focus on individual dignity. Justice Mokgoro pointed out the breadth, richness, and depth of this interpretation in the *Makwanyane* case (1995) when she conflated the concept of dignity with the African concept of "*ubuntu*." She noted:

> [g]enerally, *ubuntu* translates as humaneness. In its most fundamental sense, it translates as personhood and morality. Metaphorically, it expresses itself in *umuntu ngumuntu ngabantu*, describing the significance of group solidarity on survival issues so central to the survival of communities. While it envelops the key values of group solidarity, compassion, respect, human dignity, conformity to basic norms and collective unity, in its fundamental sense it denotes humanity and morality. Its spirit emphasizes respect for human dignity, marking a shift from confrontation to conciliation.

In doing so, Mokgoro intimated that the dignity of the community would not be fully realized if it were to uphold the death penalty. For a community to function in a moral way, it must allow for the possibility of an accused redeeming himself in the eyes of the community and being reconciled with them. This notion is a core understanding of African customary law, which focuses on reconciliation and restoration, rather than retribution. Indeed, the very idea of the Court is based on the idea of "justice in the grass," a traditional mode of indigenous justice that prioritizes the restoration of harmony to the community and does not just focus on individual harms. The Court's seal even depicts a scene where villagers are gathered to resolve a problem under a tree.

This relationship between the individual and the group was also remarked upon by the Court in *Khumalo v. Holomisa* (2002), a case involving the defamation of a public figure. There the Court explained the nature of dignity as being "not only concerned with an individual's sense of self-worth, but constitut[ing] an affirmation of the worth of human beings in our society. It includes the intrinsic worth of human beings shared by all people as well as the individual reputation of each person built upon his or her own individual achievements." The Court further noted that, "[t]he Constitution asserts dignity to contradict our past in which human dignity for black South Africans was routinely and cruelly denied. It asserts it too to inform the future, to invest in our democracy, respect for the intrinsic worth of all human beings." The Court went on to find that dignity was a "foundational" value. In contrast, freedom of speech, while undeniably important, was "not a paramount value. It must be construed in the context of the other values enshrined in our Constitution. In particular, the values of human dignity, freedom and equality." The Court therefore went on to find that the right to dignity and protection of one's good name outweighed the competing free speech rights in that case.

The approach of preferencing dignity over free speech values, was, however, recently modified by the Court in 2021 in *Qwelane v. S.A. Human Rights Commission et al;* a case involving hate speech. There the Court found that the section of the Equality Act which prohibits hate speech was constitutionally invalid because it purported to prohibit "hurtful" speech. Qwelane, a journalist, had written and published a derogatory article about gay people, and the South African Human Rights Commission initiated proceedings against him and the paper that published the article. The Commission alleged Qwelane had violated Section 10 of the 2000 Equality Act which prohibits speech that among other categories, could "reasonably be construed to demonstrate a clear intention to—(a) be hurtful." Qwelane asserted that the speech was constitutionally protected under the right to freedom of expression guaranteed by Section 16(1) of the Constitution. While acknowledging that "the purpose of hate speech regulation in South Africa is inextricably linked to our constitutional object of healing the injustices of the past and establishing a more egalitarian society," the Court concluded that "[e]xpressions that are merely hurtful, especially when understood in everyday parlance, are insufficient to constitute hate speech." The Court therefore struck down Section 10(a) of the Equality Act.

As noted, with few exceptions, the Court takes seriously its role in helping South African society transform into a community in which, not only is the dignity of the individual respected, but also the dignity of groups and communities within that society. In the 2019 case of *Maledu and Others v. Itereleng Bakgatla Mineral Resources (Pty) Limited and Another*, the Constitutional Court overruled an eviction order, permitting a mining company to evict a community of thirteen families from a farm in the Lesetlheng Community, where the company had obtained mining rights. The applicant families had claimed that they were the historically true owners of the farm, even though their purported ownership rights had never been legally recognized or recorded; they therefore asserted that the rest of the tribe did not have the right to grant the mining company a lease, as the applicant families had not given their permission for this. The Court analyzed the claims of land ownership through the lens of the Interim Protection of Informal Land Rights Act and the dignity provisions of the Constitution, as well as constitutional provisions pertaining to African customary law. According to customary law, land may be owned communally by a tribe or group within that tribe, even if that ownership has not been formally registered. In its opinion, the Court described what had happened to communities like the applicant community under apartheid. It noted that the period of history "was characterized by oppression, deprivation of a significant segment of our society and deep-rooted inequalities." In providing redress to the applicants as a community, the Court invoked "the absolute need to redress the injustices of that shameful past." It further affirmed the rights of the applicants to adhere to the communal undocumented system of land ownership that forms part of customary law, noting, "clearly the Constitution itself envisages a place for customary law in our legal system. Certain provisions of the Constitution put it beyond doubt that our . . . law specifically requires that customary law should be accommodated, not merely tolerated." The Court based its decision on the understanding that its and the Constitution's role was "the overall aim of the creation of a society in which the equal worth of all is respected." The Court therefore noted that "section 211 protects those institutions that are unique to customary law. . . . It is protected by and subject to the Constitution in its own right."

The Court's assertion of the inviolability of dignity in respect of individuals and citizens has been extended to the protection of noncitizens, refugees, and immigrants by the South African Supreme Court of Appeal. In 2004, in *Minister of Home Affairs v. Watchenuka*, the Supreme Court of Appeal upheld the rights of asylum seekers to work, study, and obtain identity documents in South Africa, while awaiting confirmation of their status, by echoing Kant to the effect that "[h]uman dignity has no nationality. It is inherent in all people, citizens and noncitizens alike—simply because they are human."

The Kantian or ontological understanding that dignity inures to each individual by virtue of their humanity seems to be a deeply held belief of some of the justices. It has been reflected in Justice Ackerman's academic publication, where he recalled that under apartheid "[b]lacks were treated as a means to an end and hardly ever as an end in themselves; an almost complete reversal of the Kantian imperative and concept of priceless inner worth and dignity" (Ackerman 2004, 650). However, the contribution of the Court has been to overlay the Kantian notion with the African concept of *ubuntu* to reflect that society itself is diminished if any individual or community is treated as less than deserving of dignity.

The Influence of the South African Court's Approach on International Human Rights Law

Although socio-economic rights have long been acknowledged in international human rights law, when it comes to practical implementation, they have historically, until relatively recently, been placed in a secondary position vis-à-vis civil and political rights. The South African Court has, however, advocated for, and upheld, the core importance of socio-economic rights as an urgent and integral part of human dignity. It has also developed the concept that the individual may choose to live her life in a community and the community has dignity rights that attach to it as part of the dignity of group recognition. Moreover, the dignity of the community may be detrimentally impacted when the dignity of a member of that community is violated—all of the foregoing elements make up the social dimension of dignity.

This recognition of socio-economic rights as integral to dignity had, until recently, not been mirrored in international human rights law. At the time that the International Covenant on Economic Social and Cultural Rights (IESCR) entered into force in 1976, Murphy and others (1992) pointed out that socio-economic rights were sometimes regarded as second-generation rights. Proponents of that position argued that attention could be given to these rights once the full complement of first-generation civil and political rights had been achieved while socialist states took the opposing view. However, restoring dignity to the "previously disadvantaged" was a key aim of the South African Constitution and Court, and socio-economic rights were integral to that restoration. International human rights law now mirrors the imperative to protect the rights of the most vulnerable. Growing awareness of income disparities, social and environmental upheaval, and other inequalities in the world, has prompted the international community to emphasize the importance of socio-economic rights, the rights of refugees, and community-based rights, such as the right to a clean environment, as all integral to dignity. This is evidenced most recently by the 2007 Declaration on the Rights of Indigenous Peoples, the 2018 UN Sustainable Development Goals, and the United Nations Human Rights Committee's General Comment No. 36 on the right to life (2018).

Most recently, the UN Sustainable Development Goals and Platform and the 2030 Agenda for Sustainable Development (UN General Assembly 2015), have stressed the human right of all peoples, particularly the most vulnerable, to dignity, peace, and prosperity. Crucial to that goal is ensuring a healthy environment; this right, along with the right to peace, speaks to the rights of communities and groups, not just individuals. It thus reflects the same social dimension that has been a concern of the South African Constitutional Court. Paragraph 7 of the Platform reiterates the "human right to safe drinking water and sanitation; and . . . [a] world where human habitats are safe, resilient and sustainable and where there is universal access to affordable, reliable and sustainable energy." Moreover, Article 8 provides for "universal respect for human rights and human dignity . . . respect for race, ethnicity and cultural diversity."

While the Court has sought to uphold dignity by assessing "the position of the complainants and whether they have suffered in the past from patterns of disadvantage" (*Hugo v. President of the Republic of South Africa*) and then determining what remedy is appropriate, the UN Human Rights Committee's General Comment No. 36 now similarly "requires States parties to take special measures of protection towards persons in situations of vulnerability." These include victims of violence, children, migrants, those with disabilities, intersex and LGBT persons, and stateless persons among others.

The HRC General Comment also points out that the "prevalence of disease, and lack of access to adequate food, water and shelter are all implicated in denying the right to live with dignity" (para. 26). The Comment goes even further by stating that exposure to gun violence, and even other forms of indirect violence like pervasive traffic and industrial accidents, all threaten the right to a life with dignity. The Comment builds on other international human rights recommendations articulated by the CEDAW Committee to claim that being exposed to violence is a form of discrimination that state parties are responsible for addressing (CEDAW Committee 2017), whether this violence is perpetrated by the state or private individuals. In General Comment 36, the Human Rights Committee also reminds states that it is irrelevant whether harmful acts or the denial of dignity are caused by private or public actors when it urges:

> Implementation of the obligation to respect and ensure the right to life, and in particular life with dignity, depends, inter alia, on measures taken by States parties to preserve the environment and protect it against harm, pollution and climate change caused by public and private actors. (para. 62)

The Human Rights Committee is reasserting the claim that, rather than being so-called "second generation rights," socio-economic and cultural rights are just as crucial to human dignity as civil and political rights. The South African Constitutional Court has been at the forefront of that approach.

Conclusion

The South African Constitution's overt endorsement of dignity as an independent right has been taken up by the Court, which has been assiduous in interpreting and applying the concept as broadly as possible, viewing itself as a guardian of dignity. It has shown that socio, economic, and cultural rights are indispensable to living a life with dignity and provided an example for other jurisdictions of how dignity rights may vest in communities as well as individuals. The Court has also espoused a belief that acknowledging and upholding the human dignity of those previously disadvantaged by apartheid can have a transformative effect on society. In recognizing individuals and communities as "persons of infinite worth," the Court has given effect to the Kantian interpretation of dignity, recognizing, in C. S. Lewis's words "there are no ordinary people" (2001).

However, as McCrudden (2008) and others have noted, the concept of dignity is extremely challenging to implement. Giving effect to dignity and defining the parameters of that right, have not been easy tasks for the South African Constitutional Court. Moreover, it is unclear whose rights would be preferred if a clash arises between an individual's right to dignity and the community's rights. Or, as Daly (1994) puts it, "[c]an a philosophy whose aim is to strengthen the community that supports its members' fulfilment also conserve and deepen personal liberty? Can communitarian philosophy also legitimate democratic institutions as it cultivates a richer and fuller moral life?" (292). The Constitutional Court seems to believe that it can, but only time will tell.

Notes

1 The Court's art collection was started by two of the justices and was designed to reflect the struggle for human rights and human dignity. A description may be found at www.constitutionhill.org.za/pages/constitutional-court-art-collection.
2 Among the rights listed are "The rights of the people shall be the same, regardless of race, color or sex." Additionally, "all laws which discriminate on the grounds of race, colour or belief shall be repealed." The Charter also provides that "All national groups shall have equal rights" and "all peoples shall have equal right to use their own language and to develop their own folk culture and customs."
3 The case was brought under the interim Constitution. In that version the equal protection, non-discrimination clause was Article 8. Under the current permanent Constitution, the same clause is now Article 9.
4 The expert witness testified, "Although it could be argued that fathers play a more significant role in the lives of older children, the primary bonding with the mother and the role of mothers as the primary nurturers and caregivers extends well into childhood."

References

Abel, Richard. 1995. *Politics by Other Means: Law in the Struggle Against Apartheid 1980–1994.* New York: Routledge.
Ackerman, Lourens. 2004. "The Legal Nature of the South African Constitutional Revolution." *New Zealand Law Review* 4: 633–79.
Chemhuru, Munamato. 2018. "African Communitarianism and Human Rights: Towards a Compatibilist View." *Theoria. A Journal of Social and Political Theory* 65 (157): 37–56.
Committee on the Elimination of Discrimination Against Women (CEDAW Committee). 2017. "General Recommendation No. 35 on Gender Based Violence against Women. C/GC/35." www.ohchr.org/en/documents/general-comments-and-recommendations/general-recommendation-no-35-2017-gender-based.
Daly, Markate. 1994. *Communitarianism: A New Public Ethics.* Belmont CA: Wadsworth Publishing Company.
Eze, Michael Onyebuchi. 2008. "What is African Communitarianism? Against Consensus as a Regulative Ideal." *South African Journal of Philosophy* 27 (4): 386–99.
Lewis, Clive Staples. 2001. *The Weight of Glory.* San Francisco: HarperOne.
Mandela, Nelson. 1993. "Speech During His Investiture as a Doctor of Laws at Soochow University, Taiwan." https://archive.nelsonmandela.org/index.php/za-com-mr-s-146.
Mandela, Nelson. 1995. "Speech at the Opening of the Constitutional Court." https://concourtblog.com/category/uncategorized/.
Mandela, Nelson. 2005. "Speech in Trafalgar Square." www.mandela.gov.za/mandela_speeches/2005/050203_poverty.htm.
McCrudden, Christopher. 2008. "Human Dignity and Judicial Interpretation of Human Rights." *European Journal of International Law* 19 (4): 655–724.

Mill, John Stuart. (1848) 1965. "Principles of Political Economy with some of their Applications to Social Philosophy." In *Books II–III*, edited by John M. Robson. Toronto: University of Toronto Press; Routledge & Kegan Paul.
Murphy, John. 1992. "Second Generation Rights and the Bill of Rights Debate in South Africa." *South African Sociological Review* 4 (2): 30–53.
South African Congress Alliance. 1955. "The Freedom Charter." www.sahistory.org.za/article/congress-people-and-freedom-charter.
United Nations Economic and Social Council. 1987. "The Limburg Principles on the Implementation of the International Covenant on Economic, Social and Cultural Rights, E/CN.4/1987/17." www.refworld.org/pdfid/48abd5790.pdf.
United Nations General Assembly. 2015. "Resolution 'Transforming Our World. The 2030 Agenda for Sustainable Development', A/RES/70/1." https://sdgs.un.org/2030agenda.
United Nations Human Rights Committee. 2018. "General Comment No 36. Article 6: The Right to Life. CCPR/C/GC 36."
World Health Organization. 2018. "Guidelines on Sanitation and Health." www.who.int/publications/i/item/9789241514705.

Case Law

The Constitutional Court of South Africa

Carmichele v. Minister of Safety and Security, 2001 (4) SA 938 (CC).
Daniels v. Scribante, 2017 (4) SA 341 (CC).
Dawood v. Minister of Home Affairs, 2000 (3) SA 936 (CC).
Govt. of the Republic of South Africa v. Grootboom, 2001 (1) SA 46 (CC).
Hoffman v. South African Airways, 2001 (1) SA 1 (CC).
Hugo v. President of the Republic of South Africa, 1997 (4) SA 1 (CC).
Khumalo v. Holomisa, 2002 (5) SA 401 (CC).
Malan v. City of Cape Town, 2014 (6) SA 315 (CC).
Maledu and Others v. Itereleng Bakgatla Mineral Resources (Pty) Limited and Another, 2019 (2) SA 1 (CC).
Mazibuko v. City of Johannesburg, 2010 (4) SA 1 (CC).
MEC for Education: KwaZulu-Natal v. Pillay, 2008 (1) SA 474 (CC).
Minister of Home Affairs v. Fourie, 2006 (1) SA 524 (CC).
Minister of Home Affairs v. Fourie et al., 2006 (1) SA 524 (CC).
National Coalition for Gay and Lesbian Equality v. Minister of Justice, 1999 (1) SA 6 (CC).
Nokotyana v Ekurhuleni Metropolitan Municipality, 2010 (4) BCLR 312 (CC).
Prinsloo v. Van der Linde, 1997 (3) SA 1012 (CC).
Qwelane v South African Human Rights Commission and Another, 2021 (6) SA 579 (CC).
S. v. Jordan, 2002 (6) SA 642 (CC).
S. v. Makwanyane, 1995 (3) SA 391 (CC).
Stanfield v. Minister of Correctional Services, 2003 (4) SA 282 (CC).

High Court of South Africa

Equal Education and Others v. Minister of Basic Education and Others, 2021 (1) SA 198 (GP).

Supreme Court of Appeal of South Africa

Minister of Home Affairs v. Watchenuka, 2004 (1) SA 21 (SCA).

9 Human Dignity as a Constitutional Value

The Viewpoint of Polish Courts

Piotr Szymaniec

Introduction

Polish lawyers began to deal more thoroughly with the concept of dignity in the transition period after 1989. The Constitution of the Polish People's Republic of 1952, like other constitutions of socialist states, did not use this term. Although it sometimes appeared in judicial decisions, it was usually linked to the protection of personal worth under civil law or to certain crimes. In official Marxist philosophy and the so-called theory of state and law,[1] the concept of dignity appeared in the context of the dignity of workers as a social class, or in terms of self-esteem or self-respect. Subsequently, beginning in the late 1970s, the democratic opposition devoted more and more attention to considerations of dignity (the term itself often appeared with an adjective, such as "civic dignity") which—as it was claimed—manifested itself in individual autonomy, in the possibility of making personal choices, and in freedom from fear and pressure from the authorities. Moreover, the references to Catholic social teaching were also apparent (Michalewska-Pawlak 2010). After the country's democratic transition began in 1989, the view that the category of dignity should be included in the new Constitution became widespread. All constitutional drafts submitted in 1993 and 1994 contained a reference to human dignity. Although their details differed, six out of the seven drafts emphasized that dignity is inviolable, and most of them also identified dignity as inalienable and as a source of individual rights (Działocha 2010; Mazurek 2001). Ultimately, the notion of dignity was introduced in Article 30 of the Polish Constitution of April 2, 1997, which states that human dignity is a source of the freedoms and rights of individuals and citizens included in the Constitution. This provision attributes three features to dignity: it is inherent, inalienable, and inviolable. Moreover, the second sentence of the mentioned article constitutes the obligation on all public authorities to respect and protect the dignity of human beings.[2] The Polish Constitutional Court has never presented a definition of human dignity. Therefore, the question should be asked whether the Court has developed its own concept of human dignity or is only using a concept taken from other legal systems. Additionally, it is worth

DOI: 10.4324/9781003307853-11

asking which philosophical concepts of dignity have influenced the views presented in Polish constitutional jurisprudence. Here, I will try to present a thorough answer to these questions.

Basic Content and Functions of the Notion of Dignity

The Constitutional Court borrows its understanding of the meaning of dignity in the Constitution from the literature commenting on Article 30. According to this view, the concept of dignity is protected by the Constitution, the entire system of positive law, and the order of natural law (although nowhere is it specified which understanding of natural law is utilized). Human dignity is inviolable, and the dignity of every human being is equal. Thus, the differentiation or grading of the dignity of individuals is not possible and not permitted from a constitutional point of view. This concept determines the manner of interpretation and application of the Constitution, as well as the scope of particular rights and freedoms contained in the Constitution (see Garlicki 2016, 32–39, 43, 45; Judgments of the Constitutional Court of Poland (CCP) SK 48/05, point 2.2 (48); SK 6/02, point 6.2). Thus, both in Polish constitutional jurisprudence and constitutional legal literature, the approach to dignity developed in German constitutional-law "doctrine" has been widely accepted on the grounds of Article 1 Section 1 of the 1949 Basic Law. The statement that human dignity should be considered as the natural-law basis of the entire positive-law system is taken directly from the works of Günter Dürig (1956). The newer views on human dignity, such as Aharon Barak's concept (2015), are virtually absent in Polish legal "doctrine."

Furthermore, the Court emphasizes that the right to respect and protection of dignity is a distinct subjective right with a normative content separate from the content of other constitutional rights of the individual (Garlicki 1999, 41–42; CCP Judgment SK 6/02; cf. Wojtyczek 2001, 205–6). Concerning this right, the Court declares as follows: "The matter of the right to dignity is, in the most general sense, the creation (guarantee) of such a situation for every human being that she will be able to pursue her personality autonomously, but above all that she will not become the target of the actions of others (especially public authorities) and will not be merely a tool in achieving their goals" (CCP Judgment SK 48/05, point 2.2 (51)).[3] This position helps the Court justify the view that Article 30 of the Constitution will only exceptionally be the sole basis for the recognition of a specific legal provision's unconstitutionality (CCP Judgment SK 6/02, point 6.2, cf. Łętowska 2003). Professor Ewa Łętowska (2003), a judge on the Constitutional Court from 2002 to 2011, generalizes the view expressed in jurisprudence, that dignity as a constitutional concept first appears as an "argument . . . of the axiological assessment of regulations and institutions belonging to the legal system."

Dignity as the Prohibition of Treating Human Beings as Mere Objects

Although Article 30 of the 1997 Polish Constitution indicates dignity as the source of all rights and freedoms of a human being and citizen, as included in the Constitution, the Constitutional Court rarely recognizes that a specific provision violates the Constitution because it undermines human dignity. According to the Court, arguments based on the violation of dignity alone would be permissible if a specific legal regulation meant that a person would only become subordinated to actions on the part of the authorities, ceasing to be their subject. This would apply to situations in which the legislator caused a person to be treated purely instrumentally or the objectification of a person occurred (CCP Judgment SK 6/02, point 6.1.). Therefore, one can find in the Court's arguments Dürig's "object-formula" (*Objektformel*), which is itself a transformation of Kant's understanding of dignity as a value that is the opposite of "price."[4] In Dürig's view, in a democratic state, an individual cannot be seen as a mere object of state power (Mahlmann 2012, 379–80; Dreier 2004, 166–68). One of the most influential Polish constitutional lawyers, Leszek Garlicki, himself a justice of the Constitutional Court from 1993 to 2001, strongly emphasizes that Dürig's formula is adequate in the context of the Polish Constitution (Garlicki 2016).

One of the more important rulings in which the Court appealed to the violation of dignity, although it did not make this the main topic of the decision, was Judgment K44/07 of September 30, 2008.[5] The subject of the ruling was to assess whether Article 122a of the Act of July 3, 2002, concerning Aviation Law, complied with the Constitution. This article, added in 2005, allowed for the destruction of a civil aircraft (including passengers and crew on board) when it was being "used for illegal activities, in particular as a means of terrorist attack from the air" and when, at the same time, this destruction was required for the security of the state. The Court ruled that this article was contrary to Article 2 (regarding a democratic state ruled by law), Article 30 (relating to dignity), and Article 38 of the Constitution (ensuring legal protection of life) in connection with Article 31 par. 3 of the Constitution (principle of proportionality). Regarding the issue of dignity, the Court pointed out that the provision being examined leads to an instrumental treatment of passengers on board the aircraft. If, the judgment noted, the law allowed the shooting down of an aircraft on which only assassins were on board, it would not raise significant controversy, because the assassins (terrorists) themselves had decided to die (CCP Judgment K 44/07, point 174). The Court in this respect followed the arguments expressed in the *Bundesverfassungsgericht* Judgment of February 15, 2006. The Court declared the incorrectness of the opinion that the passengers of the aircraft used as a tool of a terrorist attack found themselves in a life-threatening situation only as a result of the activities of terrorists. This situation also occurred because the state failed to fulfill its obligations to ensure security (CCP Judgment K 44/07, point 174). In addition, the legal protection of life, which is guaranteed in Article 38 of the Constitution, is not absolute, because in the Polish legal system there are cases when certain persons (e.g. soldiers, firemen, policemen) are required to expose their lives to danger.

Dignity as Individual Autonomy

The Polish Constitutional Court formulated a more general view of the importance of dignity as a legal category in this judgment: "Confirmation of inalienable human dignity as a constitutional principle and the subjective right of every human being—regardless of their qualifications or psychological and physical condition and current life situation—is the basis recognition of her subjectivity. This statement determines a specific way in which state authorities, including the legislature and the executive, should act. A human being should be treated as a free, autonomous entity, capable of developing her personality and shaping her behavior" (CCP Judgment K 44/07, point 173). The quoted passage suggests that the Court combines an understanding of dignity taken from Christian personalism, indicating dignity as an immanent feature of a human being, with liberal views emphasizing the importance of individual autonomy. In Polish legal literature, the view is presented that the approach to dignity proposed by personalism is the fullest one and can be expressed in legal norms (Bosek 2012, 68–69).

The denial of the autonomy of an individual's activity violates her dignity. Such a conclusion seems justified on the grounds of Judgment P. 6/01, in which the Court found unconstitutional the provisions of the Act of October 26, 1982, concerning upbringing in sobriety and counteracting alcoholism, which did not allow an application to change the court order to be submitted by a person who had been ordered to undergo rehabilitation to deal with substance addiction.

In the concept of dignity, which emerges from the jurisprudence of the Constitutional Court, two aspects can be distinguished. The first of these can be described as negative and consists of taking into account "a certain sphere of autonomy, in which a person can fully realize himself socially" (CCP Judgment K 11/00, point 173). This aspect of dignity is undoubtedly connected with a liberal understanding of freedom which emerged in the 18th century. The second aspect can be described as positive, as it includes not only the prohibition of the creation of "legal or factual situations depriving the individual of the sense of dignity" (CCP Judgment K 44/07, point 173) including the adoption of legal regulations aimed at the humiliation of human beings but also contains the obligation to create conditions under which an individual has the opportunity to develop her own personality. It is "an obligation for public authorities to take such actions that protect an individual from situations incompatible with her dignity" (CCP Judgment SK 48/05, point 2.3 (52)). It includes—as the Court points out—the guarantee of a certain minimum of material means to an individual (CPP Judgment K 11/00). Hence, one is only a step away from stating that a condition of the realization of human dignity is the existence of a social security system. These two aspects are based on two different philosophical approaches to dignity. The first refers to the Renaissance understanding of dignity as an opportunity to shape oneself—the role of a particular individual in the world. A person has dignity in the sense that he or she can decide how to develop innate abilities.[6] The second meaning recognizes dignity as a sense of self-respect that can exist, develop, and flourish only under certain social conditions, including material conditions. This understanding of dignity occurs especially in socialist and social-democratic thought.

Personal Dignity and Dignity Connected With Personality

Since the late 1980s, personalism has certainly influenced the distinction of two types of dignity in Polish legal thought (Zajadło 1989, 111; Krukowski 1997, 39–42; Mazurek 2019).[7] According to this distinction, "personal dignity" (*godność osobowa*) is inherent and inalienable; the very fact of being a human being entitles every person to it. Dignity connected with personality (*godność osobowościowa*), in turn, is of acquired character and concerns the respect to which a person must be entitled. This distinction—though differently justified—can also be found in some of the representatives of the sociological conception of dignity.[8] It is worth mentioning that the distinguished Polish sociologist Maria Ossowska presented a similar view, although she was not influenced by personalism. Ossowska claimed that dignity in the first meaning belongs to man because of "the privileged place of man in nature" (Ossowska 1972, 52). Dignity in this sense is connected with the respect that an individual enjoys in society. Franciszek Mazurek summarized this position as follows: "Dignity is recognized as a feature of personality, a need, a sense of one's identity, self-acceptance, prestige, honor as well as self-respect and respect shown by others" (Mazurek 2001, 55).

The division into personal dignity and dignity connected with personality has been accepted in Polish literature on the subject. The Constitutional Court similarly referred to it, although at the same time the Court presented various kinds of "dignity" a bit differently than the authors associated with personalism. The Court stated that the first kind of dignity—"transcendent" dignity—is an inalienable value: i.e. the legislator can never violate it, and no person can abstain from it. A human being has this dignity always, regardless of her deeds or life attitude. On the other hand, dignity in the second sense encompasses all those values that make a person respectable in society. They are, therefore, values that, in a social conviction, build the respect that every individual enjoys in society. Sometimes the Court uses the term "personality right" (clearly the translation of German *Persönlichkeitsrecht*)[9] in relation to this understanding of dignity, which includes "the values of each person's mental life and all those values that determine the subjective position of an individual in society." Therefore, it is all about the conditions under which an individual does not feel humiliated in the eyes of society. Dignity understood in this way may be affected by the actions of various persons, state bodies, as well as legislators themselves. Therefore, determining whether the actions of the authorities, including legislation, comply with Article 30 of the Constitution of the Republic of Poland requires verifying that they do not violate human dignity in this second sense (CCP Judgments K 7/01; K 10/04; Judgment SK 48/05, point 2.2 (49–50)). It must be said, however, that the Court does not always consistently apply the mentioned distinction (cf. CCP Judgment P 10/06).

Dignity in the second sense, as self-respect, was taken into account in the judgment of February 23, 2010. The Constitutional Court decided that the provision of Article 123 par. 2 of the Act of June 6, 1997 (the Executive Penal Code), which allowed the remuneration of convicted employees to be limited to no less than half of the minimum remuneration for work provided for in the relevant provisions, is unconstitutional. The Court considered this restriction to be inconsistent with the constitutional principle of equality (Article 32 of the Constitution) and indicated that sentenced persons should receive remuneration equal to at least a minimum remuneration if they are full-time employees while serving a sentence. In its argumentation, the Court referred to the concept of dignity understood as conditions of respect for the individual: "Work is often a source of satisfaction for convicts and sense of dignity of themselves, it gives them a chance for positive personality change and helps to overcome the negative psychological consequences associated with the crime and punishment" (CCP Judgment P 20/09, point 8 (42)).

Dignity and the Right to Privacy

The Constitutional Court holds the position that not all violations of the rights or freedoms of an individual violate human dignity:

> not every violation of the right to private life is tantamount to a violation of personal dignity, or more strictly: rights that result from this dignity. The right to the protection of private life, just like any other freedom and right of an individual, finds its axiological legitimacy in the dignity of a person; however, identifying the violation of any right and freedom with violation of dignity would deprive the guarantees contained in Article 30 of the Constitution of an independent significance. It would in fact render shallow and oversimplify the sense and normative content contained in the concept used by Article 30 of the Constitution. It [this concept] covers the most important values that do not use other, independent guarantees on constitutional grounds, and which affect the nature of the individual's position in society, its relation to other people and to public authority.
>
> (CCP Judgment K 7/01, point 4)

According to the Constitutional Court, equating a violation of a particular constitutional right with a violation of dignity is also not appropriate because constitutional rights—including the right to privacy—are not absolute: i.e. they may be limited in situations where it is required in a democratic state and in compliance with further requirements of the principle of proportionality (Article 31, point 3, of the Polish Constitution). The acceptance that the right to respect for dignity functions at the same level as, for example, the right to privacy, would lead to the conclusion that the right to respect for dignity may be subject to the same restrictions as other constitutional rights. This, in turn, would mean that the protection of dignity is not an absolute protection, but it is only of a relative character (CCP Judgment K 7/01, point 4). Such a position—as the Court acknowledges—would not be consistent with the content of Article 30 of the Constitution. Some restrictions on constitutional rights—the Court further argues—may even be justified. For example, people performing public functions may sometimes be forced to disclose certain information about their private sphere when it is justified by the need for transparency in public affairs. However, a person who wants to perform public functions must accept these restrictions, so this does not mean a violation of her dignity (CCP Judgment K 7/01, point 4).

Simultaneously, the Constitutional Court recognizes that there is a connection between the categories of dignity and privacy. According to the Court, the possibility of the police and other state security bodies being able to conduct unlimited surveillance would lead to a situation where the dignity of a person would be jeopardized, because the individual would be deprived of "information autonomy," which includes the protection of personal data and the principle that disclosure of information about a person is based on her consent (CCP Judgments K 4/04; K 32/04, point 3.1.). For this reason:

> Dignity of a human being requires respect for her purely personal sphere, where she is not exposed to the necessity of 'being with others' or 'sharing with others' her experiences or intimate feelings. Therefore, the private sphere is built with various circles, more or less open (from the legal point of view) to external influences, in the case of which the constitutional approval for trespassing by the authorities is not identical.
> (CCP Judgment K 32/04, point 3.2.)

Due to these findings, the Court decided that a more restrictive approach should be applied to the possibility of installing wiretaps than to interfering with the confidentiality of correspondence. On this basis, the Court found certain provisions of the Act of April 6, 1990, to be unconstitutional, as they allowed materials obtained as a result of police observation to be used for purposes other than the one for which the observation originally served.

Dignity and the Rights of Foreigners

In the case concerning the refusal of the right to a court to a foreigner illegally staying on Polish territory (CCP Judgment P 12/99), the Constitutional Court accepted that the right to a court (Article 45 paragraph 1 of the Constitution of the Republic of Poland) "may serve to protect human dignity . . . but an innate and inalienable dignity of human being is not its immediate source." In the case of this judgment, the Court adopted a positivist argument. The Court indicated that Article 30 and Article 37 par. 2 (allowing the limitation of the use of freedoms and rights set out in the Constitution in cases involving foreigners) are placed in the same chapter of the Constitution, entitled "Freedoms, rights and obligations of a person and citizen." Therefore, the rank of these two provisions is the same. In addition, Article 37 par. 2 does not contain any conditions restricting the possibility of limiting the use of constitutional rights by foreigners. This provision, for example, does not contain a list of inviolable rights. Hence, it follows that limiting a foreigner's constitutional right to a court is admissible. In this judgment, the Court did not balance rights or constitutional values and devoted only one sentence to the relation between the provision on human dignity and the right to a court.

Dignity and the Right to Life

Authors representing Christian and Catholic worldviews link the human right to life, which in their view includes the period from conception to natural death, to the concept of dignity (see Ściślicki 2013; Complak 1998, 45). However, the Constitutional Court's Judgment of May 27, 1997, which strongly restricted the admissibility of abortion in Poland,[10] referred to the notion of dignity only once, and there was no attempt to define it. The main part of the argument refers to the need to protect life in a democratic state: "The democratic state of law recognizes the person as the prime value. Their most important goods, including their life, must remain under constitutional protection at all stages of development" (CCP Judgment K 26/96). Only in the dissenting opinion (points 7–8) did Justice Leszek Garlicki present the case as a conflict between the dignity of the mother and the dignity of the fetus and come to the conclusion that there is no reason to give priority to the dignity of the fetus over the dignity of the mother.[11]

On October 22, 2020, the Constitutional Court issued a highly controversial judgment concerning the unconstitutionality of a provision that allowed for abortion in cases where the fetus had a severe and irreversible impairment or an incurable and life-threatening disease. The judgment caused a great deal of political controversy, as it was decided by judges elected by the parliamentary majority dominated by the "Law and Justice" party.[12] Moreover, in each of the largest Polish cities, for over a week, angry demonstrations and even riots against the judgment broke out, mainly conducted by young people. Although these demonstrations were inconsistent with the then-binding laws regarding the prohibition of larger assemblies during the COVID-19 pandemic, the police and other services refrained from more radical intervention.[13] In terms of legal reasoning, despite the controversies, the judgment did not add much to the position on human dignity previously expressed by the Court. The Court reaffirmed the link between dignity and the protection of life, which was stressed already in the judgment of September 30, 2008, concerning the destruction of an aircraft. The emphasis on the dignity of a fetus ("an unborn child," as it is referred to in the majority opinion) is the only novelty of the Court's reasoning (CCU Judgment K 1/20). It must be admitted, however, that this is a novelty of great practical importance.

It should also be added that arguments based on the notion of dignity to justify the legalization of euthanasia are sometimes used in Polish legal discourse (Jedlecka 2013). So far, however, these arguments have not been accepted by the courts.[14]

Dignity in the Case Law of Polish General Courts

In the jurisprudence of common courts, the concept of dignity also arose before 1989. However, the concept of dignity which arose then was narrower than that found in the jurisprudence of the Constitutional Court. It can even be said that the notion used in the case law of common courts covers only one aspect of the understanding of dignity used by the Court. The Supreme Court most fully expressed this understanding of dignity in a 1989 ruling in which it recognized dignity as a sphere of personality that "concretizes itself in the sense of self-respect of man and the expectation of respect from other people. This feeling, which is an essential element of the human psyche, is shaped by a number of different external circumstances. It is not immutable. As a product of the development of human nature, it is historically and culturally conditioned" (the Supreme Court of Poland's Decision I CR 143/89). It follows that the condition for an infringement of human dignity is not only a violation of certain rights, but also an assessment that this violation undermines, in the eyes of society, the self-esteem of a person. Simultaneously, this assessment is made not from a subjective point of view, concerning a given individual, but it is to be objectified in a certain way; i.e. it is needed to take into account the beliefs that occur in society, and thus the specific *vox populi* concerning social esteem (Jabłoński 2001). Certainly, it is not an approach to dignity taken from personalism, but a certain variant of the sociological approach to this concept. It is worth pointing out at this stage that, before 1989, such an understanding of dignity was considered to be compatible with Marxist theory. It should also be pointed out that the judicial decisions before the adoption of the current Polish Constitution, and especially before 1989, contained ambiguous, strange, and contradictory statements about dignity. For example, in one of the judgments, the Supreme Court stated that rape does not always lead to a violation of the raped person's dignity (the Supreme Court of Poland's Decision I KR 460/73, cf. Jabłoński 2001, 298–300). Therefore, it should be stated that the recognition of dignity in the Constitution of the Republic of Poland of 1997 also affects common courts, which pay more attention to this category, although they are more attached to the understanding of dignity as self-respect.

Conclusion

The Polish Constitutional Court recognizes that the ruling on the incompatibility of a provision with the Constitution of the Republic of Poland only because it infringes on dignity is possible only in specific exceptions. In judgments concerning dignity, the Court has usually considered whether there has been a violation of the provision on dignity and other provisions of the Constitution. It should be emphasized that the Court has not developed its own approach to human dignity, relying mainly on German constitutional jurisprudence and constitutional-law "doctrine." Günter Dürig's "object-formula" was introduced by the Court as a concept fully compatible with the Polish Constitution of 1997. In my view, it is connected with the Polish legal culture of the "transition" period, which was based on the assumption that, after communism, it was necessary to learn from Western legal cultures how to shape legal institutions. Because Polish legal culture had been strongly linked to Austro-German culture in the past, using German legal concepts as a pattern seemed an obvious choice.

The Court never refers to philosophical considerations about dignity in its judgments. Nevertheless, its judgments utilize elements from different views on dignity. In particular, the Court uses echoes of the Kantian understanding of dignity (seen, however, through the glass of Dürig's teachings), views influenced by personalism, and a liberal approach emphasizing the sphere of individual autonomy and the sociological concept of dignity as the entirety of conditions making a human being respectful in society. The Court's view is certainly multifaceted, but it is difficult to conclude that the Court has developed a single, coherent concept of dignity. Moreover, the Court always presents its considerations in such a way as to persuade the audience that in every judgment it discovers the objective truth about the notion of dignity contained in the Polish Constitution. The distinct feature of Polish constitutional jurisprudence is that the reasoning on human dignity is not expanded in the Court's views on such a controversial issue as abortion. One of the possible reasons is that the extensive use of the notion of dignity in such a context would make the existence of competing interpretations of human dignity rather too apparent.

Notes

1 The label "philosophy of law" was not used because it was considered to be a "bourgeois" notion.

2 Numerous provisions in the Polish legal system, both before and after the introduction of the Constitution of 1997, use the term "dignity." However, in these instances, dignity is tied not with the human person but with the characteristics of certain positions, offices, or bodies. Here, the notion of the dignity of the office of a judge, prosecutor, or juror is used. Such an understanding of dignity cannot be combined with the concept of dignity utilized in Article 30 of the Constitution (cf. Czarny 2001).

3 Some authors question the possibility of deriving a separate right to respect the dignity of an individual from Article 30 of the Constitution of the Republic of Poland (cf. Complak 1998, 48).

4 From a Kantian perspective, entities that possess the attribute of dignity are not things that can be used as a means to a specific purpose (Kant 2002, 52–54; see also Sensen 2011). Echoes of the Kantian notion of dignity can also be spotted in Polish textbooks on constitutional law, although Kant's name is rarely mentioned (cf. Dudek 2001, 51–52).

5 On this judgment cf. Szczepański 2012 and Kulesza 2009.

6 As Giovanni Pico della Mirandola (2012) explained, a human being can become everything he or she wants. Man is the only creature that has both devilish and angelic features; he decides which of them will be developed. Other beings are determined to achieve a predestined state.

7 It is not insignificant that its main proponents, Józef Krukowski and Franciszek Mazurek, were Catholic priests and professors at Catholic University of Lublin. The Constitutional Court has often cited Complak and on occasion also Mazurek.

8 Mazurek claims—similarly to other authors connected with personalism—that these two understandings of dignity are closely related to each other.

9 In German jurisprudence, *Persönlichkeitsrecht* is considered a fundamental right which is derived from Article 2 Section 1 (a right to develop one's personality) in connection with Article 1 Section 1 (the notion of dignity) of Grundgesetz.

10 As a result of this judgment, the situation specified by the Act of January 7, 1993, on family planning, protection of the human fetus, and conditions for the admission of pregnancy termination was reintroduced. Abortion is only permissible if there is a reasonable suspicion that the pregnancy is the result of rape, when the pregnancy threatens the life or health of the mother, or when there is a "high probability of a serious and irreversible impairment of the fetus or an incurable disease threatening its life" (Article 4a).

11 It is worth adding that later Leszek Garlicki questioned the view that a fetus is entitled to dignity (cf. Garlicki 2016, 44).

12 Here I will not analyze the controversies about the constitutionality of appointments of some justices of the Constitutional Court in 2015–2016.

13 Judgments of the Constitutional Court take legal effect after their publication in the Journal of Laws, and in accordance with the provisions of the Act of July 20, 2000, on the publication of normative acts and some other legal acts, the publication is ordered by the prime minister. The prime minister decided to order the publication of the judgment as late as on January 27, 2021, after the majority opinion and dissenting opinions were made public by the Constitutional Court.

14 In the Polish legal system there is no institution of civil partnership, let alone same-sex marriage. Moreover, the very issue of shaping some legal framework for same-sex relationships is met with objections not only among right-wing politicians but also among the majority of society (Centrum Badania Opinii Społecznej 2017). Both conservatives and gay activists use the ambiguous formulation of Article 18 of the Polish Constitution, which states that "Marriage, being a union of a man and a woman . . . shall be placed under the protection and care of the Republic of Poland." According to some, this article prevents the recognition of marriages

other than those created by a man and a woman. According to others, this article only grants special protection from the state to a marriage understood as a union of a man and a woman, but it does not prohibit the introduction of same-sex marriage as a legal institution. In Polish legal discourse the adherents of same-sex marriages only sometimes and very sketchily refer to the concept of dignity (Drapalska-Grochowicz 2019). Their adversaries, in turn, sometimes mention the legal notion of dignity but it is definitely not a central point of their arguments (Banaszkiewicz 2013, 610).

References

Banaszkiewicz, Bolesław. 2013. "'Małżeństwo jako związek kobiety i mężczyzny'. O niektórych implikacjach art. 18 Konstytucji RP ['Marriage as a Relationship Between a Woman and a Man.' On Some Implications of Article 18 of Polish Constitution]." *Kwartalnik Prawa Prywatnego* 22 (3): 591–656.

Barak, Aharon. 2015. *Human dignity. The Constitutional Value and the Constitutional Right.* Cambridge: Cambridge University Press.

Bosek, Leszek. 2012. *Gwarancje godności ludzkiej i ich wpływ na polskie prawo cywilne* [Guarantees of Human Dignity and Their Impact on Polish Civil Law]. Warszawa: Wydawnictwo Sejmowe.

Centrum Badania Opinii Społecznej [Public Opinion Research Center]. 2017. "Stosunek do osób o orientacji homoseksualnej i związków partnerskich. Komunikat z badan [Attitude Towards Homosexual Persons and Same-sex Partnerships. Abstract from the Research]." www.cbos.pl/SPISKOM.POL/2017/K_174_17.PDF.

Complak, Krystian. 1998. "Uwagi o godności człowieka oraz jej ochrona w świetle nowej konstytucji [Comments on Human Dignity and Its Protection in the Light of the New Constitution]." *Przegląd Sejmowy* 6 (5): 41–51.

Czarny, Piotr. 2001. "Konstytucyjne pojęcie godności człowieka a rozumienie godności w polskim języku prawnym [The Constitutional Concept of Human Dignity and the Understanding of Dignity in the Polish Legal Language]." In *Godność człowieka jako kategoria prawna (opracowania i materiały)* [Human Dignity as a Legal Category (Studies and Materials)], edited by Krystian Complak, 195–99. Wrocław: Drukarnia Centrum Handlu i Poligrafii.

Drapalska-Grochowicz, Marlena. 2019. "Kilka uwag na tle statusu prawnego związków jednopłciowych w polskim ustawodawstwie [A Few Remarks Regarding the Legal Status of Same-sex Couples in Polish Legislation]." *Młody Jurysta* 7 (2): 63–80.

Dreier, Horst. 2004. "Art. 1 I." In *Grundgesetz. Kommentar*, edited by Horst Dreier, 139–231. Tübingen: Mohr Siebeck.

Dudek, Dariusz. 2001. *Konstytucja Rzeczypospolitej Polskiej. Zagadnienia podstawowe. Wybór źródeł* [Constitution of the Republic of Poland. Fundamental issues. Selection of Sources]. Lublin: Lubelskie Wydawnictwo Prawnicze.

Dürig, Günter. 1956. "Der Grundrechtssatz von der Menschenwürde: Entwurf eines praktikablen Wertsystems der Grundrechte aus Art. 1 Abs. I in Verbindung mit Art. 19 Abs. II des Grundgesetzes." *Archiv des öffentlichen Rechts* 81 (2): 117–57.

Działocha, Kazimierz. 2010. "Idee przewodnie wolności i praw jednostki w procesie uchwalania Konstytucji RP [Guiding Ideas of Individual Freedoms and Rights in the Process of Adopting the Polish Constitution]." In *Wolności i prawa jednostki w Konstytucji RP* [Freedoms and Rights of the Individual in the Polish Constitution]. Vol. I, edited by Mariusz Jabłoński, 3–29. Warszawa: C.H. Beck.

Garlicki, Leszek. 1999. *Polskie prawo konstytucyjne. Zarys wykładu* [Polish Constitutional Law. Outline of the Lecture]. Warsawa: Liber.

Garlicki, Leszek. 2016. "Artykuł 30 (Article 30)." In *Konstytucja Rzeczypospolitej Polskiej. Komentarz* [Constitution of the Republic of Poland. Commentary]. Vol.

II, edited by Leszek Garlicki and Marek Zubik, 27–54. Warszawa: Wydawnictwo Sejmowe.

Jabłoński, Mariusz. 2001. "Pojęcie i ochrona godności człowieka w orzecznictwie organów władzy sądowniczej w Polsce [The Concept and Protection of Human Dignity in the Jurisprudence of Judicial Authorities in Poland]." In *Godność człowieka jako kategoria prawna (opracowania i materiały)* [Human Dignity as a Legal Category (Studies and Materials)], edited by Krystian Complak, 295–307. Wrocław: Drukarnia Centrum Handlu i Poligrafii.

Jedlecka, Wioletta. 2013. "Argumentacja oparta na zasadzie autonomii i godności człowieka w sporze o legalizację eutanazji [Argumentation Based on the Principle of Autonomy and Human Dignity in the Dispute about the Legalization of Euthanasia]." *Wrocławskie Studia Erazmiańskie* 7: 35–55.

Kant, Immanuel. 2002. *Groundwork for the Metaphysics of Morals.* Translated by A. W. Wood. New Haven; London: Yale University Press.

Krukowski, Józef. 1997. "Godność człowieka podstawą konstytucyjnego katalogu praw i wolności jednostki [Human Dignity as the Basis of the Constitutional Catalog of Individual Rights and Freedoms]." In *Podstawowe prawa jednostki i ich sądowa ochrona* [Fundamental Rights of the Individual and Their Judicial Protection], edited by Leszek Wiśniewski, 38–50. Warszawa: Wydawnictwo Sejmowe.

Kulesza, Jan. 2009. "Czy państwo może mordować własnych obywateli? Zestrzelenie samolotu typu *renegade* w świetle prawa karnego—zarys problemu [Can the State Murder Its Own Citizens? Shooting Down a Renegade aircraft Under Criminal Law—An Outline of the Problem]." *Czasopismo Prawa Karnego i Nauk Penalnych* 13 (3): 5–33.

Łętowska, Ewa. 2003. "O godności, jej funkcji w obrocie prawnym i promocyjnej roli Rzecznika Praw Obywatelskich [On Dignity, Its Function in Legal Relationships and the Promotional Role of the Ombudsman]." In *Godność człowieka a prawa ekonomiczne i socjalne. Księga jubileuszowa wydana w piętnastą rocznicę ustanowienia Rzecznika Praw Obywatelskich* [Human dignity and Economic and Social Rights. Jubilee Book Published on the 15th anniversary of the Establishment of the Ombudsman], 241–48. Warszawa: Biuro Rzecznika Praw Obywatelskich.

Mahlmann, Matthias. 2012. "Human Dignity and Autonomy in Modern Constitutional Orders." In *The Oxford Handbook of Comparative Constitutional Law*, edited by Michel Rosenfeld and András Sajó, 370–96. Oxford: Oxford University Press.

Mazurek, Franciszek J. 2001. *Godność osoby ludzkiej podstawą praw człowieka* [The Dignity of a Human Person as the Basis of Human Rights]. Lublin: Redakcja Wydawnictw Katolickiego Uniwersytetu Lubelskiego.

Mazurek, Franciszek J. 2019. "Pojęcie godności człowieka. Historia i miejsce w projektach konstytucji III Rzeczypospolitej [The Concept of Human Dignity. History and Place in the Draft Constitution of the Third Polish Republic]." *Roczniki Nauk Prawnych KUL* 6: 5–41.

Michalewska-Pawlak, Małgorzata. 2010. *Obywatelskość demokratyczna jako idea normatywna w koncepcjach polityczno-programowych polskiej opozycji w latach 1980–1989* [Democratic Citizenship as a Normative Idea in the Political Concepts of the Polish Opposition 1980–1989]. Gdańsk: Europejskie Centrum Solidarności.

Ossowska, Maria. 1972. *Normy moralne. Próba systematyzacji* [Moral Norms: A Tentative Systematization]. Warszawa: Państwowe Wydawnictwo Naukowe.

Pico della Mirandola, Giovanni. 2012. *Oration on the Dignity of Man.* Translated by A. R. Gaponigri. Washington, DC: Regnery Publishing.

Ściślicki, Piotr. 2013. *Prawo do życia człowieka w okresie prenatalnym. Analiza w perspektywie prawno-kulturowej—ze szczególnym uwzględnieniem personalizmu chrześcijańskiego* [The Right to Human Life in the Prenatal Period. Analysis in the Legal and Cultural Perspective—with Particular Emphasis on Christian Personalism]. Warszawa: Warszawska Firma Wydawnicza.

Sensen, Oliver. 2011. *Kant on Human Dignity*. Berlin; Boston: de Gruyter Verlag.
Szczepański, Przemysław. 2012. "Trybunał Konstytucyjny a terroryzm—analiza wybranych tez z uzasadnienia do wyroku TK 44/07 [The Constitutional Court and Terrorism—An Analysis of Selected Theses from the Judgment TK 44/07]." *Acta Universitatis Lodziensis. Folia Iuridica* 71: 113–24.
Wojtyczek, Krzysztof. 2001. "Ochrona godności człowieka, wolności i równości przy pomocy skargi konstytucyjnej w polskim systemie prawnym [Protection of Human Dignity, Freedom and Equality by Means of a Constitutional Complaint in Polish Legal System]." In *Godność człowieka jako kategoria prawna (opracowania i materiały)* [Human Dignity as a Legal Category (Studies and Materials)], edited by Krystian Complak, 200–206. Wrocław: Drukarnia Centrum Handlu i Poligrafii.
Zajadło, Jerzy. 1989. "Godność jednostki w aktach międzynarodowej ochrony praw człowieka [Dignity of a Human Being in the Acts of International Protection of Human Rights]." *Ruch Prawniczy, Ekonomiczny i Socjologiczny* 51 (2): 103–17.

Case Law and Legal Acts

Polish Legislation

Act of October 26, 1982, on the Upbringing in Sobriety and Counteracting Alcoholism. *Dziennik Ustaw* [Journal of Laws], 1993, No. 35, Item 230, as amended.
Act of April 6, 1990, on the Police. *Dziennik Ustaw* [Journal of Laws], 1990, No. 30, Item 179, as amended.
Act of January 7, 1993, on the Family Planning, Protection of the Human Fetus and Conditions for the Admission of Pregnancy Termination. *Dziennik Ustaw* [Journal of Laws], 1993, No. 17, Item 78.
Act of July 20, 2000, on the Publication of Normative Acts and Some Other Legal Acts: Consolidated Text. *Dziennik Ustaw* [Journal of Laws], 2019, Item 1461.
Act of July 3, 2002, on the Aviation Law. *Dziennik Ustaw* [Journal of Laws], 2005, No. 226, Item 1944.
Act of July 24, 2003, on the Amendment of the Executive Penal Code and Some Other Acts. *Dziennik Ustaw* [Journal of Laws], 2003, No. 142, Item 1380.

The Constitutional Court of Poland

Judgment K 26/96, May 28, 1997.
Judgment K 11/00, April 4, 2001.
Judgment K 7/01, March 5, 2003.
Judgment K 10/04 February 22, 2005.
Judgment K 4/04 June 20, 2005.
Judgment K 32/04, December 12, 2005.
Judgment K 44/07, September 30, 2008.
Judgment K 6/09, February 24, 2010.
Judgment K 1/20, October 22, 2020.
Judgment P. 12/99, November 15, 2000.
Judgment P. 6/01, November 8, 2001.
Judgment P. 10/06, October 30, 2006.
Judgment P. 20/09, February 23, 2010.
Judgment SK 6/02, October 15, 2002.
Judgment SK 48/05, July 9, 2009.

The Federal Constitutional Court of Germany

1 BvR 357/05, February 15, 2006.

The Supreme Court of Poland

Decision I CR 143/89, April 25, 1989.
Decision I KR 460/73, May 6, 1974.

Part III

Human Dignity, Religion, and Courts

10 Deliberations on Dignity

Irish Case Law Concerning Medical Interventions and Freedom of Religion, Belief, and Conscience

Michelle Flynn

Introduction

The discussion of "human dignity" has gained considerable traction in recent years, yet there remains ambiguity as to how it should function as a legal concept (Scharffs and Ochab 2022). Within the Irish context, academic debate has arisen as to whether dignity is to be understood as a foundational constitutional principle by virtue of its express invocation in the Preamble to Bunreacht na hÉireann (hereinafter referred to as the "Irish Constitution"), or as a justiciable personal right implicitly protected by virtue of Article 40.3 (Dewhurst 2019; O'Mahony 2012). The concept of human dignity can be traced back to pre-Christian thought and continues to be strongly influenced by metaphysical assumptions (Binchy 2008, 308–9; Habermas 2010, 470–71). Nevertheless, it has been argued that, in relation to the Irish Constitution, the concept of dignity that is rooted in the natural law tradition has been replaced by a more secular version (O'Mahony 2017, 183). While there are multiple philosophically and theologically inspired definitions of human dignity, given the lack of clarity concerning dignity as a legal concept, it is worthwhile examining the judicial treatment of dignity through a consideration of relevant case law in Ireland.

This chapter will examine the way in which dignity is considered in the adjudication of cases concerning the refusal by an adult on religious grounds to consent to medical treatment, in addition to parental refusal on religious grounds to consent to medical treatment in respect of a child.[1] Such cases emerge from intensely personal circumstances and often involve issues of bodily integrity, autonomy, and an individual's conscience or religious beliefs. In the case of minors, the situation is often even more complex.

Dignity: A Constitutional Principle or a Personal Right?

While human dignity became a cornerstone in national constitutions and international law[2] in the aftermath of World War II (Habermas 2010; McCrudden 2008; Shulztiner and Carmi 2014), the framers of the Irish Constitution

DOI: 10.4324/9781003307853-13

placed dignity as a founding principle in the fundamental legal document of the state as early as 1937.

The Preamble to the Irish Constitution states as follows:

> In the Name of the Most Holy Trinity, from Whom is all authority and to Whom, as our final end, all actions both of men and States must be referred,
>
> We, the people of Éire,
>
> Humbly acknowledging all our obligations to our Divine Lord, Jesus Christ, Who sustained our fathers through centuries of trial,
>
> Gratefully remembering their heroic and unremitting struggle to regain the rightful independence of our Nation,
>
> And seeking to promote the common good, with due observance of Prudence, Justice and Charity, so that the dignity and freedom of the individual may be assured, true social order attained, the unity of our country restored, and concord established with other nations,
>
> Do hereby adopt, enact, and give to ourselves this Constitution.

The concept of dignity within the Irish Constitution is thus firmly rooted within the Christian tradition. Binchy (2008) has unequivocally stated that:

> there is no great mystery about the philosophical framework of the Constitution. It is one of natural law, as developed by Aquinas, in which human beings, by virtue of their humanity rather than the gift of positive law, have rights and obligations.
>
> (311)

Kirste (2013) has similarly observed that "the Irish constitution begins with a full invocatio Dei thereby opening up a theological perspective on the constitution. In secular constitutions, a strongly religious concept of human dignity is an alien element" (71). This, therefore, provides a specific lens through which to analyze the concept of human dignity in the case law of the Irish courts. It is also of relevance that the intrinsic nature of human dignity is included in the definition provided in section 2 of the Irish Human Rights and Equality Commission Act 2014 which states that " 'dignity' means, in relation to a person, the inviolable intrinsic value, equal to other persons, that the person has and includes the recognition by other persons of such value with respect of that person."

Within the context of the Irish Constitution, Articles 40–44 contain the fundamental rights provisions. Regarding the identification of unenumerated rights, Article 40.3 provides that:

1° The State guarantees in its laws to respect, and, as far as practicable, by its laws to defend and vindicate the personal rights of the citizen.

2° The State shall, in particular, by its laws protect as best it may from unjust attack and, in the case of injustice done, vindicate the life, person, good name, and property rights of every citizen.

In the case of *Ryan v. Attorney General*, the Irish Supreme Court held that the right to bodily integrity was an "unenumerated right" within Article 40.3. The Supreme Court stated that the list of explicit rights was not exhaustive on the basis of the phrase "in particular" contained in Article 40.3.2°. The *Ryan* case was a landmark case as it recognized the "unenumerated rights doctrine" (Hogan et al. 2018, 7.3.76–7.3.94). Since then, the Irish courts have recognized a number of unenumerated rights including the right to privacy, the right to earn a livelihood, and the right of access to the courts. The method used to identify these unenumerated rights has moved from a natural law approach to one rooted in 'human personality,' however O'Mahony notes that "although it has been a less fruitful source of controversy, the notion that the Constitution protects unenumerated rights that are inherent in the human personality is suspiciously similar to natural law." (O'Mahony 2017, 181). More recently, Chief Justice Clarke in the *Climate Case Ireland* stated that he regarded the term "derived rights" as more appropriate than "unenumerated rights" for:

> it conveys that there must be some root of title in the text or structure of the Constitution from which the right in question can be derived. It may stem, for example, from a constitutional value such as dignity when taken in conjunction with other express rights or obligations. It may stem from the democratic nature of the State whose fundamental structures are set out in the Constitution. It may derive from a combination of rights, values and structure. However, it cannot derive simply from judges looking into their hearts and identifying rights which they think should be in the Constitution. It must derive from judges considering the Constitution as a whole and identifying rights which can be derived from the Constitution as a whole.
>
> (*Friends of the Irish Environment CLG v. The Government of Ireland, Ireland and the Attorney General*, para. 8.6)

There is no explicit "right to dignity" within the Irish Constitution, however in the case of *Re a Ward of Court (No. 2)* Judge Denham in the Supreme Court recognized a constitutional "right to dignity," a "right to be treated with dignity," a "right to dignity in life," and a "right to dignity in death." This tragic case centered on a woman, the ward,[3] who had been in a "near persistent vegetative state" for 23 years, and, in accordance with the express wishes of her family, the Supreme Court ordered the withdrawal of artificial nutrition and hydration to allow a natural death to occur. Judge Denham stated that:

> An unspecified right under the Constitution to all persons as human persons is dignity—to be treated with dignity. Such right is not lost by illness or accident. As long as a person is alive they have this right. Thus, the ward in this case has a right to dignity. Decision-making in relation to medical treatment is an aspect of the right to privacy; however, a component in the decision may relate to personal dignity (Re a Ward of Court (No. 2), p. 163).

In addition to recognizing a "right to be treated with dignity" and a "right to dignity," Judge Denham proceeded to list a constitutional right to "dignity in life" and "dignity in death" as factors to be considered by the Court in reaching a determination (*Re a Ward of Court (No. 2)*). In the same case, Judge O'Flaherty referred to the ward's life as "what technically is life, but life without purpose, meaning or dignity," thereby espousing a view that is inconsistent with the notion of dignity inhering in an individual (*Re a Ward of Court (No. 2)*). While the "right to dignity" and its various manifestations have been referred to in subsequent case law, Binchy has commented that:

> There has been little judicial analysis so far of the right to dignity. As we have seen, its status as a right depends on Denham J's analysis, where the logic points to its being capable of being characterised as a specific personal right falling within the protection of Article 40.3.
>
> (Binchy 2008, 325)

O'Mahony (2018) has opined that in the case of *Re a Ward of Court (No. 2)* Judge Denham adopted a loose usage of language in relation to dignity (474) and, more broadly, O'Mahony (2012) has also commented that "loose usage of the term in constitutional drafting and adjudication serves only to create confusion and uncertainty surrounding the core meaning of the term dignity" (565). Contrarily, Dewhurst (2019) has argued that Article 40.3 "is the most natural home for the right to human dignity" as it gives "clarity to the scope, content and limitations of the right, which would not have been available under the Preamble" (436).

The identification of dignity as a personal right protected within Article 40.3 gives rise to conceptual difficulties and challenges the notion of dignity as being inherent, yet there has been little judicial engagement with the distinction. For instance, human dignity as a right protected within the ambit of Article 40.3 could be subject to limitations and therefore not absolute in nature. This understanding runs counter to the notion of an ontological dignity which is inherent in every individual by virtue of being human, and thus cannot be taken away or limited. Indeed, it has been observed that "it is not obvious that a legal term can have the dual function of serving as a justification for rights and operative clauses and also constituting a right or an operative clause in itself" (Shulztiner and Carmi 2014, 481). Feldman (1999) has opined that "the notion that dignity can itself be a fundamental right is superficially appealing but ultimately unconvincing. . . . Nevertheless, human rights, when adequately protected, can improve the chances of realising the aspiration" (682). O'Mahony (2012) has similarly argued that "there is no such thing as a right to dignity: such a notion is essentially inconsistent with the invocation of human dignity as the foundational principle underlying and justifying the legal protection of human rights" (564).

In transmogrifying human dignity into a justiciable right, the concept becomes almost boundless and without any clear substantive content. Consequently, human dignity as a concept is being stretched and it is necessary to examine whether this expansion of the term may ultimately undermine or enhance its fundamental role in determining the ambit of human rights.[4]

The Irish Courts and Human Dignity

Ireland has traditionally been a religiously homogenous country with a vast majority of Roman Catholics. However, over the last 30 years there has been a significant increase in the non-Catholic population driven by both growing numbers with no religion and increases in other religions.[5] The Irish courts have been at the forefront of dealing with Ireland's considerable societal changes in recent years. The Irish Constitution is a living legal document that recognizes and protects certain fundamental human rights, and it is the role of the Irish courts to interpret the meaning of its provisions. Where a conflict arises between constitutional rights, the courts will assess the circumstances and engage in a balancing exercise to determine which constitutional right or rights should take precedence in a case.

An analysis of case law emanating from the Irish courts must be considered against the backdrop of this rapid social change, but also with the recognition that the interpretation of dignity as a legal concept is necessarily heavily informed by the theological and philosophical tradition from which it emerges. For the purposes of this discussion, the focus shall be on the role of dignity in cases that require a court to engage in a difficult balancing exercise between two human rights that go to the very core of human existence: the right to life, and the right to freedom of conscience and religion. At this juncture, it is appropriate to set out both constitutional provisions. Article 40.3.2° provides that "[t]he State shall, in particular, by its laws protect as best it may from unjust attack and, in the case of injustice done, vindicate the life, person, good name and property rights of every citizen." Article 44.2.1° provides that "[f]reedom of conscience and the free profession and practice of religion are, subject to public order and morality, guaranteed to every citizen." It is therefore clear that, within the context of the Irish Constitution, the right to freedom of conscience and religion is subject to the limitations of public order and morality.[6] Nevertheless, it has been noted that:

> Article 44.2.1 protects not only the traditional and popular religions and religious denominations—such as, for example, Roman Catholicism, the Church of Ireland and the Presbyterian Church—but perhaps just as importantly, it provides a vital safeguard for minority religions and religious denominations whose tenets are regarded by many as unconventional.
>
> (*Re Baby A.B.: Children's University Hospital Temple Street v. C.D. and E.F., para. 27*).

Presently, it is apt to refer to the case of *Re a Ward of Court (No. 2)* to draw attention to the way in which the religious beliefs of the family were held to be relevant. Under a heading titled "Spiritual aspect," Judge Denham noted that:

> The ward and her family profess the Roman Catholic faith. Great care has been taken by the mother of the ward to ensure that no steps are taken contrary to the family's faith. Evidence was given on their behalf by two theologians. This is a court of law, and the Constitution and law are applied: not moral law. However, the religious beliefs of the ward and her family are one of several factors for the Court to consider when evaluating the bona fides of the family (*Re a Ward of Court (No. 2), p. 155*).

Judge Lynch in the High Court also noted: "Another Roman Catholic moral theologian called on behalf of the institution took the opposite view. I was also supplied with a copy of a working paper prepared by the Church of Ireland discussing a statement issued in October, 1992, by the bishops of the Church of England on euthanasia" (*Re a Ward of Court (No.2)*, p. 90). In considering a range of factors, Judge Denham concluded that "the ward is a member of the Roman Catholic Church, as are her family. Great care has been taken by the family to reach a decision in accordance with the family ethic" (*Re a Ward of Court (No.2)*, p. 169). The careful attention given, by both Judge Lynch in the High Court and Judge Denham in the Supreme Court, to the religious beliefs of the family displays an acute awareness of the importance of the family's religious beliefs in reaching a decision in the matter. The role of theologians as expert witnesses and the weight attributed to that evidence is also particularly striking. Furthermore, in light of the institution's objection to the withdrawal of artificial nutrition and hydration, Judge Lynch also authorized the family to arrange for the admission of the ward to another institution which would not find it contrary to their philosophy and ethics to cease artificial nutrition and hydration. In relation to that matter, Chief Justice Hamilton in the Supreme Court observed that:

> At the substantive hearing it was accepted by the family and by all the other parties that this plea of the institution was valid and that no order should be made by the Court against the institution, the obedience to which would contravene the philosophy and code of ethics of the institution.
>
> (Re a Ward of Court (No.2), p. 110)

Thus, religious and philosophical beliefs were a significant consideration in adjudicating the case. The following cases, which span a period stretching from 2001 until 2021, are germane to this discussion as they also illustrate the approach adopted by the Irish courts.

Refusal by an Adult on Religious Grounds to Consent to Medical Treatment

The cases of *J.M. v. Board of Management of St. Vincent's Hospital and Others* and *Fitzpatrick and Ryan v. F.K. and the Attorney General* required the courts to engage in a balancing exercise between the right to life and the right to freedom of conscience and religion. Given the very serious issues at the center of both cases, it is curious that dignity is not expressly referred to at any point in either judgment. Nevertheless, it is clear from both judgments that the concept of dignity as a value is implicitly present in the judicial decision-making process.

In *J.M.*, the patient was a recently married foreign national who had adopted her husband's religion as a Jehovah's Witness. She was critically ill and required a blood transfusion and a liver transplant. The patient initially refused this treatment, then subsequently communicated to her husband that she would receive treatment, however she refused to sign the consent forms that were presented to her minutes later. There were doubts as to her capacity to make such a decision at that point, and she thereafter entered into a coma. The applicant in the case was the patient's husband who sought to have the Court place his wife in wardship. The High Court cited the decision of the Supreme Court in *Re a Ward of Court (No.2)* as authority that a competent adult who is terminally ill has the right to refuse medical treatment (*J.M. v. Board of Management of St. Vincent's Hospital and Others*). However, the Court held that no final decision to refuse treatment had in fact been made and, in exercising its *parens patriae* jurisdiction, the Court directed the provision of medical treatment including a blood transfusion and a liver transplant.

In the case of *Fitzpatrick and Ryan v. F.K. and the Attorney General*, the High Court engaged in a balancing exercise between the right to life and the right to freedom of conscience and religion. F.K. suffered a massive post-partum hemorrhage shortly after giving birth in a maternity hospital. As medical staff prepared to give her an urgent blood transfusion, they were informed that she refused to provide consent due to her religious beliefs as a Jehovah's Witness. F.K. was a foreign national from the Democratic Republic of Congo who was not proficient in the English language. She had a female "birth partner" who was present throughout the birth and acted as a translator. Before the birth, F.K. had attended several appointments at the maternity hospital and registered her religion as Roman Catholic. At the antenatal appointment, through a telephone interpreter, F.K. confirmed her medical history and her religion as Roman Catholic. Additionally, she signed a consent form to have blood samples taken from her before the birth, and those samples were subsequently taken.

In the context of the medical emergency that arose in the aftermath of giving birth, there was doubt as to whether F.K. had the capacity to understand the seriousness of the consequences of her refusal to consent, and therefore there was a concern as to whether her refusal was fully informed. The hospital made an *ex parte* application to the High Court for an order permitting the hospital to give a blood transfusion to F.K. An order was granted authorizing the hospital to give all appropriate medical treatment to F.K. and she ultimately made a full recovery. The hospital subsequently sought a number of declarations, including a declaration that it was entitled to apply for the injunction by virtue of the Irish Constitution, and that the Court was entitled and/or obliged to grant that relief. F.K. brought a counterclaim seeking declarations that the hospital had violated her constitutional rights, including her right to bodily integrity and autonomy. Furthermore, F.K. sought a declaration that the application for the *ex parte* order and the administration of a blood transfusion without her consent were incompatible with the European Convention on Human Rights. F.K. sought damages for assault, trespass to the person, and breach of her rights under the Irish Constitution and the European Convention on Human Rights.

The High Court affirmed the constitutionally protected right of a properly informed adult with full capacity to refuse medical treatment for religious or other reasons and cited with approval the Supreme Court judgment in *Re a Ward of Court (No.2)* which stated that:

> The right to life is the pre-eminent personal right. The State has guaranteed in its laws to respect this right. The respect is absolute. This right refers to all lives—all lives are respected for the benefit of the individual and for the common good. The State's respect for the life of the individual encompasses the right of the individual to, for example, refuse a blood transfusion for religious reasons. In the recognition of the individual's autonomy, life is respected (*Re a Ward of Court (No. 2), p. 160*).

Regarding freedom of conscience and religion, Judge Laffoy noted that the test for determining capacity would be fulfilled if a patient assimilated and believed the information provided by his or her doctors, but nonetheless refused medical treatment due to a religious conviction. The Court was satisfied that the hospital would have respected the wishes of any patient of the Jehovah's Witness faith who did not wish to have a blood transfusion.[7] The High Court held that the plaintiffs had acted lawfully as there was objective evidence that, at the relevant time, F.K. did not have the capacity to make a valid decision to refuse a blood transfusion. Accordingly, the Court dismissed F.K.'s counterclaim.

Parental Refusal on Religious Grounds to Consent to Medical Treatment in Respect of a Child

Regarding parental refusal on religious grounds to consent to medical treatment in respect of a child, three cases are of particular significance: *North Western Health Board v. H.W. and C.W.*, *Re Baby A. Children's University Hospital Temple Street v. C.D. and E.F.* and *In the Matter of J.J.* In addition to considerations of personal rights such as the right to bodily integrity and the right to freedom of conscience and religion, these cases also concerned Article 41.1 of the Irish Constitution which recognizes the family as the natural primary and fundamental unit group of society.[8] The former Article 42.5 of the Irish Constitution provided:

> In exceptional cases, where the parents for physical or moral reasons fail in their duty towards their children, the State as guardian of the common good, by appropriate means shall endeavour to supply the place of the parents, but always with due regard for the natural and imprescriptible rights of the child.

In 2015, Article 42.5 was repealed and replaced with a new Article 42A dedicated explicitly to the rights of the child. However, in respect of both *North Western Health Board* and *Re Baby A.B.*, Article 42.5 was in force.

In *North Western Health Board* the key question was whether the defendants, as parents, could be required by an order of the Court to permit the plaintiff to conduct a medical test on their child. The PKU test is a public health screening test for infants that can detect various rare but serious conditions. Without early detection, some of the conditions can cause either intellectual disability or life-threatening illness. The test is not compulsory, but parents are advised to consent to the test. The plaintiff, as the statutory body with responsibility for the welfare of children in its geographical area, was responsible for ensuring that infants were screened for these conditions.

The defendants were parents of a newborn infant who refused to give their consent for the PKU test which required the taking of a blood sample from their child. While the defendants had expressly stated that they had no objection to a non-invasive PKU test being conducted, such as the taking of a hair or urine sample, the blood test was supported by medical evidence as being the most effective and reliable method.

In a letter dated 11 May, 2000, the defendants wrote:

> We refuse to allow blood samples being taken, as these can only be obtained by invasive measures, such as puncturing a blood vessel. It is our strong religious belief that nobody is allowed to injure anybody else. We hope that through this clarification, court proceedings can be averted.
>
> (*North Western Health Board v. H.W. and C.W.*, p. 627–8)

The assertion of a religious motivation for the refusal of consent was not, however, reiterated in subsequent affidavits. During the hearing, the Court was informed that the refusal to provide consent for the PKU test was not religious in the sense of an identified faith, rather the objection was of a more general nature. The plaintiff applied to the High Court seeking permission to carry out the screening test and for an order restraining the infant's parents from impeding the carrying out of the test. A point of great significance is that the plaintiff sought to obtain a ruling of general application.

The High Court, in refusing the application, noted that Article 41 of the Irish Constitution placed the family in a special position as the natural primary and fundamental unit group of society which possessed rights antecedent and superior to positive law. The state's duty to vindicate the rights of children arose only in exceptional circumstances where parents had failed in their duty toward their children for physical or moral reasons. The state was not, however, entitled to intervene in every case where parental opinion differed from professional opinion or where the state viewed a parental decision as erroneous (*North Western Health Board v. II.W. and C.W.*, p. 635).

The plaintiff appealed the decision to the Supreme Court. While the Supreme Court acknowledged that this case did not engage the balancing of a religious element, it noted that a religious objection could be central in a subsequent case (*North Western Health Board v. H.W. and C.W.*, p. 753). Among several important statements made by the Court, the following observation by Judge Murphy is particularly illuminating wherein it is noted that:

> The Thomistic philosophy—the influence of which on the Constitution has been so frequently recognised in the judgments and writings of Walsh J.—confers an autonomy on parents which is clearly reflected in these express terms of the Constitution which relegate the State to a subordinate and subsidiary role.
>
> (*North Western Health Board v. H.W. and C.W.*, p. 732)

Judge Hardiman, in noting the dangers of upholding a compulsory medical examination or treatment, stated that "[a]mple scope must be given to the fundamental values of human dignity, as well as those of positive logic" (*North Western Health Board v. H.W. and C.W.*, p. 747). In the Supreme Court, three of the five-judge panel (Judge Denham (as she then was), Judge Murray and Judge Murphy) placed reliance upon the judgment of Chief Justice O'Higgins in *G. v. An Bord Uchtála* and cited with approval the following passage: "Having been born, the child has the right to be fed and to live, to be reared and educated, to have the opportunity of working and of realising his or her full personality and dignity as a human being" (*G. v. An Bord Uchtála* 1, p. 55–56). In dismissing the appeal, the Supreme Court held that it had not been established that this was an exceptional case requiring state intervention to vindicate the child's constitutional rights.

The case of *Re Baby A.B.* arose in the context of a medical emergency. The question at the center of this case was whether the state could intervene where there is parental refusal on religious grounds to consent to a blood transfusion for an infant. Three-month-old A.B. required an urgent blood transfusion due to a critical illness. The parents of A.B. refused to provide consent for the blood transfusion due to their religious beliefs as Jehovah's Witnesses. The hospital made an urgent application to the High Court for an order to permit the blood transfusion. Based on expert medical evidence which confirmed the clinical necessity for the treatment, Judge Hogan granted a declaration to the effect that it would be lawful for the hospital to administer a blood transfusion to A.B. Judge Hogan noted that Article 44.2.1° protects traditional, popular, and minority religions, and acknowledged that while the objection of Jehovah's Witnesses to the taking of blood products even to provide life-saving and essential medical treatment could be regarded as "unconventional," the Jehovah's Witnesses nevertheless:

> regard the blood prohibition as one which is not only scripturally ordained in view of the admonition in Acts 15:29 requiring Christians to "abstain from meats offered to idols, and from blood, and from things strangled, and from fornication," but is one which also poses—when it arises—a practical test of faith.
>
> (*Re baby A.B.: Children's University Hospital Temple Street v. C.D. and E.F.*, para. 28).

Judge Hogan stated that it was neither within the remit of a secular Court to determine, nor a state to prescribe, which religious views were conventional or orthodox (*Re baby A.B.: Children's University Hospital Temple Street v. C.D. and E.F.*, para. 29). Furthermore, the Court confirmed the constitutionally protected right of a properly informed adult with full capacity to refuse medical treatment, for religious or other reasons, and referred to the decision of the High Court in *Fitzpatrick and Ryan v. F.K. and the Attorney General.* However, the Court noted that in the case of minors the state had a vital interest in ensuring that children were protected, and this interest could "prevail even in the face of express and fundamental constitutional rights" (*Re baby A.B.: Children's University Hospital Temple Street v. C.D. and E.F.*, para. 35). As Article 40.3.2° was deemed to have placed a duty on the state to protect by its laws the life of every citizen, the Court accordingly had jurisdiction to override the religious objections of parents where adherence to those religious beliefs would threaten the life and general welfare of their child (*Children's University Hospital Temple Street v. C.D. and E.F.*, para. 38). It is also of note that reliance was placed upon the decision of the Supreme Court in *North Western Health Board.*

In the recent case of *In the Matter of J.J.*, the Supreme Court clarified the ambit of Article 42A which replaced the repealed Article 42.5.[9] Article 42A.1 provides that the state recognizes and affirms the natural and imprescriptible rights of all children and shall, as far as practicable, by its laws protect and vindicate those rights. Article 42A.2.1° provides that:

> In exceptional cases, where the parents, regardless of their marital status, fail in their duty towards their children to such extent that the safety or welfare of any of their children is likely to be prejudicially affected, the

> State as guardian of the common good shall, by proportionate means as provided by law, endeavour to supply the place of the parents, but always with due regard for the natural and imprescriptible rights of the child.

The question to be determined in the case of *In the Matter of J.J.* was whether the parental refusal to consent to specific medical treatment was outside the range of permissible family decision-making, thereby permitting the state to intervene. The case concerned an eleven-year-old child who, as a result of a road traffic accident in 2020, sustained severe brain injuries. Unanimous expert medical opinion concluded that neurological injuries were severe, permanent, and irreversible and that the child suffered from dystonia which involved involuntary, painful, and prolonged muscle contractions. Objective clinical assessment confirmed that the child was experiencing high levels of pain. Despite the absence of any medical evidence to support their view, the parents disagreed with the assessment and the prognosis in respect of their child. The hospital sought various orders from the High Court to administer the pain relief medication notwithstanding that the probable effect would be a reduction in the child's respiratory functions. In such an event, orders were sought to refrain from administering intensive intervention or ICU admission even if the result was death. The orders were granted by the High Court and the parents appealed the decision to the Supreme Court. The Supreme Court dismissed the appeal but varied the terms of the High Court order in declining to approve general orders regarding treatment as there was no indication that other treatments were in issue or that the parents would not consent.

The Supreme Court held that a move to palliative care did not amount to a deliberate act to end the patient's life, noting that the difference between palliative care and assisted suicide was based on intention. Within the context of Article 42A, the test is whether there is a failure of parental duty such that the safety or welfare of the child is likely to be prejudicially affected. The impact of the failure upon the child is central, rather than the motivation or reasoning of the parents. Fundamentally, the state may intervene only by proportionate means. The primacy of the parental role was reaffirmed, and the Supreme Court noted:

> The fact that part of the approach of his family may be a product of strong religious faith, to an extent not commonplace today, is something which should not be discounted, still less disparaged. The care, concern, and love displayed by his family for John are exactly the values recognised by the philosophical approach embodied in Article 41 which declares the Family to be the natural primary and fundamental unit group in society possessing rights antecedent to positive law.
>
> (*In the Matter of J.J.*, para. 149)

These cases, *North Western Health Board*, *Re Baby A.B.*, and *In the Matter of J.J.*, involved a complex analysis of core constitutional provisions arising from the question as to whether the vindication of the rights of the child required that the parental refusal on religious grounds to consent to medical treatment in respect of a child should be overridden. The judgment in *North Western Health Board* remains one of the strongest authorities in Ireland for demarcating the line between parental rights and state intervention. While in *North Western Health Board* express reference is made to dignity at numerous points, in *Re Baby A.B.* there is no explicit reference to dignity in the judgment. Nevertheless, Judge Hogan relied upon Article 40.3.2° as placing a duty upon the state to protect "the life and person of every citizen," thereby granting the Court jurisdiction to override the religious objections of the infant's parents (*Re baby A.B.: Children's University Hospital Temple Street v. C.D. and E.F.*, para. 38). Regarding *In the Matter of J.J.*, the three explicit references to dignity that arise relate to references within precedent case law.[10]

Conclusion

Within the Irish context, the question remains as to whether dignity is to be understood as being ontologically inherent or as a right that is granted. To conclude that human dignity is inherent and arises by virtue of being human, then it must be understood as being of an absolute nature. At its core is the equal value attached to all individuals by virtue of their intrinsic worth as human beings. Therefore, human dignity as an objective ontological reality may pose difficulties for the framing of certain human rights claims as it is not necessarily emancipatory (Waldron 2001).

The problematic consequence of asserting the inherent nature of human dignity thereby becomes clear when dignity is conceived of as a right. Regarding the argument that Article 40.3 "is the most natural home for the right to human dignity" as it gives "clarity to the scope, content and limitations of the right, which would not have been available under the Preamble" (Dewhurst 2019, 436), it is this author's contention that the primary purpose of human dignity within the Irish Constitution is as a foundational constitutional principle upon which human rights are premised. As a foundational constitutional principle, dignity can also operate as an interpretive tool in the adjudication of rights (O'Mahony 2018). To achieve such clarity, the conflation of dignity with certain human rights (such as autonomy, privacy, the right of the person, equality, and bodily integrity) should not go unchallenged as there is a real risk that the expansive use of the term "dignity" may empty it of its actual meaning (Corbett 2017, 125–26; Mathis 2013, 144).

The focus of this inquiry was on cases concerning the refusal by an adult on religious grounds to consent to medical treatment, in addition to parental refusal on religious grounds to consent to medical treatment in respect of a child. In each of these cases, the Court engaged in a balancing exercise to resolve the conflict between the various constitutional provisions. While dignity is referred to within some of the judgments, an in-depth discussion in any explicit form is peculiarly absent. Such an absence raises significant questions and demands further consideration. As McCrudden has observed:

> The use of dignity is particularly associated with those jurisdictions which have adopted proportionality analysis, whether that word is used or not. That is not coincidental, I think. One important institutional function for dignity is to provide a language in which courts can indicate the weighting given to particular rights and other values in this context. When a particular right or other value is described as engaging dignity, this indicates that the court considers that considerable (even in some cases overwhelming) weight should be attributed to it.
>
> (McCrudden 2008, 716)

Therefore, a particularly pertinent question arises as to whether the right to freedom of conscience and religion is perceived as not directly engaging questions of human dignity in an obvious manner. This is a question that can only be answered by considering the way in which the courts deal with human dignity in adjudicating other constitutional rights.

The ambiguous nature of dignity allows for it to serve a function as a malleable concept in human rights adjudication. McCrudden has highlighted the use of dignity as a tool in the judicial interpretation of human rights, noting that:

> It is a limited role, and (possibly) a different one from that played in philosophical, religious, and political debate, but it seems to me to go some way towards explaining its current, and I predict future, judicial popularity in human rights adjudication.
>
> (McCrudden 2008, 724)

The influence of Thomistic philosophy in the interpretation of dignity as reflecting the infinite and equal worth of each human being has impacted the judicial reasoning within each of these cases; *North Western Health Board v. H.W. and C.W.*, *J.M. v. Board of Management of St. Vincent's Hospital and Others*, *Fitzpatrick and Ryan v. F.K. and the Attorney General*, *Re baby A.B.: Children's University Hospital Temple Street v. C.D. and E.F.*, and *In the Matter of J.J.* Nevertheless, it seems necessary at this point for the Irish courts to develop a clear conceptualization of human dignity not as a right which can be invoked but rather as a value which has the important dual function of acting as the normative basis for human rights, and as a judicial interpretive tool in the identification and balancing of those rights. In so doing, the inherent dignity of the individual could be better respected and protected.

Notes

1 The following cases were selected on the basis of relevance but are by no means a comprehensive review of the entirety of the case law: *North Western Health Board v. H.W. and C.W.*, *J.M. v. Board of Management of St. Vincent's Hospital and Others*,

Fitzpatrick and Ryan v. F.K. and the Attorney General, Re baby A.B.: Children's University Hospital Temple Street v. C.D. and E.F., and *In the Matter of J.J.*

2 By way of example, the "inherent dignity" of the human person is expressly acknowledged in the Preambles to the 1948 Universal Declaration of Human Rights (UDHR), the 1966 International Covenant on Civil and Political Rights, the 1966 International Covenant on Economic, Social and Cultural Rights, and the 1989 United Nations Convention on the Rights of the Child. Indeed, Article 1 of the UDHR states that "All human beings are born free and equal in dignity and rights." More recently, Article 1 of the 2000 Charter of Fundamental Rights of the European Union states that "[h]uman dignity is inviolable. It must be respected and protected."

3 A *parens patriae* jurisdiction is exercised by the High Court in placing an individual in wardship. Wardship provides for the protection by the High Court of persons who lack the mental capacity to make decisions related to their welfare or property. Persons under 18 years of age may also be taken into wardship for reasons other than mental incapacity. Upon becoming a ward, the responsibility for all matters concerning that individual's welfare rests with the court. The Assisted Decision-Making (Capacity) Act 2015 abolished the wardship system with respect to adults and established a new statutory framework.

4 See also Justin Collings' chapter in this volume.

5 In the 2016 census, the first fall in absolute numbers of Roman Catholics in at least five decades was recorded from 3.86 million in 2011 to 3.73 million in 2016. www.cso.ie/en/releasesandpublications/ep/p-cp8iter/p8iter/p8rrc/.

6 This differs from Article 9 of the European Convention on Human Rights and Article 18 of the International Covenant on Civil and Political Rights which explicitly recognizes the absolute nature of the *forum internum* aspect of the freedom of thought, conscience, and religion and permits restrictions only with regard to the *forum externum* aspect which relates to the manifestation of one's religion or beliefs.

7 The current situation in Ireland is that the Health Service Executive (HSE), which is responsible for the provision of health and personal social services, has drafted "Essential Practice Points" concerning medical treatment of Jehovah's Witnesses. Furthermore, there are eight Hospital Liaison Committees in Ireland that provide support and guidance to a Jehovah's Witness undergoing medical procedures, and assistance in the event of an emergency or other challenging medical situation. www.hse.ie/eng/services/publications/socialinclusion/interculturalguide/jehovahswitnesses/.

8 Article 41.1 provides:

> 1 The State recognises the Family as the natural primary and fundamental unit group of Society, and as a moral institution possessing inalienable and imprescriptible rights, antecedent and superior to all positive law.
>
> 2 The State, therefore, guarantees to protect the Family in its constitution and authority, as the necessary basis of social order and as indispensable to the welfare of the Nation and the State.

9 Thirty-First Amendment of the Constitution (Children) Act 2012 was signed into law in 2015.

10 It is noted, at para. 47, that the President of the High Court had taken into account a list of factors previously noted by Judge Denham in *Re a Ward of Court (No. 2)* including the ward's constitutional right to dignity in life and death. The third explicit mention of dignity arises in para. 121 in respect of the case of *N and N. v. Health Service Executive and Others* wherein Judge Hardiman reaffirmed that the Constitution acknowledges the "natural and imprescriptible rights and the human dignity" of children.

References

Binchy, William. 2008. "Dignity as a Constitutional Concept." In *The Irish Constitution: Governance and Values*, edited by Eoin Carolan and Oran Doyle, 307–27. Dublin: Thomson Round Hall.

Corbett, Val. 2017. "The Promotion of Human Dignity: A Theory of Tort Law." *The Irish Jurist* 58: 121–52.

Dewhurst, Elaine. 2019. "Human Dignity in Ireland." In *Handbook of Human Dignity in Europe*, edited by Paolo Becchi and Klaus Mathis, 431–51. Cham: Springer International Publishing.

Feldman, David. 1999. "Human Dignity as a Legal Value-Part I." *Public Law*, 682–702.

Habermas, Jürgen. 2010. "The Concept of Human Dignity and the Realistic Utopia of Human Rights." *Metaphilosophy* 41 (4): 464–80.

Hogan, Gerard, Gerard Whyte, David Kenny, and Rachel Walsh. 2018. *Kelly: The Irish Constitution*. 5th ed. Dublin: Bloomsbury Publishing.

Kirste, Stephan. 2013. "A Legal Concept of Human Dignity as a Foundation of Law." In *Human Dignity as a Foundation of Law*, edited by Winfried Brugger and Stephan Kirste, 63–81. Stuttgart: Franz Steiner Verlag.

Mathis, Klaus. 2013. "Human Dignity as a Two-Edged Sword." In *Human Dignity as a Foundation of Law*, edited by Winfried Brugger and Stephan Kirste, 131–44. Stuttgart: Franz Steiner Verlag.

McCrudden, Christopher. 2008. "Human Dignity and Judicial Interpretation of Human Rights." *European Journal of International Law* 19 (4): 655–724.

O'Mahony, Conor. 2012. "There Is No Such Thing as a Right to Dignity." *International Journal of Constitutional Law* 10 (2): 551–74.

O'Mahony, Conor. 2017. "Unenumerated Rights after NHV." *Dublin University Law Journal* 40 (2): 171–89.

O'Mahony, Conor. 2018. "The Dignity of the Individual in Irish Constitutional Law." In *Human Dignity in Context*, edited by Dieter Grimm, Alexandra Kemmerer, and Christoph Möllers, 469–97. London: Bloomsbury Publishing.

Scharffs, Brett G., and Ewelina U. Ochab. 2022. *Dignity and International Human Rights Law: An Introduction to the Punta Del Este Declaration on Human Dignity for Everyone Everywhere*. New York: Routledge.

Shulztiner, Doron, and Guy E. Carmi. 2014. "Human Dignity in National Constitutions: Functions, Promises and Dangers." *The American Journal of Comparative Law* 62(2): 461–90.

Waldron, Jeremy. 2001. "Dignity, Rights, and Responsibilities." *Arizona State Law Journal* 43: 1107–36.

Case Law

High Court (Ireland)

Re Baby A.B. Children's University Hospital Temple Street v. C.D. and E.F. [2011] IEHC 1.

Fitzpatrick and Ryan v. F.K. and the Attorney General [2008] IEHC 104.

Supreme Court of Ireland

Friends of the Irish Environment CLG v. The Government of Ireland, Ireland and the Attorney General [2020] IESC 49 (Climate Case Ireland).

G. v. An Bord Uchtála [1980] IR 32.
In the Matter of J.J. [2021] IESC 1.
J.M. v. Board of Management of St. Vincent's Hospital and Others [2003] 1 IR 321.
N and N. v. Health Service Executive and Others [2006] IESC 60.
North Western Health Board v. H.W. and C.W. [2001] IESC 90, [2001] 3 IR 622.
Re a Ward of Court (Withholding Medical Treatment) (No. 2) [1996] 2 IR 79.

11 Religious Perspective of Human Dignity in Israeli Case Law

Haim Shapira

Introduction

Since the enactment of Basic Law: Human Dignity and Liberty, which contains the Israeli Bill of Rights,[1] human dignity has become the central concept in Israeli human rights discourse. The concept of human dignity was known in Israeli case law before the enactment of the Basic Law, but it was used only in a narrow sense, as a right against humiliation and degradation. The Basic Law establishes human dignity as a central value and the foundation of all human rights. This meaning of human dignity manifests in the Basic Law title and its opening articles.[2] The Basic Law also recognizes a specific right to dignity. Article 2 provides: "One should not violate the life, body, or dignity of a human being as such." Similarly, Article 4 provides: "Every human being is entitled to protection of his life, body, and dignity." In these two articles, "dignity" is not a general value or ground for other rights but the content of a specific right alongside "life" and "body" (Barak 2015, 280–88).

The introduction of human dignity as a general value and as a ground for human rights raises two basic questions. First, what is the content of human dignity? Is it just an expression of the inherent worth of human beings, or does it refer to a specific feature of humanity, and if yes, what feature? Second, what is the significance of grounding human rights in human dignity? Does human dignity add any meaning or value to human rights?[3] The Supreme Court of Israel dealt extensively with the interpretation of human dignity and addressed these questions. In this chapter, I introduce and analyze a certain voice within the Supreme Court that based the interpretation of human dignity on the biblical idea that human beings were created in the image of God and on the Jewish tradition that followed this idea. This approach to human dignity offers genuine answers to these basic questions and has several implications for human rights issues. This voice does not represent the mainstream in the Court, but a minority group of justices who may be characterized as "the Jewish law school" within the Court. Yet the influence of these justices extends beyond the limits of this group. Often, decisions of these justices in matters related to human dignity were accepted by other justices and became the prevalent law in these matters.

DOI: 10.4324/9781003307853-14

My purpose in this chapter is to introduce the Jewish approach to human dignity through the prism of the Israeli Supreme Court and to show its effect on Israeli case law. I point out the unique features of this interpretation and situate it in the context of the universal discourse on human dignity. I begin with a brief overview of the main approach of the Supreme Court to the interpretation of human dignity, which will make it possible to compare the Jewish interpretation with that of the mainstream in the Court. I then present the legal framework that enables judges to resort to Jewish sources. Next, I introduce the foundations of the Jewish version of human dignity and the concept of God's image. Then I move to the main part of this chapter, where I review various rulings of the Court in matters related to human dignity, which demonstrate the application of this idea.

The Main Approach to Human Dignity of the Supreme Court

The Supreme Court began engaging seriously with the concept of human dignity following the enactment of the Basic Law in 1992. Before that time, the Court rulings mentioned the concept only rarely. The Court detected the dual meaning in which this concept appears in the Basic Law, as a general value, and as a specific right. The value of human dignity was interpreted by the Court as expressing the inherent worth of human beings, but the Court underlined in particular the value of autonomy and freedom. Aharon Barak, former President of the Supreme Court wrote:

> Human dignity as a constitutional value—the humanity of man as such—means acknowledgment that the individual is a free person, who develops his body and spirit according to his own will. The will of a human being is the manifestation of his humanity.
>
> (Barak 2015, 127)

Justice Barak expressed a similar view while sitting on the bench as a justice and as President of the Court (see for example: *Vexelbaum v. Minister of Defense*; *The Movement for the Quality of Government v. The Knesset*). This view was shared by many other justices (see for example: *Anonymous v. Anonymous* (Justice Shamgar); *Taieb v. State of Israel* (Justice Cheshin). Thus, the content of human dignity according to the Court reaches beyond the value of human beings as such, embracing the values of autonomy and freedom. This meaning of human dignity has potential implications for various human rights issues because of the weight it ascribes to autonomy and to the individual's will.

A different question arises regarding the right to dignity. In this context dignity is not a ground for other rights but the content of a specific right. What exactly is the meaning of "dignity" in this context? The intuitive meaning is that of the right to be treated in a humane and dignified manner (Statman 2002, 209; Waldron 2009, 17). The classical situations in which people are exposed to inhumane or humiliating treatment are detention, incarceration, and other offensive government actions, such as searches and investigations. The right to dignity, according to this core meaning, protects against humiliation and degradation in such situations. In this vein, the Israeli Supreme Court emphasized that "human dignity includes the dignity of a person who is subject to investigation" (*Katlan v. Prison Service*). In a famous ruling, the Supreme Court held that the prohibition on torture and cruel and inhumane treatment is absolute and is not subject to any restrictions or balance. The Court also held that the General Security Service did not have the authority to employ certain methods of investigation, which entailed suffering, humiliation, and degradation (*The Public Committee Against Torture v. The Government of Israel*).

But people may be exposed to humiliation in other situations as well. They may be humiliated by the social and political order, by discrimination, or even by arbitrary treatment at the hands of the state bureaucracy (Margalit 1996). Does the right to dignity protect people in these cases as well? If so, dignity assumes a much broader meaning. The Supreme Court adopted the latter approach and construed the right to dignity in a broad manner, so that the right to dignity includes protection against all types of insults to human dignity, not only in the classical situations mentioned but in all other forms of political and social order. According to this interpretation, infringement of many other rights—such as an infringement of equality—may be considered as an insult to human dignity. One may, therefore, speak of the right to dignity as a "framework right" or a "mother right" that contains many "daughter rights," including equality, freedom of expression, freedom of religion, right to family, and more (Barak 2015, 280–301).[4]

What were the sources and principles that guided the Supreme Court in this interpretation? Before the Court was the intellectual history of human dignity and the comparative legal interpretation of this concept in other countries and international forums. But the reasoning of the Court was based on the language and structure of the Basic Law. The method that the Supreme Court embraced in this matter was purposive interpretation (Barak 2015, 69–102). According to this method, the original intentions of the legislators are less important, and what matters more is the objective purpose of the law, as defined by the Court. The Court established that the main purpose of the Basic Law is to provide a broad protection of human rights. A central consideration of the Court was the fact that the list of rights mentioned in the Basic Law was partial. Many rights that are common in other bills of rights were not included in the Basic Law because of political constraints. This absence motivated the Court to provide an interpretation that would expand the list of rights and recognize the missing ones.

The Appeal to Jewish Sources

The interpretation by the Supreme Court of human dignity was not based on Jewish tradition or on Jewish law. Nevertheless, some of the justices do occasionally resort to Jewish sources and cite them in their opinions. This is usually done for rhetorical and literary purposes, to support their decisions or embellish them with classical citations. But there is a group of justices that use Jewish law for more substantial reasons, looking for sources of guidance and inspiration. This group constitutes what we can call a "school of Jewish law" within the Court. In the course of time, different justices have belonged to this group. The most influential figure among them was Justice Menachem Elon, who served in the Supreme Court between the years 1977 and 1993. Elon was a professor of Jewish law at the Hebrew University and a leading figure in academic research in this field. On the Court, Elon developed a consistent theory of human dignity from a Jewish perspective and applied it to a range of issues. I introduce some of his rulings in this chapter.

Although only a few justices resort regularly to Jewish law, the legitimacy of turning to Jewish sources is deeply rooted in Israeli legal culture. One of the ideals of Zionism, the Jewish national movement, was to revive the ancient Jewish law and form a modern legal system based on the old one (Elon 1994, 1588–96). This ideal was not realized for various reasons that are beyond the scope of this chapter,[5] but the premise that modern Israeli law must be connected with Jewish law in one way or another has been a consensus among many legislators and judges and is indeed enshrined in legislation. The 1980 Foundations of Law Act provides that:

> where the court faced with a legal question requiring a decision, finds no answer to it in statute law or case-law or by analogy, it shall decide it in the light of the principles of freedom, justice, equity and peace of Jewish law and Israel's heritage.

In simple words, this act states that in a case of *lacunae* in the law, the Court must turn to the principles of Jewish law as a complimentary legal source. This act does not embrace Jewish law in general, but only certain principles that fit the democratic nature of the state of Israel.[6] The practical consequences of this Act, however, are limited, and courts do not apply Jewish principles frequently. There are several reasons for this, both practical and ideological. I mention here only one of them. It is not often that courts declare that they are faced with *lacunae* and must therefore fill in a missing provision. They prefer to frame their decisions as matters of interpretation. It is therefore not mandatory to take the path of the Foundations of Law Act and fill in the missing provision from Jewish principles. Nevertheless, a judge who seeks to resort to Jewish law is authorized to do so. The Foundations of Law Act is therefore an explicit source of legitimacy for using Jewish law sources.

Human Dignity in the Jewish Tradition

The term "human dignity" does not appear in the classic Hebrew sources, but the concept of human dignity, as an expression of the inherent worth of human beings, does exist in Jewish sources. The modern Hebrew term for dignity is *kavod*. In the Hebrew Bible, *kavod* means both honor and glory.[7] In rabbinic literature, we find the term *kevod ha-beriyot*, which can be rendered literally as the "honor of human beings" or "human dignity" (see, among others, Tosefta, Bava Kama 7, 10; Babylonian Talmud (BT), Berachot 19b). In modern Hebrew, human dignity is translated as *kevod ha-adam*.[8] The concept of human dignity as an expression of the inherent worth of human beings is associated in Jewish tradition with the idea that man was created in the image of God (Lorberbaum 2014). The book of Genesis (1:27) depicts the creation of man in the following words: "and God created man in His image, in the image of God He created him, male and female He created them." What can we learn from this enigmatic depiction? Scholars have pointed to the ancient Near East background of this idea. In Mesopotamia, the metaphor of God's image served to depict the special status of kings. The king was presented as the son of God who was born in his image. This description assumes an ontological hierarchy in society. Kings and princes are ontologically different from ordinary people. Against this background, the biblical story proclaims that all human beings were created in the image of God (Berman 2011; Loewenstamm 1957; Miller 1972; Speizer 1964). Thus, the first thing we can say about the idea of God's image is that it expresses the notion that every human being is inherently dignified. All human beings were born equal in dignity (Berman 2011, 15–50).

From a theological perspective, the idea of God's image raises many questions. It assumes a similarity between man and God. What is exactly this similarity? According to the plain meaning of the biblical text, the similarity is in shape, implying that God has an anthropomorphic image. But because, according to the Jewish faith, God is abstract and has no body or bodily image, the concept of God's image has been interpreted metaphorically.[9] Based on this premise, theologians and biblical commentators suggested different aspects of humanity that can be considered as "God's image." Some suggested it is the soul, others that it is rationality, and yet others that it is free will or creativity (Altman 1968, 235–59). After all, it seems that the ambiguity of the meaning of God's image is inherent already in the biblical text. Indeed, there is no certainty that the biblical story intended to make any clear statement about the image of God or His qualities. It seems more likely that the focus of the Bible here is normative. The description that man was created in the image of God was intended to express the supreme status of man (and woman) in the hierarchy of creation, and its normative implications.

The normative implication of this idea is explicit in Genesis 9:6, where the Bible says: "Whoever sheds man's blood, by man shall his blood be shed for in the image of God has God made man." The Bible derives the sanctity of life from God's image. If one takes the idea of God's image as the manifestation of humans' ontological and moral status, it is possible to derive from this idea other principles as well, including all moral duties or all human rights.

We find this line of thinking in rabbinic literature. The rabbis praised the idea that man was created in the image of God and saw it as the foundation of all moral precepts.

In the Midrash (rabbinic biblical exegesis) on the book of Leviticus, we find the following dispute (Sifra Kedoshim 2, 4, 12):

> "Love your neighbor as yourself," [Leviticus 19:18] Rabbi Akiva said: this is the great maxim of the Torah. Ben Azzay said: "This is the book of the genealogy of Adam [the day that God created man, He made him in the likeness of God, (Genesis 5:1)]" is a greater maxim.

The two second-century sages were debating what the great maxim of the Torah was.[10] They appear to have been seeking a principle that would serve as a foundation for all the commandments, or at least for all moral commandments. According to Rabbi Akiva, the founding principle is the maxim "Love your neighbor as yourself," whereas according to Ben Azzay, it is the maxim "He made him in the likeness of God." What is the difference between the two maxims? The former, the maxim in Leviticus is based on the emotion of love. It is directed to "your neighbor" or, as in the Hebrew text, to "your friend." The criterion for the proper attitude toward the other person is subjective: "as yourself." By contrast, the latter, the verse in Genesis is based on the idea that man was created "in the likeness of God." It does not require emotions but presumably deeds.[11] It is not directed at "your friend" but at all humanity. And the criterion is not subjective but objective.[12] In sum, the idea of God's image is the more inclusive and more demanding principle, but the precept "Love your neighbor as yourself" introduces the notion of love and constructs personal relations.

Do these two sages disagree, or perhaps eventually agree with each other? They do not mention any practical implication for this dispute; therefore, it may be that eventually they agree with each other. Support for this possibility may come from other sources in which Rabbi Akiva, who cites here the maxim "love your neighbor," speaks in favor of the idea that man was created in the image of God. For example: "Rabbi Akiva used to say: Beloved is man that was created in the image of God" (m. Avot 3:14). It appears therefore that both rabbis acknowledged both maxims as foundational principles. The debate between them was intended to introduce both principles and the different aspects they entail. Both maxims were accepted with no reservation in Jewish tradition.

What can we learn from the notion that human dignity is manifest in the idea or in the metaphor of God's image? The first point, which we mentioned at the outset of this section, is that the idea that man and woman were created in the image of God implies that human dignity is inherent in every human being. All human beings were born equal in worth and dignity. The idea of God's image also implies the notion that this stature of humanity is transcendent, a given beyond our choice or consent, not something that can be taken or given away. One cannot take it from any other person, and one cannot waive it or renounce one's dignity.[13]

This notion was emphasized by classic thinkers of human dignity, such as John Locke (Second Treatise of Government, II.6), and is manifest in the words of Thomas Jefferson "that all men are created equal, that they are endowed by their Creator with certain inalienable Rights." The concept of "inalienable rights" means that these rights are not ours to give away (Waldron 2011). This concept of human dignity, which is based on God's image, is therefore different from a concept of human dignity based on autonomy and free will. Human dignity that is based on free will is, in principle, subject to the individual's will, whereas human dignity that is based on God's image is not. The practical implications of each of these conceptions are more nuanced, however. Human dignity based on God's image acknowledges autonomy. Similarly, human dignity based on autonomy acknowledges the need to protect individuals' basic rights. There is therefore room left in each conception to work out the precise relations between individual responsibility on one hand and autonomy on the other hand with respect to various rights and issues.

God's Image in the Supreme Court Rulings

Now I review Supreme Court rulings that apply the principle of God's image in matters related to human dignity and human rights and consider their implications. It is important to state that the Court began to apply this principle before the enactment of Basic Law: Human Dignity and Liberty. In the period preceding the Basic Law, the constitutional language of Israeli law was lacking general principles. Turning to Jewish sources was part of the search for such principles. In the course of time, and following the enactment of the Basic Law, this concept was integrated within the new constitutional language. In each of the following sections, I begin with the period preceding the Basic Law, then move to the constitutional period following the Basic Law.

I begin with a case in which the Court laid down the foundations for the use of this principle. A political party named Kach sought election to the Knesset in 1984. Kach was an extreme nationalist Jewish party that embraced racist and anti-democratic ideas. The party incited against the Arab population in Israel and advocated depriving them of some of their rights, including citizenship. The Central Election Committee disqualified the participation of Kach in the elections on the grounds that the party manifesto contradicted the principles of the Israeli Declaration of Independence, the foundations of the democratic regime of Israel, and that the party incited hatred between different communities in Israel. The party petitioned the Supreme Court, arguing that the law did not grant the committee the power to disqualify a party for its ideological positions. The Court accepted the petition and allowed the party to participate in the elections (*Neiman v. Chair of the Central Election Committee*).[14] Simultaneously, the Court expressed its deep revulsion at the ideological worldview of the party. Some of the justices cited Jewish sources that praise human dignity and equality and condemn racism and discrimination. Justice Elon referred to the idea that man was created in the image of God:

> The idea that man was created in the image of God is a founding principle in the world of Judaism. The Torah opens with this idea and derives from its basic principles regarding the worth of man—every human being—his equality and love.
>
> (*Neiman v. Chair of the Central Election Committee*, Justice Elon's opinion, par. 10)

Justice Elon emphasized that this principle is universal and applies to every human being, whatever his or her racial, national, or religious background. Elon also cited other Jewish sources that require respecting every human being, including enemies in wartime. The motivation of Justice Elon in writing his opinion based on Jewish sources was clear. First, it was important for him to stress that the permission the Court gave the party to participate in the elections by no means legitimized the views of the party. Second, it was important for him to emphasize that the views espoused by Kach contradicted not only Israeli democracy but also Jewish tradition. Kach saw itself as a nationalist Jewish party and based its ideology on Jewish sources. Justice Elon regarded this view as a distortion of Jewish tradition. It was therefore essential for him to show that Jewish tradition stands for entirely different positions, for human dignity, equality, and love toward every human being. Justice Elon concluded that the Kach manifesto is in "a blatant contradiction with the world of Judaism" (*Neiman v. Chair of the Central Election Committee*, Justice Elon's opinion, par. 12).

Justice Elon was not alone. Justice Aharon Barak, who was part of the panel, expressed a similar position and quoted from Maimonides:

> For this reason, man was created alone in the world. This teaches us that a person who eliminates one soul from the world is considered as if he eliminated an entire world. Conversely, a person who saves one soul is considered to have saved the entire world. All the inhabitants of the world are created in the image of Adam, the first man, and yet no one person's face resembles the face of his neighbor. Therefore, each person can say: The world was created for me (Maimonides Code, Sanhedrin 12, 3).
>
> (*Neiman v. Chair of the Central Election Committee*, Justice Barak's opinion, par. 15)

Justice Barak, who represented the liberal secular pole of the Court, did not frequently cite Jewish sources in his rulings. He exceptionally did so in this case, for reasons similar to those of Justice Elon. He also wanted to denounce the manifesto of the party and to condemn its distortion of Jewish tradition. In this case, the appeal to Jewish sources was motivated by rhetorical and political reasons.

But there was something behind it. At least for Justice Elon, it reflected a sincere conviction about the role of the principle of God's image as the foundation of human rights. He would use this principle in many other cases and different contexts. In this case, he emphasized equality with respect to race and national diversity. In other cases, he would emphasize other aspects. For example, in a case that dealt with the rights of a person with a mental disability, he wrote:

> The great principle that must guide the court is that we are not authorized and are not permitted to distinguish in any form in the value of any human being, be it rich or poor, healthy in his body or having any disability, healthy in his mind or having any mental disability. All human beings were created in the image of God, and they are all equal in their dignity and worth.
>
> (*Attorney General v. John Doe*)

God's Image and Personal Liberty

Before the enactment of the Basic Law, the right to personal liberty was a judicial right. Justice Elon based this right on the idea that man was created in the image of God. The issue came up in a series of rulings that dealt with grounds for detention before trial. Until 1988, Israeli law authorized the Court to order detention before trial but did not specify the concrete grounds for such an order. Courts recognized three grounds: (1) possible disruption of legal proceedings, including escape of the defendant; (2) danger or threat to public safety; and (3) the severity of the alleged crime. Justice Elon held that courts should restrict the grounds for detention, objecting specifically to the third ground. According to him, if a defendant was not convicted, his right to liberty should not be infringed.

Our sages taught us: "Beloved is man who was created in the image of God" (Mishnah, Avot 3:14). This fundamental value is the basis and the heart of the principle of human liberty. The enjoyment of liberty by every individual, the freedom of every human being as such, is the foundation of freedom of speech and freedom of protest. From all liberties that we ought to protect, the first and foremost is the right of the lonely individual, the "gray" one, which so many are frequently indifferent to, and who is forgotten in his struggle for his liberty, that it should not be infringed; the protection of this right precedes and is indeed a condition for the right of an artist to freedom of expression or the right to protest of those who have political and other worldviews. These people are known and watched by the public, and they will not disappear from the eye that sees or from the hand that writes. Beloved is man who was created in the image of God—small as big, unknown and well known; we must protect all his rights and liberties, even when we are revolted by his actions, all the more so if these actions are only alleged, and the Court did not yet decide that he really committed them, as in the case of protecting man's liberty from detention before trial.

From Justice Elon's perspective, liberty is not just a positive right granted by law. It is a natural right granted to humans for being created in God's image. The law cannot arbitrarily deprive individuals of it for unsatisfying reasons. Justice Elon emphasized that all people of various social classes, poor and rich, unknown and well known, innocent and criminal, are equal in their worth and therefore entitled to liberty. He stressed that the right to personal freedom is the basis for all other rights and has precedence over them. He commented that the right to personal liberty precedes the right to freedom of expression, which liberal justices are wont to protect. Naturally, Justice Elon did not repudiate freedom of expression but argued that it should be secondary to the right to personal liberty. This right usually protects known people, such as artists, authors, and political activists, who are watched by the public. By contrast, the right to personal freedom protects simple men and women, "gray" people who are not famous and may even be condemned by society. It is therefore important to remember that these men and women were created in God's image and deserve the right to liberty. Justice Elon stated that according to Jewish law, an individual cannot waive his right to liberty. Legal authorities ruled out contracts in which a debtor obligated himself to be arrested if he did not pay back the debt. Justice Elon claimed that according to Jewish law, liberty is not merely a right but also an obligation.

Initially, Justice Elon found himself in the minority. Most of the justices, including liberal ones like Barak, Shamgar, and others, supported the traditional view which recognized the severity of the alleged crime as a ground for detention (*Yadlin v. State of Israel*; *State of Israel v. Yonah*; *State of Israel v. Molcho*). Following its amendment, in 1988, the Criminal Procedure Act mentioned in Art. 21 three grounds: (1) possible disruption of legal proceedings, including escape; (2) danger or threat to public safety; and (3) accusation of severe and violent crimes (specified in the Act). The act explicitly provided that in itself, the severity of a crime does not constitute grounds for detention. It was clear that the amendment was intended to settle the judicial controversy in favor of Justice Elon, but the controversy continued. Some judges interpreted the ground of "public safety" in a broad way and allowed detention for crimes that were not included in the Act. In fact, judges kept adhering to the position that the severity of the crime is a ground for detention (*State of Israel v. Leibowitz; Avitan v. State of Israel; State of Israel v. ShemTov*).

The Basic Law, which was enacted in 1992, declared a right to personal liberty and provided that it "shall not be taken or restricted by means of imprisonment, detention, extradition, or in any other manner" (Art. 5). This provision tipped the scale toward Justice Elon, and his view gradually became the majority opinion. The issue was finally decided by the enactment by the Knesset of the Criminal Procedure Act (enforcement authority and detention) 1996. This act stated three grounds for detention before trial: (1) reasonable fear that releasing the suspect would bring about disruption of proceedings or escape; (2) reasonable fear that releasing the suspect would endanger public safety or state security; and (3) the special needs of investigation. Thus, the Knesset removed the ground of "severity of crime" and the controversy ended.

The history of this issue illustrates how a minority opinion, led by Justice Elon and based on Jewish interpretation, became the majority opinion and was finally embraced by the legislature. Naturally, this position can be adopted without reasoning involving God's image, on the grounds of human dignity and liberty that are enshrined in the Basic Law. In this concrete debate, however, the position that favored the right to liberty was advanced by judges who based their opinion on this Jewish idea.

Image of God and the Right to Dignity

A right to dignity was acknowledged by the Supreme Court before the enactment of the Basic Law. At this period this right was understood to protect against humiliation and degradation, and it usually came up in cases that involved prisoner and detainee rights. In a case from 1979, the Court discussed the legitimizing of invasive searches of prisoners' bodies to ensure that they do not smuggle drugs into jail. A prisoner petitioned the Court, arguing that the search harms human dignity. The Court accepted the petition and ordered the Prison Service to stop this practice (*Katlan v. Prison Service*). Justice Barak based his decision on precedents from the United States, although it was not clear that this was indeed the common view there. Justice Haim Cohn based his decision on the right to dignity in Jewish law. He extrapolated from Jewish law the right itself as well as its power to override administrative ordinances.

The Supreme Court embraced the concept that a prisoner is deprived only of his right to personal liberty and that in principle, all other rights are protected. Naturally, restrictions on personal liberty entail restrictions on other rights as well. For example, the right to freedom of occupation cannot be exercised in jail, the right to freedom of speech cannot be exercised freely, and so on. Yet, when another right, aside from personal liberty, is restricted, it is the obligation of the authorities to justify it and explain why it is necessary to restrict that right. Dignity is one of the rights that are protected during imprisonment. Justice Haim Cohn wrote:

> A person in Israel who was incarcerated (or detained) according to law has a right to be incarcerated in such conditions that allow civilized human life. It is of no significance that this right is not enshrined in any legislative act; it is one of the fundamental rights of human beings and it is self-evident in a democratic state. It is therefore as if it were enshrined and recorded. We already have said more than once that incarceration deprives a prisoner only of his personal liberty. It does not deprive him of his personal dignity and humanity.
>
> (*Darwish v. The State of Israel*)[15]

In the *Tamir* case, the Court discussed the question of whether a prisoner has the right to receive medical treatment from his personal physician, who is not employed by the penitentiary. The Court decided that the right to medical treatment includes a right to choose a physician and receive treatment from a physician whom the prisoner trusts. The Court stated that the prisoner is not entitled to payment for this treatment but is entitled to receive the treatment at his own expense. The Court justified its decision in the following words:

> It is an established rule held by this Court that every person has a fundamental right not to have harm inflicted on his body without his consent. This right is derived from the right to personal liberty of every human being created in the image of God. This fundamental right includes the right to choose and decide which physician will provide the treatment he needs. The right to make this decision is part of his fundamental right to the integrity of his body, and his physical and mental health, and of his right not to be harmed without consent.
>
> (*State of Israel v. Tamir*)

Another prisoners' right addressed by the Court was the right to conjugal meetings. In the past, prisoners were not allowed to meet with their partners in jail. The only possibility for such meetings was during regular periods of leave that prisoners received from jail if they were eligible for them. A prisoner, who was an observant Jew, petitioned the Court based on two grounds. First, he argued that according to Jewish law, sexual relations are a religious commandment and therefore he was entitled to conjugal visits as part of his religious freedom. Second, he claimed that sexual relations are a basic human need, and therefore he was entitled to conjugal visits as part of his basic human rights. The Court was sympathetic to this claim and said:

> It is clear that preventing an adult from having sexual relations for a long period of time is serious harm to that person. . . . The deprivation of the right to have sexual relations is not part of the deprivation of the right to personal liberty and of the right to movement of a person who was sentenced to jail. The basic right to have sexual relations is protected for prisoners as well. The question is whether depriving the prisoner of the right to personal liberty affects the right to have sexual relations, and what is the nature of this effect and its measure.
>
> (*Weill v. State of Israel*)

The Court determined that, in principle, a prisoner has a right to conjugal visits. The Court was aware, however, that the realization of this right in practice requires certain arrangements, including physical facilities. The Court, therefore, dismissed this petition but nevertheless made a significant determination, establishing that prisoners have some fundamental rights that cannot be violated:

> There are some fundamental rights whose violation harms the minimal basic needs of a human being as one who was created in the image of God. Among these rights are not only the prisoner's right to food, drink, and accommodation but also civilized arrangements for supplying these needs.
>
> (*Weill v. State of Israel*)

The Court established that fulfilling these basic needs in a civilized manner constitutes an absolute right that cannot be restricted or balanced with any other considerations, including security. These rights are part of the right to dignity, and they protect the basic features of human beings who were created in the image of God. In the course of time, especially following the enactment of the Basic Law, the Israel Prison Service began allowing such visits, and since 2000, they have become part of the formal policy of the Service.

The right to dignity is relevant also in matters related to ways of punishment. What are the legitimate ways of punishment, and what are the minimal conditions that must be provided in incarceration and detention facilities? In a case dealing with these conditions, the Court cited Maimonides:

Maimonides discusses the various ways of punishment according to Jewish law and concludes:

> All of the above measures should be applied according to the judge's perception of what is an appropriate punishment for the violator in the given situation. All deeds intended for the sake of heaven and human dignity (*kevod ha-briyot*) should not be considered lightly (Sanhedrin 24: 10).
>
> (*Azazmi v. State of Israel*)

The principle of human dignity restricts ways of punishment. Cruel punishments that humiliate human beings should be prohibited. Imprisonment is in principle a legitimate punishment, but in practice, it must meet certain conditions, which may not be met in a crowded facility. This common problem brought Justice Elon to suggest that incarceration must be inflicted only on criminals who pose a threat to public safety. In other cases, he suggested we should look for other ways of punishment.

Basic Law: Human Dignity and Liberty established the right to dignity as a constitutional right. Article 2 provides: "One should not violate the life, body, or dignity of a human being as such." As noted in the introduction, the question that has arisen is: What is the meaning and scope of this right? Justice Elon suggested the following:

> Human dignity means that one should not humiliate and degrade God's image, which is inherent in human beings. Not all insults to human

> honor are included in the basic law. For example, insult to the honor of a respected man, which has a certain standing among dignified people and not among simple ones, might indeed insult his social honor (if it does so!) but it does not humiliate and degrade God's image, which is inherent in him. Therefore, such insult is not included in Basic Law: Human Dignity and Liberty.
>
> (*State of Israel v. Gueta*)

Justice Elon used the concept of God's image to make the distinction between dignity and honor.[16] The Basic Law protects only dignity, which reflects God's image. It does not protect honor, which has to do with social status. In the course of time, this narrow view was rejected by the Court, which gradually expanded the protection of the Basic Law to include social dignity as well. For example, the Court agreed that the right to a good name is part of the right to dignity. Good name includes both social honor and reputation, which is acquired by people during their lifetime and has to do also with the office and position they hold (*Senesh v. Broadcasting Authority*; *The Movement for the Quality of Government v. the Knesset*).

The *Gueta* case illustrates an instructive aspect of the right to dignity. Police officers stopped a person, suspected of being a drug dealer, and searched him. They wanted to take off his pants and asked him to go with them into a building. The suspect refused and gave his consent to be searched on the street. The officers did so and found a package of drugs on his body. The suspect argued that the search was illegal because it violated his right to dignity. The Court stated that consent is not sufficient to allow police officers or any other state officials to violate human dignity. In this case, however, the Court eventually confirmed the validity of the search because of the special circumstances of the case.

The foundation of the overarching principle of human dignity is that man was created in the image of God. From this principle, it follows that a man himself is obligated to maintain his dignity because harm to his dignity is harm to God's image. Thus, every person is obligated not to degrade himself (*State of Israel v. Gueta*).

This illuminates one of the central aspects of human dignity according to this interpretation. Human dignity that is based on God's image serves not only as a ground for rights but also for obligations: the person must protect his dignity, and therefore cannot waive this right.

God's Image and Sanctity of Life

The value of human life and the right to life occupy the top place in the hierarchy of human rights. Life is the basis and the condition of all other rights. Therefore, the right to life is the first and foremost among constitutional rights. At the same time, taking life is the most severe crime in state laws (Mathieu 2006; Tomuschat, Lagrange, and Oeter 2010). From a Jewish perspective, the value of human life is based on the special status of human beings, as created in the image of God. This connection is explicitly expressed in the book of Genesis: "Whoever sheds man's blood, by man shall his blood be shed, for in the image of God has God made man" (Genesis 9:6). Based on this verse, the rabbis drew the conclusion that "Whoever sheds blood is considered to have diminished the image of God" (Mechilta Derabi Lyshmael, Itro, Hahodesh, 8). In the Mishnah, the value of human life is illustrated as follows: "For that reason man was created alone, to teach us that whoever eliminates one soul is considered by Scripture as if he eliminated the entire world, and whoever saves one soul is considered by Scripture as if he saved the entire world" (Minshah Sanhedrin 4:5).

In *Yael Sheffer v. State of Israel*, the Supreme Court discussed the question of euthanasia. The mother of a two-year-old child, who was in a vegetative state, petitioned the Court to order the hospital to refrain from connecting the child to a ventilator and let her die peacefully. The Court defined this action as passive euthanasia.[17] At the time, the issue was not regulated by statutory law, and the Court was asked to decide the case. The Court opened the discussion with the following assumption:

> "In the image of God He created man"—this is the theoretical, philosophical foundation of the supreme value of the sanctity of life according to Jewish law. It is the sanctity of God's image in which man was created. This idea has many ramifications and shapes the unique approach of Jewish law to many issues, such as the one before us.
>
> (*Yael Sheffer v. State of Israel*, Justice Elon's opinion, par. 20)

The Court went on to elaborate on some of these ramifications. The first was that the value of human life is infinite and cannot be measured: "A basic principle of Jewish law is that the value of human life cannot be measured in quality and length. It cannot be measured or weighted. Every second of human life should be valued as many long years" (*Yael Sheffer v. State of Israel*).

Therefore, one should make every effort to save human life even when it is only for a short period of time. Furthermore, one must not cause the death of a human being even when critically ill and going to die after a short time. The Court ruled that active euthanasia, even at the patient's request, is prohibited. It is clear therefore that a guardian cannot request active euthanasia. Nevertheless, individuals have autonomy over their bodies, which means that they have a right to choose the medical treatment they want to receive. An important consideration in choosing medical treatment is preventing pain and suffering. Therefore, an individual can refuse treatment that may cause him pain or suffering, including life-saving treatment. A patient who suffers from terminal disease as well as from pain may ask not to be given life-saving treatment or not to be connected to life-saving equipment, such as a ventilator.

The Court ruled that the patient can even ask to be disconnected from such a device or machine.[18] In principle, a guardian or a parent is authorized to make such a request, but to be approved, the case must meet certain conditions of terminal disease and pain or suffering.

Another aspect must be considered. Can we assess the quality of life to determine whether life is worth saving? Is a low quality of life, such as severe disability or unconsciousness, a legitimate consideration in a decision to refrain from providing life-saving treatment? The Court warns against such a consideration:

> When one starts assessing and weighing human life, it is such assessment that would bring about the killing of people who are most damaged in their bodies and souls, and later those that are less damaged, and eventually there will be no fixed measure of what the required quality of life is. This is the way of the slippery slope.
>
> (*Yael Sheffer v. State of Israel*)

An individual can request in certain situations (or in advance, if he were to reach such a situation) not to be treated.[19] But guardians, including parents, cannot make such a request for the individual for whom they are responsible. The only case that the Court would allow is one in which a child suffers from pain and there is no hope for his recovery. But in the Sheffer case, all the medical and psychological reports showed that the infant was not suffering from any pain (*General Attorney v. Ben Ikar*).

In his search for the appropriate solution, Justice Elon reviewed the attitudes of several jurisdictions to the problem of euthanasia. He found a similarity between Jewish and American law in that both ban active but allow passive euthanasia. At the same time, he drew a fundamental distinction between the two systems. The primary principle of Jewish law is the sanctity of life, which is based on the idea that every human being was created in the image of God. This principle can be restricted by considerations of pain and suffering and the patient's will, but the fact that this is the primary principle is crucial. In American law, the primary principle is personal liberty or autonomy, which is the basis for the patient's right to refuse medical treatment. This principle may be restricted by other considerations, such as the interest of the state in protecting its citizens' lives and its medical teams, but here too, the premise that autonomy is the primary principle is significant (*Yael Sheffer v. State of Israel*, Justice Elon's opinion, par. 58). One may question Justice Elon's interpretation of American law,[20] but his words reflect his understanding of Jewish law. The value of human life is not manifested only in a right to life, but it is also a source of obligation and responsibility. He borrowed this conception from Jewish law and imparted it to Israeli law. His ruling was accepted by all and became part of Israeli case law.

Conclusion

Two approaches to human dignity are apparent in the rulings of the Israeli Supreme Court. In the mainstream approach, human dignity is based on autonomy. This approach draws from the classical liberal tradition and from the relatively new tradition of human dignity and applies it to the Israeli context in light of *Basic Law: Human Dignity and Liberty*. According to this concept, the content of human dignity is first and foremost the realization of the individual's personality and free will. Human dignity in this sense functions as the ground for all human rights. In light of this principle, human rights should also be interpreted as a manifestation of the individual's autonomy and free will. An alternative approach derives the interpretation of human dignity from the Jewish tradition. In this tradition, human dignity is based on the inherent worth of human beings, which is manifested in the idea that man was created in the image of God. According to this concept, human dignity expresses the worth and special status of human beings, beyond any individual's will or choice. Human dignity is therefore not only a ground for rights but also for obligations and responsibilities. In the present chapter, I described this approach and its effect on Israeli case law. Although this approach reflects a minority opinion within the Court, it has a significant influence on Israeli law. All the decisions mentioned in this chapter eventually became part of Israeli case law. Some expressed from the outset the majority opinion on the bench, and others were initially a minority opinion but became accepted in the course of time by the majority.

This approach introduced the notion of human dignity in Israeli law as a thick concept that includes rights and obligations. This concept follows a long tradition. The notion that some rights are inalienable in the sense that even the right bearer cannot waive them is rooted in classical writings of human rights. It was mentioned by John Locke, Thomas Jefferson, and others. In this respect, Jewish tradition converges with the human rights tradition, both rooted in the common biblical heritage. The concept of human dignity as a ground for rights and obligations follows this tradition but goes beyond it, to be interpreted and implemented in different situations. The penetration of this concept into the human rights discourse raised concerns and disputes. Some argued that human dignity is a principle that has proved to be a double-edged sword, which not only strengthens but also threatens human rights. Others have supported the weight ascribed to principles of dignity in some cases even against the individual's rights or will (Waldron 2011, 1129). Note that the acknowledgment of human dignity as a thick concept that contains rights and obligations does not in itself settle conflicts; it merely provides a rich and nuanced conception to work with in resolving difficult cases. The nature of judicial work is that it moves from case to case, laying down principles, and then further refining them. Only in retrospect can one appreciate the road that has been paved in resolving a certain type of problem. The Israeli Supreme Court laid down the conceptual foundations of human dignity as a thick concept, but there is still work to be done in implementing and refining it.

Notes

1 The enactment of this Basic Law, and of Basic Law: Freedom of Occupation, is known as the "constitutional revolution" because it authorized the Court to review primary legislation (Knesset statutes) in light of the basic laws.

2 Article 1 provides: "The basic human rights in Israel are based on the recognition of the value of the human being, the sanctity of his life, and his being a free person." The "value of human being" appears to be equal to "human dignity." Article 1a provides:

"The purpose of this Basic Law is to protect human dignity and liberty, in order to stipulate the values of the State of Israel as a Jewish and democratic state, in a Basic Law."

3 These questions can be asked in any jurisdiction or context that human dignity is related to human rights. For a general overview see McCrudden (2014).

4 The court insisted on some relation being present between these rights and human dignity. For example, in *Alice Miller v. Defense Minister* the Court concluded that Basic Law: Human Dignity and Liberty protects only against discrimination which insults human dignity. Given that, the Court held inequality in government subsidy between two types of industry does not insult dignity and is therefore not protected by the basic law.

5 For more details see Elon (1994) and Harris (2002, 21–55).

6 The Foundations of Law Act prompted a sharp judicial and academic debate. Some justices, led by Justice Menachem Elon, stood for a broad interpretation of this law (Elon 1994, 1827–40). Others, led by Justice Aharon Barak, demanded a narrow interpretation. The practical result of Barak's interpretation was that in most cases of absence of norms, judges are not obligated to resort to Jewish principles, so that the act became merely symbolic (Barak 2017).

7 In several biblical texts, it used to indicate God's special status. For example: Exodus 16:7–10; 24:16; 32:18–22. In other texts, it used to indicate human status. See especially Psalms 8:6.

8 Basic Law: Human Dignity and Liberty in Hebrew is *Kevod Ha-Adam Ve-Heruto*. Englard (1999–2000), however, draws a distinction between "*kavod*" in classical Jewish sources and that of "dignity" in modern sources including Israeli Basic Law. I think there is more affinity between the two concepts. See also on this Blidstein (2006, 97).

9 Scholars still debate when exactly this premise was accepted by all Jewish streams. One of the questions is whether in late antiquity rabbinic Judaism entirely accepted this principle. For different views see Urbach (1970, 15–52) and Lorberbaum (2015, 13–60). A debate exists also with regard to the mystical tradition. Some mystical writings depict God in anthropomorphic terms (Scholem 1941, 63–67, 1976, 153–86).

10 Compare the discussion in the New Testament: Matthew 22:34–40; Mark 12:28–34; Luke 10:25–28. Jesus is asked a similar question: "What is the great commandment in the Law?" and he mentions two commandments: "You shall love the Lord your God" and "You shall love thy neighbor as thyself."

11 Compare Kant's (2002) interpretation of this verse. He asserted that the reference to "love" should be understood as if it speaks about deeds and not about emotions (15).

12 This point was made by Midrash Bereshit Rabbah 24:7. The Midrash asks: if someone is ready to be humiliated, can he humiliate his friend? The objective criterion of God's image prevents this possibility.

13 One may ask how Jewish tradition reconciled the idea of equal dignity with the reality in which different classes of human beings were not treated equally in many aspects of their social life. I would briefly suggest two complimentary answers. First, the fact that people were not treated equally in various ways and aspects does

not deny the recognition of their core equal dignity. People could believe that all human beings are equally dignified and yet they are different in some other respects and therefore should be treated differently. Second, the idea of equal dignity is a rich and complicated idea. It has many and sometimes contradictory implications. It might be that it was not understood in the same way as we understand it today. Or, to put it in different words, it might be that it was not fully understood, and some of its implications were not yet revealed.

14 Politicians and scholars criticized the Court's decision that deviated from previous decisions which confirmed the Central Committee decisions to disqualify a party that negated the existence of Israel as a Jewish and democratic state (see *Yeredor v. Chair of the Central Election Committee*). Following the election of 1984, the Knesset amended Basic Law: Knesset and authorized the Central Election Committee to disqualify a party on the grounds that it negates the nature of Israel as a "Jewish and Democratic" state or incites to racism.

15 The statement that "this right is not enshrined in any legislative act" was true at the time when it was stated. Since 1992, it has been enshrined in Basic Law: Human Dignity and Liberty.

16 In Hebrew, both concepts are represented by the same term, *kavod*, so that the distinction is between two concepts of *kavod*.

17 As opposed to active euthanasia, such as in cases when death is caused by injection. The Court defined disconnecting from life-saving equipment, such as a ventilator, also as passive euthanasia. Some commentators, however, see this action as active euthanasia as medical personnel take an action of disconnecting.

18 The Court classified disconnection from a ventilator or a heart-lung machine as passive euthanasia because it brings the patient back to the situation before treatment. All these situations were later regulated in the Dying Patient Act 2005, which provides that one is not allowed to stop ongoing treatment; in other words, one must not disconnect a patient from a ventilator or heart-lung machine.

19 This was stated later in the 2006 Dying Patient Act.

20 The United States Declaration of Independence states that all men "are endowed by their Creator with certain inalienable rights, that among these are Life." As noted, the term "inalienable" may be understood as referring also to the right holder, in which case American law shares the conception of rights as responsibilities (Feinberg 1978).

References

Altman, Alexander. 1968. "Homo imago Dei in Jewish and Christian Theology." *The Journal of Religion* 48: 235–59.

Barak, Aharon. 2015. *Human dignity. The Constitutional Value and the Constitutional Right*. Cambridge: Cambridge University Press.

Barak, Aharon. 2017(5777). "Foundation of Law Act and Israel's Heritage." *Shenaton Ha-Mishpat Ha-Ivri* 13: 265–83 (Hebrew).

Berman, Joshua. 2011. *Created Equal: How the Bible Broke with Ancient Political Thought*. Oxford: Oxford University Press.

Blidstein, Gerald J. 2006. "Public Respect (Kevod ha-Briyot) and Human Dignity." In *Questioning Dignity: On Human Dignity as Supreme Moral Value in the Modern Society*, edited by Joseph E. David, 97–138. Jerusalem: The Israel Democracy Institute (Hebrew).

Elon, Menachem. 1994. *Jewish Law: History, Sources, Principles*. Philadelphia: The Jewish Publication Society.

Englard, Izhak. 1999–2000. "Human Dignity: From Antiquity to Israel's Constitutional Framework." *Cardozo Law Review* 21: 1903–27.

Feinberg, Joel. 1978. "Voluntary Euthanasia and the Inalienable Right to Life." *Philosophy & Public Affairs* 7: 93–123.
Harris, Ron. 2002. "Absent Minded Misses and Historical Opportunities: Jewish Law, Israeli Law and the Establishment of the State of Israel." In *On Both Sides of the Bridge: Religion and State in the Early Years of Israel*, edited by Mordechai Bar-On and Zvi Zameret. Jerusalem: Yad Ben-Zvi (Hebrew).
Kant, Immanuel. 2002. *Groundwork for the Metaphysics of Morals*. Translated by A. W. Wood. New Haven; London: Yale University Press.
Loewenstamm, S. E. 1957. "Beloved is Man that was Created in God's Image." *Tarbitz* 27 (Hebrew).
Lorberbaum, Yair. 2014. "Human Dignity in the Jewish Tradition." In *Cambridge Handbook of Human Dignity*, edited by Marcus Düwell, Jens Braarvig, Roger Brownsword, and Dietmar Mieth, 135–44. Cambridge: Cambridge University Press.
Lorberbaum, Yair. 2015. *In God's Image: Myth, Theology and Law in Classical Judaism*. Cambridge: Cambridge University Press.
Margalit, Avishai. 1996. *The Decent Society*. Translated by Naomi Goldblum. Cambridge, MA: Harvard University Press.
Mathieu, Bertrand. 2006. *The Right to Life in European Constitutional and International Case-Law*. Strasbourg: The Council of Europe Publishing.
McCrudden, Christopher. 2014. "In Pursuit of Human Dignity: An Introduction to Current Debates." In *Understating Human Dignity*, edited by Christopher McCrudden, 1–58. Oxford: Oxford University Press.
Miller, J. Maxwell. 1972. "In the 'Image' and 'Likeness' of God." *Journal of Biblical Literature* 91 (3): 289–303.
Scholem, Gershom. 1941. *Major Trends in Jewish Mysticism*. New York: Schocken Books.
Scholem, Gershom. 1976. *Elements of the Kabbalah and its Symbols*. Jerusalem: Bialik Institute (Hebrew).
Speizer, E. A., ed. 1964. *The Anchor Bible: Genesis*. New York: Doubleday.
Statman, Daniel. 2002. "Humiliation, Dignity and Self-Respect." In *The Concept of Human Dignity in Human Rights Discourse*, edited by David Kretzmer and Eckart Klein, 209–29. The Hague: Brill–Nijhoff.
Tomuschat, Christian, Evelyne Lagrange, and Stefan Oeter, eds. 2010. *The Right to Life*. The Hague: Martinus Nijhoff.
Urbach, Ephraim E. 1970. *The Sages: Their Concepts and Beliefs*. Jerusalem: Hebrew University Press.
Waldron, Jeremy. 2009. *Dignity, Rank and Rights*. Oxford: Oxford University Press.
Waldron, Jeremy. 2011. "Dignity, Rights, and Responsibilities." *Arizona State Law Journal* 43: 1107–36.

Case Law

The Supreme Court of Israel

AP 698/86 *Attorney General v. John Doe*, PD 42 (2), 661 (1986).
CA 5942/92 *Anonymous v. Anonymous*, PD 48 (3), 841 (1994).
CA 5587/97 *General Attorney v. Ben Ikar*, PD 51 (4), 830 (1997).
CA 115/00 *Taieb v. State of Israel*, PD 54 (3), 330 (2000).
CA 506/88 *Yael Sheffer v. State of Israel*, PD 48 (1), (1993).
CrimA 3734/92 *State of Israel v. Azami*, PD 46 (5), 72 (1992).
CrimA 2145/92 *State of Israel v. Gueta*, PD 46 (5), 704 (1992).
CrimA 2611/91 *State of Israel v. ShemTov*, PD 45 (3), 645 (1991).

CrimApp 496/89 *State of Israel v. Yonah*, PD 43 (2), 450 (1989).
EA 1/65 *Yeredor v. Chair of the Central Election Committee*, PD 19 (3), 365 (1965).
EA 2/84 *Neiman v. Chair of the Central Election Committee*, PD 39 (2), 225 (1985).
HCJ 4541/94 *Alice Miller v. Defense Minister*, PD 49 (4), 94 (1995).
HCJ 221/80 *Darwish v. Prison Service*, PD 35 (1), 536 (1980)
HCJ 355/79 *Katlan v. Prison Service*, PD 34 (3), 294 (1980).
HCJ 6427/02 *The Movement for the Quality of Government v. The Knesset*, PD 61 (1), 619 (2006).
HCJ 6126/94 *Senesh v. Broadcasting Authority*, PD 63 (3), 817 (1999).
HCJ 5100/94 *The Public Committee Against Torture v. The Government of Israel*, PD 53 (4), 817 (1999).
HCJ 114/86 *Weill v. State of Israel*, PD 41 (3), 477 (1987).
HJC 5688/92 *Vexelbaum v. Minister of Defense*, PD 47 (2), 812 (1992).
MiscClaim 290/76 *Yadlin v. State of Israel*, PD 31 (1).
MiscCrimApp 205/89 *State of Israel v. Leibowitz*, PD 3 (1), 441 (1989).
MiscCrimClaim 1044/82 *State of Israel v. Molcho*, PD 37 (1), 78 (1983).
PPA 4/82 *State of Israel v. Tamir*, PD 37 (1), 201 (1982).

12 Human (Personal) Dignity as an Argumentation Tool of the Russian Constitutional Court

Mikhail Antonov

Introduction

Paragraph 1 of Article 21 of the Russian Federation (the RF) Constitution sets out that human dignity shall be protected by the state, and nothing may serve as a basis for its derogation. Historically, this formulation of human dignity was informed by the German principle of *Menschenwürde,* which suggested that a human being is "not that of an isolated, sovereign individual," but rather that of an individual embedded in society and subject to societal limitations.[1] In the views of the 1993 Constitution's authors, human dignity should have played a similar role in Russian legal order—serving as the basis for other human rights (Shakhrai 2017, 146–47). Theoretically, this principle is coextensive with similar constitutional principles developed in the post-war Western legal tradition.[2] However, the normative implications of this declarative statement in Russian constitutional law are quite different from the liberal approaches generally accepted in Western jurisdictions.

This difference is not perceivable at the level of legal texts (constitutional, statutory, and others), but can be traced in mind-sets and practical uses lawyers make out of these texts. In order to better appreciate this difference, one can go from the upper levels of legal reality (that of formalized official texts) to its deeper levels beneath the legal morphology—symbols, ideas, ideals, beliefs, and collective intuitions that are later crystallized in ideological constructs and in the social practice of law (Gurvitch 1942). Such an approach opens up interesting socio-philosophical perspectives on the interplay between legal texts and "levels of depth" (Gurvitch 1942) which underpin the creation and application of constitutional law. This interplay is patent in what concerns essentially contested notions whose meaning is not firmly established in discourse and is ascertained only within social frameworks in which citizens and practitioners of law exercise their day-to-day activities (Gurvitch 1972).

The concept and interpretation of human dignity reveal conservative premises in the constitutional discourse which, in turn, reflect—to a considerable extent—the conservative attitudes of the majority of the population (Byzov 2014). These conservative attitudes are an important source of legitimacy for the political authorities. Therefore, it comes as no surprise that the political

DOI: 10.4324/9781003307853-15

regime seeks to exploit these attitudes and to support them by referring to the continued pattern of cooperation between the Russian church and the Russian state, and to the ideological constructs that result from this cooperation. Such attitudes are not taken as historical or sociological facts—they are rather reconstructed in line with the prevailing cultural patterns. These latter are established according (or at least, reveal close proximity) to the teaching of the Russian Orthodox Church (the ROC).

First, the concept of "human dignity" serves as one of the cornerstones in this strategic game because this malleable concept has many possible interpretations and therefore can work as a practical tool of ideology. Second, this concept has a huge symbolic power for building the key binary oppositions: "we and they," "true and false," and "moral and immoral." The axe of these oppositions also draws the divide between important hallmarks of normative discourse in religion and law such as "orthodox and heretic" and "legal and illegal." Third, the idea of "human dignity" is normally linked to the cultural environment, as its interpretations hinge on the prevailing social representations. In other terms, "human dignity" is usually convened in societal milieus with reference to the moral ideas, religious doctrines, mind-sets, or cultural patterns prevalent in the society. Therefore, "human dignity" can work out as a conceptual support to traditionalist discourses. And fourth, because of its symbolic and normative force, this concept can serve as an "antidote" to liberal discourses about human rights and freedoms. "Human" defines normative limits of such liberal discourses: an individual may enjoy her basic rights and freedoms only to the extent that this individual does not contradict to her "human nature."

One of the theses of this chapter is that relying on "human dignity" as a normative tool can be dangerous in cultures in which individuality is appreciated as a part of the collective—this concept can easily be invested with anti-liberal implications and work as a strong counterargument against freedom. If coupled with communitarian discourses, "human dignity" can be interpreted as "being a part of the society that makes an individual to be a human; therefore, if individuals challenge the society by their opinions or behavior, they go not only against the society but also against their own human nature." This conservative philosophy is well known in the history of ideas, from Plato or Aristotle to Burke or Eliot (Kirk 2001), and is largely supported in many religious doctrines, including that of the ROC. When an individual attempts to assert her particularity as a member of a minority group in communitarian cultures, this would expectedly trigger negative reactions in social frameworks and, finally, this individual can be held responsible for the collective's degrading her "human dignity" because she has departed from established social standards. In this sense, communitarian cultures can hijack the role of dignity in adjudication to curb minorities' rights (e.g., McCrudden 2008; Cocks 2018). This chapter will demonstrate that this is also the case in Russia: its official attitudes toward minorities are to a large extent informed by popular mind-sets, while these latter are, in turn, fostered by conservative religious dogma (Robinson 2019).

Based on this examination of the jurisprudence of the Russian Constitutional Court (the RF CC), this chapter will attempt to analytically reconstruct such connections which prepare the ground for the tacit church-state alliance against minorities. This alliance has a very long track record in Russian history and is mutually profitable: the ROC asserts its dogma and fights against sexual, religious, and other minorities with the help of the state machinery, while the state obtains an important source of legitimation in the ROC's support. This reconstruction will address deeper levels of legal reality that unveil individual and collective value systems, with reference to which Russian law deals with human dignity.

The chapter will begin with a general discussion of epistemic and normative roles of the concept of "human dignity." It will focus on the practical utilization of the concept of human dignity by the RF CC. This level of practical application will reveal several judicial strategies to use the concept of human dignity to legitimize the Court in particular, and the existing political regime in general. Using the jurisprudence of the RF CC as the background for our analysis, it will identify that there are, at least, four main goals of "human dignity" in this jurisprudence: to smooth the conflict between the liberal letter and the restrictive application of the Russian Constitution; to hide contradictions in argumentation; to assert the prevalence of collective rights over individual ones; and to re-interpret the constitutional law according to conservative ideology. After having examined these four applications, this chapter will trace their implied sources in the ROC's doctrine and, finally, will discuss how the RF CC indirectly applies this doctrine to foster a conservative reading of the Constitution to restrict the rights of minorities and to promote the conservative politics of the state.

Human Dignity as Floating Signifier

The gap between the literal meanings of the laws and their interpretation, and the selective application of Russian law is proverbial (e.g., Baekken 2019). The jurisprudence of the RF CC is a paradigmatic example of this: in penumbra and lacunae cases, the Court sometimes rules contrary to the letter of the law and even to the Constitution (Krasnov 2016). However, the RF CC does not accept that it treats the text of the Constitution as a cheap justification for de facto discretionary rulings; rather it claims to reveal, behind the constitutional text, certain underlying constitutional values and deep social meanings underpinning these values. These meanings allegedly surface through the jurisprudence of this Court.[3] In this connection, to justify their decisions in such cases, RF CC's judgments sometimes refer—directly or implicitly—to fundamentals of the social order, such as cultural and civilizational distinctiveness, social cohesion around certain values, or the collective interest understood as guiding principles of social development. The vaguer and emotionally stronger such references would be, the deeper ideological impact they would have on the population. Thus, the concept of "human dignity" enshrined in Article 21 of the RF Constitution has a wide variety of interpretations: from the symbol of individual freedom in the 1990s to the prevalence of social interest over individual rights today.

Broad concepts such as "human dignity" fit well in this interpretative strategy, as they not only admit different interpretations but also help to conceal the internal contradictions of this strategy. In this sense, "human dignity" can be considered as an "empty signifier" for Russian constitutional discourse, and might mean different things to constitutional lawyers and laypeople, or might mean whatever their interpreters want them to mean.[4] As Costas Douzinas wrote in 2000: "Symbolic excess turns the signifier 'human' into a floating signifier, into something that combatants in political, social and legal struggles want to co-opt to their cause in order to benefit from its symbolic capital" (Douzinas 2000, 255). Douzinas' words perfectly describe the strategy of the RF CC.

As a matter of fact, this concept serves as a decorative frame of reference that is evoked by the RF CC in a very broad range of cases without any normative or argumentative reason. Human dignity works as a "floating/empty signifier" and conceals the undetermined quantity of signification and is apt to receive any meaning through interpretation, thereby allowing symbolic thought to operate despite the contradiction inherent in it. Through references to "human dignity," the RF CC often seeks to reconcile the contradiction which characterizes the modern constitutional history of Russia: the contradiction between the liberal spirit and letter of the RF Constitution on the one hand, and its conservative interpretation on the other.

This use of "human dignity" equally justifies both broadening and limiting rights. Taken in the liberal sense, "dignity" would mean that any control from the part of collectivity potentially degrades individual human beings who are capable of reasonable choice; in a conservative reading, "dignity" might also imply the "social ripeness" of this individual being measured according to her ability to accept and follow common behavioral patterns. The logic of this approach has been repeatedly advocated by Valerii Zorkin, Patriarch Kirill, and other conservative thinkers: yes—they acknowledge—individuals may have human rights, but only insofar as the utilization of these rights does not deteriorate their "human dignity" (Patriarch Kirill 2016), that is the capability to live in the "image of God" and follow religiously established and socially supported moral rules.[5] In its turn, this "dignity" signifies the symbolic value attributed to individuality from the perspective of society and church.

The general philosophical justification for this approach was coined by the Court in 1995 when it formulated a lofty Kantian principle according to which a person shall never be an object for the state, but shall be treated as an entity endowed with the legal capacities equal to those of the state (Judgment of the Constitutional Court of the Russian Federation (RFCC) No. 4-P, May 3, 1995). With this interpretation, the RF CC intentionally followed the German *Bundesverfassungsgericht's* jurisprudence on *Menschenwürde* (Barak 2015). However, the practical implementation of this lofty declaration turned out to be dependent on a number of pragmatic provisos and restrictions. Taken in this broad interpretation, the conception of human dignity served for the RF CC as the central argumentation tool in a wide range of cases where its use seemed not to be logically needed: from municipal elections (RFCC Judgments no. 14-P June 22, 2010; no. 21-P December 24, 1996; no. 10-P June 7, 2000; no. 15-P June 27, 2013) to procedural details of amnesty and pardon (RFCC Judgments no. 7-P April 24, 2003; RFCC Rulings no. 406-O 11 July, 2006; no. 483-O-P April 2, 2009; no. 840-O April 22, 2014), the issue of compensation of damages (RFCC Judgment no. 16-P July 2, 2013), or tax payments (RFCC Judgment no. 9-P April 4, 1996).

In other cases where the matter touched on political issues and concerned defending the human dignity of those actors whose personalities or actions were seen as condemnable (the Alekseyev case about administrative liability for propagating non-heterosexual relations, the case of the punk group Pussy Riot's performance in the Cathedral of Christ the Saviour, etc.), the RF CC implicitly conceded degrading and discriminative treatment, weighting "dignity" as it is (the individual ability to shape oneself as a human being) with "dignity" as it ought to be (the presupposed obligation to form one's own individuality so that it is dignified in the eyes of society). "Dignity" turned out to be quite malleable at the hands of the constitutional justices: following this strategy, they managed to "link the floating and symbolic signifier to a particular signified, to arrest its constitutive indeterminacy and to achieve the partial bonding of human nature with a regional conception of humanity which will bestow upon the latter the symbolic value of the core concept, turning it into a valid instance of human nature. In doing so, characteristics of humanity, like equality and freedom, are transferred to the group that achieves recognition" (Douzinas 2000, 259). In fact, the Court implicitly linked its representations about "human dignity" with those of the ROC and thereby allowed its religious dogma to creep into law enforcement. The effect was pernicious for different categories of minorities in Russia (e.g., Antonov 2019).

Human Dignity as a Tool for Doublespeak and Education

This use of "dignity" sometimes reveals the doublespeak behind the case law of the RF CC. When the Court refers to the conception of human dignity, it phrases "human dignity" in a manner coextensive to liberal principles (individual freedom of choice, protection of minorities against the dictatorship of the majority, etc.), but normative results of this interpretation and application lead to adverse results: to judgments in which the RF CC refuses to protect human dignity, in effect. The style of argumentation typical for this strategy consists of proclaiming the unalienable character of human dignity which can never be diminished and deciding at the same time that, in a particular case, human dignity can nonetheless be disregarded. There is no argumentation of this logical jump in the decisions of the Court, but in public speeches and publications, its justices do not shy from the recognition that their understanding of "human dignity" is informed by conservative teachings of the ROC about human personality.[6]

Such abstract concepts as "human dignity" also have another dimension which is important for the RF CC to uphold its legitimacy. In its practice, the RF CC resolutely continues the Soviet legal tradition, according to which an educational function was among the most important tasks of Soviet courts (Berman 1972). Soviet courts' primary function was not so much about the settling of property, family, or inheritance disputes between Soviet citizens—their basic ideological function was to educate citizens about the supreme goals of the Soviet Union and, when possible, to reconcile their disputes with a larger view of these goals. The RF CC acts similarly when politics, national security, or traditional values, including the religion of the majority, are involved and the Court has to act as a defender of political and social order, rather than a defender of the rule of law. Lacking any serious power in checking and balancing the government and the factual ability to rule against the state, the Court readily resorts to explaining to the citizenry how law shall be appreciated, what are its moral implications, how they shall conduct their lives, etc. Its decisions are not usually so much about striking a balance between public and private interests, but rather about teaching the citizenry about the value of public interests (protection of state sovereignty, national security, etc.). For the RF CC, this role means a powerful tool for self-legitimation in the eyes of the political leadership, and the fact that the Court bows down in front of the political leaders justifies—for these political leaders—maintaining the constitutional justice as an independent branch of the judiciary.

This reading of "dignity" transpires in the RF CC's case law. One example is the 2007 Judgment on the burial of suspected terrorists where the Court rejected the petitions that protested against the inhuman treatment of the bodies of persons killed during anti-terrorist operations: human dignity includes the right to be buried according to customs and traditions, but the denial of this right to terrorists is "a specific preventive measure to counteract terrorism" (RFCC Judgment no. 8-P June 28, 2007). Other examples are the rulings concerning the transplantation of organs of dead persons without their or their relatives' consent. Agreeing that unauthorized transplantation does not fit the human dignity of the dead and his/her relatives, the RF CC in fact reasoned that these individual emotions do not count against the common interest which is pursued by society and the state: "Dignity is protected insofar as it concerns purely individual affairs, is not subject to social control and if its exercise is lawful. . . . Therefore, presumed consent to the removal of organs—aimed at developing the country's organ donation and transplantation—does not violate the Constitution" (RFCC Rulings no. 459-O December 4, 2003; no. 224-O February 10, 2016). Another example is the rulings on gay parades in which the Court proclaimed that the right to sexual self-determination of individuals is a part of their human dignity, but at the same time refused to protect this right because the prevailing negative social attitudes toward such public demonstrations by LGBT people: "human dignity implies sexual self-determination, but this shall not affect dignity of other persons and call into question the social morality as it is understood in Russian society" (RFCC Judgment no. 24-P September 23, 2014).

In all three of these cases, the Court argued in favor of individual human dignity but decided against it (in its liberal interpretation), evidently following the presupposition that dignity may have no protection if contrasted with the public interest and communitarian values. Generally speaking, this jurisprudence shows that the RF CC weighs what "human dignity" means between the prevailing (majoritarian) morality, and the morality of the relevant minorities, normally preferring the former.

It is true that in a number of politically irrelevant cases the RF CC gave protection to human dignity (in its proper meaning) against degrading treatment (Maksimenko and Novopavlovskaia 2017), such as in a case concerning the judicial rights of mentally disabled people (RFCC Judgments no. 13-P November 20, 2007; no. 15-P June 27, 2012). However, this and other similar cases do not undermine but rather confirm our hypothesis: the Court tends to identify and defend human dignity only within the limits conventionally agreed upon in society and without encroaching on the political will which endorses communitarian morality.

Human Dignity as a Tool for Propelling Socio-Economic Rights

Thirdly, the RF CC utilizes the conception of human dignity as a vehicle to affirm the priority of the socio-economical rights provided by Russian statutory and constitutional law. These rights are interpreted as basic for human existence and survival. Therefore, it is implied that they are more important for the protection of human dignity than civil and/or political rights and freedoms. Tacitly, this emphasis on socio-economic rights implies that individual rights only make sense when a person's dignity (in the sense of her dignity as a social being) is effectively guaranteed by socio-economical rights. This logic transpires in such rulings of the RF CC as the 2005 Ruling on existential minimum for pensioners (RFCC Ruling no. 17-O February 15, 2005), the 2009 Ruling on the right to housing for those who lost their living premises due to natural disasters (RFCC Ruling no. 376-O-P March 5, 2009) or a number of decisions on the matter of indexation of social payments (RFCC Judgment no. 11-P June 19, 2002; RFCC Rulings no. 787-O-O June 1, 2010; no. 89-O April 4, 2006; no. 553-O-P April 2, 2009; no. 1125-O-O October 13, 2009).

In cases when the use of individual rights could eventually harm the socio-economic rights of others (here, meaning that the subject failed to perform his or her obligations to the collective), the RF CC tends to refuse protection of those rights. Such was the case in Khodorkovskiy's trial where the RF CC stressed the social importance of the distribution of the funds expropriated from YUKOS (the Russian state would be unable to pay pensions and other social subventions unless it expropriated the funds collected by Khodorkovskiy by means of tax evasion). In this sense, the Court also perpetuated the logic of Soviet jurisprudence, which insists on the priority of socio-economic rights over political rights and individual freedoms, and underscored the normative reciprocity between rights granted to individuals by the community and individual's obligations toward the community. In other words, private property, personal freedom, and other human rights belonging to a person may obtain legal protection only insofar as they do not contravene the socio-economic rights of pensioners and other vulnerable categories, and the collective rights of the Russian population in general.

Human Dignity as a Framework for a Conservative Interpretation of the Constitution

The fourth application is connected to the interpretational strategy of the RF CC to imbue the liberal wording of the RF Constitution with conservative meanings through the utilization of such "essentially contestable notions" as sovereignty, tradition, (human) dignity, identity, and so forth. This strategy tends to reject universalism in interpreting legal principles and underscores the national specificity in this regard. Such a pursuit of "constitutional identity" and other strategic tools of the RF CC have much in common with similar trends in the constitutional law of other European countries. However, in the Russian context, it leads to a profound reinterpretation of the concept of human dignity in a communitarian sense. Human dignity is often taken to mean a reflection of individual obligations toward the community, and in this light, dignity becomes dependent on whether an individual and her choices are congruent with the collective's values or not.

This approach is apparently shared by the justices of the RF CC and by the constitutional scholars who work closely with the Court. In a commentary to the RF Constitution edited by Chief Justice Zorkin, Professor Vladimir Kruss, commenting on Article 21 of the Constitution, symptomatically expresses this "constitutional understanding" of human dignity:

> The problem of human dignity includes the idea that recognition of dignity obtains the practical meaning only relatively to a particular social level (quality) and condition of life of a concrete human being. In this sense, philosophical and socio-cultural ideas about human dignity do matter. The liberal individualism displays the subjective and self-satisfactory understanding of human nature for which the main goal is to constantly strive for the unreachable horizon of ultimate material prosperity. Perception of human dignity in our cultural tradition is combined with the idea that the value and objectives of free development of every man shall include the active and consolidated participation in the creation of preconditions not only for material prosperity but also for the spiritual health of the nation.
>
> (Zorkin 2011)

The same argument is voiced by RF CC Justice Nikolai Bondar:

> However, some significant particularities of the constitutional formulation of human dignity can be connected with national and religious traditions, with concrete historical specificities of countries. . . . The formally legal qualities of this concept were developed in Russian socio-cultural milieu in a close connection with moral and ethical principles, with deep national traditions based on thrust to good and justice (the Preamble to the Constitution): this substantially strengthens the axiological background of the constitutional concept of human dignity.
>
> (Bondar' 2017)

Human dignity as perceived by each individual human being is not as important as collective values and, thus, should cede in the case of a conflict (Krasnov 2013). A plethora of cases illustrate this conservative underpinning of the interpretation of human rights, the right to human dignity among them, in the jurisprudence of the RF CC (Antonov 2014).

Chief Justice Zorkin himself has on many occasions underscored that he distinguishes two levels of the Constitution: the formal level and the deep level. In his 2018 article, the Chief Justice explained that the latter, the "deep legal meaning" of the Constitution is revealed by the RF CC by adapting the constitutional text to the "social and legal realities" (Zorkin 2018, 6). This objective implies that the Court defends Russia's national interests against the threats of globalization by "reformulating, at the level of mass consciousness, its own religious, national or regional identity, by reestablishing its own traditional values" (Zorkin 2018, 6). It is the majority opinion that shapes the normativity of Russian law, and this majoritarian normativity decides to what extent minority rights shall be protected (Zorkin 2018, 6).

Using the metaphor of the deep state (e.g., Lofgren 2016), one can describe the results of this reinterpretation in terms of "deep Constitution," which reincarnates the spiritual continuity of the Russian people and claims to be a compendium of supra-statutory principles with the supreme binding force. This compendium is unconceivable for Chief Justice Zorkin without Orthodoxy, and it comes as no surprise that not only does the RF CC's understanding of human dignity not coincide with the ROC's doctrine, nor does it benefit from some abstract "religious" or "spiritual" arguments, but it is directly inspired by the ROC.

In his latest book, Zorkin mentions "leaders of the public opinion who have the wide possibilities of influencing that allows that the states and social institutions exist" (Zorkin 2021, 148). It is these leaders who shall have the decisive role in the interpretation of the Constitution which is the "historically established and developing set of principles and norms which characterizes the given society and which is accepted by the majority" (Zorkin 2021, 148). Although he does not explicitly mention the ROC and its factual role as a "moral entrepreneur" in Russian society, the Chief Justice evidently means the ROC when he considers the restoration of the bases of moral regulation and the adjustment of legal mechanisms so that they correspond to the informal moral mechanisms as the key objective (Zorkin 2021, 148). Here, it belongs to the ROC as to one of the "leaders of the public opinion" to guarantee the links between conservative interpretation of the Constitution and Orthodoxy.

One cannot fail to notice that there will inevitably be conflict between the deep Constitution described by the Chief Justice and the formal Constitution: the latter proclaims and guarantees individual rights and freedoms against the dictates of the state and of the "silent majority," while the former condemns these rights and freedoms as the expression of antisocial individualism if they are exercised against traditional values. This cleavage is often underscored not only by Zorkin but also in other numerous political narratives in which Russian society is described as traditionalist, sharing the common Orthodox values and instinctively resisting the godless liberal narratives about the sacredness of individual choice (e.g., Chapnin 2020). This can explain why the constitutional interpretation in Russia is actually so deeply influenced by the social philosophy of the ROC.

The Christian Orthodox Roots of the Constitutional Interpretation of Human Dignity

All four of these applications of human dignity unveil the intrinsic connection between the interpretation of this concept in Russian constitutional law and in the doctrine of the ROC. This latter doctrine is implicitly based on the similar communitarian presumption of the priority of obligations over rights and on the justification of principles by the communitarian morality seen as a precondition of the legal effect of these principles. The doctrine is intimately connected with anti-liberal political attitudes in a number of regards (minority rights, secular state, dominant religion, etc.).

The main assertion of this doctrine in 2008 *Russian Orthodox Church's Basic Teaching on Human Dignity, Freedom and Rights* (the Basic Teaching) is that it is possible to accept the liberal Constitution and liberal principles enshrined in it under the condition of their conservative interpretation in line with the ROC's communitarian social philosophy. In other words, the Basic Teaching implicitly rectifies the Constitution through its broad interpretation corresponding to the "Russian historical tradition" and "traditional values." Even if the RF CC normally does not mention the ROC's doctrine in its case law, a number of plausible connections can be reconstructed through the analysis of similarities between the philosophical presuppositions that underpin the Court's jurisprudence and the writings of Court's judges and constitutional lawyers on the one hand, and the ideas set out in the Basic Teaching on the other.

There are a number of key propositions from the 2008 Basic Teaching which are selected as central by its authors (they are marked in bold) to illustrate the main tenets of the ROC's communitarian social philosophy and which at the same time point to the thematic axes around which the interpretation of human dignity is construed in the RF CC's jurisprudence.

The Basic Teaching's main presupposition underscores the interdependence between the right to dignity and its moral justification: "a human being preserves his God-given dignity and grows in it only if he lives in accordance with moral norms because these norms express the primordial and therefore authentic human nature not darkened by sin. There appears a direct link between human dignity and morality. Moreover, the acknowledgement of personal dignity implies the assertion of personal responsibility" (Chapter 1).

This interpretation results in two substantial reservations imposed on those who would want to take advantage of their constitutional right to human dignity: the subject shall live according to moral norms and shall assume responsibility for the use of dignity before the church and the collective. Therefore, all those persons whose values and choices might be morally reproachable and who do not assume moral responsibility for their actions that can be qualified as "wrongdoing"—e.g., behavior and opinions of sexual minorities, atheists, non-Christians, or non-traditional religious denominations—can by default be excluded from the privileges conferred by the constitutional right to dignity.

This interpretation is confirmed in the following part (Chapter 2) of the Basic Teaching where its authors assert that "freedom of choice will inevitably disappear if the choice is made in favor of evil. Evil and freedom are incompatible. . . . Free adherence to goodness and the truth is impossible without the freedom of choice, just as a free choice loses its value and meaning if it is made in favor of evil." In other words, only morally commendable rights are justified, and this justification is derived from the correct (approved by the Church) morality and serves as a condition of the validity of rights and freedoms.

This presupposition logically leads to normative constraints on the constitutional right to human dignity in the system of human rights: "the political and legal institution of human rights can promote the good goals of protecting human dignity and contribute to the spiritual and ethical development of the personality. To make it possible the implementation of human rights should not come into conflict with God-established moral norms and traditional morality based on them. One's human rights cannot be set against the values and interests of one's homeland, community, and family" (Chapter 2). This is a quite expectable normative framework within which the right to human dignity is dependent on a person's adherence to the system of conservative values and his or her actions in line with these values.

In the Declaration on Human Rights and Dignity adopted by the World Russian People's Council (2006) under the guidance of the ROC, this idea is laid down even more strongly. Human dignity is not innate—it is acquired only by "doing good." Therefore, "dignity" is not a natural right, but a positive evaluation of a person by the community—a religious community of true believers. Furthermore, the authors of this declaration draw a distinction between the worth and dignity of human beings: "Worth is given, while dignity is acquired."

The same (or a very similar) conservative reading not infrequently serves as a background for further identification of legal principles by Russian courts and in particular by the RF CC. This coincidence does not seem to be random, as both institutions (the RF CC and the ROC) pursue basically the same goal of establishing Russia's identity. Alexander Agadjanian describes the Russian Orthodox Church's strategy as protection of traditional identity through resistance to global liberal secularism, which includes insulating itself from some external (outside of Russia) influences (Agadjanian 2003, 339). A short glance at the public narratives of Russian political leaders leaves no doubt that they appropriated the same approach, and the RF CC in its argumentation cannot neglect this collusion between the Russian state and the ROC (Agadjanian 2017; Blitt 2022; Curanović 2019; Koellner and Benovska 2021; Stoeckl 2020).

Conclusion

The conception of human dignity plays a particular role, allowing the RF CC to make connections between the signifier and the signified, without being bound by the interpretative constraints that delimit the interpretational discretion of judges in the Western legal tradition. Thereby, the RF CC gets a tool that at the same time helps to adjust its jurisprudence to informal or semi-formal political directives and to reassert its symbolic ("hegemonic") power in the normative field. The concept of "human dignity" can be effectively applied here as an empty signifier to help courts justify their contradictory decisions in similar cases (e.g., different applications of the same legal rules in cases with "traditional religious denominations" and with religious minorities).

At face value, the conservative logic—as applied to the issue of human dignity—is simple: Russia does not endorse the Western emphasis on individual rights to the possible detriment of collective rights and interests, as, in the "Russian legal tradition," individual rights have never been accepted as constitutive elements of the legal order. Prioritizing individual interests can split the organic collective whole and lead to the destruction of the whole of society which cannot survive if it loses its integrity and cohesion; or, at least, it can impede organic social development.

Such empty signifiers as "human dignity," "sovereignty," or "tradition" work in the RF CC's jurisprudence as argumentative vehicles for this coordination between legal texts and legal culture. Such methodological tenets are advantageous for great historical narratives and discourses about the civilizational role of Russia that, unsurprisingly, also become the foundational narratives for the legal system. Practically applied to the concept of human dignity, this philosophy means that judges do not have unfettered discretion when they deal with the interpretation of this concept. In order to make good interpretations, they have to check how their decisions contribute to reaching the ultimate objectives of Russian organic development and whether these decisions fit the "collective consciousness" reflecting this development and revealing its objectives.

Our analysis shows how the RF CC utilizes the concept of human dignity as an empty signifier to the effect that, in fact, it excludes its application in cases where the protection of rights may result in challenging established behavioral patterns and opinions. According to this reinterpretation, in a conflict between individual rights and collective interests, the former shall be defeated. To defend this reinterpretation, the Court chose to deny the universality of "human dignity," arguing that national states have the unrestrained power to make exceptions in human rights protection with a view to protect national interests, cultural specificity, and other similar reasons.

Following this strategy, the RF CC pragmatically extended its scope of competencies, de facto assuming an ideological function (there are many scientific works whose authors assert that "constitutional ideology" is a necessary prerequisite of Russia's legal development and does not fall under the ban on state ideology in Art.13 of the RF Constitution)—at the same time, encapsulating itself from normative criticism from within or from without. In terms of competence, no other opinion can prevail over the Court's opinion.

This is the main premise in the long contentious debates with the European Court of Human Rights (ECtHR), culminating in the RF CC's famous 2015 judgment concerning the prevalence of constitutional interpretations rendered by the Constitutional Court over international law and the ECtHR case law (RFCC Judgment no. 21-P July 14, 2015). To a certain extent, this conflict can be seen as a struggle for the decisionist power to make exceptions from legal rules—the power that the RF CC unambiguously considers as its exclusive prerogative.

Human dignity is in fact used by the RF CC as a floating signifier, with its ability to conceal inconsistencies in reasoning. One can distinguish several normative properties of human dignity as it is utilized by the RF CC. "Human dignity":

- Has no clear-cut legal framework and can be interpreted only by referring to extra-legal ethical or religious ideas;
- Combines heterogeneous ideologies and allows to choose the meaning which is required from the RF CC depending on the political situation;
- Excludes logical verification of coherence and thereby provides leeway for concealing contradictions in argumentation;
- Can serve as a tool for evolutive interpretation and, as a result, can be utilized by the Court to uphold its legitimacy.

These properties invest "human dignity" with a potentially very strong normative force. This force can be utilized both for liberal and illiberal interpretations of constitutional law. The case law of the RF CC and the narratives of its justices demonstrate an evident proclivity to illiberalism which is justified by the religious reading of "human dignity" in line with the ROC's conservative philosophy.

"The publication was prepared within the framework of the Academic Fund Program at HSE University (grant No. 24-00-032)"

Notes

1 See for example: 4 BVerfGE 7, 15 (1954).
2 Human dignity was also discussed in the pre-revolutionary Russian legal philosophy, especially by Vladimir Soloviev and such his followers as Pavel Novgorodtsev (Walicki 1992).
3 Surely, the RF CC is not the only court that utilizes this argumentation tool. There might be some situations where courts, especially constitutional courts, have to decide *contra legem* or use dynamic interpretation of constitutional provisions.
4 As defined by Laclau, "An empty signifier can, consequently, only emerge if there is a structural impossibility in signification as such, and only if this impossibility can signify itself as an interruption (subversion, distortion, etcetera) of the structure of the sign" (Laclau 1996).
5 This view is also reflected in the 2008 Basic Teachings of the Russian Orthodox Church on Human Dignity, Freedom and Human Rights which underscores (part IV, last paragraph) that "The social value and effectiveness of the entire human rights system depend on the extent to which it helps to create conditions for personal growth in the God-given dignity and relates to the responsibility of a person for his actions before God and his neighbors."
6 E.g., the conservative diatribes of Chief Justice Zorkin (Antonov 2017).

References

Agadjanian, Alexander. 2003. "Breakthrough to Modernity, Apologia for Traditionalism: The Russian Orthodox View of Society and Culture in Comparative Perspective." *Religion, State & Society* 31 (4): 327–46.

Agadjanian, Alexander. 2017. "Tradition, Morality and Community: Elaborating Orthodox Identity in Putin's Russia." *Religion, State & Society* 45: 39–60.

Antonov, Mikhail. 2014. "Conservatism in Russia and Sovereignty in Human Rights." *Review of Central and East European Law* 39 (1): 1–40.

Antonov, Mikhail. 2017. "Philosophy Behind Human Rights: Valerii Zorkin vs. the West?" In *Russia and the European Court of Human Rights: The Strasbourg Effect*, edited by Lauri Mälksoo and Wolfgang Benedek, 150–87. Cambridge: Cambridge University Press.

Antonov, Mikhail. 2019. "Religion, Sexual Minorities, and the Rule of Law in Russia." *Journal of Law, Religion and State* 7 (2): 152–83.

Baekken, Hovard. 2019. *Law and Power in Russia: Sense of Quasi-Legal Practice.* Abingdon: Routledge.

Barak, Aaron. 2015. *Human Dignity: The Constitutional Value and the Constitutional Right*, 225–42. Cambridge: Cambridge University Press.

Berman, Harold J. 1972. "The Educational Role of the Soviet Court." *The International and Comparative Law Quarterly* 21 (1): 81–94.

Blitt, Robert C. 2022. "Russia's 2020 Constitutional Amendments and the Entrenchment of the Moscow Patriarchate as a Lever of Foreign Policy Soft Power." In *The Geopolitics of Religious Soft Power: How States Use Religion in Foreign Policy*, edited Peter Mandaville. New York: Oxford University Press (forthcoming). https://papers.ssrn.com/sol3/papers.cfm?abstract_id=3930235

Bondar', Nikolai. 2017. "Konstitutsionnaia kategoriia dostoinstva lichnosti v tsennostnom izmerenii: sudebnaia praktika [The Constitutional Category of Human Dignity in the Axiological Dimension: The Court Practice]." *Konstitutzionnoe I munitsipalnoeuteo* 4: 19–31.

Byzov, Leontii. 2014. "Novoe konservativnoe bol'shinstvo kak sotsialno-politicheskii fenomen [The New Conservative Majority as a Social and Political Phenomenon]." *Mir Rossii* 4: 6–34.

Chapnin, Sergey. 2020. "The Rhetoric of Traditional Values in Contemporary Russia". In *Postsecular Conflicts. Debating Tradition in Russia and the United States*, edited by Kristina Stoeckl and Dmitry Uzlaner, 128–38. Innsbruck: Innsbruck University Press.

Cocks, Joan. 2018. "Dignity and the Limits of Liberal Individualism." *Law, Culture and the Humanities* 14 (3): 353–64.

Curanović, Alicja. 2019. "Guided by a 'Symphony of Views': The Russian Orthodox Church's Role in Building Russia's Symbolic Capital." In *On Multiple Secularisms and Entanglements: Orthodox Religion and Politics in Eastern Europe*, edited by Tobias Koellner, 195–213. London; New York: Routledge.

Douzinas, Costas. 2000. *The End of Human Rights. Critical Legal Thought at the Turn of the Century.* Oxford; Portland: Hart Publishing.

Gurvitch, Georges. 1942. *The Sociology of Law.* New York: Philosophical. Library.

Gurvitch, Georges. 1972. *The Social Frameworks of Knowledge.* New York: Harper & Row.

Kirk, Russell. 2001. *The Conservative Mind: From Burke to Eliot.* 7th ed. Washington, DC: Gateway Editions.

Koellner, Tobias, and Milena Benovska. 2021. "Continuity and Change in Orthodox Christianity in Contemporary Russia: Enduring Legacies and New Developments in the Making." *Religions* 12 (12): 1053.

Krasnov, Mikhail. 2013. "Khristianskoe mirovozzrenie i prava cheloveka [Christian World Outlook and Human Rights]." *Rex russica* 5: 465–77.

Krasnov, Mikhail. 2016. "Tolkovaniia Konstitutsii kak ee fakticheskie popravki [Interpretations of the Constitution as Its Factual Amendments]." *Sravnitelnoe konstitutsionnoe obozreniie* 1: 77–91.

Laclau, Ernesto. 1996. *Emancipation(s).* London; New York: Verso.

Lofgren, Mike. 2016. *The Deep State: The Fall of the Constitution and the Rise of a Shadow Government.* New York: Penguin Publishing Group.

Maksimenko, Aleksandr, and Elena Novopavlovskaia. 2017. "Okhrana dostoinstva lichnosti v deiatelnosti Konstitutsionnogo Suda RF [Human Dignity under Protection of the RF Constitutional Court]." *Vestnik Voronezhskogo instituta MVD* 3: 140–47.

McCrudden, Christopher. 2008. "Human Dignity and Judicial Interpretation of Human Rights." *European Journal of International Law* 19 (4): 655–724.

Patriarch Kirill. 2016. *Svoboda i otvetstvennost': v poiskakh garmonii. Prava cheloveka i dostoinstvo lichnosti* [Freedom and Responsibility: in the Search of Harmony. Human Rights and Personal Dignity]. Moscow: Izdatelstvo Moskovskoi Patriarchii.

Robinson, Paul. 2019. *Russian Conservatism.* Ithaca; London: Cornell University Press.

The Russian Orthodox Church. 2008. *Basic Teaching on Human Dignity, Freedom and Rights.* The ROC Department for External Relations. https://old.mospat.ru/en/documents/dignity-freedom-rights/.

Shakhrai, Sergey. 2017. *Konstitutsionnoeuteo Rossiiskoi Federatsii* [Constitutional Law of the Russian Federation]. 4th ed. Moscow: Statut.

Stoeckl, Kristina. 2020. "Russian Orthodoxy and Secularism." *Brill Research Perspectives in Religion and Politics* 1: 1–75.

Walicki, Andrzej. 1992. *Legal Philosophies of Russian Liberalism*. Notre Dame, IN: University of Notre Dame Press.
World Russian People's Council. 2006. *Declaration on Human Rights and Dignity*. The ROC Department for External Relations. https://mospat.ru/en/news/74568/.
Zorkin, Valerii, ed. 2011. *Kommentarii k Kostitutzii Rossiiskoi Federatsii (postateinyi)* [A Commentary to the Constitution of the Russian Federation (Article-by-Article)]. 2nd ed. Moscow: Norma, Infra-M.
Zorkin, Valerii. 2018. "Konstitutsiia RF—pravovaia osnova integratsii rossiiskogo obshchestva [The RF Constitution as the Legal Basis for Integration of the Russian Society]." *Gosudarstvo i pravo* 12: 5–17.
Zorkin, Valerii. 2021. *Constitutional Justice: Procedure and Meaning* [Konstitutsionnoe pravosudie: protsedura i smysl]. Saint Petersburg: KS RF.

Case Law

The Federal Constitutional Court of Germany

4 bVerfGE 7 (1954).

The Constitutional Court of the Russian Federation

Judgment no. 4-P. May 3, 1995.
Judgment no. 9-P. April 4, 1996.
Judgment no. 21-P. December 24, 1997.
Judgment no. 10-P. June 7, 2000.
Judgment no. 11-P. June 19, 2002
Judgment no. 7-P. April 24, 2003.
Judgment no. 8-P. June 28, 2007.
Judgment no. 13-P. November 20, 2007.
Judgment no. 14-P. June 22, 2010.
Judgment no. 16-P. July 2, 2013.
Judgment no. 15-P. June 27, 2013.
Judgment no. 24-P. September 23, 2014.
Judgment no. 21-P. July 14, 2015.
Ruling no. 459-O. December 4, 2003.
Ruling no. 17-O. February 15, 2005.
Ruling no. 89-O. April 4, 2006.
Ruling no. 406-O. July 11, 2006.
Ruling no. 376-O-P. March 5, 2009.
Ruling no. 483-O-P. April 2, 2009.
Ruling no. 553-O-P. April 2, 2009.
Ruling no. 1125-O-O. October 13, 2009.
Ruling no. 787-O-O. June 1, 2010.
Ruling no. 840-O. April 22, 2014.

Part IV

Human Dignity and Social Rights Protection

13 The Judicial Use of Human Dignity in Social Rights Issues

A European Perspective

Giorgio Repetto

Human Dignity in Contemporary Constitutionalism: Enthusiasm or Suspicion?

Both in contemporary legal discourse and in judicial applications worldwide, human dignity stands nowadays as an overarching value. Its composite moral foundations have not prevented it from becoming a standard in adjudicating fundamental rights. In addition to this, its diversified dimensions of application made the recourse to it viable in disparate situations: one can invoke the protection of dignity against the intrusion of public authority in his or her personal domain as well as against degrading practices put forth by state and non-state actors and ask, on this basis, for positive obligations for public authorities (Cohn and Grimm 2013). Moreover, human dignity is supposed to act both as an instrument aimed at protecting *individual* liberty and autonomy and as a basis of moral justification for the introduction of public policies aimed at safeguarding *objective* values. It is commonplace in legal discourse that on some debated issues, like abortion, human dignity may be invoked at the same time as a vehicle of empowerment or as an instrument of constraint (Brownsword 2012, 20).

The risk of such a reversibility of the argument by dignity seems to be part of a larger problem. The global spread of dignity as a guiding rhetoric for human rights protection has definitely shown that its use as a cluster of judicial arguments has traveled in several directions around the globe (Barak 2015; Barroso 2012; Jackson 2004); one could say that the motor of human dignity has shifted from those European countries that made it the cornerstone of their constitutions after World War II to some new "importers countries" like South Africa, Israel, Canada and, to a certain degree, the USA (Carozza 2011).

This dissemination of human dignity in judicial reasoning has given rise to opposite narratives about the reasons for such a success story. On one side of the spectrum, a more enthusiastic position makes human dignity one of the basic traits of liberal constitutionalism, centered upon values like the rule of law and the respect for human rights and personal autonomy. In doing so, it sets the premises for a detachment of human rights from the decision

DOI: 10.4324/9781003307853-17

of political actors and their conveyance in the hands of a new judicial order (Dupré 2015; Mahlmann 2008). At the opposite end of the spectrum, a demystifying rhetoric has emerged, according to which human dignity is the Trojan horse of a broader depoliticization project, relying upon an increasing and irresistible *montée en puissance* of human rights narrative (Douzinas 2007, 54).

Against this background, my intention is to demonstrate whether and to what extent human dignity is a viable legal basis for promoting social rights and welfare policies. In doing so, I move from the assumption that the dignity of the individual in the social field (i.e. "social dignity") is a distinct feature of the European constitutional tradition since it reflects, at a closer view, a distinctive bond between individual autonomy (as enshrined in fundamental rights guaranteed at both national and supranational, i.e. regional levels) and solidarity as a heritage of a shared duty to provide for the common good. This link between autonomy and solidarity is mediated by the value of human dignity, but it requires an ongoing reassessment of its institutional premises, that is, a balance between political decision and judicial reasoning.

In Part 2, I try to briefly sketch out the main aspects of this theoretical debate, although my intention is rather to focus on the legal implications thereof. In Part 3, I delve into an overview of the judicial applications of human dignity in social rights and welfare policies in four European countries: France, Italy, Germany, and the United Kingdom. The German and the UK cases in particular reveal the basic variables of and the different reactions to a fully fledged utilization of human dignity as a legal basis in the field of social policies. In Part 4, I offer some concluding remarks about the legal epistemology of human dignity in social rights issues and the opportunity to refer to it as a moral and legal basis for promoting individual rights and social integration via judicial decisions.

Beyond Individual Dignity: What Status Does Human Dignity Have in the Social Field?

It is common knowledge that dignity was first introduced as a normative concept by Immanuel Kant. Although references to dignity are long-standing and far-reaching in the Western tradition and many traces of it can be seen in other cultures, the modern usage of the word and its conceptualization almost entirely coincide with the Kantian theory. As is well known, the absoluteness of the Kantian *Würde* (dignity), the relationship between means and ends that it endorses, and the centrality of the individual as a moral agent have jointly led to the conclusion that human dignity can first and foremost be addressed in terms of individual autonomy (Kant 1997). For a long time, theoretical reflections have highlighted that the absoluteness of dignity works at its best when it opposes the individual agent (as the bearer of rights) and the public authority (as the source of power threatening the absoluteness of moral individuality). Within such a liberal arrangement, there is no place for establishing a link between dignity and the social field, although the position of Kant insisted on a broader notion of autonomy, encompassing moral duties (Augsberg 2018).

In more recent years, the philosophical debate about the widespread diffusion of dignity and its multipurpose nature has called into question its relationship with welfare policies and social rights. More recent philosophical strains have highlighted the need to encompass dignity within a broader reading, according to which the respect of individual autonomy implies some necessary conditions for one's self-fulfilling project (Gewirth 1978). In this light, human dignity becomes the source of both rights and duties, since the mutual respect for autonomy calls for a limitation on individual actions that may infringe on others' rights. The insistence on duties as a distinctive component of autonomy and dignity reveals the intention to provide the latter with some distributive intent. Human dignity is not a persistent and immutable quality of individuals, but rather is a set of entitlements that have to be safeguarded from the intrusions of private and public actors; therefore it needs to be arranged at an institutional level. A step forward in this direction is made by those scholars who stress the insufficiency of a utilitarian approach, centered upon the maximization of individual good or benefit, which is accused of underestimating the cooperative potential of public institutions. Their coordinated action is able to overcome the theoretical and practical shortcomings of a purely horizontal dimension of individual aid which, in doing so, provides a basis for the arrangement of public services like healthcare, pensions, and social support for disadvantaged people (Steigleder 2014).

Such a philosophical foundation is in line with those international legal trends aimed at elevating social rights to the level of human rights. The right to access health services, the right to an education, the right to housing, and the right to fair working conditions have been part of many global and regional covenants for decades—since (at least) the 1966 International Covenant on Economic, Social and Cultural Rights. Against this background, it comes as no surprise that human dignity has been invoked in judicial decisions as a guarantee for the right to have essential needs satisfied. In the *Guatemala Street Children Case*, the Inter-American Court of Human Rights asserted that the right to life "includes not only the right of every human being not to be deprived of his life arbitrarily, but also the right that he will not be prevented from having access to the conditions that guarantee a dignified existence" (par. 144). In a similar vein, the Indian Supreme Court has interpreted the right to life and personal liberty by stating that it includes "the right to live with human dignity and all that goes along with it, namely, the bare necessities of life such as adequate nutrition, clothing and shelter over the head and facilities for reading, writing and expressing oneself in diverse forms" (*Mullin v. The Administrator. Union Territory of Delhi* 516, 518). Similar decisions have been taken on similar grounds in countries like Hungary (see the Constitution Court of Hungary's Decision 32/1998 (VI. 25), 251; Decision 42/2000 (XI. 8)) and South Africa (see *Government of the Republic of South Africa v.*

Grootboom), thereby contributing in the last 20 years to the emergence of a human dignity judicial canon within global constitutional law.

Although these evolutions have contributed to the enrichment of human dignity's multifaceted texture, one can read behind them a certain vague and erratic attitude: their capacity to stand as the flagship of civilization and of political and socio-economic life seems to be at odds with the context in which they are called to deploy their effects. Their high moral ambitions are likely to elevate their judicial proclamation from the harsh political situations surrounding them, and in this way they may be captured by the aspirational intent of such social rights claims. Quite paradoxically, this can alternatively lead to their ineffectiveness or rather to a reversal of the message they are called to uphold. A striking example comes again from Hungary: in 1998 and 2000, the local Constitutional Court delivered some pioneering decisions that emphasized in terms of a dignitarian mandate the duty of the state to secure a minimum livelihood through all the welfare benefits necessary for the realization of the right to human dignity, in particular for the right to provide a shelter for homeless persons (see the Constitution Court of Hungary's Decision 32/1998 (VI. 25), 251 and Decision 42/2000 (XI. 8)). On 4 June, 2019, after the entry into force of a new Fundamental law in 2011 and the packing of the Constitutional Court, this judicial body delivered an astonishing decision according to which the criminalization and eventual imprisonment of homeless people was in line with the Constitution: according to the majority, "nobody has the right to poverty and homelessness, this condition is not part of the right to human dignity" (see the Constitution Court of Hungary's Decision 19/2019. (VI. 18.) ABH 2019, 493; Chronowski and Halmai 2019).

Social Dignity as a Defining Feature of European Constitutionalism: Trends and Challenges

When the relationship between human dignity and social rights is considered from a legal point of view, and from the perspective of constitutional law in particular, a few preliminary observations should be made. Human dignity emerged as a distinct legal component of modern constitutions after World War II, even though previous references had been made in other constitutional texts (such as Spain and Ireland).

The close connection between human dignity and social rights should thus not be surprising if one focuses on the constitutional ideas that prevailed in the aftermath of World War II (Oehling De Los Reyes 2011, 135). At an international level, Art. 1 of the Universal Declaration of Human Rights paved the way for dignity to take on an increasingly important role by stating that "All human beings are born free and equal in dignity and rights." Even before this, a new legal and theoretical strain had emerged, according to which human dignity had to be grasped within the social and relational contexts the individuals lived in so that a more individualist approach had to be abandoned.[1] The Italian (1948) and German (1949) Constitutions were, among others, strongly committed to the idea that the protection of the individual could not be left solely to the dynamics of social interactions anymore and had to be taken under the control of the public authorities. In Germany, this approach has been realized thanks to the combination of Art. 1 of the Basic Law (BL) and the principle of social state enshrined in Art. 20 BL. In the Italian Constitution, meanwhile, human dignity is more immediately related to its social dimension: it is mentioned with regard to the principle of equality in Art. 3 ("equal social dignity"), as a limit to the freedom of economic actors (Art. 41, par. 2), or as a basic yardstick indicating the minimum threshold for wages (Art. 36). In the French system, human dignity is not directly mentioned by the Constitution (both 1946 and 1958) and the protection of social rights emerges indirectly from the Preamble to the 1946 Constitution.[2]

If we move to the judicial applications of human dignity in the social field, however, the connection between human dignity and social rights is much more blurred.

The German example is quite revealing. Despite the clear connection between *Menschenwürde* and the principle of the social state, the Federal Constitutional Court highlighted from the very beginning that the public authority (i.e. Parliament) has a duty to provide the individual with social services (*Leistungspflicht*), but this duty is not directly enforceable by the individual, since it stands as a purely objective constitutional mandate (BVerfGE 1, 97, par. 104, BVerwGE, 159, par. 161). In extreme circumstances, the individual can bring a claim against manifestly insufficient legislation, but the burden of proof is high since the individual has to demonstrate that such a shortcoming was related to an arbitrary inaction of the legislative power (BVerfGE 33, 44, par. 51; 71, 39, par. 58; 75, 108, par. 157). This could be partly related to the absence of a constitutional catalog of socio-economic rights at the federal level since the related clauses are enshrined in the constitutions of the German *Länder*.

A turning point in this field was the decision taken in 2010 by the Federal Constitutional Court in the social minimum case (*Existenzminimum*). In that case, the Court clearly stated that each and every individual has a right to state benefits that:

> covers those means which are vital to maintain an existence that is in line with human dignity. It guarantees the whole subsistence minimum by a uniform fundamental rights guarantee which encompasses both the physical existence of the individual, that is food, clothing, household goods, housing, heating, hygiene and health . . . and ensuring the possibility to maintain inter-human relationships and a minimum of participation in social, cultural and political life.
>
> (BVerfGE 125, 175, par. 136)

Two aspects of this seminal decision need to be highlighted.

The influence of human dignity in fostering a socially inclusive measure can be perceived at its clearest when the Court emphasizes the relational potential of such an intervention, which should not be limited to providing the individual with material goods and services, but should instead be directed to "maintain[ing] inter-human relationships and a minimum of participation in social, cultural and political life." In so doing, the Court seeks to detach social benefits from the most classical (German) domain of the social state, where public intervention in favor of disadvantaged people is traditionally considered (since the Bismarck era) a distinctive policy with some authoritarian traits. The shift from such a traditional "duty of intervention" to a multifaceted idea of the individual and its basic needs is, according to many, the contribution delivered by the notion of human dignity and the underlying idea of individual autonomy enshrined therein (Baldus 2016, 230; Eichenhofer 2009, 218). A social intervention aimed at respecting human dignity must not simply concede a subsidy but must put the individual in a condition to help himself or herself re-establish the conditions for a dignified life in the social environment (Denninger 2011; Neumann 1995, 428).

At the same time, this decision and the one taken in 2012 with regard to the social benefits of asylum seekers (bVerfGE 132, 134) show, at a deeper glance, the continuity with the previous approach of the German Federal Constitutional Court. The right of individuals is not considered even today in terms of a fully fledged right to assistance (*Leistungsrecht*), but in a more modest right of the individual "to be assured" (*Gewährleistungsrecht*) in the enjoyment of services that embody the social minimum in terms that do not violate their human dignity. Many commentators have argued that such a terminological shift is not just a sign of legal pedantry, since it reflects the intimate nature of the constitutional mandate emerging from Art. 1 BL in the social field (Mayen 2012, 1458). On the one hand, human dignity does not stand anymore on a terrain separated from social dynamics; it does not convey a barely natural law perspective but must be grasped in the light of the problems of associated life. On the other hand, human dignity sets a limit to the freedom of political actors to address measures and instruments for the advancement of social inclusion, but this limit is *not* absolute. A public authority has a duty to justify the breadth of its interventions. It must respect some substantial and procedural standards, but its discretion as to the evaluation of the compatibility of such measures, e.g., with budgetary requirements, must be safeguarded (BVerfGE 125, 175, par. 222, 224). The absoluteness of human dignity, therefore, is not deemed to be able *per se* to set an absolute limit upon the freedom of assessment of political actors.

This conclusion needs to be emphasized at a more general level. As we will see, the German case shows the deepest and closest relationship between a strong vision of human dignity and social rights and measures aimed at contrasting poverty and favoring social inclusion. But the epilogue of such a brief survey demonstrates that the intimate meaning of dignity seems to be at odds with its standing as a guiding principle in the field of social measures since these ones forcefully require a graduation, a selection of interventions for which the human dignity and its absoluteness are not able to offer a valid yardstick.[3]

Despite this, the German case represents, in my view, a successful way of dealing with dignity in the social field, although the impression is that such an outcome has been made possible by decades of legislative interventions in the social field (in the framework of the "social code"[4]) which paved the way to a judicial decision aimed at securing social minimum as an individual right.

The French case demonstrates that the existence of legislation in the social field and the commitment of public institutions to social goals does not lead *per se* to establishing a link with human dignity. Even though the French *Conseil constitutionnel* referred in a pair of cases to the *dignité de la personne humaine* as a value, among others, safeguarding the social right to housing,[5] there is a widespread consensus that human dignity has not yet emerged as a basic value capable of offering protection against social exclusion (Dupéré 2008). Despite of this, many authors have stressed the growing importance of human dignity in legislation concerning socio-economic issues (Hennette-Vauchez 2014),[6] although such an outcome is deemed to cause a dilution of human dignity's absolute nature (Mathieu 1998, 50).[7]

The Italian system has traditionally shown a different approach with regard to the role played by human dignity in the judicial protection of socio-economic rights. As was stated earlier, unlike France, the Italian Constitution makes several mentions of dignity in relation to the social dimension of fundamental rights. Despite this, an overview of case law from the Italian Constitutional Court reveals that such a principle is rarely invoked in the field of social rights (as well as in human rights litigation in general). The scant reference to human dignity in this field can be explained by two different reasons. On the one hand, the Constitutional Court has traditionally given Parliament a lot of leeway about whether, how, and to what extent to introduce legislation aimed at granting social rights. In particular, the Court has developed a broad range of interpretive techniques aimed at securing a priority in the legislative evaluation of social policies, among which the principle of graduality must be mentioned. According to this principle, in the first instance it is up to the political authority to decide whether and to what extent the promotion of social goals is compatible with budget considerations and the macroeconomic framework in general.[8] Such an evaluation can be reviewed by the Court only in case of a manifestly arbitrary assessment, but it must be added that the Court has rarely reversed such assessments.[9] On the other hand, a judicial correction of legislative choices is possible with regard to sectoral decisions, i.e. when a certain social benefit must be granted to other groups or categories that Parliament decided to ignore or treat less favorably than others. In such cases, the potential of human dignity as a tool aimed at securing social rights has been absorbed by the principle of equality and its connected interpretive technique of "reasonableness" (*ragionevolezza*, an Italian version of proportionality), whose basic meaning must be intended as a quest for systemic coherence upon the legislator.[10] With regard to both aspects, the Italian version of *dignità umana* reveals the weakness of judicial responses whenever the legislative decision enjoys a margin of choice and intervention in the social field which is counterbalanced only in a limited measure by judicial actors. Rather than enabling the courts to set a core content of social rights and services that could not be lowered by the political authority, human dignity acts as a value justifying political choices, albeit with a very narrow oppositive content (Messineo 2012).

Against these backgrounds that share a basically sympathetic approach toward human dignity, the UK case could be invoked as a laboratory in which the recourse to dignity enters the scene as a "legal irritant" (Teubner 1998).

The emergence of dignity in UK law was mainly vehiculated by the entry into force of the Human Rights Act of 1998, which nationalized the standards set forth in Articles 2 (right to life) and 3 (prohibition of cruel and degrading treatments) of the European Convention on Human Rights and Fundamental Freedoms (ECHR). At such a general level, the entrance into UK law of a principle like human dignity in its "continental fashion" raised concerns in those scholars who promptly argued that this risked conferring to this principle an overinclusive stance. In particular, a moral content that is too broad was charged with delivering a paternalistic attitude to the protection of fundamental rights and, in this way, human dignity as a "German legal concept" threatened to replace, according to many, the prerogative of Parliamentary sovereignty in the establishment of the common good on the basis of political representation (Feldman 1999, 698). The evolution of the judicial applications in the following years showed a growing inclination to refer to human dignity in those areas covered by Art. 2 and 3 ECHR (see *R (Daly) v. Secretary of State for the Home Department* (2001) UKHL; *R v. Ian McLoughlin*; *R v. Lee William Newell* (2014) EWCA Crim; *Regina v. Secretary of State for the Home Department ex parte Limbuela* (2005) UKHL), but one could not argue that such a principle has become commonplace in judicial reasoning.

First, even from a perspective aimed at safeguarding a moral reading of the institutional balance between the judicial power and sovereignty of Parliament, the UK example reveals a resistance against the empowerment of human dignity through judicial decisions not so different from the one at stake in the aforementioned continental systems.

If we then turn to the relationship between human dignity and social rights, things appear even more blurred. In the evolution of the UK system after 1945, social dignity has been often invoked as a guiding idea of the legislative process establishing a new public service aimed at securing individual security in the framework of a dignified citizenship (Marshall 1950). The approval of seminal legislation like the 1944 Education Act, the 1946 National Health Service Act, and the 1946 New Towns Act shows that the commitment of the English Parliament to human dignity had a clear social attitude that was not related to an authoritarian tradition (as in Germany), but rather with the idea of a (then) "new" relationship between the individual and society. Sovereignty of Parliament, in this field, means that social forces have conferred some basic choices to political actors as to the inclusion of disadvantaged classes in the social realm. In so doing, dignity acts as a guiding principle since its core content is supported by a wide ranging political and social context. Therefore, it is not surprising that when such a social and political consensus vanishes, human dignity has "to cope with an attack on its whole underlying premise, namely that the electors have (through their government) any responsibility at all for the welfare of their neighbours and co-nationals" (Gearty 2004, 89).

Within this framework, the judicial application of human dignity in the social field has been marked in recent years by a reluctance to move beyond the narrow margins of the "degrading treatments" referred to in Art. 3 ECHR; whereas, if other ECHR rights are invoked (for example Art. 8, *Right to respect for private and family life*), the respect of human dignity is balanced against the need to preserve limited public resources.[11] As a brief analysis of judicial decisions shows, human dignity has currently lost most of its social traits and seems rather limited to preserving individual liberty and autonomy when they are at stake "into the realms of social responsibility" (Hale 2009, 107).

What can be learned from the adventure of human dignity in the United Kingdom is that its inability to stand as an autonomous legal basis for the promotion of social rights is related to its dependence on the value choices that prevail in a society at a given time. Rather than the bare institutional divide between judges and Parliament, much more revealing is the fact that dignity has increasingly shifted away from the domain of legislative enactment of social goals and moved into a realm where individuals engage each other's rights and duties in a process of social responsibility. All of this can obviously be related to a process of impoverishment of the social dimension of legislative decisions, but such an outcome testifies one more time the clash between the absoluteness of human dignity, its aim to define the essence of human nature, and the floating historical and social conditions and factors that make an individual life a dignified component of the social world (Sypnowich 1990, 101). In the words of a German constitutional judge referred to by Baroness Hale of Richmond: "can human dignity keep its universal quality if we try to use it in a court to win cases?" (Hale 2009, 106).

As it emerges from the overview of other experiences (McCrudden 2008, 700), the principle of human dignity is not able *per se* to give a final answer to the question concerning whether and to what extent social rights and social equality should be constitutive of a political community. It probably can set some limits in cases of treatments endangering minimal conditions of existence in a given social context (Leijten 2015; Young 2008), but beyond these very minimum thresholds, there is a lot of political leeway. This should not sound like a plea to ignore the contribution of human dignity in the social field, but rather as a confirmation that "dignity appears to become other than impossibly vague only when it is tethered to a coherent community of interpretation" (McCrudden 2008, 723).

Therefore, the idea of a dignified social life should aim at revitalizing the link between human rights and the political context: in this framework, the question as to whether and how to give a distinctive place to human dignity remains open.

Questioning Human Dignity as a Flagship for Social Protection

The relationship between human dignity and social rights is therefore not straightforward. As this brief comparative survey shows, in the four European countries that I have examined, the role of human dignity shows many differences besides a minor set of common traits. Even with the aim of methodologically justifying the comparison among these four countries, the impression is that these similarities do not rely exclusively upon the common European and Western democratic heritage of these legal systems, but rather on a functional trait, which remains crucial in order to understand human dignity as a constitutional principle in the social field. In the aforementioned contexts, judicial assessment of individual dignity does not exhaust the semantic meaning and the legal potential of the constitutional principle at stake, because it is always the outcome of a more complex interaction between judicial actors and political bodies. Due to the peculiar aspects of social dignity, it is hardly identifiable a decision that imposes duties of protection that fall largely beyond (or rather, do prescind from) the decision of democratically accountable political organs, whereas dignity-based claims with respect to civil and political rights are more suited to be protected by the judiciary.

This can lead to dissatisfaction. Unlike the pioneering decisions delivered in India, in the Guatemala Street Children case, in South Africa or in Hungary, "old" European countries seem much more hesitant to confer to human dignity a counter-majoritarian role, able to reverse decisions taken by political actors. In my view, this is not a shortcoming, but on the contrary, a sign of the proper way in which human dignity should drive the arrangement of social rights and policies.[12]

In current debates, human dignity seems to be captured by contrasting logic. On the one hand, dignity and autonomy operate as the bulwarks of a growing individualism in which freedom of will risks progressively eroding the premises of a democratic society lived *in common*. In this vein, social dignity should be called upon to uphold individual self-determination through the arranging of individual benefits and services aimed at exclusively self-promoting the individual without the need to refer all of this to a common political endeavor. In this way, the risk is that human dignity vehiculates in the social field the same "detachment from history" that Charles Taylor had critically highlighted some decades ago in terms of a "view from nowhere" (Taylor 1991). On the other hand, the recourse to human dignity sometimes risks overcharging its meaning and its potential in terms of moral perfectionism, according to which a "dignified life" coincides with aspirational attitudes that may alternatively be grounded on the reproduction of an ideal world (in a

Platonian fashion) or in the tendency to progressively imitate a transcendent order (in an *Augustinian* fashion). If such total views of common order and good life are transposed into legal reasoning and legal justification, they can lead to separate public deliberation over the common good from the basic preconditions of democratic life (the rule of law, the rights of minorities, freedom of expression, the separation of powers) (Nettesheim 2019, 8).

Against this background, the notion of social dignity emerging in Europe shows a much more balanced nature. My opinion is that it can be grasped in terms of a second-order principle, which is unlikely to be invoked as an immediately enforceable legal yardstick since its main function is rather to steer constitutional conflicts in favor of a solution that is capable of maximizing both individual autonomy and public solidarity (Alexy 2002). In a few words, it is a meta-principle that seeks to constantly reconnect the individual and the public according to different constitutional geometries and proportions. I would like to finally stress four main aspects of this approach:

1) Although, in the countries considered, human dignity is not *per se* a valid yardstick for justifying social policies and for ensuring the enjoyment of social rights, it is not deprived of any legal meaning. On the contrary, it can be invoked as both a lever for protecting basic human needs that coincide with a minimum threshold of citizenship and human rights (like the basic income regulations) and as a moral argument for addressing such relief in the direction of *individual self-empowerment*. Human dignity is at odds with the idea that social rights are instruments for governing social and political conflicts and not individual entitlements for promoting individual flourishing within the social and political community (Mahlmann 2012).
2) Human dignity in the social field *mediates between freedom and equality*. In the countries considered, the recourse to human dignity paves the way for different strategies of balancing the commitment to individual freedom and the constitutional mandate to preserve an acceptable degree of social homogeneity. There can be different degrees and different solutions for the same questions, but human dignity remains a sort of "shadow principle" that preserves the need not to entirely compress one side of the balance (freedom) against the other (equality). The different ideas of the relationship between the common good and individual liberty emerge in constitutional texts but their development and reassessment are demanded by the institutional *liaison* between legislators and judges (Cohn and Grimm 2013, 197). None of them has the last word as to whether and to what extent human dignity has been respected or not: the legislator without the judge is deprived of the capacity to deal with a variety of situations, whereas the judge without the legislator remains unable to offer general responses and to take into account all conflicting interests.
3) Human dignity seeks to *balance individual autonomy and the pursuit of community interests*. Thanks to its nature as a "shadow principle," human dignity does not offer a final say as to how such conflicting values should

be reconciled. Political constitutions do not aim to decide every aspect of social life, since they offer rather an institutional framework within which many actors are called to interact in order to keep an ongoing conversation about the founding elements of social and political life. In doing so, they are limited by basic constraints, such as (among others) the separation of powers and the respect of fundamental rights of the individual. In this framework, human dignity enters the scene in different ways, depending on whether its role has a prominent position (e.g. Germany and Italy) or a hidden place (France and the UK). In any case, its function has some basic tenets, in that it sets the outer limits of what political authorities are basically prevented from doing with regard to the impairment of that line dividing the individual autonomy from the interests of the community (Khaitan 2012, 15). That line can be drawn according to different proportions between the areas of individual and community, as the German and the UK cases clearly demonstrate. Human dignity can alternatively be invoked in order to promote individual self-help or commitment to the enhancement of public services. But the role and logic of the functioning of human dignity remain quite similar.

4) At a deeper level, social dignity does not have a clear and fully fledged status since it is called to strike a balance between two radically incompatible dimensions: the *absoluteness of its moral aspiration vs. the situatedness of the social sphere*. Such incommensurability of human dignity is a *fil rouge* that dominated legal and philosophical reflections in the 20th century (Bloch 1986), but its implications do affect legal and political systems in several ways. The impossibility of using human dignity as a valid yardstick for assessing in quantitative terms what is "basic" in basic income regulations is a clear example of such a problem. The need for judicial decisions to refer to political discretion in order to find a useful yardstick for assessing (though not exclusively) what respects human dignity (and what does not) tells us something relevant about the place of human dignity in social issues. Even though in other fields human dignity can be strictly connected with other fundamental rights and can even act (in the words of Aharon Barak) as a "mother right," i.e. as a source of unenumerated rights, in the social field, its connection with fundamental rights is inevitably looser, since it rather operates as a constitutional mandate acting *behind* fundamental rights (Nettesheim 2019, 10), tracing the outer boundaries of their mutual relationships and conferring different mandates upon the institutional actors whose decisions should forge the social dimension of modern democracies.

Notes

1 It suffices here to mention two authors like Jacques Maritain and George Gurvitch, both highlighting that human dignity did not coincide with the qualities and entitlements of an abstract individual, but had to be grasped within the intertwinement between individuals and groups in a given society. Both authors moved thus from

a pluralist and anti-statist approach: see Maritain (1973) (whose concept of dignity is explored by Valadier 2014) and Gurvitch (1946), whose *Bill of Social Rights* at Art. 1 reads: "The goal of society is the fraternity of men and groups, which can be fulfilled only through variety in unity. – i.e. through a plurality of equalitarian associations protecting the liberty and human dignity of each member and integrated in the national community" (74).

2 It must however be remembered that a strong connection between social rights and human dignity emerged in several clauses of the first draft of the 1946 Constitution: Art. 22 read as follows: "Every human being has rights that guarantee his full physical, intellectual and moral development, while respecting his integrity and dignity." Art. 27 stated that "Neither working time nor working conditions should infringe on workers' health, dignity or familial life." Finally, Art. 28 stated that both men and women should earn wages that allow them to live a "dignified life." As well known, this draft has been repealed by the people of France on a referendum held on April 19, 1946.

3 See Neumann (1995) explicitly referring to the Kantian idea of the incommensurability of human dignity (428), and Huster (2018, 415).

4 The "social code" (*Sozialgesetzbuch*) is a formal codification of federal legislative rules in the field of social protection.

5 See the Constitutional Council of France's decisions No 94–359 DC and No 98–403 DC. In both cases, dignity was invoked in horizontal relationships, since the right to housing had to be balanced against the right to the property of other individuals.

6 E.g. the imposition of working conditions contrary to human dignity became a criminal offence in 1992 (Art. 225-13/225-16 of the French Criminal Code); a 1998 law proclaims that "the fight against social exclusion is a national imperative grounded on the respect of all human beings' equal dignity" (The Constitutional Council of France's decision No. 98-657).

7 It comes thus as no surprise that the recent proposal to amend the 1958 French Constitution with the introduction of the principle of human dignity raised some concerns: see Belaich (2018).

8 See, among others, decisions Nos. 128/1973, 374/1988, 455/1990, 30/2004. In more recent times, an explicit statement as to the role of the legislator in determining the objective meaning of human dignity as a limit to economic activity is made with decision No. 141/2019, concerning the role of sex workers.

9 An exception is to be seen in a well-known decision concerning the right to housing (dec. no. 404/1988, quoting the previous dec. no. 217/88), according to which, though in a quite declamatory fashion, the Constitutional Court stated that human dignity is the goal that steers the action of public activity in pursuing the enhancement of fundamental social rights of the individuals. For a critical stance on this argument, see Bognetti (2005, 97).

10 An example of this can be seen in dec. no. 432/2005, concerning the constitutionality of a regional law that deprived foreign people with disabilities of using public transport. Whereas the core content of the right to health (Art. 32) has to be enjoyed by non-citizens too, the right to movement falls outside of this domain since it aims at different purposes. Despite this, the Italian Constitutional Court has declared the legislation unconstitutional since, beyond the respect of human dignity, the legislative assessment ran counter the principle of proportionality and reasonableness.

11 Among others see: *R (Q, D, J, M, F and B) v. Secretary of State for the Home Department* (2003) [EWHC 195, *R (McDonald) v. Royal Borough of Kensington and Chelsea* (2011) UKSC; for an overview see Gearty (2013) and Miller (2016); on recent trends see Meers (2018).

12 According to Hofmann (1993), human dignity could stand as a binding legal principle only if proclaimed by a humanity which is politically unified (366).

References

Alexy, Robert. 2002. *A Theory of Constitutional Rights.* Translated by Julian Rivers. Oxford: Oxford University Press.

Augsberg, Ino. 2018. "'The Moral Feeling Within Me': On Kant's Concept of Human Freedom and Dignity as Auto-Heteronomy." In *Human Dignity in Context. Explorations of a Contested Concept*, edited by Dieter Grimm and Alexandra Kemmerer, 55–68. Baden-Baden; Oxford: Nomos and Hart.

Baldus, Manfred. 2016. *Kämpfe um die Menschenwürde. Die Debatten seit 1949.* Frankfurt am Main: Suhrkamp.

Barak, Aharon. 2015. *Human Dignity. The Constitutional Value and the Constitutional Right.* Cambridge: Cambridge University Press.

Barroso, Luis Roberto. 2012. "Here, There and Everywhere: Human Dignity in Contemporary Law and in Transnational Discourse." *Boston College International and Comparative Law Review* 35 (2): 331–93.

Belaich, Charlotte. 2018. "L'inscription de la dignité humaine dans la Constitution fait debat." *Libération*, July 19, 2018.

Bloch, Ernst. 1986. *Natural Law and Human Dignity.* Translated by Dennis J. Schmidt. Boston: MIT Press.

Bognetti, Giovanni. 2005. "The Concept of Human Dignity in European and US Constitutionalism." In *European and US Constitutionalism*, edited by Georg Nolte, 85–107. Cambridge: Cambridge University Press.

Brownsword, Roger. 2012. "Bioethics Today, Bioethics Tomorrow: Stem Cell Research and the 'Dignitarian Alliance'." *Notre Dame Journal of Ethics and Public Policy* 17 (1): 15–51.

Carozza, Paolo. 2011. "Human dignity in Constitutional Adjudication." In *Research Handbook in Comparative Constitutional Law*, edited by Tom Ginsburg and Rosalind Dixon, 459–72. Cheltenham: Edward Elgar.

Chronowski, Nóra, and Gábor Halmai. 2019. "Human Dignity for Good Hungarians Only." *Verfassungsblog*, June 11, 2019. https://verfassungsblog.de/human-dignity-for-good-hungarians-only/.

Cohn, Margit, and Dieter Grimm. 2013. "'Human Dignity' As a Constitutional Doctrine." In *Routledge Handbook of Comparative Law*, edited by Mark Tushnet, Thomas Fleiner, and Cheryl Saunders, 193–205. London; New York: Routledge.

Denninger, Erhard. 2011. "Der Menschenwürdesatz im Grundgesetz und seine Entwicklungen in der Verfassungsrechtsprechung." In *Nachdenken über Eigentum. Festschrift für Alexander von Brünneck zur Vollendung seines siebzigsten Lebensjahres*, edited by Franz-Joseph Peine and Heinrich Amadeus Wolff, 397–411. Baden-Baden: Nomos.

Douzinas, Costas. 2007. *Human Rights and Empire. The Political Philosophy of Cosmopolitanism.* London; New York: Routledge.

Dupéré, Olivier. 2008. "Dignité de la personne humaine et logement decent." Communication au VIIe Congrès français de droit constitutionnel. Association française de droit cconstitutionnel, Paris, Septembre 17–25, 2008. www.droitconstitutionnel.org//congresParis/comC8/DupereTXT.pdf.

Dupré, Catherine. 2015. *The Age of Dignity.* Oxford; Portland: Hart.

Eichenhofer, Eberhard. 2009. "Sozialrechtlicher Gehalt der Menschenwürde." In *Das Dogma der Unantastbarkeit. Eine Auseinandersetzung mit der Absolutheitsanspruch der Würde*, edited by Rolf Gröschner and Oliver W. Lembcke, 215–34. Tübingen: Mohr Siebeck.

Feldman, David. 1999. "Human Dignity as a Legal Value. Part I." *Public Law*, 682–702.

Gearty, Conor. 2004. "The Principle of Human Dignity." In *Principles of Human Rights Adjudication*, edited by Conor Gearty, 84–114. Oxford: Oxford University Press.

Gearty, Conor. 2013. "Socio-Economic Rights, Basic Needs, and Human Dignity: A Perspective from Law's Front Line." In *Understanding Human Dignity*, edited by Christopher McCrudden, 155–72. Oxford: Oxford University Press.

Gewirth, Alan. 1978. *Reason and Morality*. Chicago: University of Chicago Press.

Gurvitch, George. 1946. *The Bill of Social Rights*. New York: International Universities Press.

Hale, Brenda. 2009. "Guest Editorial. Dignity." *Journal of Social Welfare and Family Law* 31 (2): 101–8.

Hennette-Vauchez, Stéphanie. 2014. "Human Dignity in French Law." In *Cambridge Handbook of Human Dignity. Interdisciplinary Perspectives*, edited by Marcus Düwell, Jens Braarvig, Roger Brownsword, and Dietmar Mieth, 368–74. Cambridge: Cambridge University Press.

Hofmann, Hasso. 1993. "Die versprochene Menschenwürde." *Archiv des öffentlichen Rechts* 118 (3): 353–77.

Huster, Stefan. 2018. "The Universality of Human Dignity and the Relativity of Social Rights." In *Human Dignity in Context. Explorations of a Contested Concept*, edited by Dieter Grimm and Alexandra Kemmerer, 415–20. Baden-Baden; Oxford: Nomos and Hart.

Jackson, Vicki. 2004. "Constitutional Dialogue and Human Dignity: States and Transnational Constitutional Discourse." *Montana Law Review* 65: 15–40.

Kant, Immanuel. (1785) 1997. *Groundwork for the Metaphysics of Morals*. Translated by Mary J. Gregor. Cambridge: Cambridge University Press.

Khaitan, Tarunabh. 2012. "Dignity as an Expressive Norm: Neither Vacuous nor a Panacea." *Oxford Journal of Legal Studies* 32 (1): 1–19.

Leijten, Ingrid. 2015. "The German Right to an *Existenzminimum*, Human Dignity, and the Possibility of Minimum Core Socioeconomic Rights Protection." *German Law Journal* 16 (1): 23–48.

Mahlmann, Matthias. 2008. *Elemente einer ethischen Theorie der Grundrechte*. Baden-Baden: Nomos.

Mahlmann, Matthias. 2012. "Human Dignity and Autonomy in Modern Constitutional Orders." In *Oxford Handbook of Comparative Constitutional Law*, edited by Michel Rosenfeld and Andras Sajó, 371–96. Oxford: Oxford University Press.

Maritain, Jacques. 1973. *Integral Humanism*. Translated by J. W. Evans. Notre Dame, IN: University of Notre Dame Press.

Marshall, Thomas Humphrey. 1950. *Citizenship and Social Class*. London: Pluto.

Mathieu, Bertrand. 1998. *Constitution et ethique biomédicale*. Paris: La Documentation Française.

Mayen, Thomas. 2012. "Das Grundrecht auf Gewährleistung eines menschenwürdigen Existenzminimums. Gewährleistungsrecht als leistungsrechtliche Grundrechtsdimension." In *Der grundrechtsgeprägte Verfassungsstaat. Festschrift für Klaus Stern zum 80. Geburtstag*, edited by Michael Sachs und Helmut Siekmann, 1451–74. Berlin: Duncker & Humblot.

McCrudden, Christopher. 2008. "Human Dignity and Judicial Interpretation of Human Rights." *European Journal of International Law* 19 (4): 655–724.

Meers, Jed. 2018. "United Kingdom." In *Social Rights in Europe in an Age of Austerity*, edited by Stefano Civitarese Matteucci and Simon Halliday, 122–46. London; New York: Routledge.

Messineo, Donato. 2012. *La garanzia del "contenuto essenziale" dei diritti fondamentali*. Turin: Giappichelli.

Miller, Jacinta. 2016. "Dignity: A Relevant Normative Value in 'Access to Healthcare and Social Care' Litigation in the United Kingdom?" In *Justiciability of Human Rights Law in Domestic Jurisdictions*, edited by Alice Diver and Jacinta Miller, 71–90. Heidelberg: Springer.

Nettesheim, Martin. 2019. ""Leben in Würde": Art. 1 Abs. 1 GG als Grundrecht hinter den Grundrechten." *JuristenZeitung* 74 (1): 1–11.

Neumann, Volker. 1995. "Menschenwürde und Existenzminimum." *Neue Zeitschrift für Verwaltungsrecht* 14 (5): 426–32.

Oehling De Los Reyes, Alberto. 2011. "El concepto constitucional de dignidad de la persona. Forma de comprensión y modelos predominantutetioneptión en la Europa continental." *Revista Española de Derecho Constitucional* 91 (enero–abril): 135–78.

Steigleder, Klaus. 2014. "Human Dignity and Social Welfare." In *Cambridge Handbook of Human Dignity. Interdisciplinary Perspectives*, edited by Marcus Düwell, Jens Braarvig, Roger Brownsword, and Dietmar Mieth, 471–76. Cambridge: Cambridge University Press.

Sypnowich, Christine. 1990. *The Concept of Socialist Law*. Oxford: Clarendon.

Taylor, Charles. 1991. *The Malaise of Modernity*. Concord: Anansi.

Teubner, Gunther. 1998. "Legal Irritants: Good Faith in British Law or How Unifying Law Ends Up in New Differences." *Modern Law Review* 61 (1): 11–32.

Valadier, Paul. 2014. "Jacques Maritain's Personalist Conception of Human Dignity." In *Cambridge Handbook of Human Dignity. Interdisciplinary Perspectives*, edited by Marcus Düwell, Jens Braarvig, Roger Brownsword, and Dietmar Mieth, 260–68. Cambridge: Cambridge University Press.

Young, Katharine G. 2008. "The Minimum Core of Economic and Social Rights: A Concept in Search of Content." *The Yale Journal of International Law* 33: 113–75.

Case Law

The Constitutional Council of France

Décision January 19, 1995, n. 94-359 DC, *Loi relative à la diversité de l'habitat*.

Décision July 29, 1998, n. 98-403 DC, *Loi d'orientation relativeute lutte contre les exclusions*.

The Constitutional Court of Hungary

Decision 32/1998 (VI. 25.) AB, ABH 1998, 251.

Decision 42/2000 (XI. 8) AB, 5/G/1998.

Decision 19/2019 (VI. 18) ABH 2019, 493.

The Supreme Court of India

Francis Coralie Mullin vs The Administrator, Union Territory of Delhi, 1981 AIR 746, 1981 SCR (2) 516.

The Inter-American Court of Human Rights

Villagran Morales v. Guatemala ("Street Children Case"), Judgment November 19, 1999.

The Constitutional Court of Italy

Judgment no. 128/1973.

Judgment no. 217/1988.

Judgment no. 374/1988.

Judgment no. 404/1988.

Judgment no. 455/1990.
Judgment no. 30/2004.
Judgment no. 432/2005.
Judgment no. 141/2019.

The Federal Constitutional Tribunal of Germany

Judgment December 19, 1951, 1 BvR 220/51, *Hinterbliebenenrente* (BVerfGE 1, 97).
Judgment April 12, 1972, 2 BvF 2/72, *Deutscher Osten* (BVerfGE 33, 44).
Judgment October 15, 1985, 2 BvL 4/83 (BVerfGE 71, 39).
Judgment April 8, 1987, 2 BvR 909, 934, 935, 936, 938, 941, 942, 947/82, 64/83 and 142/84, *Künstlersozialversicherungsgesetz* (BVerfGE 75, 108).
Judgment February 9, 2010, 1 BvL 1, 3, 4/09, *Hartz IV* (BVerfGE 125, 175).
Judgment July 18, 2012, 1 BvL 10/10, 2/11, *Asylbewerberleistungsgesetz* (BVerfGE 132, 134).

The German Federal Administrative Tribunal

Judgment June 24, 1954, V C 78.54 (BVerwGE, 1, 159).

The Constitutional Court of South Africa

Government of the Republic of South Africa v. Grootboom 2001 1 SA 46 (CC).

The Court of Appeal, Civil Division (The United Kingdom)

R (Q, D, J, M, F and B) v. Secretary of State for the Home Department, [2003] EWHC 195.

The Court of Appeal, Criminal Division (The United Kingdom)

R v Ian McLoughlin e R v. Lee William Newell, [2014] EWCA Crim 188.

The House of Lords (The United Kingdom)

R (Daly) v. Secretary of State for the Home Department, [2001] UKHL 26.
Regina v. Secretary of State for the Home Department ex parte Limbuela, [2005] UKHL 66.

The Supreme Court of the United Kingdom

R (McDonald) v. Royal Borough of Kensington and Chelsea, [2011] UKSC 33.

14 Dignity as a Shield

The Putative Dignitarian Discourse on Protecting Migrant Domestic Workers in Singapore

Eugene K. B. Tan

Introduction

More than a decade ago, the World Bank (2009) underscored the importance of migration and argued for facilitating the voluntary movement of people as part of the larger process of development. The 2009 *Human Development Report* (UNDP 2009) observed that one out of seven persons (or one billion people) in the world was a migrant. It noted that migration had significant human development potential for both receiving and sending countries. Allowing for migration—both within and between countries—can increase people's freedom and improve the lives of millions around the world. In a similar vein, the United Nations Economic and Social Commission for Asia and the Pacific (UN-ESCAP 2008) observed that international migration had become "a structural and permanent element of societies and economies" in the Asia-Pacific region. This was particularly so in East and Southeast Asia, where the region's demographic trends and economic disparities had stimulated transnational labor movements. The larger context was the "geoeconomics of international migrations" which was shifting from South-North to South-South (Sassen 2007, 134). A striking characteristic of migration trends and patterns—especially in Asia—is the feminization of migratory movements over the last three decades.[1]

This chapter considers the legal regime governing female migrant domestic workers (MDWs) who form a significantly important part of the domestic care economy in Singapore, and the courts' tentative engagement with a dignitarian discourse as an integral part of dispensing justice in egregious cases of abuse of MDWs. Although there is no specific mention of dignity as an enumerated right in Singapore's Constitution, this does not mean that dignity is not recognized in Singapore law. Moreover, Singapore courts have invoked the principle of dignity in a series of cases involving offenses against MDWs. This chapter also examines the judicial treatment of dignity vis-à-vis MDWs that undergirds the evolving discourse on dignity buttresses and enhances the regulatory framework protecting the basic rights and interests of MDWs.

Part II of this chapter briefly discusses human dignity and overviews the backdrop of both permanent and work migration in Singapore, including the

DOI: 10.4324/9781003307853-18

considerable number of MDWs providing care to Singaporean households. Part III examines the law and policy that regulate the employment of female MDWs in Singapore. I argue that the overarching framework consciously avoids a rights-centric approach in the management of MDWs. While providing basic protection to MDWs, it is primarily about ensuring that the presence of such workers in Singapore is temporary. Undergirding the regulatory framework is the centrality of the contractual approach in which the granting of a work permit to work in Singapore requires the quid pro quo from an MDW agreeing to a transient status in Singapore. Singapore's legal regime for the MDWs strongly emphasizes not only regulation and responsibilities (on the part of both the MDW and her employer) but also surveillance to ensure that the contractual requirements of employment are observed. In particular, the conditions attached to the work permits instrumentally exclude these workers from making their transient presence in Singapore into anything substantive such as being conferred citizenship or even permanent residence rights.

Part IV explores the putative human dignity discourse, particularly in MDW abuse cases, in Singapore courts. Beyond the judicial perspective of dignity, civil society advocacy for and the promotion of the interests and welfare of MDWs also rely on human dignity broadly conceived (even if dignity itself is not articulated). In the main, advocacy efforts by civil society organizations seek to get the government and employers to adopt a basic level of rights recognition through education rather than robust rights assertion. Confrontation is seen as an ineffective way of mutually protecting the rights and welfare of the workers and the larger societal interests.

On Dignity—A Brief Overview[2]

Much as a person's dignity is certainly worth protecting, human dignity is often said to be indeterminate. But dignity features prominently in human rights law instruments and in many national constitutions: see, for example, the Preamble to the Charter of the United Nations 1945, the Preamble and Article 1 of the Universal Declaration of Human Rights 1948, the International Covenant on Civil and Political Rights 1966 (ICCPR), and the International Covenant on Economic, Social and Cultural Rights 1966 (ICESCR). While this chapter does not engage in the debate of what constitutes dignity and its legal effects, it regards dignity as a norm that is not only expressive but also functional in that it helps to give effect to and is complementary of rights (see also Khaitan 2012).

To be sure, the law does seek to protect dignity; indeed, it would be a travesty of justice if the law is reduced to or seen as embodying rights only but not dignity. In other words, dignity should be conceived as the basis of rights; often dignity is manifested whenever a right is given effect. The ICCPR, for example, states that the body of civil and political rights contained therein "derive from the inherent dignity of the human person." McCrudden (2008) highlights the four functions of dignity: (1) providing a key rationale for why humans should have rights; (2) aiding the identification of a catalog of specific rights; (3) an "interpretative principle" to analyze and develop further the catalog of rights generated by the principle; and (4) as a right or obligation with specific content. In shIrt, dignity is treated as a means to an end and an end in itself. Jeremy Waldron (2012) understands dignity as:

> [T]he status of a person predicated on the fact that she is recognized as having the ability to control and regulate her actions in accordance with her own apprehension of norms and reasons that apply to her; it assumes she is capable of giving and entitled to give an account of herself (and of the way in which she is regulating her actions and organizing her life), an account that others are to pay attention to; and it means finally that she has the wherewithal to demand that her agency and her presence among us as a human being be taken seriously and accommodated in the lives of others, in others' attitudes and actions towards her, and in social life generally.

However one defines or characterizes dignity, a key element is that of an individual's inherent value and worth by virtue of being a human person, with the individual and others recognizing and giving effect to the individual's inherent value and worth. One specific challenge for the use of dignity in rights adjudication is determining its actual and probative jurisprudential content and giving effect to it such that it has a distinct identity and role. Dignity must establish its *sui generis* credentials and not be conflated with values and concepts like equality, autonomy, and accountability, much as they may overlap. The Canadian Supreme Court puts it well: "[H]uman dignity is an abstract and subjective notion . . . it has also proved to be an *additional* burden on equality claimants" (*R v. Kapp*, para. 22).

This chapter does not argue that dignity is the silver bullet; rather, dignity complements rights and can add that sharp edge in dealing with the violation of rights and the consequences that flow thereon. Dignity, for example, can provide "an invaluable criterion for evaluating laws, policies, and government actions for how well they accord with human rights standards."[3] The importance of dignity cannot be understated. On the one hand, it represents an aspirational calling to go beyond what the letter of the law mandates. On the other hand, dignity possesses a trip-wire quality in providing a sense of how the curtailing or disregard of one's rights can trigger adverse impacts on those affected. Conflict is often the natural consequence of violations or the lack of recognition of dignity. This is often manifested in the lack of respect accorded to a person and her identity, beliefs, and values. This will only escalate the conflict and deepen the differences and divide. Put simply, human dignity can be conceived as a legal idea that integrates and influences legal institutions and rights. Human dignity empowers the individual, as a bearer of dignity and rights, and acts as a constraint against inappropriate conduct whether proscribed by law or not.

In the case of MDW abuse in Singapore, the dignitarian discourse has provided a complementary mode to the understanding of the limited rights that MDWs have and how the law and the judiciary working together can aid in the protection of these workers from the indignities that they may suffer. The emancipatory notion of human dignity can further promote the rights, needs, and interests of the MDWs. This subtle emphasis on dignity can enhance workplace protection for the MDWs operating in a very regimented legal regime, which often consigns them to the slipstream of Singaporean society. Before proceeding further, the contextual setting of immigration vis-à-vis Singapore society that MDWs are a part of is outlined next.

Immigration as a Defining Feature of Singapore Society[4]

The immigration of new citizens and temporary workers has become the primary means by which the population in Singapore is replenished and maintained for its economic and demographic requirements. Slightly more than one in three persons living in Singapore are foreigners (i.e., noncitizens, including permanent residents).[5] The vast majority of these foreigners are transient workers on short-term work permits. Of these, about 235,000—all women—are employed as domestic help (or "maids" in local parlance).

Singapore is also severely under-reproducing. In 2021, Singapore's total fertility rate (TFR) was 1.10 (i.e., 1.10 babies per resident woman), among the lowest in the world. Hence, there is a pressing need to increase Singapore's population and to import foreign workers at all levels to meet Singapore's economic needs (NPTD 2013). Given the political sensitivities connected with immigration, the Singapore government must be selective in admitting permanent residents and naturalized citizens.

About one in five households in Singapore employ at least one MDW (Tseng 2022), demonstrating the impact of what has been popularly referred to as "global care chains" and "transnational mothering" (Ehrenreich and Hochschild 2003; Parreñas 2001).[6] It is no exaggeration to say that MDWs occupy a niche in the Singaporean labor force and household today. The relative ease and affordability of hiring MDWs have been a boon for many Singaporean households, especially dual-income ones, enabling many Singaporean women to seek paid employment outside the home. The demand for MDWs has been projected to be about 300,000 MDWs by 2030 (NPTD 2012, para. 18). It is likely, however, that this figure will be reached even before 2030 as more Singaporean married women work and as Singapore ages rapidly (Rozario and Hong 2019).

To help regulate the demand for MDWs (and other transient workers) by reducing excessive reliance on them, the government imposes an MDW monthly levy of SGD300 (normal rate).[7] The MDW levy is put in place to ensure that only employers who need and have the financial capability to employ an MDW can do so. Work permits for employment as MDWs are issued only to females from approved source countries. Most MDWs in

Singapore come from the Philippines and Indonesia, with smaller numbers from Sri Lanka and Myanmar (Burma). In addition, the regulatory framework is conspicuously legalistic and requires vigilant surveillance and control.

Regulating Through Contractualism, Surveillance, Control, and Exclusion

Singapore's ready acceptance of transient migrant workers co-exists with an extensive surveillance system to ensure that these workers do not become permanent residents or citizens. The trade-off between openness and rights characterizes the labor immigration policies of many high-income countries, including Singapore (Ruhs 2013; Lee 2019). Transient migrant workers, including MDWs, are given work permits to work in Singapore on the condition that they will leave the country at the end of their work contracts. Even before entering Singapore for employment, they must also agree to not make any claim to Singapore citizenship. Significantly, Singapore does not subscribe to the principle that a foreigner, by virtue of having worked and lived for an extended period in Singapore, acquires a moral or legal entitlement to rights of membership, including citizenship. For Singapore, affording the rights of citizenship or permanent residence is a prerogative of national sovereignty, not one of moral equity earned or conferred benevolently on migrants.

As such, borders become "central places of anxiety about control and sovereignty" (Ferguson and Mironesco 2008, 7). Border controls inform us why and how a state governs access to and control over matters such as employment, family unification, residency, citizenship, and the like, which many citizens take for granted.[8] While most transient workers in Singapore are not preoccupied with making Singapore their permanent home, their expectations are nonetheless adroitly managed from the outset. The conditions attached to their work permits ensure that the workers are fully alive to this reality of exclusion through a contractual undertaking that they will not be able to secure full membership in the Singapore polity (see also Dobbs and Loh 2019).

This overarching message that transient foreign workers are not considered for inclusion into Singapore society is reinforced by the marriage restriction policy, another onerous condition governing the conduct of transient foreign workers. Under this policy, a foreign work-permit holder "shall not go through any form of marriage under any law, religion, custom or usage with a Singapore Citizen or Permanent Resident in or outside Singapore without the prior approval of the Controller [of Immigration], while he/she holds a Work Permit, and also after his/her Work Permit has expired or has or revoked."[9] Those who marry a Singapore resident without approval during the course of their employment in Singapore will be repatriated and disallowed future entry into Singapore. The marriage restriction policy helps ensure that temporary labor migration of MDWs does not become permanent through marriages with Singapore residents.

Thus, the particularist immigration and employment regulations effectively operate as a de facto family law and citizenship law. These conditions apply even *after* the foreign worker's work permit has expired or has been canceled or revoked.[10] This severe approach to the marriage restriction policy had been justified as follows:

> So imagine if every other ex-work permit holder were to marry a Singaporean, we would not be able to manage our social services and social system. . . . Even though we want to increase our population size, we have to ensure that those who want to live and have families in Singapore can look after themselves, their children and their families. That is the basic premise that we all must understand. . . . Singaporeans do have human rights to be able to look after ourselves and manage our limited resources and to ensure that those legitimate Singaporeans would be well looked after and would not exact too much of our social system.
>
> (Hawazi 2004)

For MDWs, the regulatory framework extends to the surveillance of their physical bodies. MDWs are required to go for a six-monthly medical examination (6ME) by a registered Singapore doctor "to screen for infectious diseases and pregnancies." An MDW who fails the 6ME will be repatriated immediately. According to the Manpower Ministry in 2014:

> The 6ME helps to ensure that [M]DWs do not carry infectious diseases such as HIV [sic] or TB, which might harm them or the people they come into contact with. This is especially important as they work in a residential environment and may have contact with children. A pregnancy test is also required for the [M]DWs. An [M]DW who fails the 6ME should be repatriated immediately.[11]

More recently, the authorities have also mandated the use of 6ME to better detect cases of abuse. Since September, 2021, doctors must check for suspicious signs of injuries, weight loss, and warning signs of abusive conditions. Such check-ups at the doctor's clinics will be conducted without the employers present (The Straits Times 2021).

In addition, the law stipulates that an MDW "shall not become pregnant or deliver any child in Singapore during and after the validity period of her Work Permit, unless she is a Work Permit holder who is already married to a Singapore Citizen or Permanent Resident with the approval of the Controller."[12] Another condition is that the "foreign employee shall not be involved in any illegal, immoral or undesirable activities, including breaking up families in Singapore."[13] Taken collectively, the work permit conditions reify the stereotype of MDWs' disposition and intention to be dependents of the state and/or their Singapore spouses. The fear of migrants as potential burdens to and parasitic on Singapore society is therefore managed through a rigorous gatekeeping and surveillance function, whereby the granting of citizen or permanent resident status is a means of determining who gets to enjoy additional rights and benefits such as social services, government subsidies, and grants.

The Singapore government is alive to the potential of international marriages becoming an arena of contention over rights, privileges, and access to employment, government services, and assistance. It ensures that contestation is reduced, if not pre-empted, by resolutely maintaining a marital union regime that heavily regulates marriages involving Singapore residents and MDWs. Thus, immigration and employment laws and regulations in Singapore retain their utility as a strategic gatekeeping tool to the Singaporean body polity (Tan 2008).

While a liberal approach advocates the granting of citizenship rights to foreign workers who have lived and worked for an extended period, such a position is untenable in Singapore. Instead, what immigration policies and laws do is circumscribe in clear and rigid terms the place of transient migrant workers within the nation-state. Through its conferment of legal status and rights, immigrant status and citizenship create boundaries that seek to include members and exclude non-members based on ascribed attributes, identities, and values. This regulatory framework may have unwittingly spawned the unfortunate cases of migrant workers being poorly treated over the years. Reports of migrant workers being unpaid, abandoned, or housed in poor conditions are regularly covered in the local media. Scholars have noted the precariousness of migrant workers—their work and their existence—in which stakeholders condone the production of precarity (Chin 2019; Wajihad and Tutt 2019).

However, there is no widespread public clamor yet for removing such onerous conditions of employment. At one level, it may reflect the indifference or even apathy of the average Singaporean towards human rights, especially when it concerns foreign workers with a transient presence in Singapore performing menial jobs.[14] At another level, it may well reflect a situation in which all parties, including the MDWs and the authorities, are fully aware of their respective legal positions. Even where rights are fully in play—and even then, asymmetrically since migrant workers have to accept the conditions without question if they are to obtain their work permits—they are focused almost exclusively on contractual rights of the Singapore state vis-à-vis the contractual responsibilities of the transient migrant workers. The promotion and protection of human rights vis-à-vis the MDWs have not entered the public discourse in Singapore in any significant way (see further Tan 2010).

Such a contractual approach, rather than a rights-centric approach, is preferred when it comes to the management of MDWs. The admission of transient workers into Singapore is seen solely in transactional terms. Moreover, caregiving provided by MDWs is increasingly marketized: a legal agreement in which the rights of residence are pre-empted and explicitly excluded from the outset. The fact that MDWs are admitted into the country as transient workers, on renewable short-term employment contracts, is relied upon to justify a differential regime—one where regulations are more prominent than rights.

Matters are further complicated by the workplaces of the MDWs, which are also their employers' homes. MDWs are required by law to reside at the homes of their employers.[15] Despite their spending most of their time in the employer's home, this state of affairs of being "at home" and yet being an outsider in the intimate domain of the home only reinforces their separate and, often, marginal status. The abiding association of MDWs with the domestic sphere—buttressing the notions of privacy, harmony, familial obligations, and responsibilities—often denies such workers access to a range of rights since the home is not perceived as an appropriate setting for the prescriptive structuring of an employer-employee relationship, especially one that is heavily rights-based.

The MDWs' regulatory framework invariably highlights their marginality and functionality in the overall employment and immigration regimes (Yeoh 2006). The employment opportunity afforded to an MDW is beneficently characterized as a privilege provided by Singapore. The quid pro quo for an MDW is contractually agreeing to not seek and secure extra-employment rights and privileges, such as Singaporean permanent residency or citizenship as well as access to public resources such as subsidies and budgetary handouts. The contractual approach taken to their securing legal permission to work in Singapore further relegates the concerns of justice and fairness, moral rights, and access to political membership. Put simply, these concerns are perceived to be marginal, if not nonexistent, in such a contractualist regime. From a policy perspective, expectations are better managed when all parties concerned are fully appraised of their contractual rights and responsibilities right from the outset. By contrast, an insistence on unenumerated rights in an intimate setting like the domestic household is seen as setting the stage for disputes, confrontation, and disharmony.

Singapore's laws governing transient, low-skilled workers in Singapore reveal the long-standing ideological, economic, and socio-cultural underpinnings of such laws (Wee 1995).[16] To reiterate, the physical transience of MDWs in Singapore is secured through the work permit system. They are also not permitted to bring their spouses and children to live in Singapore. The MDW's work permit is tied to her employer, and as such she cannot freely enter the local employment market as a free, autonomous agent. The employer can revoke the MDW's work permit unilaterally at any time; such a revocation would result in the immediate repatriation of the MDW. Unlike other work-permit holders, MDWs are excluded from Singapore's Employment Act 1968.[17] As such, MDWs do not possess clear state-sanctioned rights with regard to standard employment conditions such as wages, regular time off, and working (and living) conditions. The Manpower Ministry explained the particularistic regime governing the MDWs' employment conditions in the following terms[18]:

> [I]t is not practical to regulate specific aspects of domestic work i.e. hours of work, work on a rest day and on public holidays. It would also

be difficult to enforce the terms of the Employment Act for domestic workers as:

- They work in a home environment; and
- The habits of households vary.

For example, it would be hard to compute overtime payments as domestic workers' work/free time are difficult to define and regulate in the same way as employees working in offices or factories.

The government requires employers of MDWs to post a SGD5,000 security bond for each MDW to ensure that employers are responsible for their MDWs complying with the conditions of their employment. Such an arrangement provides the employer with a lot of control over the employment fate of the MDW. It also serves the function of ensuring that employers of MDWs arrange for the orderly repatriation of MDWs at the end of their service contracts, rather than abandoning them.[19] Notwithstanding the good intentions behind the security deposit, this only heightens the tendency of employers of MDWs, on the pain of losing their security deposits, to excessively regulate the lives of their MDWs to engender good behavior. Some employers deny their MDWs time off from work (rest days in regular employment parlance) fearing that they may be in bad company or engage in activities that would breach the conditions attached to the work permits. Consequently, despite the sizable number of MDWs, they are rendered disproportionately invisible.

Legal Protection of MDWs and A Putative Discourse of Human Dignity

Although Singapore's regulatory framework for MDWs is austere, MDWs do receive protection under Singapore's laws, principally through the Employment of Foreign Manpower Act 1990.[20] Employers are required to provide adequate rest and meals for their MDWs and ensure worker safety, proper housing, and prompt salary payments. Despite the government's policy preference not to couch an elaborate rights discourse within the regulatory regime governing MDWs, the government does not tolerate any abuse or exploitation of MDWs. In 1998, in response to more maid abuse cases, the Singapore Parliament amended the Penal Code[21] to provide that employers of domestic workers (regardless of whether she is a local or a foreigner) and members of their households who commit specified offenses against the domestic workers will be liable to be punished with one-and-a-half times the amount of punishment to which they would otherwise have been liable for those specified offenses. In moving the legislative amendments, the Minister for Home Affairs Wong Kan Seng (1998) observed that:

> Domestic maids are female, work within the confines of their employers' homes for 24 hours of the day, and except during their time off,

> are isolated from the rest of society nearly all the time, and depend on their employer for food and lodging. Maids are therefore more vulnerable to abuse by employers and their immediate family members than any other categories of employees. All employers have an obligation to treat their maids humanely and decently. . . . Maid abuse runs counter to Singapore's aspiration to become a gracious and civil society. Abuse of foreign domestic maids can also damage our international reputation and bilateral relations.

In recent years, the courts have come out strongly in support of the government's deterrent stance in MDW abuse cases and have imposed deterrent sanctions against employers convicted of abusing their MDWs. In the case of *ADF v. Public Prosecutor*, Singapore's apex court, the Court of Appeal, reviewed the sentencing principles relevant to an accused being convicted of voluntarily causing hurt to a domestic worker. It stated that:

> In a case of domestic maid abuse, ordinarily, the principles of deterrence and retribution take precedence. A deterrent sentence signifies that there is a public interest to protect over and above the ordinary punishment of criminal behaviour. *The protection of domestic maids from abuse by their employers is always a matter of public interest, given their vulnerable status and the prevalence of such relationships in Singapore.* No employer or household member has the right to engage in abusive behaviour against a domestic maid. All maids should be treated fairly, with dignity and respect. . . . The courts have unwaveringly recognised domestic maids as vulnerable victims and a category of persons in need of constant protection.
>
> (*ADF v. Public Prosecutor*, para. 55, 61, emphasis in original)

Although the Court did not engage in a discourse on rights, it was evident that the *raison d'être* of human dignity and respect exerted a strong influence in the Court meting out the punishment to the offenders. In the leading judgment, Judge of Appeal VK Rajah stated:

> The courts in Singapore have consistently adopted a firm and uncompromising stance in cases involving domestic maid abuse. There is an irrefutably sound basis for this: a maid in agreeing to provide domestic services to a household has neither sold herself nor agreed to be treated as a chattel devoid of human emotion. No employer (or other household member) has the right to treat a maid as such. An agreement for the sale of services does not amount to a license to abuse and/or cause hurt. Domestic maids deserve to be treated with fairness, respect and dignity. A maid's role of servitude in a household does not mean that she is any less worthy of protection by the law. On the contrary, the susceptibility of domestic maids to abuse in such a patently unequal relationship with their employers warrants special protection. Not all cases of maid abuse

> come to light as the abuse is usually perpetrated in the confines and the privacy of the home. If and when such cases are detected and brought to the attention of the courts, judges are duty-bound to impose deterrent sentences on all errant employers or members of their household. This will send an unequivocal and irrevocable signal that such conduct will not only be denounced but also severely punished.
>
> (*ADF v. Public Prosecutor*, para. 159)

Judge of Appeal Andrew Phang further noted the principal societal concerns in MDW abuse cases where:

> the existing relationship between an employer and an employee has not only broken down but has deteriorated into one where the former abuses the latter in a manner that is repugnant to all notions of common humanity. That this is a situation which is abhorrent to all civilized societies is a proposition which is self-evident and rests on the premise that all human beings are worthy of dignity and respect. Looked at in this light, no complex theory is needed to justify the need for employers to treat their maids with dignity and respect, and to refrain (on pain of legal sanction) from abusing them. Put simply, all human beings in every society are worthy of dignity and respect, and they therefore cannot—and must not—be subject to any form of abuse whatsoever (whether it be physical or non-physical). This is an irreducible and non-negotiable proposition.
>
> (*ADF v. Public Prosecutor*, para. 219–220)

Subsequent MDW abuse cases have applied the notion of "human dignity" similarly without further explication. In *Public Prosecutor v. Lim Choon Hong and Another*, the maltreatment of the MDW, through intentional starvation, had caused the domestic worker's weight to drop from 49 kg to 29 kg. The Court held that the respondents subjected the victim to systematic cruelty and the denial of her basic human dignity.[22] In delivering judgment, Chief Justice Sundaresh Menon noted at the commencement of his judgment that:

> As a country with a scarcity of human resources, we depend on foreigners who come here to undertake work. With rising levels of affluence and the opportunity for families to enjoy double incomes, very much of the menial work in our country is done by foreign workers. Foreign domestic workers are pervasive in many segments of Singapore's society. In some senses, the work opportunities this presents provides economic incentives for nationals of other countries who seek to work their way out of their own difficult conditions.
>
> *It is imperative in this milieu of circumstances that we as a society ensure that these foreign workers are treated decently and accorded the sort of guarantees of human dignity that we would accord to any human being.* This is

> important for several reasons but in my judgment, one consideration of special significance is what this says about ourselves as a society. We too have progressed as a nation from the direst of circumstances just 52 years ago. *If we reach the point where we do not set our face firmly against the treatment of our fellow human beings in a way that reasonable people would regard as not being in keeping with the most basic standards of decency, then we have condemned ourselves* (*Public Prosecutor v. Lim Choon Hong and Another*, para. 1–2, emphasis added).

In another recent case of MDW abuse, the High Court condemned the humiliating treatment of the MDW as "a serious affront to her dignity" (*Tay Wee Kiat and Another v. Public Prosecutor and Another*, para. 79). Degrading treatment was also condemned as it denied the MDW of "the basic dignity of a human being" (*Tay Wee Kiat and Another v. Public Prosecutor and Another Appeal*, para. 69).

The lack of articulation on the substantive content of dignity is also seen in non-MDW abuse cases where dignity has also been merely referenced. The opportunity to consider and develop the doctrine of human dignity in other areas has not been taken advantage of so far. For example, on the tort of malicious falsehood, the Court noted in one case that where there was malicious prosecution, the state would be held accountable for the acts of prosecutors who did not enjoy absolute immunity "for violating the liberty of the person and the human dignity arising from botched prosecution" (*Lee Tat Development Pte Ltd v. Management Corporation Strata Title Plan No 301*, para. 72).[23] In *ACB v. Thomson Medical Pte Ltd and Others*, a case of wrongful fertilization, the apex court discussed "human dignity" in relation to the concept of "autonomy": [Proponents of the "thicker" view of autonomy] "would argue that a conception of autonomy which gives effect to a person's long-term goals is ultimately more productive of liberty and human dignity than one which focuses on his immediate volitions, which can be motivated by the exigencies of the moment" (para. 117). The Court also emphasized that "The life of every person carries with it its own inestimable value and dignity and the worth of a person can neither be enlarged nor its importance abridged by any pronouncement of this court" (para. 210). However, the Court ultimately did not decide the case on the principle of autonomy, finding it too "nebulous."

Human dignity was also raised by litigants challenging the constitutionality of section 377A of the Penal Code, which had then criminalized consensual sex between two adult males. In *Tan Eng Hong v. Attorney-General*, counsel for the applicant contended that the protection accorded by Singapore's Constitution Article 9(1) (right to life and liberty) does not only cover "mere existence" and "must extend to all those faculties by which life is enjoyed," including "privacy, human dignity, individual autonomy and the human need for an intimate personal sphere." Both counsel and the Court, however, did not elaborate on the notion of human dignity. The apex court affirmed the trial court's interpretation that "our courts have eschewed such wide interpretations" of the terms "life" and "personal liberty" in Art 9(1)" (para. 120). In *Lee*

Hsien Loong v. Ngerng Yi Ling Roy, a case of defamation brought by the prime minister against a blogger, the Court cited with approval three arguments for the justifications for the right of free speech guaranteed by Article 14 of the Singapore Constitution: the arguments from truth, democracy, and human dignity (para. 97). While the Court elaborated on the arguments from truth and democracy, it did not, however, elaborate on the human dignity argument. Similarly, in *UKM v. Attorney-General*, a case on the adoption of the biological child of a gay man who was birthed in the US by a surrogate mother, the Court noted with a high level of abstraction that, "At a fundamental level, surrogacy, especially commercial surrogacy, implicates issues of human dignity and autonomy. Some object that surrogacy commodifies children by treating them as products to be manufactured to fulfill a consumer demand and goods to be bought and sold" (para. 181).

Taken together, the passing reference to and the inadequate engagement of human dignity by the courts in these cases is not surprising. Despite its ambiguity, human dignity is hard to disagree with. As there is yet to be a landmark case, dignity as a legal concept or doctrine is still in search of substantive content in Singapore, and its use thus far is heavily confined to the abuse of vulnerable persons, especially MDWs. As criminal cases, MDW abuse cases are also widely reported in the local media for deterrent and educational purposes. Further, as a deterrent, all convicted employers and their spouses are permanently barred from employing MDWs. Yet, the regulatory regime does not have the reach that is needed since the cloistered domestic setting does not always facilitate the enforcement actions that can prevent the mistreatment of the MDWs. The Chief Justice in *Janardana Jayasankarr v. Public Prosecutor* noted the vulnerability of MDWs:

> The special provision enacted for the abuse of this class of victim stems from the recognition that domestic helpers are particularly vulnerable to abuse by their employers and their immediate family members (see *Singapore Parliamentary Debates, Official Report* (April 20, 1998) vol 68 at col 1923 (Mr Wong Kan Seng, Minister for Home Affairs)). This is so for several reasons, of which I will mention just three:
>
> (a) First, domestic helpers are in a foreign land and will often not have the time or opportunity to develop familiarity or a support network. Domestic helpers who have just arrived in Singapore or have only been working here for a few months, such as the victim in this case, are especially vulnerable.
> (b) Second, they are in an inherently unequal position of subordination in relation to their employers.
> (c) Third, the abuse will usually take place in the privacy of the employer's home and without the presence of any independent witnesses. This not only makes the offense very difficult to detect but also invariably increases the difficulty of prosecuting such offenses because it

> will usually be a case of one's word against that of the other. This, coupled with the fear of jeopardizing their prospects of employment as well as the general fear of the employer engendered by the situation they find themselves in, is likely to discourage victims from making a complaint.

The upshot of this is that domestic helpers usually do not have a voice and, in many senses, are dependent on the good faith of their employers. It is critical that the law steps in to protect domestic helpers from being abused by their employers, who are the very people who should be taking care of them. Deterrence therefore takes center stage where such abuse has taken place and offenders can expect a stiff sentence (para. 3–4).

Cheah (2022) notes that state actors—such as the courts—may call for MDWs to be recognized as "human beings with aspirations, interests, intellect and more." She argues that for MDWs to be truly treated with dignity and have their rights respected, the laws and policies enabling their abasement and exploitation must change (153). She observes that judicial decisions "can go further to protect and empower MDWs by explaining that such fair, respectful, and dignified treatment is owed to MDWs as a matter of right rather than charity or morality. Recognizing MDWs as rights-bearing agents is particularly salient given the severe power imbalance between MDWs and their employers" (Cheah 2022, 167).

Nevertheless, the Singapore courts in the cases discussed have demonstrated that the MDWs, as an integral part of many Singaporean households and workforce, are valuable in two ways. They are useful for the valuable services they render at significant personal expense, not least being away from kith and kin in a foreign land with a vastly different way of life. Moreover, the courts have also recognized, through the concept of human dignity, that MDWs are individuals with dignity and are valued for their own sake and deserving of respect.[24] In this regard, human dignity is endowed in the Singapore legal context as a legal and ethical imperative. This conscious use of human dignity in the Court's argumentation and reasoning reflects the close connections between dignity and rights, and dignity and vulnerability.

Dignity Discourse as Rights Consciousness

Evident from the discussion is the nascent but uncertain status of the doctrine of dignity in Singapore jurisprudence. The dignitarian discourse is widely accepted in MDW abuse cases but hardly engaged in almost all other cases. The Singapore Constitution makes no reference to dignity. It is thus far a tentative judge-made doctrine, situationally contingent and most applicable to a specific group of vulnerable persons, namely MDWs. Singapore's limited jurisprudential discourse on dignity appears to point to dignity as an adjunct to a rights-centric approach. Its primary use has been to justify a heavier punishment in egregious cases of MDW abuse. Where an employer has not fulfilled his legal responsibilities *qua* employer, it could amount to having little or no regard for the dignity of the victim in egregious cases. Beyond MDW abuse cases, however, human dignity appears to be of limited use and may even present additional difficulties in interpreting and developing further the suite of rights generated by the doctrine.

Notwithstanding its uncertain status, the putative conception of dignity in Singapore's jurisprudence recognizes that when abuses are committed against vulnerable persons, the dignity of society is denigrated. Dignity may well have a greater role in the future development of Singaporean jurisprudence, especially where the rights of vulnerable people have been affected adversely or where the applicable legislation is apparently lacking. For instance, in sentencing, the vulnerability of the victim is considered. This entails considering the characteristics of the victim and the degree of exploitation by the offender as an integral part of the fact-sensitive exercise. In the MDW abuse cases, the courts have consistently treated the vulnerability of the victim to be a specified aggravating factor, where there is either a high degree of victim vulnerability or a high degree of exploitation by the offender of the victim's circumstances. In such instances, the offender would be treated in law as being more morally culpable. This is where the need to send a stronger deterrent signal that such acts will not be tolerated is most strongly manifested.[25]

Following the lead of the courts, the Singapore legislature also enacted tougher provisions in MDW abuse cases. While the law does not categorize them as "vulnerable persons," they are effectively treated as such. Before 2019, the Penal Code provided enhanced punishments for a specified list of offenses committed against MDWs by their employers or members of the employer's household. Introduced in 1998, the former section 73 of the Penal Code recognized that due to their circumstances, MDWs who "work within the confines of their employers' home for 24 hours of the day, and except during their time off, are isolated from the rest of society nearly all the time, and depend on their employer for food and lodging," are "more vulnerable to abuse by employers and their immediate family members, than any other categories of employees" (Wong 1998). Hence, Parliament passed the amendments for the enhancement of penalties for certain offenses committed against MDW by one-and-a-half times to "signal clearly to employers of domestic maids that the Government takes a serious view of maid abuse" (Wong 1998). The courts had adopted a similar stance and applied section 73 to enhance sentences.

For example, then Chief Justice Yong Pung How said "[a]n employer should not exploit his maid's dependence on him for food and lodging, for these are basic rights. A maid's abased social status does not mean that she is any less of a human being and any less protected by the law" (*Farida Begam d/o Mohd Artham v. Public Prosecutor*, para. 27). The courts have also acknowledged "there is ordinarily a pressing need for general deterrence in cases of maid abuse." As "a class of highly vulnerable victims," their employers "can subject them to strict control, which means that abuse can go unreported and undetected for long periods of time" (*Soh Mei Yun v. Public Prosecutor*, para. 44).

In 2019, after a major review of the Penal Code, Parliament further enhanced the penalties for the abuse of MDWs. The Penal Code Review Committee (PCRC) had earlier recommended that the extension of the extant section 73 "to cover all offences in the Penal Code for which there could be a natural victim. This would provide full protection to domestic maids who are exploited, abused, or mistreated by their employers" (PCRC 2018). Secondly, the PCRC recommended the enhancement of maximum punishments that offenders would be liable to from one-and-a-half to two times. The PCRC opined that this would "signal society's strong disapprobation of such offences and strengthen the deterrent effect of s 73. The enhancements would also be consistent with similar enhancements to offences committed against children and vulnerable persons." Thirdly, the PCRC proposed the expansion of the scope of offenders covered by s 73 to include the following: (i) Someone who acted in a similar capacity as the employer, and whose orders the domestic maid had reasonable grounds for believing she was expected to obey, and (ii) the agent of the domestic maid, or someone who was acting in a similar capacity as the agent and whose orders the domestic maid has reasonable grounds for believing she is expected to obey (PCRC 2018, 139). Parliament repealed the former s 73 and a new s 73 incorporating the recommendations into law was enacted in 2019.[26]

Civil Society and the Dignitarian Discourse

Organized labor in the MDW sector is not permitted in Singapore. The limited framework of rights for MDWs in Singapore has resulted in local non-governmental organizations concerned with the welfare of MDWs filling the gap by focusing on generating rights consciousness within the Singaporean public. This ought to be distinguished from the robust assertion of rights. The effort revolves around trying to make rights real and meaningful for vulnerable workers by going beyond what the law requires. What is clear is that the advocacy discourse by civil society groups employs the language of welfare, humane treatment, and dignity (see Cheah 2009; Lyons 2005). The concern with the welfare and dignity of MDWs provides a non-threatening segue to raise the issue of rights. A fair assessment would be that the various civil society organizations, through their advocacy and educational programs, have contributed to the issues facing MDWs being kept on the agenda of the relevant authorities and in the public consciousness. There have been improvements in the regulatory regime on the employment conditions of MDWs. To be sure, there is still a long way to go. As emphasis shifts toward the care of caregivers, a focus on the needs of MDWs (Goh 2019) as part of the dignitarian approach to work and inclusive practices is required.

Given the sizable number of migrant workers in Singapore, the Singapore government is concerned with the foreign policy dimension should these workers be mistreated. In recent years, the government has sought to educate Singaporeans and MDWs alike on their roles and responsibilities. For example, all first-time employers of MDWs, as well as those who change MDWs frequently, are required to attend a compulsory orientation program. The program emphasizes the obligations and responsibilities of employers toward their MDWs.[27] Following in the footsteps of the Migrant Workers Centre (MWC), the Centre for Domestic Employees (CDE) was established in January, 2016, by the National Trades Union Congress (NTUC).[28] The MWC's objectives are three-fold: (1) To champion the fair treatment of MDWs through a "balanced and pragmatic approach towards issues resolution, humanitarian aid, social integration, and support"; (2) to develop partnerships with service/training providers to facilitate the up-skilling of domestic employees' personal effectiveness and enhancing their emotional resilience; and (3) to engage all stakeholders proactively to harmonize the relationship among all concerned parties so as to engender mutual understanding and respect.[29] At the governmental level since 2009, the Ministerial Steering Committee on Foreign Worker Management, chaired by the Manpower Minister, coordinates the whole-of-government efforts to ensure that the migrant workers' issues are properly managed.

The thrust of migrant worker management is on enhancing the regulatory framework rather than on advocating rights. It is also about appealing to the employers' sense of responsibility, rather than fear of punitive sanctions, for compliance. An exhortation a decade ago was revealing: "The way we treat migrant workers in Singapore reflects our maturity as a society. Migrant workers have traveled, sometimes thousands of miles, to a country with unfamiliar customs and languages, to create a better future for their families" (see Hawazi 2009). Such exhortations are repeated regularly such as during the COVID-19 pandemic.[30]

Conclusion

The dignitarian discourse in Singapore, for now, is an inchoate one. This is perhaps not unexpected. Beyond Singapore, there is skepticism and disagreement about the concept because of its subjectivity which is compounded by a lack of universal consensus on its substantive content and how it could form a viable basis for interpreting and applying rights. In Singapore, human dignity is engaged, albeit superficially, most often in MDW abuse cases. Flagged in other cases involving fundamental liberties, the discourse remains largely tentative. Nevertheless, given the courts' acknowledgment of the principle of dignity, the discourse can only develop further. Human dignity can provide the requisite legal and moral standard for determining the proper relationship between two parties where there is an asymmetry of power. For now, the dignitarian discourse appears to be an adjunct of and augments the limited rights framework. It is hoped that judges further utilize the dignitarian discourse as a complement to the rights analysis. In this way, the measure of rights provided for in a constitutional provision, common law, or a piece of legislation can be enjoyed in full measure by the rights-bearer.

Immigration is often rationalized as being good for Singapore and its people. But excluded from this narrative are the transient migrant workers, including the MDWs. Yet, because they are needed to ensure that the more glamorous engines of the economy can roar, heavy reliance is placed on the work contracts that an MDW enters into with the authorities and their employers with regard to her macro- and micro-existence during the tenure of her employment. This abiding reliance on an MDW agreeing to the conditions that come with her work permit highlights the prominence of a market fundamentalism based on contracts. Furthermore, with the objective to exclude, the restrictions and the surveillance mandated that flow from the issuance of the work permits can be described as the governmentality of exclusion. This extension of border control to the personal realm (through the regular medical examinations required) and the extra-territorial reach (via the marriage restriction policy) suggest the prominence of control and discipline, highlighting the paradigm of exclusion through regulation. However, it is in such a regulatory regime that human dignity can play a significant role in the promotion and protection of the rights of the MDWs.

Thus far, rights talk is largely absent or deliberately muted in the public discussion on the betterment of welfare for MDWs. The government has also resisted framing the MDW issues as one pivoting on rights. Dignity, however, is also relied upon by the courts to buttress and enhance the regulatory approach, providing that humane touch and the courts' exhortation to employers to do right. Public education rather than coercive law is its preferred approach. The dignitarian discourse suggests that the protection of MDWs can be enhanced in conjunction with a calibrated emphasis on rights to deliver outcomes that will benefit the MDWs and the regulatory framework. There is much to be said, in law and in policy, for the dignity of work as an aspect of the identity and inherent worth of a human being. The Singapore judiciary has provided a foundation for the concept of human dignity to be more prominent in its jurisprudence and to better interpret the rights and responsibilities of employers and MDWs. It is not so much about dignity playing *a* role in rights protection but *the* role that it should play. Ultimately, when dignity is a pervasive value in interpreting and applying the law, the full measure of the rights of MDWs can be safeguarded.

Notes

1 See Sassen (2008), Piper (2008) and Morrison, Schiff, and Sjoblo (2008) on the feminization of migratory flows.

2 The various chapters in this edited volume provide a rich survey of various leading theories and understanding of human dignity and its role in the promotion and protection of rights.

3 See 2018 *Punta Del Este Declaration on Human Dignity for Everyone Everywhere*, an initiative seeking to revitalize human rights through engaging the notion of human dignity. For further discussion of this initiative and on how human dignity has been used to strengthen human rights, see Scharffs and Ochab (2021).

4 On some of the politically charged issues on immigration in Singapore, see Tan (2014a).
5 The data in this section are taken from NPTD (2021).
6 On the East Asian context, see Ochiai et al. (2008), Ochiai (2009).
7 See Lee (2019) on the evolution of the levy scheme in Singapore.
8 This was vividly demonstrated during the COVID-19 pandemic that began in early 2020 when border controls and closures for extended periods were the norm.
9 See paragraph 6 of Part VI of the Fourth Schedule to the Employment of Foreign Manpower (Work Passes) Regulations 2012; available online at www.mom.gov.sg/-/media/mom/documents/services-forms/passes/wpspassconditions.pdf.
10 Of course, there is nothing to stop a former MDW from marrying a Singapore resident outside of Singapore. However, the prospect of the former MDW being allowed to subsequently reside in Singapore with her husband may be practically non-existent. See further Tan (2014b).
11 Previously available on the Ministry of Manpower website: Last accessed March 1, 2014, www.mom.gov.sg/foreign-manpower/passes-visas/work-permit-fdw/inform-mom/Pages/medical-examination.aspx. See also Ministry of Manpower website: www.mom.gov.sg/passes-and-permits/work-permit-for-foreign-domestic-worker/eligibility-and-requirements/six-monthly-medical-examination.
12 See paragraph 7 of Part VI of the Fourth Schedule to the Employment of Foreign Manpower (Work Passes) Regulations 2012; available online at www.mom.gov.sg/-/media/mom/documents/services-forms/passes/wpspassconditions.pdf.
13 See paragraph 8 of Part VI of the Fourth Schedule of the Employment of Foreign Manpower (Work Passes) Regulations 2012; available online at www.mom.gov.sg/-/media/mom/documents/services-forms/passes/wpspassconditions.pdf.
14 Bell (2006) notes the apparent lack of concern with the "permanent second-class citizenship" for foreign domestic workers in Singapore and Hong Kong.
15 See paragraph 5 of Part I of the Fourth Schedule of the Employment of Foreign Manpower (Work Passes) Regulations 2012; available online at www.mom.gov.sg/-/media/mom/documents/services-forms/passes/wpspassconditions.pdf.
16 On the government's reticence and reluctance to regulate the work conditions of the MDWs, see Teo and Piper (2009).
17 Section 67 of the Act provides that the Manpower Minister may apply all or any of the provisions in the legislation to domestic workers.
18 See "Employers' Guidelines: Employment Laws and Contracts"; available online at www.mom.gov.sg/publish/momportal/en/communities/work_pass/foreign_domestic_workers/employers__guidelines/Employment_Laws_and_Contracts.html.
19 The Manpower Ministry would forfeit only half of the security deposit if the employer had made reasonable efforts to locate the worker.
20 See also the subsidiary legislation, Employment of Foreign Manpower (Work Passes) Regulations 2012 (S569 of 2012).
21 The Penal Code 1871 is Singapore's primary criminal law legislation.
22 This case involved prosecution for a far less serious offense under s 22(1)(a) of the Employment of Foreign Manpower Act (Cap 91A, 2009 Rev Ed) ("EFMA") read with reg 4(2) of the Employment of Foreign Manpower (Work Passes) Regulations 2012 (S 569/2012), punishable under s 22(1)(i) of the EFMA which carries a maximum imprisonment term of only 12 months.
23 The apex court was citing with approval Okpaluba (2013).
24 See also Etinson (2020) on the rich normative content of dignity and its call to envisage humanity as a society of equals.
25 Domestic worker abuse is often talked of in terms of physical abuse. It remains to be seen how the courts would deal with emotional abuse, which is much harder to prove. A local NGO has organised the various types of emotional abuse documented among domestic workers into three main categories: (1) terrorising

behaviour, which are threatening/intimidating words and actions that are insulting or cause fear, diminished confidence and sadness; (2) control by the employer resulting in the MDW's social isolation and/or invasion of privacy and surveillance; (3) degradation, which targets the domestic workers' identities and is detrimental to their self-esteem, including causing domestic workers' loss of dignity. See the June 2022 report by Humanitarian Organization for Migration Economics (HOME), *Invisible Wounds: Emotional Abuse of Migrant Domestic Workers in Singapore*; available online at www.home.org.sg/s/Invisible-Wounds-Emotional-Abuse-of-Migrant-Domestic-Workers-in-Singapore.pdf.

26 See section 15 of Criminal Law Reform Act 2019, which came into force on 1 January, 2020. The law also changed the term describing the MDW from "domestic maid" to "domestic worker" although the definition remained unchanged: "any female house servant employed in, or in connection with, the domestic services of her employer's private dwelling house and who is required to reside in her employer's private dwelling house". This change is long overdue and emphasizes the centrality of the dignity of work and, hence, the dignity of the MDW.

27 For some of the measures taken in recent years by the government, see Singapore's reports for its periodic reviews under the Convention on the Elimination of all Forms of Discrimination Against Women (CEDAW) framework at www.msf.gov.sg/policies/Women-Celebrating-Women/International-Obligations/Pages/default.aspx. See also shadow reports submitted to the UN Committee on CEDAW.

28 The NTUC is the umbrella trade union movement in Singapore.

29 Taken from CDE's website at http://cde.org.sg/wps/portal/cde/home/aboutus/aboutcde.

30 For example, when migrant worker dormitories were locked down to contain the spread of infections there, the Prime Minister in his live broadcast to the nation, highlighted the need to protect the migrant workers. He said, "We are paying close attention to the welfare of the foreign workers. They came to Singapore to work hard for a living, and provide for their families back home. They have played an important part building our HDB flats, Changi Airport, MRT lines. We have worked with their employers to make sure they will be paid their salaries, and can remit money home. We will provide them with the medical care and treatment that they need. If any of their family members watch my video, let me say this to them: We appreciate the work and contributions of your sons, fathers, husbands in Singapore. We feel responsible for their well-being. We will do our best to take care of their health, livelihood and welfare here, and to let them go home, safe and sound, to you. On behalf of all Singaporeans, I wish you well." See Prime Minister Lee Hsien Loong's remarks on the COVID-19 situation in Singapore, delivered on April 10, 2020; available online at www.pmo.gov.sg/Newsroom/PM-Lee-Hsien-Loong-on-the-COVID-19-situation-in-Singapore-on-10-April-2020.

References

Bell, Daniel A. 2006. "Justice for Migrant Workers? The Case of Migrant Domestic Workers in East Asia." In *Beyond Liberal Democracy: Political Thinking for an East Asian Context*, edited by Daniel A. Bell, 281–322. Princeton, NJ: Princeton University Press.

Cheah, Wui Ling. 2009. "Migrant Workers as Citizens within the ASEAN Landscape: International Law and the Singapore Experiment." *Chinese Journal of International Law* 8 (1): 205–31.

Cheah, Wui Ling. 2022. "CEDAW and Transformative Judicial Obligations: The Vulnerable Migrant Domestic Worker and Root Causes of Abuse." *Michigan Journal of International Law* 43: 129–70.

Chin, Chuanfei. 2019. "Precarious Work and its Complicit Network: Migrant Labour in Singapore." *Journal of Contemporary Asia* 49 (4): 528–51.

Dobbs, Stephen, and Kah Seng Loh. 2019. "Open or Bordered? Singapore, Industrialization and Malaysian Workers." *Asian Studies Review* 43 (2): 206–23.

Ehrenreich, Barbara, and Arlie Russell Hochschild, eds. 2003. *Global Woman: Nannies, Maids, and Sex Workers in the New Economy*. New York: Henry Holt.

Etinson, Adam. 2020. "What's So Special About Human Dignity." *Philosophy & Public Affairs* 48 (4): 353–81.

Ferguson, Kathy E., and Monique Mironesco, eds. 2008. *Gender and Globalization in Asia and the Pacific*. Honolulu, HI: Hawaii University Press.

Goh, Daniel P. S. 2019. "Super-diversity and the Bio-politics of Migrant Worker Exclusion in Singapore." *Identities: Global Studies in Culture and Power* 26 (3): 356–73.

Hawazi, Daipi. 2004. *Parliamentary Debates Singapore Official Report*, vol. 78, col. 666 (September 21). Senior Parliamentary Secretary of the Ministry of Manpower.

Hawazi, Daipi. 2009. "Speech by Senior Parliamentary Secretary for Manpower and Health at the Migrant Workers Carnival and Launch of the Migrant Workers Centre." *Ministry of Manpower Website*, April 26, 2009. www.mom.gov.sg/newsroom/speeches/2009/speech-by-mr-hawazi-daipi-senior-parliamentary-secretary--at-the-migrant-workers-carnival-and-launch-of-the-migrant-workers-centre-26-april-2009-705-pm-scal-recreation-centre.

Khaitan, Tarunabh. 2012. "Dignity as an Expressive Norm: Neither Vacuous nor a Panacea." *Oxford Journal of Legal Studies* 32 (1): 1–19.

Lee, Jack Jin Gary. 2019. "Why Developmental States Accept Guest Workers: Bureaucratic Policy-Making and the Politics of Labor Migration in Singapore." *Journal of Ethnic and Migration Studies* 45 (13): 2508–26.

Lyons, Lenore. 2005. "Transient Workers Count Too? The Intersection of Citizenship and Gender in Singapore's Civil Society." *SOJOURN: Journal of Social Issues in Southeast Asia* 20 (2): 208–48.

Lyons, Leonore. 2009. "Transcending the Border: Transnational Imperatives in Singapore's Migrant Worker Rights Movement." *Critical Asian Studies* 41 (1): 89–112.

McCrudden, Christopher. 2008. "Human Dignity and Judicial Interpretation of Human Rights." *European Journal of International Law* 19 (3): 655–724.

Morrison, Andrew R., Maurice Schiff, and Mirja Sjoblo, eds. 2008. *The International Migration of Women*. Washington, DC; New York: The World Bank and Palgrave Macmillan.

National Population and Talent Division (NPTD). 2012. Occasional Paper: "Projection of Foreign Manpower Demand for Healthcare Sector, Construction Workers and Foreign Domestic Workers." www.strategygroup.gov.sg/images/Press%20Release%20images/PDFs/occasional-paper-projection-of-foreign-manpower-demand-healthcare-construction-foreign-domestic-workers.pdf.

National Population and Talent Division (NPTD). 2013. *White Paper on A Sustainable Population for a Dynamic Singapore ["Population White Paper"]*. Singapore: Prime Minister's Office.

National Population and Talent Division (NPTD). 2021. *Population in Brief 2021*. Singapore: Prime Minister's Office. www.population.gov.sg/files/media-centre/publications/Population-in-brief-2021.pdf.

Ochiai, Emiko. 2009. "Care Diamonds and Welfare Regimes in East and South-east Asian Societies: Bridging Family and Welfare Sociology." *International Journal of Japanese Sociology* 18 (1): 60–78.

Ochiai, Emiko, Yamane Mari, Miyasaka Yasuko, Zhou Weihong, Onode Setsuko, Kiwaki Nachiko, Fujita Michiyo, and Hong Sang Ook. 2008. "Gender Roles and Childcare Networks in East and Southeast Asian Societies." In *Asia's New Mothers: Crafting Gender Roles and Childcare Networks in East and Southeast Asian Societies*, edited by Emiko Ochiai and Barbara Maloney, 31–70. Folkestone: Global Oriental.

Okpaluba, Chuks. 2013. "'Prosecution' in an Action for Malicious Prosecution: A Discussion of Recent Commonwealth Case Law." *Journal of South African Law* 2: 236–56.

Parreñas, Rhacel Salazar. 2001. *Servants of Globalization: Women, Migration and Domestic Work*. Stanford, CA: Stanford University Press.

Penal Code Review Committee. 2018. "Penal Code Review Committee Report." Accessed November 3, 2018. www.mha.gov.sg/docs/default-source/default-document-library/penal-code-review-committee-report3d9709ea6f13421b92d3ef8af69a4ad0.pdf.

Piper, Nicola. 2008. "Feminisation of Migration and the Social Dimensions of Development: The Asian Case." *Third World Quarterly* 29 (7): 1287–303.

Rozario, Philip A., and Song-lee Hong. 2019. "Foreign Domestic Workers and Eldercare in Singapore: Who Hires Them?" *Journal of Aging & Social Policy* 31 (3): 197–210.

Ruhs, Martin. 2013. *The Price of Rights: Regulating International Labour Migration*. Princeton, NJ: Princeton University Press.

Sassen, Saskia. 2007. *A Sociology of Globalization*. New York: Norton.

Sassen, Saskia. 2008. "Two Stops in Today's New Global Geographies: Shaping Novel Labor Supplies and Employment Regimes." *American Behavioral Scientist* 52 (3): 457–96.

Scharffs, Brett G., and Ewelina U. Ochab. 2021. *Dignity and International Human Rights Law: An Introduction to the Punta del Este Declaration on Human Dignity for Everyone Everywhere*. London; New York: Routledge.

The Straits Times. 2021. "Medical Check-Ups for Maids Enhanced to Better Detect Abuse." August 6.

Tan, Eugene K. B. 2008. "A Union of Gender Equality and Pragmatic Patriarchy: International Marriages and Citizenship Laws in Singapore." *Citizenship Studies* 12 (1): 73–89.

Tan, Eugene K. B. 2010. "Managing Female Foreign Domestic Workers in Singapore: Economic Pragmatism, Coercive Legal Regulation, or Human Rights?" *Israel Law Review* 43 (1): 99–125.

Tan, Eugene K. B. 2014a. "Angst, Anxieties, and Anger in a Global City: Coping with and Rightsizing the Immigration Imperative in Singapore." In *Immigration in Singapore*, edited by Norman Vasu, Yeap Su Yin, and Chan Wen Ling, 37–66. Amsterdam: Amsterdam University Press.

Tan, Eugene K. B. 2014b. "Troublesome Women and the Nanny State: Drawing Boundaries and Legislating Bifurcated Belonging in Patriarchal Singapore." *Intersections: Gender and Sexuality in Asia and the Pacific* 36. http://intersections.anu.edu.au/issue36/tan.htm.

Teo, Youyenn, and Nicola Piper. 2009. "Foreigners in Our Homes: Linking Migration and Family Policies in Singapore." *Population, Space and Place* 15 (2): 147–59.

Tseng, Cherie. 2022. "Commentary: Is It Time for Us to Explore Live-Out Arragments for Maids." *CNA*, September 19, 2022. www.channelnewsasia.com/commentary/maid-domestic-work-part-time-salary-leave-mom-employer-2942781.

United Nations Development Program (UNDP). 2009. *Human Development Report 2009—Overcoming Barriers: Human Mobility and Development*. New York: UNDP.

United Nations Economic and Social Commission for Asia and the Pacific (UN-ESCAP). 2008. "Key Trends and Challenges on International Migration and Development in Asia and the Pacific." Report Prepared for the Asia-Pacific High-Level Meeting on International Migration and Development, Bangkok, September 22–23, 2008.

Wajihad, Hamid, and Dylan Tutt. 2019. "'Thrown Away Like a Banana Leaf': Precarity of Labour and Precarity of Place for Tamil Migrant Construction Workers in Singapore." *Construction Management and Economics* 37 (9): 513–36.

Waldron, Jeremy. 2012. "How Law Protects Dignity." *Cambridge Law Journal* 71 (1): 200–222.

Wee, Vivienne. 1995. "Children, Population Policy, and the State in Singapore." In *Children and the Politics of Culture*, edited by Sharon Stephens, 184–217. Princeton, NJ: Princeton University Press.

Wong, Kan Seng. 1998. *Singapore Parliamentary Debates, Official Reports*, vol. 68, cols. 1923–1924. Minister for Home Affairs.

World Bank. 2009. *World Development Report 2009: Reshaping Economic Geography*. Washington, DC: World Bank.

Yeoh, Brenda S. A. 2006. "Bifurcated Labor: The Unequal Incorporation of Transmigrants in Singapore." *Tijdschrift voor Economische en Sociale Geografie* 97 (1): 26–37.

Case Law

The Court of Appeal of Singapore:

ACB v. Thomson Medical Pte Ltd and others [2017] 1 SLR 918.
ADF v. Public Prosecutor [2010] 1 SLR 874.
Lee Tat Development Pte Ltd v. Management Corporation Strata Title Plan No 301 [2018] 2 SLR 866.
Tan Eng Hong v. Attorney-General [2012] 4 SLR 476.

The Hight Court of Singapore

Farida Begam d/o Mohd Artham v. Public Prosecutor [2001] 3 SLR(R) 592.
Janardana Jayasankarr v. Public Prosecutor [2016] 4 SLR 1288.
Lee Hsien Loong v Roy Ngerng Yi Ling [2016] 1 SLR 1321.
Public Prosecutor v Lim Choon Hong and another [2017] 5 SLR 989.
Soh Mei Yun v. Public Prosecutor [2014] 3 SLR 299.
Tay Wee Kiat and another v. Public Prosecutor and Another Appeal [2018] 4 SLR 1315.
UKM v. Attorney-General [2019] 3 SLR 874.

The Supreme Court of Canada

R v. Kapp 2008 SCC 41.

15 Conclusion

Human Dignity on the Ground of Adjudication

Brett G. Scharffs, Andrea Pin, and Dmytro Vovk

Human dignity is not just a staple of contemporary adjudication at the national, supranational, and international levels. As a matter of fact, it has also become one of its drivers, as cases centered around dignity have promoted the judicialization of politically, culturally, and socially divisive disputes. As such, dignity has had its share of praise and criticism as a substantial part of modern human rights adjudication. Although the chapters in this book inevitably focus on only a small portion of the jurisdictions that have made recourse to the concept of human dignity in their case law, they nonetheless provide insights both on the success and the shortcomings of dignity-based litigation around the globe.

Dignity Everywhere?

Dignity-based litigation crosses borders and cultures. As this and other books have shown, distinct narratives of dignity have surfaced in the late-20th early-21st century in the four corners of the world, spanning the Middle East, Russia, Singapore, Latin America, and South Africa. Now, dignity is not just a predominantly European concept—if it ever was—with ramifications in the offspring of that continent across the globe. Given the worldwide success of the concept, the German constitutional culture has been immensely influential in spreading the concept of dignity around the world in the aftermath of World War II and remains a point of reference for any global discourse on dignity, but at this point Germany is probably no longer the yardstick against which the judicial treatment of dignity should be measured. Many more state, supranational, and international jurisdictions now provide useful examples of courts that have to deal with dignity-centered cases.

The spread of such a concept on the one hand is inevitable. The idea of *human* dignity is one of the most universalizable legal concepts, as it captures the idea that human beings have an intrinsic worthiness that the law should recognize and protect, regardless of their social, political, and economic situation (Kateb 2011). The spread of human dignity is therefore both a result and a catalyst of judicial rulings and judicial dialogue among jurisdictions.

DOI: 10.4324/9781003307853-19

However, such a widespread recourse to human dignity in adjudication has not resulted in a homogenization of the concept, which remains to a certain degree amorphous and dependent on context. Human dignity has, in fact, discharged several—even opposite—roles depending on the circumstances, even within the same jurisdiction, as happened in Ireland (Kenny 2013).

Dignity in Everything?

Different jurisdictions have leveraged dignity for a variety of reasons. As judges assess specific controversies according to how cases are brought to them, their analyses of dignity have constantly focused on specific angles. Many chapters of this book testify that some topics have become quite common denominators in dignity-based adjudication in several jurisdictions, while some others are still characteristic of specific national cultures. For example, the treatment of terrorists and the ethnic divide have kept the Israeli Supreme Court occupied for decades now, and it is no surprise that several legal systems have struggled to cope with migration and refugees. This is a cross-jurisdictional issue, as it addresses a global phenomenon that covers legal systems as different as the EU and Singapore.

An equally cross-jurisdictional phenomenon, which is also connected with migration, is adjudication centered around the economic dimension of dignity. Interestingly enough, even countries with a long and well-established tradition of dignity-based adjudication and a solid welfare system such as Germany have recently struggled to reconcile the impact of the 2008 economic crisis with the crisis of social welfare and the protection of human dignity.

Whose Dignity?

If courts have been prone to use the concept of dignity, they have often been pressed to do so. Once dignity-centered litigation took off, the parties—as well as amici curiae, where they are admitted—have intensively exploited such a concept to make or to strengthen their arguments even when courts hesitate to espouse dignity-related arguments (Annicchino 2021; Relaño Pastor 2021). A dignity-based adjudication is therefore the product of constitutional and legal texts as well as of judicial practice and dignity-based judicial claims.

The piecemeal development of dignity-based judicial narratives in courts has shown the slow development of different understandings of dignity. Many of them have been articulated in accordance with the predominant local culture. A more holistic understanding of dignity is traceable in South Africa, where it seems to respond to the needs of the local communitarian culture. Germany's traditional preoccupation with social rights is reflected in the thread of cases revolving around dignity at the German Constitutional Court. Singapore's immigration cases on dignity are reflective of the country's status as a global hub and the shifting culture of hospitality toward immigrant workers. Irish and Israeli understandings of dignity can be read in light of the cultural and spiritual forces that have given shape to those jurisdictions at different times. Russia's case law leverages dignity to curb human rights claims for a wide array of reasons, spanning from security concerns to a religiously informed public morality.

Although courts have leveraged social assumptions about human dignity, they have normally avoided explicit generalizations and theorizations of human dignity beyond what was at stake before them—the only notable and almost universally valid exception being the widespread recourse to Immanuel Kant's philosophy. As courts are tasked with solving disputes, they have resented providing strong philosophical foundations or comprehensive anthropological considerations about the worthiness of human beings. Although some chapters have reverse-engineered their legal reasoning and speculated about their theoretical underpinnings, they had to put together the pieces of a judicial puzzle made up of various judicial rulings.

Going beyond what was necessary to solve cases would have probably also backfired in courts. As the Polish case about abortion demonstrates, couching extremely sensitive topics in terms of dignity may incite controversy (Szymaniec 2021). Reading divisive issues in terms of dignity can convey the impression that courts are using dignity in a partisan way. In this respect, it seems that courts are avoiding as much as they can responding to the emphasis that individuals and groups are giving to the dignitary components of their claims.

Compared to what state courts have done with dignity, much more difficult has been the job of supranational courts. As they host several states, they are normally committed to respecting a variety of worldviews and political and legal cultures. Dignity-based complaints in such courts are not just divisive within jurisdictions, but often across jurisdictions. Partisanship in reading dignity within such contexts may not just empoison the concept; it can trigger broader opposition to the institution and alienate entire states, as happened with the British case about the life-sentenced prisoners' right to release or to have their sentence reviewed (*Vinter v UK*). It is therefore not a surprise that supranational courts have tried not to embrace substantive conceptions of dignity but have either accepted a national understanding of it or acknowledged that the concept itself is capable of conveying different values and meanings.

The Job of Dignity

At a superficial level, the chapters of this book seem to testify that dignity does not possess an intrinsic normative value. Its content is opaque, as its meaning and legal significance change with the context, the circumstances, and even the institutional expediency of deciding a case on the grounds of dignity. Dignity often absorbs and drives the most pressing interests and priorities of a certain place, time, or social component—such as the need to protect the environment or migrants' rights, or fight discriminatory practices. Pushed by waves of dignity-based judicial claims, courts themselves often shy away from providing definitive answers about the scope and content of human dignity.

As the concept of dignity is obfuscated by agendas that are dependent on time and place, the accusation that dignity is amorphous seems well founded. But the fact that dignity is so polysemic and malleable should not blind us to the fact that dignity, in fact, discharges an important role *in* judicial litigation and *for* judicial litigation.

First, dignity encapsulates the tensions of a certain legal environment. It is therefore an important heuristic tool, as it can help define a political and legal culture. If it is not capable of concretely deciding cases, it is certainly a way in which parties and judges signal the particular importance of a certain subject for the whole society. The chapters of this book to a large extent map out not just the uses of dignity, but also into which camps each jurisdiction is investing many of its cultural and legal resources. The opaqueness of the concept within a certain jurisdiction reflects the cultural and political disagreements over its meaning and legal ramifications.

Second, its amorphousness is also relative. In several jurisdictions, there are fields in which there seems to be a large convergence—at least within the judiciary—that dignity is at stake. In such cases, courts have easily found that someone's dignity has been blatantly violated. It is instead when a variety of worldviews come into conflict and contend that someone's dignity has been violated that courts mitigate the impact of the concept, avoid deciding only on the basis of dignity, and leave room for further rumination around the concept. In other words, when the deployment or any sharp definition of dignity would trigger controversy, then judges usually prefer not to pin down its exact contours, as this would make the concept partisan and delegitimize the judiciary at once. The idea of dignity does not seem to lose teeth because it is amorphous—on the contrary, it becomes amorphous in order to respect the political, cultural, and ideological diversity that inhabits a certain legal order: courts often appear conscious of the fact that the various components of a society must see themselves reflected in how dignity is defined and utilized.

Third, and relatedly, the judicial treatment of dignity is a reminder of the scope and limits of adjudication. In many instances, those who make dignity-based claims weaponize this concept not just to win in court; they often argue that their claim has a social significance that extends beyond the case at stake. Claiming that dignity is involved in a case surmises that a judicial loss would be a judicial humiliation—and perhaps even a social humiliation. One of the drivers of dignity-based litigation is the quest for social recognition, and several dignity-centered legal controversies can be also seen as power struggles in judicial robes in which one or each party complains about its own vulnerability. This puts courts in a difficult institutional position, as their rulings can become political statements that can engulf wider society—and, perhaps paradoxically, deny the social recognition many parties look for through litigation.

Finally, critiques of dignity are hardly a surprise given the mounting critiques of human rights. Both dignity and human rights have lately been subject to intense scrutiny, and skepticism has grown around them as a category and as a tool to provide justice. As rights are often seen as "absolute," they often work as trump cards, capable of tilting the balance in adjudication no matter the collateral effects they might have.[1] And, if rights are absolute, human dignity is even more so (Kateb 2011). Debates on the limits of dignity, on its proper judicial utilization, and on whether dignity should be treated as an absolute or requires balancing are therefore also part and parcel of the contemporary debate on the limits of rights-based adjudication.

The delicacy—even the opaqueness—with which many courts have treated dignity, however, suggests that, in several circumstances, they have been wary of giving it a specific meaning, precisely in order to protect themselves from accusations of unfairness and the broader society from polarization. They seem to understand that the concept is capable of hosting different worldviews and therefore try to preserve it also as an instrument to mitigate social conflict. Dignity may not win cases, but it may facilitate conversations. The lack of a well-defined constitutional meaning for the word "dignity" may have an institutional meaning, after all. The issue is, of course, whether such conversations can or should take place in courts.

Note

1 On the role of rights as trumps, see Greene (2018).

References

Annicchino, Pasquale. 2021. "Friends of the Court: Christian Conservative Arguments on Human Dignity Before the U.S. Supreme Court and the European Court of Human Rights." *BYU Law Review* 46 (2021): 1155–82.

Greene, Jamal. 2018. "The Supreme Court 2017 Term—Foreword: Rights as Trumps?" *Harvard Law Review* 132 (1): 28–132.

Kateb, George. 2011. *Human Dignity*. Cambridge, MA; London: Belknap Press.

Kenny, David. 2013. "Recent Developments in the Right of the Person in Article 40.3: *Fleming v. Ireland* and the Spectre of Unenumerated Rights." *Dublin University Law Journal* 36: 322–39.

Relaño Pastor, Eugenia. 2021. "Christian Faith-Based Organizations as Third Party Interveners at the European Court of Human Rights." *BYU Law Review* 46 (2021): 1329–68.

Szymaniec, Piotr. 2021. "Constitutionality of Abortion: Legal Analysis of the Recent Case in Poland." *Talk About: Law and Religion*, April 20, 2021. https://talkabout.iclrs.org/2021/04/20/constitutionality-of-abortion/.

Index

9781032310572